FOR HISTORY'S SAKE

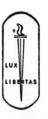

THE UNIVERSITY OF
NORTH CAROLINA PRESS · CHAPEL HILL

FOR HISTORY'S SAKE

THE PRESERVATION AND PUBLICATION OF NORTH CAROLINA HISTORY

1663-1903

H. G. JONES

To

the memory of

MARY GIVENS BRYAN

1910-1964

State Archivist of Georgia, 1951-1964
President of The Society of American Archivists, 1959-1960

COLLEAGUE AND FRIEND

Preface

In 1964, the North Carolina State Department of Archives and History received the first Distinguished Service Award ever given by the Society of American Archivists. The award, which cited the department for "outstanding service to the American people and exemplary contributions to the archival profession" by developing over a period of years "an archival program of such depth and scope as to warrant especial recognition," is but another evidence that North Carolina has, in the twentieth century, effectively provided for the preservation and administration of her public records. But it was not always so. Notwithstanding efforts of individual historians and public officials, the State gave only sporadic and sometimes ineffectual attention to the proper care of the records until 1903 when it established the North Carolina Historical Commission (now the Department of Archives and History).

This study seeks to tell the story of the public records from 1663 to 1903—their creation, preservation, destruction, use, and publication. Inextricably woven into the chronicle are the various factors which influenced record making, preservation, and utilization. Among these factors are the laws governing the records, the repeated moving of the records due to changing the seat of government or because of threats brought on by war, the conditions of buildings housing the records and the calamities that befell them, the care or neglect with which custodians tended the records, and the efforts of individuals who sought to provide greater security for the records. The historians who made first extensive research use of the archives play an increasingly important role as the narrative progresses, for it was they who stimulated interest in the records as sources of history. Only those historians who used the original sources in the writing—or intended writing—of general state histories are included; those who wrote first-hand accounts without reference to the records, or who wrote on subjects of restricted scope, are omitted. Thus while Francis Lister Hawks is included, John Lawson is not. Some consideration is given to private manuscripts in the nineteenth century, but only because at that time little or no distinction was made between private papers and public records. Finally, considerable space is devoted to the activities of historical societies and the eventual establishment of the state archival-historical agency. All of these subjects have been of primary concern to me during the past decade in my position as state archivist.

No detailed analysis of the public records of an American state appears to have been made previously; consequently I have had no prototype to follow. The need for such works is great, however, and it is hoped that the present publication will stimulate the production of similar but better studies for the other states of the Union.

This book has been made possible only by the encouragement and assistance of Christopher Crittenden, my superior officer and director of the State Department of Archives and History, and Robert H. Woody, my graduate advisor in the Duke University Department of History. To them I express publicly my profound appreciation.

C. F. W. Coker and Beth G. Crabtree of the State Department of Archives and History gave me much assistance. The former made helpful suggestions for improving the manuscript, the latter prepared the index, and both assisted in the proofreading. William S. Powell, librarian of the North Carolina Collection at The University of North Carolina at Chapel Hill, gave me his usual wise counsel.

I am also indebted to two personal as well as professional friends who read an earlier draft of the manuscript and who gave me valuable advice—Ernst Posner, the "dean" of American archivists, and Oliver Wendell Holmes, director of the National Historical Publications Commission. Carolyn Andrews Wallace, curator of manuscripts in the Southern Historical Collection, and members of my own staff in the State Department of Archives and History led me to sources that otherwise I might have missed. Finally, I express my appreciation to my assistant, Julius Howard Avant, who went beyond the call of duty in checking details, typing, and proofreading.

Raleigh, North Carolina   H. G. JONES
July 1, 1966

Contents

Illustrations

The endpaper: *View of Raleigh, 1872,* by C. Drie
(Courtesy State Department of Archives and History)

Introduction

Historians charge that North Carolinians, until recent decades, have shown little interest in preserving the written record of their heritage. Upon that alleged indifference has been blamed the dearth of dependable published histories and, in fact, most writers have justified the shortcomings of their own works on the grounds that documentary sources were lacking. Inasmuch as most of the complaints have been directed toward public officials, the implication is clear that the public records have not been adequately cared for.

A study concerned largely with the subject of public records needs to begin with a definition of the term. A widely accepted definition of "records" is as follows:

All books, papers, maps, photographs, or other documentary materials, regardless of physical form or characteristics, made or received by any public or private institution in pursuance of its legal obligations or in connection with the transaction of its proper business and preserved or appropriate for preservation by that institution or its legitimate successor as evidence of its functions, policies, decisions, procedures, operations, or other activities or because of the informational value of the data contained therein.[1]

The prefix "public" narrows this definition to the records of government.

The proliferation of public records in recent decades has been so great that, in common usage, "records" have come to cover many documentary materials which are of short-term administrative value only and consequently subject to orderly destruction by competent authority after they have served their usefulness. Because historians deal primarily with those records of continuing

1. T. R. Schellenberg, *Modern Archives: Principles and Techniques* (Chicago: University of Chicago Press, 1956), p. 16.

historical value, the limiting term of "archives" is more appropriate in referring to documentary materials preserved for evi-
dential and informational content. The word "archives," as used
in this book, refers to the *permanently valuable* records, in whatever form, that have been created or received by a governmental
body—the Colony and State of North Carolina or one of its sub-
divisions—for its official purposes and made a part of its official
documentation.

This rather thin line of distinction between the two defini-
tions suggests a question as to why within the text the words will
be used interchangeably. The reason is a utilitarian one: "Records" become "archives" only when they are so designated by an
appropriate authority. One such authority is a law which pre-
scribes the permanent preservation of a particular record. Another is an official agency which, by law, is charged with the
responsibility of determining what records are to be kept permanently. Very few laws specified such permanent preservation,
and it was not until 1903 that a public agency was established
with the primary responsibility of preserving records for historical purposes. Consequently, prior to the twentieth century,
the determination of what records were archives was generally
not made.

Record keeping was usually a by-product of the more important primary functions of public officials in the early days of the
Colony. Several officers such as the secretary of the Province and
the register of the precincts, however, were mainly recording
officials and their duties pertained almost solely to the creation,
preservation, and utilization of records. Even so, there was no
one agency with authority over all records of government, and
consequently the records were created and kept as well or as badly
as the particular occupant of the office saw fit. Nearly all office
holders were amateurs, and their frequent replacement resulted
in a difficult task, at best, in caring adequately for the records.
Thus inexperience, lack of interest, and frequent turnover among
officials, coupled with inadequate facilities for the protection of
the records, resulted in losses of much documentary evidence
of the Colony's government.

North Carolina was not unique in this respect. Notwithstanding strenuous efforts on the part of some farsighted officials and historians, it was not until the close of the nineteenth century that any state in the Union finally created an archival agency with sufficient legal authority to cope with the problem of preserving the archives of state government. Thus, the North Carolina Historical Commission in 1903 was, in effect, one of the earliest such agencies established in the United States.[2] It preceded by thirty-one years the formal establishment of the National Archives, and, interestingly enough, furnished the first Archivist of the United States.

A study of the public archives neither corroborates unreservedly the traditional charges that North Carolinians have neglected their history nor exonerates them entirely from the charges. It does reveal, however, that during the first two and a half centuries both public officials and the citizenry paid too little attention to their historical source materials. This inattention led to the loss of many irreplaceable public records. On the other hand, those losses were remarkably few in comparison with the entire body of the State's historical records. The fact that an estimated 20,000,-000 pages of official records are now preserved in the State Archives—with many more millions of pages still housed in public offices—supports a general conclusion that historians have exaggerated their claims that until the twentieth century North Carolinians were a people without interest in their history and the sources thereof.

Yet, had it not been for the criticism of nineteenth-century

2. No detailed study appears to have been made previously of the public archives of a particular state. In 1961, however, the Society of American Archivists, by means of a grant from the Council on Library Resources, Incorporated, inaugurated a study of archival programs in the fifty states. Ernst Posner, formerly a state archivist at the Privy State Archives in Berlin-Dahlem, who came to the United States in 1939 and established at The American University, Washington, D.C., the first formal training course in archival administration, was appointed director of the study. His report, *American State Archives* (Chicago: University of Chicago Press, 1964), includes a valuable survey of the development of archival programs in the various states. For brief surveys of the archival programs of the American states, see also H. G. Jones, "State Archival-Records Management Programs in the United States," *Archivum*, XI (1961), 135-42; and H. G. Jones (ed.), *Guide to State and Provincial Archival Agencies* (Raleigh: Society of American Archivists, 1961).

historians, the verdict would not be so favorable to the State of North Carolina. For it was those historians—men like Archibald D. Murphey, John H. Wheeler, and David L. Swain—who badgered government officials into positive steps toward a more orderly preservation of the public archives, and it was they who laid the groundwork for the success of William L. Saunders and Walter Clark in acquiring from England copies of records relating to North Carolina and in making the early records available in published form. They collected private papers as well as public documents that had fallen into private hands, thus laying the foundations for modern manuscript repositories; they wrote; they exhorted; they organized historical societies. And they eventually brought about the establishment of a state archival-historical agency through whose efforts the public archives of North Carolina are being preserved and made available for research. All in all, the public archives of North Carolina—both state and local—have fared better than the critics in her midst have admitted. Had it not been for their agitation, however, it is unlikely that this statement would be true.

PART ONE

THE PUBLIC ARCHIVES

1663-1903

I

Record Keeping in Proprietary Carolina
1663-1728

The first permanent English settlement in the area now known as North Carolina preceded by only a few years the issuance of the Carolina Charter of March 24, 1663, by the Crown to eight Lords Proprietors. Except for an ill-fated attempt of a small band of New Englanders to settle on the Cape Fear River—a venture whose records are as meager as its lasting effects upon North Carolina—only a few hardy families from Virginia had pushed to the south and taken up lands in the Albemarle Sound area. A few land grants had been issued for this otherwise unsettled section by Virginia Governor William Berkeley and they had been recorded in the secretary's office at Jamestown.[1]

Even earlier expeditions had led to records—both public and private—relating to the vast land to the south of Virginia. But none of these records remained on Carolina soil and few, if any, returned to the place of their origin. It is perhaps justifiable, therefore, that any study of the public and private records begin with the formal establishment of government in North Carolina. Happily, the Charter of 1663 provides a beginning, for that document marks the origin of organized government.

1. Wesley Frank Craven, *The Southern Colonies in the Seventeenth Century 1607-1689*, Vol. I of *A History of the South*, ed. Wendell H. Stephenson and E. Merton Coulter (10 vols.; Baton Rouge: Louisiana State University Press, 1948–), p. 318. Cited hereafter as Craven, *Southern Colonies*. See also Elizabeth Gregory McPherson, "Nathaniell Batts, Landholder on Pasquotank River, 1660," *North Carolina Historical Review*, XLIII (Winter, 1966), 66-81.

The Charter does not contain the word "record," and it specifically directs the keeping of but one record—the laws to be made by the Lords Proprietors "with the advice, assent, and approbation of the Freemen. . . ."[2] This provision for a legislative assembly, along with other authorizations including the granting of lands, the establishing of courts, the awarding of titles of nobility, the creating of towns, and the appointing of officers, carried the assumption that civilized government would create records of its functions. This assumption made unnecessary explicit requirements for record keeping. The Charter, after all, was a grant of land and authority over that land. Except for requiring the Proprietors to grant their subjects certain accepted rights of Englishmen, the Charter was designed to permit the Proprietors to establish a government of their choice so long as it was not inconsistent with the restrictions contained therein. The mechanics of record keeping therefore was not a fit subject for the Charter and omission of detail simply emphasized the acceptance of record making as an appropriate and necessary function of government.

That the Proprietors recognized the necessity of written records is evident from the minutes of their first recorded meeting on May 23, 1663, at which time they appointed an "Ingeneir & Surveyo[r]" for Carolina and provided that the Province be "bounded & leyed out" into settlements. It was required that land in each settlement be reserved for "the Court howses & howses for publique meetings."[3] This first mention of buildings for public offices was in sharp contrast to the later lack of concern for public buildings on the part of the settlers. At the same time it emphasized the Proprietors' chief interest in the establishment of land policies and orderly government. Like the older colonies to the north, the records of early Carolina "reveal a

2. Mattie Erma Edwards Parker (ed.), *The Colonial Records of North Carolina: North Carolina Charters and Constitutions, 1578-1698* (Raleigh: Carolina Charter Tercentenary Commission, 1963), p. 78. Cited hereafter as Parker, *Charters.*

3. William L. Saunders (ed.), *The Colonial Records of North Carolina* (10 vols.; Raleigh: State of North Carolina, 1886-90), I, 34. Cited hereafter as Saunders, *Colonial Records.* The Proprietors at the same meeting ordered maps of the Province to be printed and "some declaration drawne to invyte the planters" to come to Carolina.

concern chiefly for the adjustment of land policies and of the machinery of government to the peculiar requirements of expanding frontiers."[4]

By far the preponderance of instructions on record keeping in the early years of the Colony related directly to the granting of lands. As early as September 8, 1663, the Proprietors, while authorizing the appointment of a governor for Albemarle by Sir William Berkeley of Virginia, reserved for themselves the right to appoint a secretary and surveyor—the two key officials in land transactions.[5] These same instructions outlined the procedure for granting land and keeping records thereof: The governor and Council issued warrants which were entered with the surveyor who ran out the land, drew a "small plot of the same," and certified to the secretary the bounds of the land surveyed. This certificate was to be recorded "in a booke to be kept for the purpose" by the secretary who in turn certified to the governor and Council that the survey had been made. The secretary prepared the formal grant which was signed and sealed by the governor. All grants were issued with provision for a quitrent. A fee was allowed officials for each step of the procedure in which they were involved. Here, in the early years of the Colony, was established a fee system that was to remain a source of conflict between the people and the government throughout the entire colonial period, both proprietary and royal.

The certificate of appointment on December 3, 1664, of Peter Carteret as secretary and chief registrar for Albemarle, in addition to authorizing him to be present at all meetings of the governor and Council "and to take & keep an exact Register of all theire acts orders & constitutions," again outlined the responsibility of the secretary in keeping the land records "in yo[r] said office that recourse may bee thereupon had upon all occasions. . . ."[6]

4. Craven, *Southern Colonies,* p. 310.

5. Saunders, *Colonial Records,* I, 52-53. A "Monsiear Lepreyrie" was appointed surveyor and Richard Cobthorp secretary. See also Lawrence N. Morgan, *Land Tenure in Proprietary North Carolina* ("The James Sprunt Historical Publications," Vol. XII, No. 1 [Chapel Hill: The University of North Carolina Press, 1912]), p. 49.

6. William S. Powell (ed.), *Ye Countie of Albemarle in Carolina: A Collection of Documents 1664-1675* (Raleigh: State Department of Archives and History,

For the first two years government in the Albemarle was based on such temporary authorizations and instructions. But in 1665, the Proprietors issued their "Concessions and Agreement" between themselves and Major William Yeamans who had been appointed governor of the group from Barbados who were attempting a settlement in the County of Clarendon on the Cape Fear. This document, however, extended as well to the government of the Albemarle[7] and is recognized as the first constitution or over-all plan of government put into effect in Carolina.[8]

The third item of the "Concessions and Agreement" again spelled out the responsibility of the secretary who was to

. . . keep exact entries in fair books of all public affairs of the said Counties and, to avoid deceits and Lawsuits, . . . record and enter all Grants of Land from the Lords to the planter, and all conveyances of Land, house, or houses from man to man; As also, all Leases for land, house, or houses made or to be made by the Landlord to any tenant for more than one year; which Conveyance or Lease shall be first acknowledged by the Grantor or Lessor, or proved by the oath of two witnesses to the conveyance or Lease, before the Governor or some Chief Judge of a Court for the time being; who shall, Under his hand, Upon the backside of the said deed or Lease, Attest the acknowledgement or proof, as aforesaid, which shall be warrant for the Registers to record the same; which Conveyance or Lease so recorded shall be good and effectual in Law, notwithstanding any other Conveyance, deed, or Lease for the said Land, house, or for any part there [sic], although dated before the Conveyance, deed, or Lease so recorded as aforesaid.[9]

Instructions for the issuance of warrants and grants of land were again outlined, generally in conformity with the previous temporary instructions except that the keeping of the secretary's land records was made more explicit. He was to record certifi-

---

1958), p. 5. Cited hereafter as Powell, *Albemarle*. Similar instructions had been given earlier, on November 14, 1664, to Robert Samford (or Sandford) as secretary and chief registrar of the County of Clarendon. On the latter date John Vassall was appointed surveyor general of Clarendon with similar instructions. See Saunders, *Colonial Records*, I, 72-73.

7. Parker, *Charters*, p. 107.

8. An earlier plan, "A Declaration and Proposals to All That Will Plant in Carolina," had been issued in 1663, but was never put into effect since no colonies were founded under it. Parker, *Charters*, p. 107.

9. Parker, *Charters*, p. 112.

cates "in a book to be prepared for that purpose, with an Alphabetical table referring to the book, That so the Certificate may be the easier found, and then to file the Certificates and the same to keep Safely. . . ."[10] The accepted form for a land grant was included. That the general provisions of the "Concessions and Agreement" were still in effect in 1667 is indicated in the instructions to Governor Samuel Stephens in that year.[11]

Until 1669, the County of Albemarle had not been subdivided for administrative purposes even though the revised Charter of 1665 had authorized the division of the Province into "several counties, baronies, and colonies."[12] Consequently the recording of real estate had remained the responsibility of the "chief register" or secretary of the county. The promulgation of the first of several "Fundamental Constitutions of Carolina," sometimes called the "Grand Model," on July 21, 1669, however, again provided for the division of the colony into counties, seigniories, baronies, precincts, and colonies. Albemarle already constituted one county, and it was soon divided into four precincts —Chowan, Currituck, Pasquotank, and Perquimans. Like most other provisions of the Fundamental Constitutions, the authorization for creation of seigniories, baronies, and colonies was never carried out.

The importance of the establishment of precincts can hardly be overestimated for they later were to become counties, thereby forming a vital subdivision of the government of the Colony and State. It was to be in the precinct—later county—that land records, and most other records relating to real estate, vital statistics, and estates were to be recorded.

Of particular relevance was Item 74 which provided that "There shall be a Registry in every precinct, wherein shall be enrolled all deeds, Leases, Judgments, or other conveyances which may concern any of the land within the Said Precinct; and all

10. Parker, *Charters*, pp. 125-26.
11. Lords Proprietors' Instructions to Samuel Stephens, Governor of Albemarle, October 8, 1667, in Thurmond Chatham Collection, State Department of Archives and History, Raleigh. Cited hereafter as Chatham Collection. The State Department of Archives and History hereafter will be cited as State Archives. See also Powell, *Albemarle*, p. 26.
12. Parker, *Charters*, p. 90.

Such conveyances not so entered or Registered shall not be of force against any person not privy to the Said contract or conveyance." The freeholders of each precinct were to nominate three men, each with at least three hundred acres freehold, one of whom the chief justice's court was to choose as register of the precinct.[13]

Although Albemarle County was divided in 1670,[14] precinct registers appear not to have been appointed for several years. Upon their appointment, however, the precinct registers took over the responsibility for recording land transfers from person to person, though the secretary continued to handle the initial grants from the Proprietors and later the Crown and State. The earliest extant deed book is Book A, Perquimans Precinct. Although this book was not begun until 1681, it recorded deeds issued as early as 1662.

Thus it was that the granting of land and the entering of the grants came to constitute not only the most important records of the early colonial period, but also perhaps the most important function of government other than the keeping of law and order. The fees—along with those for other entry making—supported all the public officials from the governor down to precinct register. Under the laws of 1715, the following fees were charged for land transactions: governor, 10s. for signing grants of 640 acres; surveyor, £1 13s. 4d. for surveying a thousand acres and under; secretary, 9s. for a patent in paper or 11s. for a patent in parchment, 5s. 2d. for a warrant for surveying land and making return, 5s. for recording the surveyor's return, 5s. for assignment of warrant, and 1s. for a certificate or patent of land; and precinct register, 2s. 6d. for registering a conveyance and 2s. 6d. for a copy thereof.[15]

Although some changes were made in the procedure for keeping land records, the general characteristics of granting and enter-

13. Parker, *Charters*, p. 147.

14. David Leroy Corbitt, *The Formation of North Carolina Counties 1663-1943* (Raleigh: State Department of Archives and History, 1950), p. 65.

15. Laws of 1715, c. 58, in Walter Clark (ed.), *The State Records of North Carolina* (16 vols.; Winston, Goldsboro, and Charlotte: State of North Carolina, 1895-1907), XXIII, 83 ff. Cited hereafter as Clark, *State Records*. The "Laws of 1715" probably constituted a code of laws, many of which had been passed at previous sessions. A new set of fees was established from time to time. See, for instance, Laws of 1722, c. 6, in Clark, *State Records*, XXV, 179 ff.

ing lands were thus established early in the proprietary period and continued until the creation of the independent State of North Carolina. The precincts became counties in 1738, but their functions were not changed greatly. The system of recording titles and registering deeds, at that period not generally followed in England, is due to a clause in the Fundamental Constitutions. It appears to have originated from the customs of Holland, and it may be that this was the most enduring contribution of the ill-fated Fundamental Constitutions.[16]

Recording of wills and settlements of estates down to 1760 was a responsibility of the secretary of the Province. The oldest extant will, that of Mary Fortsen dated January 28, 1663, was recorded November 15, 1665.[17] The usual procedure was for a will to be proved by the governor, but by 1715 an act had been passed authorizing its proving by the General Court or a precinct court, although letters of administration were to be signed only by the governor "and only issueing out of the Secretary's office and countersigned by the Secretary or Deputy."[18] The governor was allowed a fee of 10s. for the probate and the secretary 5s. for recording the will and the copy of the probate.[19]

The requirement for recording vital statistics appeared in the Fundamental Constitutions of 1669. Article 77 provided for a "registry in every Colony, wherein shall be Recorded all the Births, Marriages, and deaths that shall happen within the said Colony."[20] Because "colonies" were never officially established in Carolina, this responsibility devolved upon the precinct, though

16. Clark, *State Records*, XXV, iii. See also William Conrad Guess, *County Government in North Carolina* ("The James Sprunt Historical Publications," Vol. XI, No. 1 [Chapel Hill: The University of North Carolina Press, 1911]), p. 13. Cited hereafter as Guess, *County Government*. For a discussion of land registration in an American colony and the European background of the system, see S. G. Nissenson, "The Development of a Land Registry System in New York," *New York History*, XX (1939), 16-42.

17. Will of Mary Fortsen, original manuscript in Secretary of State's Papers, North Carolina Wills, State Archives.

18. Laws of 1715, c. 48, in James Iredell (comp.), *Laws of the State of North-Carolina* (Edenton: Hodge & Wills, 1791), pp. 28-30. Cited hereafter as Iredell, *Laws*.

19. Laws of 1715, c. 58, in Clark, *State Records*, XXIII, 83-87.

20. Parker, *Charters*, p. 147. A revision in the second Fundamental Constitutions established a registry in each seigniory and barony also, but these units of government were never organized. Parker, *Charters*, p. 162.

only one such record—that for Perquimans Precinct covering the period 1659 to 1820—has come to light.[21]

The provision, while specific,[22] was never enforced throughout the Province. An act of 1669 or before[23] provided for couples to be married before the governor or a member of the Council who would give certificate thereof, "and the said Certificate being registered in the Secretary's Office or by the Register of the precinct or in such other Office as shall hereafter for that use be provided" should be lawful evidence of marriage. The act was among six reconfirmed by the legislative session of 1715.[24] In the latter year also was passed an act providing that the register in each precinct record births, burials, and marriages "till there be a Clerk of the Parish Church. . . ."[25] In the same year the fees for vital records were, for the governor, 10s. for marriage license; and for the register, 1s. for registering every birth, burial, or marriage, and 2s. 6d. for each copy.[26] While the scarcity of records created under provisions of these laws is no proof that the laws were not observed, this fact plus comments from later colonial officials make it clear that the registration of vital records was carelessly done, if at all.

Next in importance to the records relating to the citizen's birth, marriage, land ownership, death, and estate settlement came the records of the General Assembly and the laws thereof. The first General Assembly met in present Pasquotank County

21. This register is identified as having originated in Berkeley Parish. J. R. B. Hathaway (ed.), *North Carolina Historical and Genealogical Register*, III (1903), 199-220, 363-410. Cited hereafter as Hathaway, *Register*. The records, bound in two volumes under the title of "Perquimans Precinct Births, Marriages, Deaths, and Flesh Marks," are now in the State Archives.

22. The law provided, "The time of every one's Age shall be Recorded from the day that his Birth is entered in the Registry, and not before"; "No Marriage shall be lawful . . . till both the parties mutually own it before the Colony Register, and he enter it, with the names of the Father and mother of such party"; and "No man shall administer to the goods, or have right to them, or enter upon the Estate, of any person deceased till his death be Registered in the Colony Registry." Parker, *Charters*, p. 147-48.

23. Saunders, *Colonial Records*, I, 184; Clark, *State Records*, XXV, 119. The act was either ratified or confirmed in 1669; it may have been passed at a previous session.

24. Laws of 1715, c. 1, in Clark, *State Records*, XXIII, 1.

25. Laws of 1715, c. 28, in Iredell, *Laws*, pp. 22-25.

26. Laws of 1715, c. 58, in Clark, *State Records*, XXIII, 83-87.

in 1665. From that time forward the legislature—composed of the Council made up of the governor and members appointed by the Proprietors and the Lower House made up of elected freeholders and referred to variously as the "General Assembly," "House of Burgesses," and just the "Assembly"—made such laws as the Proprietors might approve. It may be assumed that each session produced journals of the two bodies but such journals are not extant for many of the early sessions. The secretary appears to have been the clerk of the Upper House in the proprietary period, but the Lower House had its own clerk.

That the journals were not always accurately kept is indicated in a dispute arising in 1716 in which the governor laid before the Council some papers said to be a copy of the journal of the Lower House wherein "amongst other things" were contained four resolves concerning the "deplorable Circumstances of this Governmt. . . ." The Council reported that ". . . the said Resolves and Every of them were Clandestinly obteyned and entered in the said Journal on purpose of Torment and Create Differences unreasonable Jealousies and Contempt of yᵉ authorityes of this Governmᵗ for that no such resolves were ever Published at the same Assembly nor Communicated to yᵉ upper house at the time of yᵉ Setting of yᵉ said Assembly. . . ."[27] Again, in 1718, Maurice Moore and Edward Moseley were committed to the custody of the provost marshal for "illegally possessing themselves of the Sectys Office the Journals at the Council and several other papers Relateing to the government lodged at Sandy Point the Dwelling house of Capt John Lovick Deputy Secty. . . ." The Council ruled that Moore and Moseley were "guilty of a high Crime, and misdemeaners being not only tending to the manifest Injury of the people and Subverting the quiet of the goverment [*sic*] but a high contempt and dishonor of the Supreme authority thereof in entring into the Offices Aforsd and detaining near twenty four hours the records papers and Journals aforsd. . . ."[28] Moseley was convicted and fined for the act in the General Court.[29]

27. Council Journal, December 30, 1718, in Saunders, *Colonial Records*, II, 244.
28. Council Journal, December 30, 1718, in Saunders, *Colonial Records*, II, 321.
29. Saunders, *Colonial Records*, II, 329.

Less than ten years later, in 1728, John Leatry, clerk of the
Lower House, was accused of "having given Copies of the Proceedings of the Late Assembly which he [the governor] believeth
doth not agree with the original minutes of the proceedings of
the Assembly. . . ." Upon a request that he produce the originals,
Leatry reported that "they were at his Lodgings for his more
ready making out of Copies for such as wanted them. . . ," where-
upon he was sternly warned by the governor and Council "that
it was their unanimous Opinion that he ought not to remove
them from the office appointed for keeping them least [sic]
some accident might happen to them. . . ." The incident also
brought to light the clerk's failure to give security for the per-
formance of his duties and the attorney general was ordered to
prosecute him therefor, in spite of Leatry's contention that such
security was not required since he was appointed by the representatives of the people.[30]

Of greater significance to the growing population of the
Province than the journals were the laws themselves. There was
no printing press in North Carolina until 1749, and none of the
laws is known to have been printed during the proprietary period.
A law of 1720 provided that the clerk of the Lower House was
within ten days after ratification of the act to send "faire Copies
. . . to the Clerks of every precinct Court in this Gov'mt, who are
forthwith required to publish the Same by affixing a Note at the
precinct Court House and all other publick places, as Churches,
Reading meeting house Doors, in their Several precincts."[31]
This appears to have been the usual way of circulating the laws.
In addition to the inaccuracies that inevitably crept into the
handwritten copies, it is likely that only a small minority of the
people were cognizant of the laws in force. Indeed, it is doubtful
if the officials themselves knew what laws had been passed. An
unidentified official wrote in 1729 that the confirmed laws of
1715 had been "out of use and lost for above 20 years when upon
a revival [sic] of the whole body of Laws in 1715 an old copy was

30. Saunders, *Colonial Records*, II, 767.
31. Clark, *State Records*, XXV, 166.

produced and transcribed into the Law Book the original of them are entirely lost and they are become quite obsolete."[32]

Following the first revisal of the laws in 1715, at which time many were omitted as being "obsolete," there appears to have been a greater effort to circulate up-to-date manuscript copies. In 1718, Deputy Secretary John Lovick received from Edward Moseley thirty pounds for five copies of the laws, "2 of them being in ye book of Claimes Novr 1717 & other 2 since."[33] One manuscript volume of the laws, including those confirmed in 1715 and those passed at subsequent assemblies through 1723, which appears to have been sent to the clerk of court in Bertie Precinct, is preserved in the State Department of Archives and History.[34]

The Charter of 1663 authorized the establishment of various courts in the Province,[35] and the Fundamental Constitutions of 1669 made provision for a complicated system of courts which was never carried out. Instead, there gradually developed during the proprietary period a court system, the most important body of which was the General Court, made up of the governor and a varying number of deputies of the Lords Proprietors. Beginning in 1697, however, judges especially commissioned by the governor made up the court. Finally, after 1712, the chief justice and from two to four associate justices comprised the General Court.[36] This was both an appellate court for cases tried in the precinct courts and also a court of original jurisdiction in major cases. The secretary of the Province appears to have served both as clerk of the pleas and clerk of the Crown in handling the records of the General Court.[37] Although the bulk of the provincial court records of the proprietary period were those created

32. Saunders, *Colonial Records*, III, 176.

33. Hathaway, *Register*, III, 148.

34. This manuscript volume, untitled and unpaged and containing later scribblings, is in an advanced state of deterioration. It has deliberately not been restored.

35. Charter of 1663, as contained in Parker, *Charters*, p. 79.

36. Charles C. Crittenden and Dan Lacy (eds.), *The Historical Records of North Carolina: The County Records* (3 vols.; Raleigh: North Carolina Historical Commission, 1938-39), I, 58. Cited hereafter as Crittenden and Lacy, *Historical Records*. See also Minutes of the General Court, *passim*, in State Archives, and Saunders, *Colonial Records*, II, 80.

37. Clark, *State Records*, XXIII, 252; XXV, 222.

by the General Court, there were other provincial courts, including those of the Admiralty and Chancery, and records of some of these courts have been preserved in the State Archives for as early as 1665.

Although county courts were provided for in the Fundamental Constitutions,[38] such courts appear to have been held in Albemarle County only from 1682 until 1694.[39] The Proprietors in 1691 gave instructions to Governor Philip Ludwell that "All processes and actions to be tryed in the County Courts and pleas &c. shall be entred and records kept of them by the Clearke of that County Court where the Action is to be tryed the Clearks of the respective County Courts shall be appointed by the Chief Judge or sheriff w[ch] Clearkes are to be sworne for the due Execution of his office and give security by his owne bond."[40]

Thus, except for the brief life of the county courts, there was no intermediate jurisdiction between the precinct courts and the General Court. These precinct courts became, therefore, the courts that most frequently touched the lives of the people. A precinct court, as provided for in the Fundamental Constitutions,[41] was to be composed of a steward and four justices. The precinct clerk gradually became an important local official, and his appointment devolved upon the secretary of the Province until 1761 when the office of clerk of the pleas was created with power to appoint the county (formerly precinct) clerks.[42] The clerk's duties were to keep the records of the court and especially to transcribe the minutes which were required to be read in open court and duly corrected prior to their signing by the justices.[43] Minutes have been preserved for the Perquimans Precinct Court for as early as 1688.

38. Parker, *Charters,* p. 143.

39. Memorandum from Mattie Erma Parker [Editor of the Colonial Records Project, State Department of Archives and History] to the Advisory Editorial Board, November 29, 1965, in State Archivist's Files, State Archives; Paul M. McCain, "The County Court in North Carolina Before 1750" (unpublished Ph.D. dissertation, Duke University, 1950), p. 22, n. 44.

40. Instructions to Col. Philip Ludwell, Governor of Carolina, November 8, 1691, in Saunders, *Colonial Records,* I, 375.

41. Parker, *Charters,* p. 144.

42. Saunders, *Colonial Records,* VII, 482; Clark, *State Records,* XXIII, 566.

43. Guess, *County Government,* p. 22.

To the precinct court belonged not only trial jurisdiction over routine cases but also the responsibility for administering the affairs of the precinct (later county). Beginning in the eighteenth century it appointed and controlled administrators, executors, and guardians; probated wills; recorded real estate transactions; levied taxes; granted licenses; appointed road overseers; and in general served as the administrative body of the precinct.[44] Its records, therefore, comprise a valuable chronicle of the history of the people and their local government.

One of the earliest offices created in the Province was that of sheriff, among whose duties was that of collecting the quitrents for the Proprietors.[45] The task of listing tithables fell to the constable who made returns to the treasurer of the precinct who in turn collected the taxes.[46] Among the early records extant are tax lists which often form the only census of the citizens of the Province.

A variety of other records were provided for during the proprietary period. The governor was required to keep the Lords Proprietors informed of the affairs in the Colony through reports and correspondence—a requirement of great importance inasmuch as the papers preserved in England in many instances now comprise the only records of certain periods of the early history of the Province. The secretary, in addition to the duties of record keeping already outlined, was required to "keep exact Enteryes in faire books of all publicke affaires. . . ."[47] He also was to enter all "actions Pleas &c. to be tryed before" the governor;[48] to keep all other records required of him and to "deliver them safe and entire when demanded by their Lordships or any other person or

44. Saunders, *Colonial Records*, VII, 480-81.
45. Instructions to Governor Samuel Stephens, January, 1670, in Chatham Collection, State Archives. See also Powell, *Albemarle*, p. 35. Later this duty fell upon the receiver general who was to collect rents due the Crown. See Saunders, *Colonial Records*, III, xiii.
46. Laws of 1715, c. 51, in Iredell, *Laws*, p. 31. See also Saunders, *Colonial Records*, II, 889.
47. Lords Proprietors' Instructions to Governor Samuel Stephens, October 8, 1667, in Chatham Collection, State Archives. See also Powell, *Albemarle*, p. 26.
48. Instructions to Governor Philip Ludwell, November 8, 1691, in Saunders, *Colonial Records*, I, 575.

persons authorized by them";[49] to file papers and surveys of the boundaries of the Colony;[50] to keep records of bonds of public officers;[51] and to keep other such records as the governor and Council might direct.

Records relating to religion also were to be kept. The Fundamental Constitutions of 1669 provided that "The terms of admittance and communion with any church or profession shall be written in a book and therein be Subscribed by all the members of the said church or profession," and that a religious record "of every church or profession shall be kept by the public Register of the Precinct where they reside." The protection of the laws was to be denied to any person seventeen years of age or over whose name had not been so recorded. A true copy of the Fundamental Constitutions was to be kept in a "great book" by the register of every precinct and to be subscribed by all persons seventeen years of age or older. Aliens were to be registered by the precinct register.[52] Few of these provisions were carried out in practice, however. Clerks of the church were named, and that their duties extended to other than things relating to record keeping is indicated by the requirement that the clerk of St. Paul's Parish in Chowan Precinct ". . . keep the Keys of the Church and keep the Church clean and keep the woods fired at the time of the year round the Chappell also to provide water for the baptizing of Children, and to attend the Chappell every Lords Day, when the Minister is here to officiate as a Clerk, and when the Minister is absent to read divine Service, and a Sermon &c. to keep the Vestry Journal and to attend the Vestry at their meetings."[53]

The collection of import and export duties by the "naval officer" or collector of customs was another function necessitating the keeping of records. An audit was required quarterly.[54]

49. "Further Additional Instructions to Colonel Edward Tynte Governor of South & North Carolina," March 24, 1708/9, in Saunders, *Colonial Records*, I, 706.
50. Council Journal, August 11, 1714, in Saunders, *Colonial Records*, II, 141.
51. Laws of 1715, c. 12, in Clark, *State Records*, XXIII, 15.
52. Parker, *Charters*, pp. 149-51.
53. Minutes of a meeting of the St. Paul's Parish Vestry, Chowan Precinct, March 9, 1703/4, in Saunders, *Colonial Records*, I, 597.
54. Saunders, *Colonial Records*, II, 498, 567.

These records were required of colonial office holders either by statute, instructions, or other directives, references to which have been preserved. Other records were created, perhaps without directives, for the simple reason that they were found to be necessary in the administration of government. Some of these have been preserved.

But it seemed to be easier to create records than to care for them. The reason was twofold: First, public officers were usually chosen for political reasons rather than for their qualifications and there were frequent charges of neglect; and second, there was no fixed seat of government for either the Colony or the precincts in the early decades, and consequently records were carted around from place to place with the resultant loss of many.

In addition to the complaints voiced over the falsifying of legislative journals,[55] charges of abuses in record keeping are frequent in the colonial records. In 1711, the General Assembly passed an act

> . . . for redressing several grievances, abuses and illegal proceedings whereby the poor Inhabitants have been wronged in their Titles of Land, as in the payments of certain sums of money extorted from them without sufficient acquittances . . . and for the better discovery of what sum or sums of money are in the hands of the said Thomas Cary [Hyde's predecessor as governor] (the Land Office with all books, records, and papers thereunto belonging being feloniously detained or otherwise imbeziled by Mr Em^ll Low) so that a true account thereof cannot be had.[56]

In connection with the charge, Governor Edward Hyde alleged that "Coll: Cary made clarke of Pemplico Court in Bath County" was well known "for forging of false Judgements and razing of records which most in that Court are now raz'd . . . [and] when I compelled him to deliver them, abundance of records was not only razed but whole councells cut out of the Booke[.]"[57] Three

55. See above, p. 11.
56. Saunders, *Colonial Records*, I, 792.
57. Edward Hyde to "My Lord," August 22, 1711, in Saunders, *Colonial Records*, I, 802. It should be remembered that this act was passed just after the "Cary Rebellion" in which the leaders of the Colony divided sharply over issues other than record keeping, and the charges against Cary may have been politically inspired. They are cited here not for their truthfulness but because they were contained in a public law.

years later Edward Moseley was accused of refusing to deliver to the secretary the papers relating to the boundary between North Carolina and Virginia, and was ordered to do so.[58] Furthermore, a scribe noted the following in the General Court Minutes: "Mem—it appears that all the Records of the Court from March 1707 to March 1715 wch. includes the time wherein Mr. Moseley presided in the Genll Court is all taken out & destroyed."[59] An act of 1715, undoubtedly as a result of similar experiences, required that outgoing registers deliver to the precinct register "all papers & Records which shall be in their Custody and which of right belong and appertain to the said office under the penalty of Fifty pounds."[60] Tobias Knight, secretary of the Province, was charged with being an accessory of pirates in 1719[61] and a few months later William Duckenfield "appear'd and desir'd to be made Secretary of North Carolina Mr Knight the Secretary being very ill[.]" In what may have been an action of significance, the Proprietors at a meeting on July 31, 1719, ordered "that the said Duckingfield be minuted to be Secretary when the Lords shall be informed that Mr Knight is dead, he giving security for the due execution of his office."[62]

In 1725, the Council ordered that all books and papers belonging to the collector of custom's office be delivered to the new appointee, Christopher Gale, along with "all Records Books and other papers belonging to the General Court Office. . . ."[63] Three years later Governor Richard Everard charged that he, Everard, put certain records in the hands of Attorney General William Little "for the use of the publick and not for his own private use," and asked for a warrant for their return.[64] In the same year the Lords Proprietors reported to the Privy Council that an accurate

58. Council Journal, August 11, 1714, in Saunders, *Colonial Records,* II, 142.

59. General Court Minutes, 1695-1703, State Archives.

60. Laws of 1715, c. 38, in Clark, *State Records,* XXIII, 50. See also Iredell, *Laws,* pp. 22-25.

61. Council Journal, April 4, 1719, in Saunders, *Colonial Records,* II, 329.

62. Minutes of a meeting of the Lords Proprietors, July 31, 1719, in Saunders, *Colonial Records,* II, 350.

63. Council Journal, July 17, 1725, in Saunders, *Colonial Records,* II, 567.

64. Minutes of a General Court of Oyer and Terminer and General Sessions, July 30, 1728, in Saunders, *Colonial Records,* II, 825. The court required that the books be delivered, but then returned them to the attorney general.

account of neither the quitrent arrears owed to the Proprietors nor the claims of the officers was possible "for want of a proper Register. . . ."[65]

In the light of twentieth-century emphasis on the right of the people to have access to the public records, it is interesting to note that, in 1712, the Lords Proprietors instructed the governor "to take care that all persons may be admitted to Peruse y[e] Publick Records of our Province provided they make such Perusal in the place where the same are Constantly kept & pay the Customary & usual Fees."[66]

Perhaps a greater villain than corrupt officials was the absence of a provincial capital or fixed courthouse during the early years. Both the legislature and the precinct courts held their sessions in the homes of substantial planters, and probably no building reserved for public use was constructed prior to 1700. The intentions of the Proprietors seem to have been to provide for such buildings, however, as is evidenced by perhaps the first reference to the erection of a seat of government, in 1670. They wrote to Governor Samuel Stephens:

And for as much as we out of o[r] abundant desire to have y[e] County of Albemarle in a safe & flowrishing Condition are Resolved wth y[e] first money that we shall receive of our quitt rents fines or forfeitures to Erect a State house for reception of y[e] Govern[r]: Councell & assembly in their times of meeting alsoe a prison & a Church w[ch] being placed whereon of yo[r] public storehouses is we Judge will conduce much to y[e] speedy building of a Towne:—We desire that yo[u] will alsoe as above send us the opinions of yo[r]: selves & the Assembly in what place it is most Convenient for the Country to have theise buildings erected. . . .[67]

In 1676, the Proprietors asked the Assembly to erect a town on Roanoke Island "which wee would have the Cheife towne and

65. Lords Proprietors to Privy Council, 1728, in Saunders, *Colonial Records,* II, 721.

66. "Instructions for Ye Honble Edwd Hyde Esqr Governr of North Carolina," January 24, 1711/12, in Saunders, *Colonial Records,* I, 845. The cynic might interpret this instruction as an effort to improve the income of the various office holders by encouraging greater use of the records by the public, thus increasing the amount of fees collected.

67. Lords Proprietors to Governor Samuel Stephens and the Council, January, 1670, in Chatham Collection, State Archives. See also Powell, *Albemarle,* p. 35.

the place where the Councell assemble [*sic*] should meete. . . ."[68]
Instructions to Captain Henry Wilkinson, "Governor of that
Part of the Province of Carolina that Lyes 5. miles South of the
River of Pemlico and from Thence to Virginia," in 1681, contained a requirement that "You are to choose some fitting place
in a Collony whereon to build the cheefe Towne of Albemarle
in the choyce of which you have regard to health plenty and easy
access you are to endeavor to gett the Parliament to rayse where-
withall to build a house for the meeting of the Councell and
Parliament in said Towne and when the said house is erected
the Council and Parliament are allways to sitt there and allso the
Surveyors Registers and Secretarys offices are there to be kept
and in no other place. . . ."[69] But these and perhaps other instructions were not immediately carried out. The public officials
continued to keep their records in their homes or in other locations convenient to themselves. The General Assembly and the
courts, too, met in private homes prior to the construction of
public buildings. The date and location of the earliest public
building in Carolina are not known, although the minute book
of the Perquimans Precinct Court indicates that a meeting was
held in 1701 in the "Gran Court House for ye p^{r}cinct of Piquim-
ons."[70] Around the turn of the century the "Grand Assembly"
ordered the erection of a "Corte House 60 foot long, 20 foot wide,
9½ foot pitch" in Chowan Precinct.[71] The courthouse was to
have "two roomes and an entry to the Secretary's office and one
to the office of the Clerke of the Assembly"—a requirement that

68. Saunders, *Colonial Records,* I, 229.
69. Instructions to Captain Henry Wilkinson, 1681, in Saunders, *Colonial Records,* I, 336.
70. Perquimans Precinct Court Minutes, October 14, 1701, in State Archives. The fact that subsequent courts met in private homes raises some doubt as to the dependability of this reference in the court minutes. It seems strange that only one session would have been held in a "Gran Court House." Could this reference have been simply a mischievous clerk's way of ridiculing an undesirable and perhaps dilapidated meeting place?
71. Fred A. Olds, *Story of the Counties of North Carolina with Other Data* (Oxford, N. C.: Oxford Orphanage Press, 1921), p. 22. Cited hereafter as Olds, *Story of the Counties.* The original document which Olds quoted has not been found. The date of the order is not known, but it must have been before 1706 when William Wilkinson, one of the commissioners appointed to contract for the construction of the building, died.

clearly indicated that the proposed building was intended for use by the provincial government. In 1712, the General Assembly ordered construction of a courthouse and an assembly house on Queen Anne's Creek in Chowan.[72] But there is no record of such buildings until November 11, 1718, when the Council met "at the Court House in Chowan."[73] The following year the General Court met at the "Court House at Queen Annes Creek,"[74] and a "Craven Court House" appears to have existed by that time also.[75] A law of 1720 referred to the "Gen'll Court House in Chowan and at Bath Town,"[76] but these courthouses may have served the precincts as well.

In 1722, an act provided for the construction of precinct courthouses with dimensions not less than twenty-four by sixteen feet, the cost to be defrayed by a poll tax of up to 5s. per year.[77] Of even more significance, however, was another law passed that year. It required that the offices of the chief justice, secretary, attorney general, surveyor general, provost marshal, escheator general, collector, comptroller, naval officer, and receiver of powder be kept in Edenton. But there was an important proviso: The officers were not obliged to obey the law "until there shall be a Councill Room & Gaol built in the said Town."[78]

In 1725, the Council met for the first time in the "Council

72. Olds, *Story of the Counties*, p. 22. Olds does not indicate the source of this statement.

73. Saunders, *Colonial Records*, II, 314. The Craven Precinct Court, noting in 1714 that "by misfortune of the War in this Government with the Indians, the office of the aforesaid Precinct of Craven being burnt," authorized the re-recording of a deed originally recorded in 1711. Craven Precinct Deed Book 2, p. 626, Craven County Courthouse, New Bern; Minutes of the Craven Precinct Court of Pleas and Quarter Sessions, 1714, p. 132 (reverse), State Archives. This "office" of Craven was probably the home of the precinct register rather than a specially-constructed public building. I am indebted to Charles R. Holloman, editor of *We the People*, for calling this entry to my attention.

74. Minutes of the General Court, July 28, 1719, in Saunders, *Colonial Records*, II, 357.

75. Alonzo T. Dill, *Governor Tryon and His Palace* (Chapel Hill: The University of North Carolina Press, 1955), p. 57. Cited hereafter as Dill, *Governor Tryon*.

76. Laws of 1720, c. 1, in Clark, *State Records*, XXV, 165.

77. Laws of 1722, c. 8, in Clark, *State Records*, XXIII, 101. See also Iredell, *Laws*, p. 39.

78. Laws of 1722, c. 4, in Clark, *State Records*, XXV, 177-78.

Chamber" in Edenton,[79] and in the following year the Lower
House met at the "Usuall Place at Queen Annes Creek."[80] Although there is not conclusive proof that provincial buildings
had been erected for the General Assembly, evidence supports
this assumption.[81] Thus, at the earliest, the Colony was sixty-
two years old before public buildings were provided specifically
for its legislative branch.

Fires and other calamities, in addition to human neglect, undoubtedly resulted in the loss of records in the proprietary period.
One instance occurred in 1714 when Indians burned the house
of John Lillington in which he had temporarily stored surveys of
Bath County, making a resurvey necessary.[82]

By the end of the proprietary period in 1728, even if it had
legislative halls, the Colony of North Carolina had no buildings
for executive officers of the Province, few courthouses of any
kind and none worthy of the name, no newspapers or printing
presses, no paper mills, and few records. Except for the reports
and correspondence sent to the Proprietors,[83] there existed probably no single complete series of records for the Colony—not even
of the laws. The few records that had been kept were scattered
throughout the Province in the hands of officials and former
officials. It is not surprising, therefore, that upon the discovery
and publication of a group of significant documents relating to
the Lords Proprietors, a twentieth-century historian commented,
". . . the scarcity of surviving records of the seventeenth century
makes it impossible to be certain about a number of points in our
earliest history. The very fact, however, that the twenty-eight

79. Council Journal, April 3, 1725, in Saunders, *Colonial Records*, II, 562.
80. Journal of the Lower House, April 5, 1726, in Saunders, *Colonial Records*,
II, 608.
81. In 1733, there were a "Council House" and an "Assembly House" at Edenton. See below, p. 38. These may have been the same buildings as those referred
to in 1725 and 1726, but proof is lacking.
82. Council Journal, August 11, 1714, in Saunders, *Colonial Records*, II, 141.
83. Much of this material is now being uncovered by the Colonial Records
Project of the State Department of Archives and History. This project began
in 1961 by the now extinct Carolina Charter Tercentenary Commission and was
transferred to the State Department of Archives and History on January 1, 1964.
The first volume of a projected new series of the colonial records was published
in 1963.

documents published here have been unknown for so long gives hope that others may yet come to light."[84]

Unfortunately for North Carolina history, however, the lack of concern—or of corrective action—for properly keeping the records of the Province did not end with the proprietary period.

84. Powell, *Albemarle*, p. xxiv.

II

Record Keeping in the Royal Period

1729-1776

The hopes of the Lords Proprietors for a flourishing and profitable colony in Carolina were never achieved. Their visionary feudal system, as contemplated in the various Fundamental Constitutions, came to virtually naught. The recalcitrant settlers were frequently embroiled in political and economic struggles with the Proprietors' appointed officials and at least two of these struggles have gone down in history as "rebellions." Life was crude; government was just as primitive. Unrealistic policies, incapable administrators, and settlers determined to remain virtually ungoverned, coupled with the conspiracy of geography against the development of seaports and inland transportation, all contributed to the unruliness of the Carolinians. Laws were made and disregarded; the officials had neither the determination nor the ability to enforce them.

Because of the substantial settlement of the Cooper and Ashley River areas to the south, the Proprietors in 1712 provided for separate governors for North and South Carolina. It might have been hoped that the separation of the widely settled areas would lead to a tightening of governmental control over the portion of the Carolina grant to be referred to hereafter as North Carolina. Perhaps it did, because there was a perceptible increase in the productivity of the General Assembly beginning in 1715. Laws were revised and increasing attention was given to the problems confronting the Colony. But six decades after the granting of the Carolina Charter, North Carolina could still boast of no public building for its administrative records and no adequate system of enforcement of its laws and recording of its actions. Quitrents, the chief source of income for the Proprietors, were largely unpaid and uncollectible because of the inability of the officials to maintain accurate land records and to enforce the rent laws.

It is perhaps not surprising, therefore, that several of the Proprietors[1] expressed an interest in the sale of their land to the Crown. All but one—the Earl of Granville—agreed in 1728 to sell their shares for £2,500 (approximately $12,500) each, and, in 1729, the Crown assumed ownership of all of Carolina except a one-eighth share remaining with Granville's heirs. But it was not until 1744 that this one-eighth share—known as the Granville District—was laid off, thus assigning to private ownership the lands between the Virginia boundary southward to an east-west line running approximately through the town of Bath. Thus, after 1744, though the Crown retained governmental jurisdiction over all the Province, Lord Granville owned the land for approximately half of North Carolina—the most valuable half at that.

Just as in the proprietary period, so also under royal ownership the problem of land and taxes continued as the chief concern of government. As has been seen, early instructions attempted to place all registration of land grants and transfers in the office of the "chief register" or secretary of the Province. While the issuance of grants from the Proprietors remained a function of that office, as early as 1681 precinct registers had assumed the recording of land transfers from person to person.[2] Afterward there was no central registration of land transfers, a deficiency which resulted in the inability of the Proprietors to levy and collect more than a portion of the quitrents due them. Such was the confusion that in 1728 the Proprietors told the Privy Council that for want of a proper register they could not closely estimate

1. From 1663 to 1728 the eight shares of the Carolina grant were inherited in part by nearly fifty different persons. See William S. Powell, *The Proprietors of Carolina* (Raleigh: Carolina Charter Tercentenary Commission, 1963), p. 6.
2. See above, p. 8.

the arrears due them in quitrents. They wrote, "[J]udging upon a strict enquiry Much more will be found due to them, yet it is drawn according to the best calculation they have been able to make under the long destracted state of affairs in Carolina. . . ."[3]

In an effort to bring order out of the confused state of land affairs, one of the earliest actions of the new government was to order that no more land be granted until further notice. But the secretary, John Lovick, was accused of violating the order "in a very Contemptable manner." He was reminded by the president of the Council that the recording and copying of such orders were "not meerly (ex gratia Curia) to be granted or not to be granted at his Pleasure Whose Business it is to Record and give Copys out of His Office. . . ."[4] The fact that the secretary's office derived much of its income from fees in connection with land grants undoubtedly played a role in the reluctance of that officer to discontinue grants. Displeasure at the operation of the secretary's office led Governor George Burrington, the first royal governor, to report to the Board of Trade in 1732:

I have altered the Method used heretofore in this Government, [which] was to leave sign'd Warrants in the Secretary's hands to fill up as any man came for them, and very often the Deputy Surveyors, kept numbers in their Possession, by which they made considerable advantages, by their management some people were injured, and other benefitted, to put an end to all unfair Practices, the warrants are now filled up before my signing, and Directed only to the Surveyor General, Who afterwards gives Direction to his Deputy's, All the Warrants made out are entered in a book at the Secretary's office, when I sign them they are entered in another I keep on purpose, and when they come to the Surveyor's hands he do's the same[.][5]

The commission of the new secretary, Nathaniel Rice, contained instructions that he adhere strictly to established procedures in receiving certificates, issuing warrants, and preparing grants.[6]

3. Petition of Lords Proprietors to Privy Council, 1728, in Saunders, *Colonial Records,* II, 721.

4. Saunders, *Colonial Records,* III, 14.

5. Governor George Burrington to Board of Trade, February 20, 1731/32, in Saunders, *Colonial Records,* III, 337.

6. Commission to Nathaniel Rice as secretary, May 11, 1731, in Saunders, *Colonial Records,* III, 633-34.

A veiled accusation of mismanagement in the surveyor general's office was made before the Council in 1731 when it was charged that Edward Moseley, the former occupant of that office, had not delivered the papers relating to the office in spite of repeated demands.[7] A few years later the receiver general came in for similar criticism. The papers relating to the quitrents were demanded of the heirs of the deceased receiver general, but "no more than three loose sheets of paper which gave no manner of light into that Affaire" were turned in.[8] In an effort to obtain a central registration of land, Governor Burrington urged the Crown to appoint a general register for the Colony to replace the ten precinct registers.[9] While this suggestion was not heeded, there was established the post of auditor general in whose office all land grants should also be recorded for rent purposes.[10] This law was never effectively carried out because of repeated legislation delaying the time for enrolling the lands.[11]

The Crown, in a further effort to determine land ownership in the Colony, instructed Burrington to transmit to the Board of Trade a map of the whole Province showing the various plantations.[12] Such a map was prepared in 1733 by Edward Moseley, but within twenty years Governor Gabriel Johnston was complaining that it was "very deficient, especially in the back settlements, [where] many thousand persons have sat down there since that map was published."[13]

Evidence that the Lower House on occasion could be concerned with the records of the Province emerged early in the royal period. On May 1, 1668, the Proprietors had issued to the

7. Council Journal, April 22, 1731, in Saunders, *Colonial Records*, III, 217.

8. Governor Gabriel Johnston to Board of Trade, October 15, 1736, in Saunders, *Colonial Records*, IV, 173.

9. Governor Burrington to———, September 3, 1730, in Saunders, *Colonial Records*, III, 88.

10. Council Journal, December 9, 1735, in Saunders, *Colonial Records*, IV, 74.

11. See, for instance, Laws of 1741, c. 10, in Clark, *State Records*, XXIII, 169.

12. Instructions to Governor Burrington, 1730, in Saunders, *Colonial Records*, III, 115.

13. Governor Johnston to Board of Trade, February 15, 1750/51, in Saunders, *Colonial Records*, IV, 1073. The Moseley map was titled "A New and Correct Map of the Province of North Carolina. By Edward Moseley, late Surveyor General of the said Province. 1733."

"Grand Assembly" of Albemarle the "Great Deed of Grant" under which the people of that county were permitted to hold their lands under the same terms as the inhabitants of Virginia.[14] These terms permitted the payment of quitrents in specie or commodities. But in the 1730's there was an attempt by the Crown to require payment of quitrents only in currency.[15] The reaction of the populace was vehement. The Lower House in 1731 ordered that the "Great Deed of Grant" be delivered and copied in the journal after which the original was to be kept in the possession of the speaker.[16] Two years later Governor Burrington reported to the General Assembly that "after three days labour, our search proved in vain and we could not find any Copy of that Deed, or anything relateing to it[.]"[17] That it was found two months later, however, was indicated in a letter from the Board of Trade acknowledging a copy of the document, but questioning the authority of the Proprietors to issue it.[18] The controversy was still raging in 1743 when again the original document was ordered kept in the possession of Cullen Pollock.[19]

Neither Burrington nor his successor, Gabriel Johnston, was successful in obtaining the proper registration of land and the preparation of a rent roll. Many grantees mistakenly assumed that their grants were complete upon the return of the warrants to the secretary's office, and, in 1753, the secretary was ordered to publish in the *No^{th}-Carolina Gazette,* the only newspaper in the Colony, a list of warrants in his office for which completed patents had not been issued.[20]

Perhaps the third royal governor, Arthur Dobbs, made the most valiant efforts on behalf of the Crown. Soon after arriving in the Province in 1754, he wrote:

14. Records of Perquimans County, Book A, No. 66, Perquimans County Courthouse, Hertford, North Carolina.

15. Saunders, *Colonial Records,* III, 613-22.

16. Saunders, *Colonial Records,* III, 288-92.

17. Governor Burrington to General Assembly, November 8, 1733, in Saunders, *Colonial Records,* III, 621.

18. J. Willes to———, January 7, 1733/34, in Saunders, *Colonial Records,* III, 623.

19. Lower House Journal, July 26, 1743, in Saunders, *Colonial Records,* IV, 650.

20. Council Journal, September 29, 1753, in Saunders, *Colonial Records,* V, 36.

. . . I shall find great difficulty in getting a proper rent-roll, there is not one plot or chart of any Survey lodged in any office, in the King's part of this Province, there being only one which is annexed to the Patent, the only entry in the Secretary's or Auditors Office, being only the bearings of the lines, as entered in the Patents, so that upon reexamining the Patents to get duplicates of the Charts, which I must do, before I can do justice to the Crown, I am afraid it will appear that different Surveyors have entered into the surveys of those who went before them, & that the plots will not talley with each other as they ought, but probably may overlap one another & in many cases there may be great Vacancies not granted at all, but occupied by the neighbouring Patentees, but I am determined to go through them regularly County by County until I can compleat the rent roll & keep all the Officers to their duty, & after properly dividing the Counties, when I give them Charters, & fixing the boundaries of each County, I will have duplicates of every chart lodged in the proper office to prevent future frauds, for want of proper places to keep the Offices in & to preserve records upon account of the changeable state of this Province, whenever a Receiver General, Surveyor General, Secretary or Auditor dies, all papers die with them, for the Successors say they have got no papers, or if any those very insignificant, from their Predecessors, which I must beg leave to say is owing to the Appointment of improper persons who know nothing of the Business, & therefore neglect it, & leave it all to their Deputies or Clerks, who only work for themselves, & not for the Publick; every Officer or Clerk going to his Plantation, & neglecting the publick business—.[21]

The opposition of powerful forces in the Colony was destined to defeat Dobbs's well-meaning enthusiasm. After his death and the assumption of the governorship by William Tryon, the rent roll still had not been prepared.

An interesting account of the careless handling of the land records was told in 1767 when it was alleged that fourteen volumes "in Folio Bound in Leather, and two stitched in sheets," purporting to be the rent roll, were delivered by John Rutherford, the receiver general, to the auditor's office. The latter's deputy complained that "from great appearance of rain and to prevent Books of such labour and consequence to the Crown suf-

21. Governor Arthur Dobbs to Board of Trade, December 19, 1754, in Saunders, *Colonial Records*, V, 156-57. See also Desmond Clarke, *Arthur Dobbs, Esquire: 1689-1765* (Chapel Hill: The University of North Carolina Press, 1957), p. 141. Cited hereafter as Clarke, *Arthur Dobbs*.

fering by being exposed in an open cart," he accepted them, but upon a closer look, the deputy concluded that the books were not completely finished nor fit to be received into the auditor's office. Rutherford replied that he had not meant for the books to be considered as complete and that it would take him "a few years" to complete the list due to the failure of the county registers to make proper returns of their conveyances. The Council thereupon ordered that the secretary require "in the most express terms from the registers of the Counties in his Majestys district, that they deliver to the Secretarys office Extracts of the several Conveyances in their respective offices. . . ."[22]

The preamble of an act in 1770 again blamed much of the confusion and neglect upon the county officials. It referred to "the Neglect and Mismanagement of Persons, who have heretofore been Registers in this Province," and stated that "many of the Books wherein the Conveyances of Lands within Several of the Counties are Registered, are so abused and defaced, as to be almost unintelligible, and in Danger of being entirely lost, and are some of them removed to, and dispersed in other Counties. . . ." The justices of the counties concerned were to appoint persons to "collect together all the Books or Papers, wherein are registered the Conveyances of land . . . and to make a Fair Copy of the same into a Book or Books, well bound in Calf or Vellum," which were to be certified by a committee appointed for the purpose.[23]

Thus by the outbreak of the Revolution there was still lacking an adequate registry of the real estate of the Province and a rent roll by which the quitrents could be effectively collected. The ingenuity of the landowners, coupled with the ineffectiveness of the officials—both provincial and county—made neither possible.

The treasurers of the Province, charged with the responsibility of collecting the taxes from the counties, also found ways of evading their instructions for keeping and reporting their accounts. In 1751, Governor Johnston wrote the Board of Trade,

22. Saunders, *Colonial Records*, VII, 524-26. The county clerks were also required to report on devises of land by wills to the secretary.
23. Laws of 1770, c. 40, in Clark, *State Records*, XXIII, 842.

"As to the Treasurers accounts I believe there never was any sent home from this Country either before my coming to the Government or since, but I shall take care they shall be sent for the future. . . ."[24]

Statutory requirements that the precinct register record births, deaths, and marriages were not carried out generally in spite of the fact that fees were established for such registrations.[25] In 1731, Governor Burrington wrote, "According to the 85th Instruction there is allready a Law of the Country for registering all Births and Burials in each Parish; tho little taken notice of it,"[26] and, in 1755, Governor Dobbs complained to the Board of Trade that "it is not possible for me to get a return of the number of Births and Burials as there are no Parish Clerks or any Registry of them until I can get a Law pass'd for that purpose."[27] Twelve years later Governor Tryon wrote:

There is no regular register of births, burials or marriages kept in any county in the province although prescribed by some of our acts of Assembly and a fee established for it. The reason of this neglect is chiefly owing to the extensive residence of most of the parishioners from the parish clerks or readers in their respective parishes or counties many of which are from forty to fifty miles square and upwards, besides most families having a private burying place on their plantations.[28]

While North Carolinians would have to wait until the twentieth century for the establishment of a registry of births and deaths,[29] Governor Johnston was successful in securing the passage of legislation for the issuance of marriage permits. In 1740, the

24. Governor Johnston to Board of Trade, September 16, 1751, in Saunders, *Colonial Records,* IV, 1075.

25. See, for example, Laws of 1722, c. 6, in Clark, *State Records,* XXV, 179 ff., and Laws of 1736, c. 1, in Clark, *State Records,* XXV, 220 ff. The 1736 act omitted a fee for recording death records.

26. Governor Burrington to Duke of Newcastle, July 2, 1731, in Saunders, *Colonial Records,* III, 153. Burrington erred as to the number of the instruction; it should have been the eighty-eighth.

27. Governor Dobbs to Board of Trade, February 8, 1755, in Saunders, *Colonial Records,* V, 331.

28. Governor William Tryon, "A View of the Polity of . . . North Carolina" (1767), in Saunders, *Colonial Records,* VII, 488.

29. It was not until 1913 that North Carolina began on a state-wide basis to record births and deaths.

governor complained of "the many notorious abuses, which attend the present method of granting Licenses for Marriages and Ordinarie Keepers,"[30] a statement perhaps indicative of the governor's equation of the two types of licenses. The following year was passed an act providing that all marriage permits be issued by the clerk of the court of the county in which the female made her usual residence. The licenses were actually in the form of a bond, first made out to the King and later to the governor, in the amount of £50 and to be signed by the groom and a bondsman guaranteeing that there was no legal impediment to the marriage and that the groom would show up for the wedding. The publication of banns in the church was made legal substitute for the bond. The county clerk collected 25s. for each bond, 20s. of which he remitted to the governor. The minister received 10s. if the marriage were performed by license and 5s. if by banns; the justice of the peace received 5s. and the minister or reader 1s. 6d. for publishing the banns and granting a certificate.[31] This act was the first effective legislation concerning marriage records, and one bond has been preserved for as early as 1741. There was unfortunately no requirement that a register be kept of the bonds issued; consequently only a few marriage records have been preserved for the period prior to 1760. The method of requiring bonds continued in North Carolina until 1868 when the State's second constitution abolished it in favor of the license-register system used until the present day.

In one phase of record keeping, government under royal rule made progress. As has been seen, there was no printing press in the Colony and neither the journals of the Assembly nor the laws had been printed.[32] Manuscript copies of the laws were prepared and sent to each precinct (later county). The journals were copied by hand and sent to the Proprietors in London,

30. Saunders, *Colonial Records,* IV, 472.

31. Laws of 1741, c. 1, in Clark, *State Records,* XXIII, 158-61. Later the clerk himself signed the bond in place of the governor. Not until 1962 was there a central registration of marriage records in North Carolina.

32. The journal of a special session of the Lower House was printed in Williamsburg, Virginia, in 1740. See below, p. 35, n. 48.

along with copies of the laws. Sometimes copies were also sent to the Board of Trade even prior to 1729.[33]

As for the journals and papers of the Assembly, the clerk of each house was required to prepare them, and in some instances to purchase the blank books and collect a 25 per cent profit on the purchases.[34] But the clerks were not always dependable. For instance, in 1739, the Lower House resolved, "This House taking into consideration the ilconveniency they lye under for want of the Clerk Mr John Prat together with the records and papers belonging to this House thought proper to address his Excellency the Governor . . . in order to obtain a Press warrant to expedite the messenger to bring said Prat before them." The former clerk produced "several Books & Papers belonging to this House there not being all he had in his Custody," and the Lower House relented and authorized Pratt to keep the records so long as they were available to the House on call.[35]

The secretary was instructed by the Board of Trade in 1754 to transcribe all acts and orders of the General Assembly, together with a copy of the journals of the Council and required that all such transcripts and copies "be fairly abstracted in the margins to the end the same may be transmitted unto Our Commiss^{rs} for Trade and Plantations . . . upon pain of incurring the forfeiture of his place." The clerk of the Lower House was instructed to provide similar copies of the journals of that body.[36] Four years later the Lower House authorized its clerk to make copies of legislative papers for use in court, but the originals were required to remain in his custody.[37] In 1769, it was necessary for the Lower House to take action to recover its records from the executors of William Herritage, former clerk of the body, and the new clerk was ordered to take an "inventory or schedule thereof."[38]

33. See, for example, Saunders, *Colonial Records,* III, 62-63.
34. See Saunders, *Colonial Records,* IV, 412.
35. Saunders, *Colonial Records,* IV, 386-88. It would appear that Pratt kept the records either in his house or place of business.
36. Instructions to Governor Arthur Dobbs, June 17, 1754, in Saunders, *Colonial Records,* V, 1119.
37. Saunders, *Colonial Records,* V, 1085.
38. Saunders, *Colonial Records,* VIII, 125.

In spite of repeated instructions and complaints concerning
the copying and circulation of the laws, and in spite of Governor
Burrington's claim that he was confined to his pen "twenty hours
in every day and night" in transcribing them himself,[39] Governor
Johnston in 1736 wrote that "upon the strictest enquiry I can't
find that there is one compleat Copy of them in any place, neither
have I yet seen two copies of them which perfectly agree. . . ."
He told the General Assembly, ". . . the Laws are dispersed up
and down in different Places on [sic] loose Papers, some of them
contradictory, others unintelligible, and even from the plainest
and best of them, the vilest and most notorious malefactors not
only may, but actually have escaped with impunity, by reasons
of the insufficiency of the Publick Prisons. . . ."[40] The legislators
promised remedial action. Three years later the Lower House,
noting the "ill consequences this Province lyes under, for want of
Coppy of the several Laws now in force, since the year one thousand seven hundred and thirty three, being delivered to the
severall County Courts of this Province," asked their clerk to
obtain a copy of the laws from the secretary's office for which he,
the clerk, would be paid. But the Upper House objected on the
grounds that the payment should be to the secretary, not to the
clerk.[41] A similar request by the Lower House the following
year met the same fate.[42] Again in 1740, Governor Johnston
wrote that he had given orders to the secretary to transcribe a
copy of "what they here call their Laws." The laws passed under
the Proprietors he said were "of dubious Authority none of them
printed and the written copies very different from one another."[43]
He had traveled through the Province and heard complaints every-
where "of their wanting Copys of the Laws."[44]

39. Governor Burrington to Board of Trade, February 20, 1731/32, in Saunders,
Colonial Records, III, 335.

40. Governor Johnston to Upper House, September, 1736, in Saunders, *Colonial
Records,* IV, 227-31.

41. Saunders, *Colonial Records,* IV, 376.

42. Saunders, *Colonial Records,* IV, 573.

43. Governor Johnston to Board of Trade, December 17, 1740, in Saunders,
Colonial Records, IV, 423.

44. Governor Johnston to General Assembly, February 7, 1740, in Saunders,
Colonial Records, IV, 471.

Finally, in 1746, Governor Johnston obtained passage of an act appointing commissioners to revise and print the laws of the Province.[45] The revisal, credited largely to Samuel Swann, was approved by the General Assembly in 1749.[46] The same year an act was passed encouraging James Davis, a twenty-seven-year-old Virginia printer, to settle in North Carolina and to handle the public printing.[47] He was to be paid £160 proclamation money for printing and distributing the laws and other public documents. By June, 1749, Davis had set up his press in New Bern and his first imprint, the journal of the 1749 legislative session, appeared later in the year.[48]

Following approval of the revisal in 1749, Governor Johnston told the General Assembly, "It is with great satisfaction that I now congratulate you on finishing the revisal of your Laws in order to their being printed, a work earnestly desired by and zealously struggled for by every honest man, for these fifteen years past but never could be got accomplished till now. . . ." He laid the blame for the delay upon the "low intrigues of a restless sett of Men, who will always find their account in keeping the Country in ignorance and confusion."[49] The revisal came off Davis' press in 1751.[50] For the first time, the colony had a published set of its laws in force.

45. Laws of 1746, c. 1, in Clark, *State Records*, XXIII, 268.
46. Saunders, *Colonial Records*, IV, 1009.
47. Laws of 1749, c. 3, in Clark, *State Records*, XXIII, 314.
48. [North Carolina, General Assembly], *The Journal of the House of Burgesses of the Province of North-Carolina* (Newbern: James Davis, 1749). The journal of a special proceeding of the House of Burgesses had been printed in the shop of William Parks at Williamsburg, Virginia, in 1740. [North Carolina, General Assembly], *True and Faithful Narrative of the Proceedings of the House of Burgesses of North-Carolina, Met in Assembly for the Said Province at New-Bern, February 5th, 1739, on the Articles of Complaint Exhibited Before Them Against the Honourable William Smith, Esq., Chief Justice of the Said Province* (Williamsburg, Virginia: William Parks, 1740).
49. Governor Johnston to General Assembly, October, 1749, in Saunders, *Colonial Records*, IV, 1009. He was referring to the delegates from the Albemarle counties who had boycotted the Assembly since 1746.
50. [North Carolina, General Assembly], *Collection of All the Public Acts of Assembly in the Province of North Carolina Now in Force and Use, Together with the Titles of all Such Laws As Are Obsolete, Expir'd or Repeal'd and Also an Exact Table of the Titles of the Acts in Force; Revised by Commissioners Appointed by an Act of the General Assembly of the Said Province for that Purpose, and Examined with the Records and Confirmed in Full Assembly* (Newbern: James Davis, 1751).

Of particular importance to the Proprietors, and later to the Crown, was the transmission of official reports and instructions to and from England. As early as 1675 the Committee for Trade and Foreign Plantations[51] announced its authority to send for "all Bookes, Papers and other writings concerning any of his Majesty's said Plantations in whosesover [*sic*] custody they shall bee informed the same doe remayne. . . ." Upon the purchase of seven-eighths of the Colony by the Crown in 1729, communication with the Board became even more important. The carrying of such papers was largely the responsibility of captains of vessels plying between the countries, but the need for land conveyance of communications was recognized during the proprietary period by a law which provided that in time of war letters to or from the Crown's service, the governor, or other public officers or field officers of the militia, should be conveyed from plantation to plantation by the owner of each under penalty of £5 for each default.[52] Governor Burrington in 1729 complained that for two years he had received but one letter in answer to hundreds sent to England and "that Letter came into the hands of a gentleman in Virginia who detained the same till a Messinger from me went on purpose for it."[53] Governor Johnston in 1747 also complained that "many Paquets addressed to your Board [of Trade] from this Province have miscarried. . . ."[54] Two years later the Board of Trade charged that "no letters or public papers of any kind" had been received from Governor Johnston from December, 1741, to June, 1746, and only four letters and several journals since then.[55]

While these complaints probably indicated as much the failure of the officials to send communications as the failure of the

51. The name of the Committee was changed to that of the Board of Trade in 1696. The latter name is used in this book as a general rule.

52. Laws of 1715, c. 56, in Clark, *State Records*, XXIII, 81; Saunders, *Colonial Records*, II, 888. A similar law had been passed in Virginia as early as 1658. William Smith, "The Colonial Post-Office," *American Historical Review*, XXI (January, 1916), 265. Cited hereafter as Smith, "Colonial Post-Office."

53. Governor Burrington to Lords Proprietors, August, 1729, in Saunders, *Colonial Records*, III, 28.

54. Governor Johnston to Board of Trade, January 20, 1746/47, in Saunders, *Colonial Records*, IV, 844.

55. Board of Trade to Duke of Bedford, February 20, 1748/49, in Saunders, *Colonial Records*, IV, 931.

vessels and couriers to deliver them, they nevertheless pointed up the absence of an effective postal system within the Colony. Not until 1738—almost a century after the first crude post office had been established in Massachusetts—were there regular monthly post riders in North Carolina. In that year William Parks, printer of the *Virginia Gazette* in Williamsburg, Virginia, was commissioned by Alexander Spotswood, deputy postmaster general of the Colonies, "to carry on a stage from Williamsburg to Edenton in North Carolina" once a month.[56] The mail route, however, went no farther south than Edenton, and after one night's stay the rider returned via Norfolk on his route back to Williamsburg where the mail made connections with the north. Dr. Abraham Blacknall was made postmaster of Edenton. The following year another post route was established from Charleston, South Carolina, via Cape Fear to Edenton and return, thus providing mail connections both north and south. It was reported that the postage for one trip on the latter route amounted to £80.[57]

The first postal route appears to have been discontinued sometime within the following sixteen years, for, in 1755, Governor Dobbs reported to the General Assembly that "there is no Established Post thro [*sic*] this Province" and recommended the appointment of James Davis, the printer, to convey by messenger all public letters, expresses, and dispatches relating to the Province every fifteen days to Suffolk, Virginia, and Wilmington, North Carolina. The Assembly thereupon appointed Davis at an annual salary of £100 6s. 8d. proclamation money.[58] A more-or-less regular postal service appears to have been provided in North Carolina thereafter, and, by 1774, there was a weekly post route through the Colony.[59]

56. *Virginia Gazette* (Williamsburg, Virginia), April 28, 1738. For a study of the early postal system in Virginia, see Fairfax Harrison, "The Colonial Post Office in Virginia," *William and Mary Quarterly*, IV (April, 1924), 73-92. The word "stage" should not be interpreted as a stagecoach, but rather as a route or portion of a route. The mail was carried by a rider on horseback.

57. *Virginia Gazette*, May 25, June 22, 1739.

58. Saunders, *Colonial Records*, V, 516-17. Saunders, in his preface (V, xxvi), is of course in error when he credits James Davis with conducting the first post route.

59. Smith, "Colonial Post-Office," p. 273.

Edenton had been designated the capital of the Colony in 1722[60] but no buildings had been provided for the executive officers. Consequently their records had continued throughout the proprietary period to be kept in their homes or places of business. The provincial courts had met in the courthouse in Edenton at least as early as 1719,[61] probably sharing the building with the precinct court.

The General Assembly, however, fared somewhat better. As has been pointed out, buildings may have been erected as early as 1725 for the two houses, but if not, such buildings certainly were provided by 1733 when one Christopher Becket was allowed £12 per year "for his care in keeping the Doors & Windows of the Council House and Assembly House when those Houses are not used."[62] Repairs were also authorized for the "Council House, Court House and Goal."[63] The wording of the law of 1722 and the omission of the "Assembly House" in Governor Burrington's reference lends credence to the conclusion that the "Goal" (jail) served as a meeting place for the Lower House and also possibly the General Court.[64] Thus, by 1733, crude though they may have been, North Carolina had provided regular meeting places for the General Assembly and provincial courts at Edenton.

So long as the center of population remained around Albemarle Sound, Edenton served conveniently as the seat of government. But after the Crown took over the Colony, a tide of settlers arrived year by year and soon the population was spread from Virginia to the South Carolina border, clustered largely on both sides of the sounds and streams. No longer was Edenton the center of the Colony.

Gabriel Johnston assumed office as governor in 1734. A strong-willed Scotsman with a particular interest in the Cape Fear region, within three years he persuaded the General Assembly to hold a

60. Laws of 1722, c. 4, in Clark, *State Records*, XXV, 177-78.
61. Saunders, *Colonial Records*, II, 357.
62. Council Journal, July 9, 1733, in Saunders, *Colonial Records*, III, 544.
63. Saunders, *Colonial Records*, III, 547.
64. See Governor Burrington to Board of Trade, November 11, 1735, in Saunders, *Colonial Records*, IV, 23.

meeting in New Bern.[65] Calling that town "the most central place of the Province," he set out to fix it as the new capital. "There is not a place of the whole Government fit to keep any one Office in," he complained to the Board of Trade.[66] But the Albemarle representatives, predominant in the Assembly, would not hear to moving the capital and in 1739 they passed an act "to erect a sufficient Goal, and an Office or Place for safe Keeping the Records of the General Court, and for repairing the Court House at Edenton."[67] Another act the following year provided "that the Places already laid out, as by the Plan of the said Town [Edenton] may more fully appear, for Streets, Passages, Church, Governour's House, Court House, Burying Place, Market Place, Prison, Council Room, and Town Common, be reserved for those Uses, and no other."[68] In 1740, the Lower House, indignant over Johnston's attempt to move the seat of government, adopted the following address to the governor:

This House having resolved that Edenton is the proper place where the Secretary's Office of this Province ought to be kept and that all records, wills and other papers in any ways relating to the said office ought to be kept and deposited there and being informed that most of the records and other papers formerly kept at Edenton and belonging to the said office is removed and kept at Cape Fear chiefly at the Secretary's House and under the care and management of persons deputed by the Secretary that great Mischief may arise to the people of this province by loosing, altering or erasing the said Records on which the propertys of the people of this Province intirely depend or in case of the death of the Secretary the said Records and Papers may fall into such hands as by unfair practices may secrete, alter or erase the records and papers belonging to the said Office to the great prejudice of the Inhabitants of this Province[,]

Humbly address your Excellency will be pleased to order and direct the Secretary to deposite in such time as your Excellency shall think proper all the records and papers aforesaid or take such measures as you shall think proper that two Members appointed by this House

65. The first meeting outside the Albemarle was in March, 1737, at New Bern. Dill, *Governor Tryon*, p. 105.

66. Governor Johnston to Board of Trade, March 11, 1736/37, in Saunders, *Colonial Records*, IV, 243.

67. Saunders, *Colonial Records*, IV, 363.

68. Laws of 1740, c. 1, in Clark, *State Records*, XXIII, 137.

may inspect and take a list or catalogue of all records and other material papers belonging to the said Office to prevent any future Mischiefs by removing the said Records and papers or otherwise.[69]

On the same day, the Lower House again ordered that the Council Chamber in Edenton be repaired and that the sheriff of Chowan County "take care of and keep clean and lock the Court House and Council Chamber in Edenton unless at Publick times."[70]

Governor Johnston's preference for New Bern as the capital appears to have been only a temporary one. He divulged his true aim to the Board of Trade in 1740 when he wrote that he had been able "tho not without great opposition to get a law passed for establishing a Town on the Forks of Cape Fear River which is the most commodious in every respect, of any situation in the Province." The town was Wilmington, where he succeeded in calling a scantly-attended Assembly in 1741.[71] "In a year or two," he wrote, "I hope to get all the Publick Business done there. But this must be done by Degrees."[72] His intentions temporarily remained unknown to the Albemarle delegates, but they recognized the untenable position for retaining Edenton as the capital. Consequently they shifted their support to Bath. When the General Assembly meeting in Edenton was prorogued in 1743 to convene the following year in Bath,[73] the legislature bade a permanent farewell, unknowingly, to its traditional meeting place.

The governor's concern for removing the seat of government was not altogether for selfish reasons. True, he had personal interests in the Cape Fear region, but he repeatedly decried the miserable state of the records of the Colony. To the Board of Trade, he wrote, "I cannot help here remarking another great Impediment to the dispatch of publick business [in addition to the lack of copies of the laws] in the Colony because I am afraid it may make me often appear culpable to your Lordships when

69. Saunders, *Colonial Records,* IV, 572.
70. Saunders, *Colonial Records,* IV, 573.
71. Saunders, *Colonial Records,* IV, 597.
72. Governor Johnston to Board of Trade, December 17, 1740, in Saunders, *Colonial Records,* IV, 423-24.
73. Saunders, *Colonial Records,* IV, 719.

I am really innocent. And that is that the Papers and Records of the several offices are so dispersed that I am frequently obliged to send from one end of the province to another for them." This situation was owing to the want of a town where all the offices could be kept. "But the people both here and in Virginia are very far from being fond of Towns," he lamented.[74]

When the legislature met at Bath in February, 1744, Johnston told the members that it was high time that a new capital be fixed:

> When all the parts of this Province except such as were contiguous to the Virginia Line was but thinly inhabited, when your dealings were but small and navigation inconsiderable, when the soil of the whole province was the property of the Crown, there was then no great hardships in continuing the seat of Government where it has been for several years past in allowing the Officers to keep the public Records in their private Houses and giving their attendance twice or thrice in a year at Publick times. But now Gen^t when the Province is peopled quite up to the head of Pedee River which was formerly reconed in South Carolina when the number of the people towards that Colony are so much increased when your commerce and navigation are so considerable augmented and so large a portion of the Lands in the Neighborhood of Virginia are no longer his Majesties property.
>
> In these circumstances it is highly necessary to appoint a place nearer the centre of the Country where his Majestie's Courts may be held where Offices may be built for keeping the publick registers and Officers obliged to give constant attendance for the dispatch of Business without hurry or confusion.[75]

The Upper House promised due consideration to his recommendation "as far as the publick debts already contracted and the difficulties attending the payment of publick Taxes will admit. . . ."[76] A bill to carry out the governor's request died in the Lower House.[77]

Bitter toward the recalcitrant legislature, the governor warned

74. Governor Johnston to Board of Trade, December 17, 1740, in Saunders, *Colonial Records*, IV, 423-24.
75. Governor Johnston's message to General Assembly, February 23, 1743/44, in Saunders, *Colonial Records*, IV, 721.
76. Saunders, *Colonial Records*, IV, 722.
77. Saunders, *Colonial Records*, IV, 731.

the Assembly meeting in New Bern the following November,
"I am sensible I have it in my power to settle this point with
the advice of his Majestie's Council, but I assure you I cannot
without great regret determine a matter that is of so much consequence to every man in the Province without your consent and
concurrence which I shall always be glad to be guided by." Again,
he blamed the lack of a seat of government for the misfortunes
of the Province. "It is impossible to finish any matter as it
ought to be while we go on in this itinerant way," he said, claiming that "we have now tryed every Town in the Colony and it is
high time to settle somewhere."[78] This time the Lower House
passed a bill for fixing the seat of government, but it appears to
have died in the Upper House.[79] Again, at its June, 1746, session,
the Upper House demanded New Bern as the capital and the
Lower House just as adamantly held out for Bath. The impasse
could not be compromised and the Assembly was prorogued with
no action on the question.[80]

The predominance of Albemarle men in the legislature frus-
trated Governor Johnston's attempt to move the capital to New
Bern or Wilmington. From the proprietary days the Albemarle
precincts (now counties) had been privileged to send five representatives each to the Lower House. Bertie, because it was created
from an Albemarle precinct, sent three, but all the others to the
south and west were allowed only two representatives each. Consequently, in 1746, the Lower House consisted of thirty-one members from the seven Albemarle counties and one borough[81] and
only twenty-three members from the remainder of the Colony—
by then ten counties and three towns.[82]

Another of Johnston's prime objectives was opposed by the
Albemarle representatives: the preparation of an adequate rent

78. Governor Johnston's message to General Assembly, New Bern, November
16, 1744, in Saunders, *Colonial Records,* IV, 735.

79. Saunders, *Colonial Records,* IV, 742, 787. This bill probably would have
fixed Bath as the seat, though the text has not been preserved.

80. Saunders, *Colonial Records,* IV, 833.

81. The counties of Currituck, Pasquotank, Perquimans, Chowan, Bertie,
Northampton, and Tyrrell, and the borough of Edenton.

82. The counties of Hyde, Beaufort, Edgecombe, Granville, Johnston, Craven,
Carteret, Onslow, New Hanover, and Bladen, and the boroughs of Bath, New
Bern, and Wilmington.

roll which would make possible the collection of the long-overdue quitrents. The northern counties clung to their claim that the "Great Deed of Grant" of 1668 had, for all time, allowed them to hold their lands for a quitrent payable in commodities.[83] It is not surprising, then, that the governor should look upon the northerners as obstructionists whose continued dominance in the legislature blocked all his efforts to rescue the Colony from its lethargy and lawlessness. The governor, an intensely practical man, could not but recognize the possibility of aligning himself with the underrepresented non-Albemarle counties in his efforts to govern the Colony.

Faced with opposition of the Albemarle representatives to his plan to move the capital, to prepare a quitrent roll, to emit more paper money, and to reduce their representation, Johnston (whose salary was eight years in arrears because of his inability to collect the quitrents[84]) boldly called for the November, 1746, session of the Assembly to meet in distant Wilmington. He was probably aware that the Albemarle delegates had vowed not to attend a session that far away from their homes. Consequently not a single northern representative and only fourteen others were present when the Lower House proceeded with business on November 21.[85] By December 5, the Assembly had passed and the governor had signed a bill fixing New Bern as the seat of government.[86]

But Johnston was no more ingenious than his Albemarle antagonists who appealed to the Crown for a disallowance of the act, sent an agent to represent their cause in London, and boycotted the General Assembly for the next eight years. In 1750, the attorney and solicitor generals in London expressed to the Board of Trade their opinion that the act had been "passed by Managem[t] Precipitation and Surprize when very few Members were present" and that the governor "by his Instructions ought

83. See above, pp. 27-28.
84. Saunders, *Colonial Records,* IV, 792.
85. Saunders, *Colonial Records,* IV, 839; Lawrence Lee, *The Lower Cape Fear in Colonial Days* (Chapel Hill: The University of North Carolina Press, 1965), p. 129. Cited hereafter as Lee, *Lower Cape Fear.*
86. Saunders, *Colonial Records,* IV, 843.

not to have assented to them."[87]   But it was not until March
14, 1754, that the Board finally transmitted to the Colony official
notification that the bill had been disallowed on the grounds that
it was a prerogative of the Crown to determine the seat of government and that the Assembly had no authority to pass the act.[88]
In the meantime, the Colony had remained in a state of "Civil
Rebellion"[89] with the Albemarle region refusing to send representatives to the Assembly. Governor Johnston died in 1752
and was succeeded as chief executive by Nathaniel Rice, president of the Council. Rice too died shortly thereafter, and Matthew Rowan, next in seniority on the Council, became head of
the government in January, 1753.[90]

During the eight-year struggle between the governor and the
Albemarle, the public records continued to suffer. A legislative
committee complained that "the uncertain and Itinerant condition of the Secretary's office and the carrying of Records & other
Papers from place to place over great Ferrys and on Horseback
whereby the Titules of many People may become precarious is a
very great Grievance."[91] A few days later the secretary admitted
that he had lost a record book "in Carrying from one place to
another or mislaid. . . ."[92] Two years later Governor Johnston
wrote: "The Publick Records lye in a miserable condition one
part of them at Edenton near the Virginia Line in a place without
Lock or Key; a great part of them in the Secretarys House at Cape
Fear above Two Hundred Miles Distance from the other Some
few of 'em at the Clerk of the Council's house at Newbern, so
that in whatever part of the Colony a man happens to be, if he
wants to consult any paper or record he must send some Hundred
of Miles before he can come at it."[93]

87. Saunders, *Colonial Records*, IV, 1223-24.
88. Saunders, *Colonial Records*, V, 108. The order in council on April 8,
1754, formally repealed the seat of government act as well as another act of the
1746 legislature that would have reduced the number of representatives from the
Albemarle counties to two each. See Saunders, *Colonial Records*, V, 117, 1119.
89. Saunders, *Colonial Records*, IV, 1166.
90. Saunders, *Colonial Records*, IV, 1314; V, 17-18.
91. Lower House Journal, June 13, 1746, in Saunders, *Colonial Records*, IV, 825.
92. Council Journal, June 28, 1746, in Saunders, *Colonial Records*, IV, 807.
93. Governor Johnston to Board of Trade, December 28, 1748, in Saunders,
Colonial Records, IV, 1165.

A resolution of the General Assembly in 1750, not anticipating the ultimate disallowance of the seat of government act, required that the provincial buildings at New Bern be constructed of brick and consist of a courthouse fifty feet by thirty feet, a council house thirty feet by twenty feet, and a house for the officers thirty feet by twenty feet, all to be "placed in a regular manner, upon such lots as they shall procure in Newbern."[94] During the same session a committee was appointed to inquire into "the reasons why the said publick buildings have not been erected and built. . . ."[95] The next year four lots in New Bern were purchased.[96] About the same time the governor claimed that there was not in the Province

. . . one Publick Office, nor one place to keep any record of Publick Papers, they all lye disperst in private Houses and we must often send a hundred miles for a Paper that is wanted, as long as these points are unknown at home it is a wonder to me we have been able to observe any regularity at all or indeed to keep up the face of Government, we shall not be able to do so long, but must disband of course, five years is a long time for such a wild uncivilized Country as this to be kept in suspense on matters so essential to the very being of Government.[97]

In the same year one of the deputy secretaries was charged with having offices at Brunswick, Edenton, New Bern, and a fourth in Edgecombe County.[98] Matthew Rowan, upon becoming head of the government, wrote, "The publick Papers have come thro' so many hands of late that I am the less surprised at so few of them being delivered to me; but I shall cause strict search to be made and the Papers of the late Governor & President by their executors for such as yet remain that I may have all the directions necessary for promoting His Majesty's service and obeying your Lordships commands."[99]

94. Saunders, *Colonial Records*, IV, 1062-63.
95. Saunders, *Colonial Records*, IV, 1052.
96. Council Journal, October 10, 1751, in Saunders, *Colonial Records*, IV, 1269.
97. Governor Johnston to Board of Trade, September 16, 1751, in Saunders, *Colonial Records*, IV, 1075.
98. Saunders, *Colonial Records*, IV, 1138.
99. Matthew Rowan to Board of Trade, February 14, 1753, in Saunders, *Colonial Records*, V, 18.

When Governor Arthur Dobbs arrived in the Colony late in
1754, the population had reached about 100,000 and settlement
had been extended more than 200 miles to the foothills of the
mountains to the west.[100] The Province was no longer a series
of settlements along the coast and rivers, and no longer was any
coastal town its center. It is not surprising, therefore, that the
new governor looked westward for an appropriate location of the
capital.

Within ten days after his arrival,[101] Dobbs had run squarely
into the seat of government problem. He wrote, ". . . none of
the Council, nor publick Officers reside here [in New Bern],
being all dispersed, 7 of the Council near Cape Fear, 2 at Edenton, one at present in Virginia, 2 in England," and that no meeting could be held of the Council without sending expresses
"which travel very slow & at great expense; and no fund for
contingencies to pay it."[102] Later he claimed that upon his arrival
he had not found

. . . one publick Office erected for records in all the Province, . . . So
that all publick papers were removed from place to place as Assemblies were changed and held in four different Vallages at the pleasure of
the Governor, as he was obliged or disobliged with the people of the
Province, so that almost all the publick records were in a manner lost
or destroyed, for each person coming into Office kept his Papers in
his house or cabbin, or in any small room he could hire and at his
death no enquiry was made and his executors embezzled or destroyed
most of the papers, so that very few came into the hands of his successor, nor had the Governor any house and not above one Church
roofed and seated in the Province.[103]

The governor lost no time in determining to fix the seat of
government, and his promptness in suggesting its approximate
location indicates that he had considered the matter of location
prior to his coming to America. He recommended that it be

100. Saunders estimated that about 20 per cent of the white population in
1753 lived westward from a line drawn from Hillsborough to Fayetteville. Saunders, *Colonial Records*, V, xxxix.

101. Saunders, *Colonial Records*, V, iv.

102. Governor Dobbs to Board of Trade, November 9, 1754, in Saunders,
Colonial Records, V, 146.

103. Governor Dobbs to Earl of Loudoun, July 10, 1756, in Saunders, *Colonial
Records*, V, 595.

. . . upon News river, above this town [New Bern], as far as it may be navigable for flat bottom boats, in case I find the Lands good, and situation healthy, as it will be nearer the back settlements which increase very fast, and is most central, and this town [New Bern] will still be the place where the merchants will reside and ships be entered, and both the gentlemen to northward and southward, seem to like it as the great Ferries at Edenton and Bath will be avoided; and it will be equally near to Cape Fear, as this place, and more healthy[.][104]

He proposed that the officers of the Province, including at least five members of the Council, be required to live at the capital town.

Early in 1755, the governor traveled up the Neuse River and selected as his choice for the capital a place at Stringer's Ferry on the north side of the river, "healthy high and well watered, about 50 miles by water and 40 by land above Newbern, to which small craft Periaguas and Canoes or flats may come in the dryest summer which may easily be made fit for larger Vessels, which is agreeable to the whole Province, north, south and west. . . ."[105] He asked for the Board of Trade's approval. Impatient because he had not received a reply, Dobbs in August wrote again, saying that approval was "highly necessary . . . as all our offices are in great confusion, & don't know where to fix them."[106] By March of the following year, the Governor was getting more impatient and complained that "we have no convenient houses here but most indifferent houses not 30 feet long and 20 feet wide exposed to the Weather and none can be undertaken until the place is determined. . . ."[107] Finally, in July, 1756, the Board wrote the governor that it did not feel that the Crown should fix the seat of government without having the sense of the next session of the General Assembly.[108] Dobbs took the Board's recommendation

104. Governor Dobbs to Board of Trade, November 9, 1754, in Saunders, *Colonial Records*, V, 147.

105. Governor Dobbs to Board of Trade, May 19, 1755, in Saunders, *Colonial Records*, V, 344.

106. Governor Dobbs to Board of Trade, August 24, 1755, in Saunders, *Colonial Records*, V, 364.

107. Governor Dobbs to Board of Trade, March 15, 1756, in Saunders, *Colonial Records*, V, 573.

108. Board of Trade to Governor Arthur Dobbs, July 29, 1756, in Saunders,

to the Assembly in October, 1756, with the request that it view
several locations along the Neuse. Both houses responded and a
committee was appointed to select the site.[109] But it was not until
December 22, 1758, that the bill finally was passed to build the
capital city at "Tower Hill," the site recommended three years
earlier by the governor.[110]

Except for what appears to have been cupidity on the part of
the governor, North Carolina's capital town might indeed have
been built at "Tower Hill." But his zeal was his undoing. Anticipating that the Crown would choose Tower Hill, Dobbs
shrewdly bought up the land without divulging to the previous
owner what he had in mind. When finally the site was chosen by
the Legislature, he offered to sell the property at the same price
he paid for it.[111] Whether or not the governor ever imagined
that he might personally profit from his plan is not proved, but
the very possibility led to the eventual defeat of the proposal.

The 1758 act provided for the purchase of 850 acres from
Dobbs, 400 acres of which was to be used for establishment of
"George City" in which were to be built "a Governor's House,
and Offices, a House for holding Assemblies, and a Secretary's
Office."[112] Many delegates, especially those from the coast, were
dissatisfied with the law establishing the capital at Tower Hill,
and the intimation that Governor Dobbs had pursued the entire
plan for personal profit and with ulterior motives was widespread.
These suspicions may have reached London, though the Board of
Trade in 1759 rebuked the governor on the grounds that they
had intended for the Assembly only to advise on the location, not
to determine it. The latter decision was one for the Crown, it
said.[113] Thus the bill was suspended and the Colony was still

---

Colonial Records, V, 608. See also Board of Trade to Dobbs, August 6, 1755, in
Saunders, *Colonial Records,* V, 417. Dobbs, in his address to the Assembly in
December, 1754, had asked only for funds with which to construct the buildings;
he reserved to the Crown the right to fix the place for the capital.

109. Saunders, *Colonial Records,* V, 674, 683.

110. Saunders, *Colonial Records,* V, 1036; Clark, *State Records,* XXV, 373 ff.

111. Saunders, *Colonial Records,* V, 1069-70. See also Clarke, *Arthur Dobbs,*
p. 151.

112. Laws of 1758, c. 3, in Clark, *State Records,* XXV, 373 ff.

113. Board of Trade to Governor Arthur Dobbs, June 1, 1759, in Saunders,
Colonial Records, VI, 46.

without a capital. Faced with this rebuke for doing what he had conceived to be his instructions, it is not surprising that the governor took particular offense when in 1760 the Lower House condemned him for having the records of the secretary's office removed to Cape Fear. He charged that the failure of the Crown to assent to the 1758 act had prevented the construction of any building for the public records, and that "Wilmington to which the Records are removed is the most opulent town in the Province, . . . the inhabitants of which are the persons chiefly interested in this Office. . . ." He asked, since the secretary's records should be near the seat of government and since no seat of government had yet been fixed, "where then cou'd I fix the keeping of the Records and Papers but at Wilmington, a place in every respect so advantageously circumstanced[?]"[114]

By 1762, the General Assembly, probably thoroughly disgusted with the confusion, had addressed a resolution to the Crown asking that the 1758 act be disallowed and that New Bern be fixed as the seat of government.[115] A similar resolution was passed later in the same year[116] and the governor was requested[117] to assist in persuading the Crown on this course. But Dobbs was adamant. He wrote that he would not support New Bern as the capital, giving its unhealthy qualities as his reason.[118] Several "southern" members objected to the address and charged that it was carried by only a small majority in the Lower House and by the deciding vote of the presiding officer of the Council.[119] Thereupon the governor demanded that he be paid for the land as provided for in the 1758 act, with interest, and in May, 1764, he was ordered paid accordingly.[120] Thus ended another attempt to obtain a capital for the Province.

Meanwhile, complaints against the handling of the public records continued. The secretary pointed out in 1762 that there

114. Saunders, *Colonial Records,* VI, 300-1, 412.
115. Saunders, *Colonial Records,* VI, 831-35.
116. Saunders, *Colonial Records,* VI, 927.
117. Saunders, *Colonial Records,* VI, 934.
118. Governor Dobbs to Board of Trade, February 23, 1763, in Saunders, *Colonial Records,* VI, 967.
119. Saunders, *Colonial Records,* VI, xxiv-v.
120. Saunders, *Colonial Records,* VI, xxv.

were various records belonging to his office lodged in the towns
of Halifax and New Bern and that the office was then held by the
direction of the governor at Wilmington "and as great Inconven-
ience must arise to those persons who have Business to Transact
in the said Office from part of the Records being Lodged in several parts of this province," he sought Council approval of his
plan to consolidate the records at Wilmington. His request was
granted and it was ordered that "all papers and Books of Record
belonging to the secretary's office in this province wheresoever
in this province to be found" be lodged there.[121] Shortly thereafter the Council noted that the secretary had taken "into his
possession Sundry books and papers at New Bern without any
Account being taken of them," and ordered that he "do not open
the Sundry Packages containing the said Books and papers but in
the Presence of two people and that they draw out the List thereof upon Oath."[122] In 1763, the deputy secretary produced a
". . . List of all the Books of Record for this Province and also of
all Wills Bonds Inventories and other papers belonging to the
Secretary's Office which have been brought from Newbern and
Halifax and are now Lodged in the Secretarys Office which at
the request formerly made by the Secretary for the said province
is Entered upon the Council Journals that it may appear what
Books of Records and papers are to be found in the Secretary's
Office."[123]

James Davis, the New Bern printer and an increasingly important leader, entered the affray in 1764 with an essay in his
paper, *The North-Carolina Magazine*. The capital had, in effect,
been transferred by Dobbs to Wilmington, Davis charged, and "a
CART dispatched to Newbern for the PUBLIC RECORDS." He
warned representatives of the northern counties to attend the
coming session of the Assembly "to a Man" lest Wilmington be
permanently fixed as the capital. Turning to the records, he
questioned, "Can you Contentedly, see the Province in this Dis-
contented State! Can you see the PUBLIC RECORDS Carted
from Place to Place, and your Properties and Estates trusted to

121. Council Journal, November 18, 1762, in Saunders, *Colonial Records,* VI, 768.
122. Council Journal, January 1, 1763, in Saunders, *Colonial Records,* VI, 1008.
123. Council Journal, December 22, 1763, in Saunders, *Colonial Records,* VI, 1017.

the Mercy of a Shower of Rain, and at the Discretion of a Cart-Driver? Forbid it Heaven! O Tempora!"[124]

Lieutenant Governor William Tryon succeeded to the governorship upon the death of Governor Dobbs in 1765. He lost no time in recommending to the Board of Trade that New Bern be fixed as the "properest" place for carrying on public business.[125] His campaign for that city during the following year was successful, and on December 1, 1766, he gave his assent to an act for the erection of a building in New Bern for the governor. To cost £5,000, the building was to be financed by a poll tax of 8d. for two years and a 2d. per gallon tax on wine, rum, and distilled liquors imported into the Colony during the same period.[126] The following month, however, Tryon wrote that the appropriation would be short of the amount required. John Hawks, who had come with Tryon to North Carolina, designed the building.[127] And right he was on the cost, for, in 1768, an additional act was required to increase the appropriation by £10,000 and to increase the poll tax to 2s. 6d. for three years.[128] The building was occupied by Tryon in mid-1770, and on December 5, 1770, the Council met in it for the first time.[129]

The "palace," as Tryon began calling it in 1770, was designed primarily as a residence and office for the governor, but it also provided a Council chamber and an office for the governor's private secretary. The Lower House met there only for the opening ceremony each session, then probably moved into the courthouse for its sessions. There were no offices in the palace for the secretary of the Province or any of the other provincial officials.[130] In effect, the sumptuous edifice did little to correct the problem of the public records.

124. [James Davis], "Newbern's Remembrancer: Or, An Essay on the Seat of Government," *The North-Carolina Magazine* (New Bern), I (August 17-24, 1764), 94 ff.

125. Governor Tryon to Board of Trade, April 1, 1765, in Saunders, *Colonial Records*, VII, 146.

126. Laws of 1766, c. 2, in Clark, *State Records*, XXIII, 664.

127. Governor Tryon to Earl of Shelburne, January 31, 1767, in Saunders, *Colonial Records*, VII, 431.

128. Laws of 1766 [1768], c. 5, in Clark, *State Records*, XXIII, 711.

129. Dill, *Governor Tryon*, p. 116.

130. Dill, *Governor Tryon*, pp. 116-17.

The story of the citizens' reaction to the building of the palace does not belong to the story of the public records. Suffice it to say here that the resentment in the back country against the heavy taxes and against the extravagance of the building contributed mightily to the War of the Regulation in 1771.[131]

While New Bern was being fixed as the capital, the problem of the public records continued. The secretary was ordered in 1766 to "remove to Newbern . . . the Council Journals, Chancery Docket and all papers relative to the Respective Courts to be held there."[132] The following April, the secretary complained of "the inconveniency and irregularity of attending his office from being constantly open and for want of proper hours being appointed for their doing business." It was ordered that the clerks attend the office from 9:00 A.M. to noon and from 2:00 to 5:00 P.M. "on which hours the Clerks are Ordered punctually to attend daily Sunday and Holidays excepted."[133]

In 1768, the Lower House heard the complaint of its clerk about the need for a proper place for depositing and keeping safe the papers and journals of the Assembly "several of which in part are eaten by rats and mice and some totally destroyed, and those journals that are perfect lie in small paper books, so that an application of the members of the House and others for papers and copies thereof, proves almost fruitless[.]" Thereupon the clerk was ordered to provide a house in New Bern for an office "and that such Clerk lock up all papers in his Custody, belonging to this House, and file the same in order, in proper cases to be by him furnished; and also a large folio book, and enter all the journals since April Session, 1760, therein. . . ."[134]

Early in 1771, the Assembly directed that the secretary "employ carriages for the removal of all the Records and papers now in the Secretary's Office at Wilmington, and have them safely conveyed to New Bern and make a claim for defraying the ex-

131. For a study of the role of the palace in the "War of the Regulation," see Elmer D. Johnson, "The War of the Regulation: Its Place in History" (unpublished M.A. thesis, The University of North Carolina, 1942).

132. Council Journal, September 27, 1766, in Saunders, *Colonial Records*, VII, 259.

133. April 23, 1767, in Saunders, *Colonial Records*, VII, 450.

134. House Journal, November 29, 1768, in Saunders, *Colonial Records*, VII, 963.

pense thereof, And on their arrival at New Bern provide a proper place for the safe keeping of the same." The records had safely arrived in town by January 21 when Secretary Robert Palmer was ordered paid £50 for their removal.[135] The land records, which made up most of the records formerly in Wilmington, were housed in the east wing of the palace, but the remainder of the secretary's records were housed elsewhere in New Bern.[136]

At last—after more than a hundred years of wandering—the few records preserved by the Colony of North Carolina had found a home. But the clouds of revolution were forming and the new capital of New Bern was to enjoy its honor for only a few years.

135. Voucher showing payment to Robert Palmer, January 21, 1771, in Legis-lative Papers, 1771, State Archives. The moving of the records involved two armed guards and two carts. See also Saunders, *Colonial Records*, VIII, 371, 445, 480.

136. Dill, *Governor Tryon*, p. 117.

III

War and Its Aftermath: Dislocation and Settlement

1774-1794

In better times, the people in 1771 might have breathed a sigh of relief. At last their officers, courts, legislature, and—most important of all—the records of the Colony had been centralized in one town. A magnificent structure had been provided as a home for the governor and as a meeting place for the Council. Even so, Governor Tryon's Palace was not the "first permanent capitol" of North Carolina. In the first place, the town of Edenton had been fixed by law as the capital of the Colony in 1722 and buildings for the legislative and judicial branches had been provided at least as early as 1733.[1] In the second place, Tryon Palace was primarily a residence for the governor and provided neither office facilities for the other administrative and judicial officials nor chambers for the Lower House or the courts. Furthermore, the building was destined to be used for perhaps no more than ten of the twenty-three years from 1771 to 1794 when the newly-created town of Raleigh became the "unalterable" seat of government.

Be that as it may, the auspicious opening of the new "capitol" in 1771 came in abnormal times. Tryon soon left the Colony to become governor of New York. His successor, Josiah Martin, arrived just as sounds of revolution were heard.

1. See above, p. 38.

War alone would have caused serious problems in the preservation of records. But for North Carolina the problems were multiplied by two other factors: the confused government of the Colony from 1774 to 1776, and the itinerant nature of the government from 1775 to 1794. These factors, coupled with frequent changes of officials and complications wrought by enemy threats within the State, resulted in the loss of many of the valuable records of the first century as well as of contemporary records.

As the American colonies moved toward armed resistance to the British, North Carolina played its role. The First Provincial Congress met in New Bern in August, 1774, and appointed delegates to the Continental Congress. In April, 1775, the Second Provincial Congress met at New Bern simultaneously with the General Assembly and composed mostly of the same delegates. The latter Congress endorsed the creation of a committee of safety for each county and borough town, one for each of the six military districts, and one for the entire Province. Governor Martin, angered by the disloyalty of the Assembly, dissolved it. This adjournment of the Legislature marked the end of royal rule in North Carolina; within the year almost twenty counties and four towns had set up safety committees. On May 24, 1775, Governor Martin fled to Fort Johnston, leaving the government in the hands of the colonists. The committees ruled the Colony during much of 1775, and from August 20 to September 10, 1775, the Third Provincial Congress met at Hillsborough with every county and borough town represented. This gathering established an elaborate form of government comprising the Provincial Congress composed of five members from each county and one from each borough and the Provincial Council (which was to be the executive branch of government), consisting of thirteen members. Committees of safety were to continue to function in the counties, towns, and military districts. From April 4 to May 14, 1776, the Fourth Provincial Congress met at Halifax and passed the "Halifax Resolves" authorizing North Carolina's delegates to the Continental Congress to "concur" in voting for independence from Great Britain. This Congress made further changes in the structure of government, establishing the Executive Council composed of the president and six councillors. But the Council of Safety remained the dominant force and its president, Cornelius Harnett, was virtually governor of the Colony. Finally, during its session from November 12 to December 23, 1776, at Halifax, the Fifth Provincial Congress adopted a constitution for the new State.[2]

During the period from April, 1775, until the new General Assembly under the Constitution met in New Bern in April, 1777, if virtual anarchy did not exist in civil government, it did tend to prevail insofar as the making and keeping of the official records were concerned. Sessions of the congresses were held in three different towns; the composition of the congresses and councils and committees tended to be fluid and indefinite; and the lack of a single executive authority tended to cause a lessening of the sense of responsibility on the part of office holders. The impact of these factors was certainly of consequence, though it is difficult to assess the damage. Records that failed to survive the Revolution may have survived the interregnum between colony and state.

With the acceptance of the Constitution, a new era might have begun for the archives[3] of the State. Out of the chaos of the preceding two years came in 1777 a new government with more clearly defined duties for officials, all of whom were to be appointed by the Assembly. There were to be a governor chosen annually, a council of seven to aid him (but independent of him), a secretary of state to serve for three years, a treasurer to serve for one year, and an attorney general to be chosen for a term of good behavior. Richard Caswell, perhaps the most popular man in the State at the time, was chosen governor, and James Glasgow was elected to the important post of secretary of state.

In colonial times copies of important documents were often required to be sent to England. Following independence, this

2. Hugh Talmage Lefler and Albert Ray Newsome, *North Carolina: The History of a Southern State* (Chapel Hill: The University of North Carolina Press, 1954), pp. 190 ff. Cited hereafter as Lefler and Newsome, *North Carolina*.
3. The term "archives" means, in the modern sense, the *permanently valuable* records of a government, organization, business, etc. For the purpose of this study, however, the terms "archives" and "records" will be used interchangeably.

requirement ended and the State was now "on its own" in the matter of making and keeping records. Historians of the twentieth century were able to turn to London to find valuable documents relating to the colonial history of North Carolina— documents which were not to be found in the archives of the State. For records after 1775, the historian finds that his source is, except for an occasional alienation of public records, in the State. For the historian, independence brought mixed blessings.

The problems of wartime government are not proper subjects for consideration here, but it is appropriate to mention some of the handicaps under which the new state was to operate. Record keeping in the colonial period, as poor as it was, nevertheless was based largely upon instructions from the Proprietors and later the Crown. Under the Constitution of 1776, such matters were left solely to the determination of the state government. In practice, the experience of colonial record keeping was to a large extent followed. Nevertheless, there were important new requirements for which there had not been adequate colonial experience. Armies were created, necessitating complicated record-keeping procedures. Strict controls had to be extended over requisitions, taxes, and other aspects of life; these required records. The State was one of several co-operating states; correspondence, reports, and negotiations required more paper work. The Granville District, comprising more than half the area, now belonged to the State. And the problems of the records were complicated by the abnormalities of the times.

The story of public records for the last quarter of the eighteenth century is inextricably involved with the movements of the legislatures, courts, committees, councils, and executive officers. Documentary evidence is insufficient to determine in many instances just what records were involved in the transfer of the government from one place to another, but a casual reader might be led to think that they remained aboard wagons and carts for much of the war.

Even before the declaration of independence, the Provincial Council directed that "all the public records of what nature soever in the Custody of the Secretary be immediately removed and kept in some Secure place by Mr. Christopher [Neale] who is hereby required to see this Necessary order carried into Execution, and in Case of Necessity to [call] on the Col°. of the Militia for sufficient force for such purpose."[4] The following year Neale was paid £176 for "receiving, removing & keeping the records of Secretary's Office."[5] The Council of Safety met at Whitfield's Ferry on the Neuse River in Dobbs County in June-August, 1776, and Simon Totwine was hired to take "Papers and Records" from that place to Halifax "and back again."[6] On November 1, 1777, William Sconyears was paid £4 10s. for himself and horse to remove the "Public papers from New Bern to Kingston & from Kingston to New Bern."[7] The Assembly held two sessions in New Bern that year. At about the same time, Jarvis Buxton was allowed £6 7s. for work done and materials furnished in enlarging the secretary's office, presumably at New Bern.[8] Toward the end of the war Secretary Glasgow was apparently keeping his office at his home near present-day Kinston.

The State's new government was less than a year old when the westerners, still chafing under the necessity of traveling to the coast to attend sessions of the Legislature and to carry on their business with government officers, introduced a bill to move the

4. Resolution of Provincial Council, March 3, 1776, in Treasurer's and Comptroller's Papers, Executive Offices, State Archives.

5. Voucher dated August 16, 1777, in Treasurer's and Comptroller's Papers, Accounts, State Archives. Where Neale kept the records during that period is not definitely known, but in March, 1777, he was appointed clerk of the Craven County Court, and he may have moved them into the courthouse in New Bern. The following year he was made deputy secretary of state. Clark, *State Records*, XI, 710; XIII, 177.

An interesting paper has been located among the records of the Fifth Provincial Congress which met in Halifax in November, 1776, and which adopted the new state constitution. The paper, apparently a wrapper from a bundle of correspondence between Cornelius Harnett, president of the Council of Safety, and William Hooper, a North Carolina delegate to the Continental Congress, contains the blunt warning, "Death to take any of these papers out of the file without leave." The original paper is framed and hangs in the Search Room of the State Archives.

6. Voucher dated August 13, 1776, in Treasurer's and Comptroller's Papers, Executive Offices, State Archives.

7. Receipt, dated November 1, 1777, in Treasurer's and Comptroller's Papers, Executive Offices, State Archives.

8. Voucher of Jarvis Buxton, 1777, in Treasurer's and Comptroller's Papers, Executive Offices, State Archives.

capital from New Bern to the newly-erected town of Smithfield on the Neuse River. The bill, passed on first reading in the Senate on December 6, 1777, stated that it was ". . . absolutely necessary for the Ease of the People and the Conveniency of transacting publick Business, that the seat of Government should be fixed in the most central and convenient Part of this State, and that a fit and commodious House for the setting and Holding of Assemblies, a Secretary's Office, a Land Office and a Treasurer's Office, and other necessary and convenient publick Buildings, should be erected with all convenient Expedition." Smithfield, it said, was "nearly central" to most of the inhabitants, and "hath been found to be healthy and agreeable; having the natural advantage of a pleasant situation, temperate Air, high and dry Land, and wholesome Springs." A week later, the bill was rejected.[9] But the struggle over the capital, stilled for a few years by the construction of the magnificent palace at New Bern, had been rejoined.

Although the Legislature met in New Bern in 1777 and for the April-May session in 1778,[10] the August session in 1778 was moved to Hillsborough. For the next six years only one session—that of 1780—was held in New Bern. In fact, for all intents and purposes, the palace was tenantless until 1783,[11] the governors preferring to remain at home or to rove with the assemblies. During these years the people of the State were in a large measure governed locally and had little information on what was going on about them. Only one newspaper is believed to have been published in the State from 1778 to 1783.

Sessions in 1779 were held in Halifax (January-February), Smithfield (April-May), and again in Halifax (October-November). At Smithfield the westerners obtained passage of a resolution to appoint commissioners to study the possibility of putting the capital in Wake, Johnston, or Chatham counties. The commissioners appear to have met in October and recommended

9. Original bill in Legislative Papers, 1777, State Archives.
10. The easterners were strong enough to require the establishment of the office of Court of Chancery and Equity at New Bern during this session. See original bill in Legislative Papers, 1778, State Archives.
11. Dill, *Governor Tryon*, p. 210.

Wake County.[12] A bill, presumably the commission's draft, passed on first reading but was rejected on second reading in the House of Commons. One of its purposes was the "preservation of public papers."[13]

In April, 1780, the Assembly returned to New Bern only to find the determined westerners still carrying on the battle to move the capital inland. Another bill, including the statement that "the fixing the Seat of Government for this State would tend greatly to the Preservation of the public papers thereof," would again have appointed commissioners from the six military districts to choose the site and contract for land. But this bill, too, after passing first reading, was rejected in the House of Commons.[14] Again in the fall, the Assembly moved to Hillsborough, and in January, 1781, to Halifax.

Between 1774 and February, 1781, the provincial congresses and general assemblies had met at New Bern six times, Halifax five times, Hillsborough three times, and Smithfield once. In addition, the Provincial Council and the Committee of Safety had met at other places. Thus the government of the Colony and State was indeed an itinerant one, and in the words of a twentieth-century historian, "The migrations of legislatures from town to town, the residence of the governor and other administrative officials at different places, the location of government records in private homes, and the hauling of these records 'in a common cart' from town to town did not make for efficiency in government and were a serious obstacle to business."[15]

An interesting commentary on this roving of the government lies in the fact that, except for periodic Tory threats within the State and the major British invasion of 1781, there was relatively little military danger to the government. The movements, therefore, appear to have been the result of the whims or convenience

12. See four vouchers for payment of the commissioners in Treasurer's and Comptroller's Papers, Capital Buildings, State Archives. See also Dill, *Governor Tryon,* p. 242.

13. Clark, *State Records,* XIII, 860, 955, 966-67. See also Dill, *Governor Tryon,* p. 242.

14. Original bill in Legislative Papers, 1780, State Archives.

15. Lefler and Newsome, *North Carolina,* p. 244.

of the legislators. The security of the records was a secondary consideration. Had the offices of the governor, secretary, and treasurer remained in New Bern until 1781, the records might have been more secure. But even so, when the General Assembly met, many current records had to be available for consultation. Likewise, meetings of the Provincial Council, the Committee of Safety, and the Council of State required availability of certain records. Thus, even if the executive offices had been located constantly in one place, the itinerant nature of the executive and legislative branches would have dictated frequent movements of records.

The year 1781, however, brought another danger. In January the British occupied Wilmington and began their attacks inland. The West was invaded from South Carolina. By spring much of the State was in enemy hands. So great was the threat that on February 4, 1781, the Assembly, noting that "it may be necessary in these times of difficulty and danger, to remove the public Records and Papers in the Secretary's office papers belonging to the General Assembly, the Public Accounts and all other public papers, to a place of safety," authorized the governor, with the advice of the Council of State, to remove the records and papers "to such place or places of security and safety as he shall judge proper."[16] A guard from the militia was authorized to escort the records. In April, 1781, meeting in New Bern, a "Council Extraordinary" directed that the public records in the secretary's office be removed to some place of security.[17]

The threat of British occupation of New Bern led Governor Abner Nash to flee from that town to Tarborough on April 17, 1781,[18] and on April 28, Captain James Haven[19] was put into the service of "removal of the Publick Records in the Secretary's

16. Clark, *State Records*, XVII, 664, 672, 751.

17. Richard Caswell to Alexander Martin, April 27, 1782, in Secretary of State's Papers, Correspondence, 1782, State Archives. Caswell's letter was written a year after the action.

18. Nash to General Richard Caswell, April 17, 1781, in Governor's Papers, 1781 (G.P. 6), State Archives.

19. The identity of Captain Haven has not been established. It is conjectured that he was a member of the militia in view of the legislative resolution's authorization that a guard be procured from the militia.

Office." Here begins one of the most interesting efforts in the history of the State to preserve its records.[20]

The records at New Bern were packed aboard at least two wagons and the long journey of the archives of the Colony and State of North Carolina began. The two "waggoners" included one Godfrey Williams of Beaufort County, and horses were impressed from, among others not known, John Tillery of Halifax County and James Ransome of Warren County.[21]

On May 6, Haven and the wagons crossed Tar River at Atkins' Ferry and on May 8, corn for the teams was purchased from Thomas Hill of Franklin County. Though proof is lacking, it is conjectured that one wagon, drawn by the horses belonging to Tillery and Ransome, picked up additional records at Tarborough where the late assembly had met.

Crossing into Virginia, the wagons were in Mecklenburg County on May 10, Charlotte County May 15, Bedford County May 21, Botetourt three days later, Montgomery June 7, and Washington County, Virginia, on June 13. By June 20, the records had arrived in Sullivan County in what later was to be Tennessee and on June 24, General Campbell Smith was paid 240 "Carolina Dollars" for "work done on the Waggons." Captain Haven's duties terminated on June 25 and he returned home. [22] Williams and the horses remained in service until Oc-

20. It is unfortunate that documentary evidence fails to reveal just what records were moved. However, from the paucity of records for a year following the removal (1781-82), it may be assumed that practically all of the important records were so removed. The imminent threat of the British adds to this presumption.

21. This identification of Tillery and Ransome is based on information contained in the Census of 1790. Absolute proof is lacking.

22. The story of the movement of the archives is told graphically by a claim filed by Haven and Williams and paid by the State on April 27, 1782. This two-page claim is found in the Treasurer's and Comptroller's Papers, Executive Offices, State Archives. See also, in same source, certificates of impressment of horses from John Tillery and James Ransome, both dated October 10, 1781.

It is interesting to note that North Carolina earlier had played a role in the protection of the records of the secretary of state of Georgia. In 1778, the Georgia records were taken by Secretary of State John Milton to Charleston. When that city was threatened by the British, Milton took the records by wagon to New Bern where they were placed in the care of Governor Abner Nash. Finally, as the British troops neared New Bern, these records were sent to Baltimore where they remained until 1783. Hugh M'Call, *The History of Georgia Containing Brief Sketches of the Most Remarkable Events Up to the Present Day (1784)* (reprint;

Dr. The State of North Carolina In Accts with

Capt. James Haven for the removal of the Publick

Records in Secetarys Office

1781			Continental Money	Specie
May 6	For Cash pd Atkins for Ferreges of the Waggons across Tar River		100	
8	paid Thomas Hill for Corn for Teams		180	
10	do Asa Roberts for do Mecklenburg		600	300
12	do John Hogan		380	180
15	do Thomas Jones do Charlote		650	320
19	do William Bryan		464	282
21	do John Going do Bedford		320	160
24	do Capt. Johnston do Botetort		400	200
27	do John Church		600	300
29	do Alexr Bame		500	250
June 5	do John Crispin		600	300
7	do John Adams do Montgomery		530	265
11	do James McGavock do		650	325
13	do Capt Arthur Campbell Washington		500	250
	do Isaac Crow do		300	150
	do Capt Thompson do		500	250
	do Bryan do		380	140
20	do Robert Ellisons do Sullivan		800	400
24	do John Loughlin 2 bbl		1000	500
	do paid Genl Campbell Smith for Work done on the Waggons		240	120
	To pay of my self and Horse from the 28th April Until the 22 of July 60 days a 7/6			
	To the Rations of my self and two Waggoners 60 days — a 3/ a day			
	To my Expences Home		4000	2000

Nov. 25th personally appeared before me James Haven who was appointed for the Removal of the Publick Records belonging to the Secretarys Office and made oath that the Money as above Charged was necessarily advanced for the Publick together with the Rations received of the [...] & the pay for the above Time due James Haven

Willson Spright Jr   (Turn ova)

As British troops approached New Bern in 1781, a "Council Extraordinary" directed that the records in the office of the Secretary of State be evacuated. The claims of James Haven and Godfrey Williams permit the tracing of the westward route of the wagons carrying the records: through the Virginia counties of Mecklenburg, Charlotte, Bedford, Botetourt, and Washington, and finally into Sullivan County, North Carolina (now Tennessee). The original claims are in the Treasurer's and Comptroller's Papers, State Archives.

tober, by which time the records had apparently been returned to North Carolina.

There is at least one other recorded instance of the evacuation of records from the State. When the British approached Hillsborough early in 1781, Memucan Hunt, the auditor for the Hillsborough District, rushed his records northward. Shortly thereafter he sent a wagon to bring "the Public papers from Virginia, where they had been carried to prevent falling into the hands of the Enemy. . . ." He retained the records at his home near Williamsborough in what is now Vance County until October, 1783, when he transported them "about 43 miles" to Hillsborough.[23]

The Assembly met early in 1781 in Halifax. Meanwhile, British forces under Cornwallis swept through the Piedmont to the Virginia border, engaged the American troops at Guilford Courthouse, marched on to Wilmington to join other British forces there, and threatened the entire East. In June, the Assembly met uneasily at the Joel Lane homestead in Wake County where it adopted a resolution calling attention to the "alarming situation of our Enemies" and asking the commanding officer of the Hillsborough District to make a "general return to this Assembly of all the troops, arms, &c and their disposition now in actual service for its defence and security."[24] Well might the legislators have been apprehensive, because on September 12, 1781, Governor Thomas Burke was captured in Hillsborough by a Tory unit under command of Colonel David Fanning.[25] The county records, before Fanning's arrival, were said to have been buried in the woods near Hillsborough.[26]

Atlanta: A. B. Caldwell, 1909), p. 469; Allen D. Candler (ed.), *The Colonial Records of the State of Georgia* (25 vols.; Atlanta: The Franklin Printing and Publishing Company, 1904-13), I, [i]; Mary Givens Bryan (ed.), *Abstracts of Colonial Wills of the State of Georgia, 1733-1777* (Atlanta: Atlanta Town Committee of the National Society, Colonial Dames of America, 1962), p. v.

23. Claim of Memucan Hunt, dated May 13, 1784, in Treasurer's and Comptroller's Papers, Executive Offices, State Archives. See also account of Memucan Hunt, May 31, 1784, in Clark, *State Records*, XIX, 684.

24. Resolution in Legislative Papers, 1781, State Archives.

25. Hugh F. Rankin, *North Carolina in the American Revolution* (Raleigh: State Department of Archives and History, 1959), p. 69.

26. Olds, *Story of the Counties*, p. 48.

With Cornwallis' surrender at Yorktown in the fall, and except for threats from Tory bands in the West, the State was at last in no great danger from the enemy. It is unfortunate, however, that few records covering the period 1781-82 have survived— so few, in fact, as to arouse suspicion that unrecorded losses may well have occurred from the action of enemy troops. At least one loss, however, is known to have occurred in 1781. Brigadier General John Ashe, former treasurer of the southern district, had buried his papers in an "untight Casket" upon the approach of British troops. Ashe died, and when the cache was finally located and exhumed the papers had all rotted.[27]

The 1782 session of the Assembly was held at Hillsborough, which, in spite of the war's end, was designated the place for future meetings. In 1783, too, the Legislature met at Hillsborough, but the 1782 resolution was repealed.[28] The Assembly again was free to rove. And as if to prove its indecision, the House rejected on second reading a new bill that would have established an undesignated town "for public offices, keeping the public Records and for the accommodation of the two houses of the General Assembly."[29] Three months later one Jephtha Rice was paid 9s. and three quarts of rum for "bringing public papers from Hillsborough to Kingston." In October, one Drewry Andrews was paid £9 "for a Cart to bring down public papers from the State Auditors &c."[30]

Though the Assembly was not yet ready to choose the location of the government, it did return to Hillsborough in April, 1784, but the following month it rejected a bill to authorize repairs to the public buildings in that town. In June, following adjournment of the Assembly, "8/13 of a Load" of public papers was taken from Hillsborough to Kinston[31] and in October the As-

27. Clark, *State Records,* XX, 316.

28. Resolution in Legislative Papers, 1783, State Archives. In another action, the Assembly appointed commissioners to consider the expediency of selling the Tryon Palace in 1782. Clark, *State Records,* XVI, 128. Dill says nothing came of this effort to sell the palace. Dill, *Governor Tryon,* p. 247.

29. Clark, *State Records,* XIX, 279, 303, 326.

30. Account of the comptroller, 1783, in Treasurer's and Comptroller's Papers, Accounts, State Archives.

31. Receipt of Alexander Mebane, 1784, in Treasurer's and Comptroller's Papers, Executive Offices, State Archives. During or soon after the Revolution, the "g" was dropped from "Kingston."

sembly met in New Bern for the first time since 1780 and the second time since 1778. Again in 1785, the session was held in New Bern, and Francis Child, the comptroller, claimed expenses for "finding a Cart, Horses, and Driver to carry the Comptrollers Books and Papers to New Bern."[32] In March, 1786, he made a claim for carrying the continental money "consisting of a Hogshead and Barrel full from Kinston to New Bern."[33] Late in 1786, the Assembly journeyed to Fayetteville and there, as the session dragged on into 1787, members appeared to be on the verge of fixing Hillsborough as the capital. The secretary of state, treasurer, and comptroller were directed to "reside and constantly keep their respective offices at the Town of Hillsborough in order that those offices may be convenient to the greater part of the Inhabitants of the State."[34] In July, Comptroller Francis Child wrote that he was going to Hillsborough in order to accommodate himself with an office and to engage wagons for the purpose of conveying his papers from Kinston where they were then located. He estimated that it would require five or six wagons. As if objecting to the Assembly's action, he wrote that "when the General Assembly passed the Resolve it was just on their breaking up, and in the hurry of Business."[35] Child still had not moved his records to Hillsborough as late as December, 1787. Obviously irritated, the Assembly, then meeting in Tarborough, passed a resolution providing "that the Comptroller be and is hereby directed to have the whole of the Public Papers in his office, or charge, removed to the Town of Hillsborough on or before the first day of April next."[36] On the same date, the Assembly directed the secretary of state to continue his office and public papers "where the same have usually been kept until the Seat of Government shall be fixed, or the General Assembly shall otherwise direct."[37] This too, presumably, was Hillsborough.

32. Claim of Francis Child, 1785, in Treasurer's and Comptroller's Papers, Executive Offices, State Archives.

33. Claim of Francis Child, 1786, in Treasurer's and Comptroller's Papers, Executive Offices, State Archives.

34. Clark, *State Records*, XVIII, 444.

35. Child to Governor Caswell, July 11, 1787, in Clark, *State Records*, XX, 736-37.

36. Clark, *State Records*, XX, 282.

37. Clark, *State Records*, XX, 281.

At the Tarborough session, a bill was introduced which expressed the exasperation of the people over the lack of a fixed seat of government. It stated, ". . . the Citizens of this State are greatly incommoded by the officers of Government residing in different parts, and . . . the public papers, vouchers, Books and accounts are not preserved in particular offices, but are scattered over the face of the Country in different hands, whence the State is exposed to great frauds and its revenue is neglected or misapplied insomuch that the public debt seems to be increasing while the Citizens are grieved by heavy Taxes. . . ." The bill stated further in its preamble that ". . . it is found to be impracticable to remove the public Records and papers every year to a new station without great expence danger and Loss," and that "it is necessary that proper offices for the safe keeping of the public papers, as well as a good and convenient House for the residence of the Governor should be provided. . . ." It called for the appointment of commissioners to report on needs and costs at the next General Assembly, but the name of the city was left blank.[38]

The Assembly rejected the bill and chose instead to hand the perennial problem to a convention being called to meet the following year to consider adoption of the proposed federal constitution.[39] The Convention met in Hillsborough on July 28, 1788, and following lengthy and heated discussion, finally voted to fix the capital within ten miles of Isaac Hunter's plantation in Wake County, the exact location to be left to the determination of the General Assembly.[40] It was not until 1792 that Joel Lane's plantation was finally chosen.[41]

In the meantime, the General Assembly continued its migra-

38. Original bill, dated December 11, 1787, in Legislative Papers, 1787, State Archives.

39. The ordinance is printed in Francois-Xavier Martin (comp.), *Public Acts of the General Assembly of North-Carolina* (2 vols. in 1; Newbern: Martin & Ogden, 1804), I, 459. Cited hereafter as Martin, *Public Acts*.

40. [North Carolina], *The Journal of the Convention of North-Carolina at a Convention Begun and Held at Hillsborough, on the Twenty-First Day of July, in the Year of Our Lord One Thousand Seven Hundred and Eighty-Eight . . .* (Hillsborough: Robert Ferguson, n.d.), pp. 12-13. Cited hereafter as *Journal of the Convention [1788]*.

41. See below, p. 75.

tions, meeting in Fayetteville from 1788 through 1790, New Bern in 1791 and 1792, again in Fayetteville in 1793, and then holding a last meeting in New Bern in June, 1794. All the while the public records were shifted from one place to another.[42]

The meandering of the government throughout the war and postwar periods makes impossible a clear picture of what records were where at a particular time. For instance, the comptroller was required to present certain papers to the General Assembly, as were other officers, but it is doubtful that he carried with him more than those needed in that particular session. The remainder, presumably, were left in his office or home. The frequent references to removal of records indicate that his papers were probably scattered in more than one place. The secretary of state too appears to have had his records in more than one location. Though the state papers were taken to the West in 1781, eight years later the secretary of state moved from New Bern "the residue of the papers of the Assembly & while a province," a reference that indicates that at least some legislative records had not been moved upon the capture of the town by the British.

Just as it is impossible from documentary evidence to get a clear picture of the various locations of records, so it is not clear just how the records were kept in the offices. Nowhere, of course,

42. To trace the movement of the records from 1787 to 1792, see the following in Treasurer's and Comptroller's Papers, State Archives: payment to a Mr. Marley for moving the treasurer's papers from Fayetteville to Hillsborough in 1789; receipt from John Armstrong for payment for moving "public papers" from Hillsborough to Fayetteville in 1789; payment to James Walker for "cartage of Money & Books from Fayette" in 1790; payment to H. Bailey for removal of the same from Tarborough to Hillsborough the same year; payment to Henry Aaron for carting "an Iron Chest" from Halifax to Hillsborough in 1790; vouchers for repairs to the "Blue House" in Hillsborough in 1790 (the comptroller had his office in the Blue House); receipt of Frederick Taylor and James Pratt for 12s. and three quarts of rum for serving as guard to escort the treasurer's and comptroller's papers and "returning back"; receipt of John Faddis for carrying and guarding the papers of the treasurer and comptroller from Fayetteville to Hillsborough the same year and another of Frederick Taylor and James Pratt for "liquor and forage" for escorting and guarding the papers of the two offices from Fayetteville to Hillsborough; receipt of Will Lytle in 1791 for removing the treasurer's papers from Hillsborough to New Bern; and receipt of Harrison Baily for transporting public papers in 1792 from New Bern to Hillsborough. See also allowance to Thomas Bridges for removing the records of the clerk of the House of Commons from Fayetteville to Tarborough, December 20, 1787, and allowance in favor of William Muzzle and others for conveying the treasurer's papers from Hillsborough to Fayetteville in 1788, in Clark, *State Records*, XX, 269, 590.

is the term "file cabinet" found, but there are frequent references to "chests" and "chair boxes." For example, in 1784, one William White was paid for a chest and for "Mending a Chair that was broke in going after public papers. . . ."[43] The following year money was being kept in a "Hogshead and Barrel."[44] In 1789, payment was authorized for an "Iron Chest," a hasp for the chest, and a "Blankett to wrap books in. . . ."[45] Secretary James Glasgow purchased two boxes "to hold the papers"[46] and, in 1790, Henry Aaron transported an iron chest containing records.[47] A portion of the money paid Joel Lane for the land upon which Raleigh was to be built was "taken from the Chair Box."[48]

State offices were probably set up insofar as practicable in county courthouses in the towns in which the assemblies met. In Hillsborough, the "Blue House" was utilized for at least some of the executive offices.[49] The treasurer, during the Fayetteville session of the Legislature in 1790, transacted treasury business in a room in the house of Lee DeKeysar.[50] It would be a reasonable assumption that where space was not available in the courthouses, the offices were located in homes or stores.

Little also is known—except for internal evidence in the papers that have survived—of the papers, inks, and other record-keeping materials used during the period. There are references to "a bound Journal & Ledger of the best kind," bound books, paper, quills,[51] and other strictly clerical supplies. During the

43. Bill of William White, 1784, in Treasurer's and Comptroller's Papers, Executive Offices, State Archives.

44. Claim of Francis Child, 1785, in Treasurer's and Comptroller's Papers, Executive Offices, State Archives.

45. Account of Treasurer John Haywood, 1789, in Treasurer's and Comptroller's Papers, Executive Offices, State Archives.

46. Account of secretary of state, in Treasurer's and Comptroller's Papers, Executive Offices, State Archives.

47. Account of Treasurer John Haywood, 1790, in Treasurer's and Comptroller's Papers, Executive Offices, State Archives.

48. Voucher, showing payment to Joel Lane, 1792, in Treasurer's and Comptroller's Papers, Capital Buildings, State Archives.

49. Voucher, showing payment for repairs to the Blue House, 1790, in Treasurer's and Comptroller's Papers, Capital Buildings, State Archives.

50. Receipt of Lee DeKeysar, 1790, in Treasurer's and Comptroller's Papers, Executive Offices, State Archives.

51. Account of Treasurer John Haywood, Treasurer's and Comptroller's Papers, Executive Offices, State Archives.

war, paper was scarce, and the General Assembly encouraged John Hulgon to operate a paper mill at Hillsborough as early as 1777.[52]

While the constantly-changing location of the public offices created the most frustrating problem in preserving records, other problems persisted. Under the new constitution, the officials continued on the fee system[53] and record-keeping procedures appear to have been little changed from earlier practices except for the absence of copies being sent to England. A perennial problem was the private possession of public records. In 1777, one James Green, Jr., was directed to deliver to the secretary of state "Records and papers relative to the late Assemblies of this State; also a great number of commissaries and paymasters bonds. . . ."[54] Ten years later a resolution required the secretary of state to "call on all Persons having in their hands books of record belonging to his office" to deliver the same to his office,[55] and in 1789 William Boyd of Beaufort County was directed to turn over to the secretary of state "several ancient records, patents, deeds, &c."[56]

Land records of the erstwhile Granville District were, according to a legislative resolution passed in 1783, "scattered throughout the State" and many were "in a ruinous condition. . . ."[57] In 1787, the secretary again was directed to "demand & receive of such Persons as have in their possession, the record Books of Earl Granville's office. . . ."[58] Another resolution the same session observed that ". . . it is represented . . . that there are in the possession of divers Persons in this State, Books of record wherein are entered or recorded Patents issued or granted under the former Government, and the record Books properly belonging to Lord Granville's office, which of right should be deposited in the Secretaries office of this State," and required such persons to

52. Clark, *State Records,* XII, 413. Hulgon's name is spelled variously as Holgun, Holgan, and Hogan.

53. See bill to regulate fees of officers, May, 1782, in Legislative Papers, 1782, State Archives. See also Clark, *State Records,* XXIV, 445.

54. Clark, *State Records,* XII, 428, 430. Green was also directed to turn over "the robes and gown in his possession."

55. Clark, *State Records,* XX, 464.

56. Clark, *State Records,* XXI, 333.

57. Clark, *State Records,* XIX, 230 ff. See also original act, dated May 17, 1783, in Secretary of State's Papers, Miscellaneous Papers, 1750-1902, State Archives.

58. Clark, *State Records,* XX, 269.

turn them over to the secretary "at their peril."[59] Special acts were passed to permit the re-recording of Granville grants when properly proved,[60] because some of the books belonging to the secretary's office in which they were formerly recorded had been lost or destroyed.[61]

The practice of delivering the original acts of the Assembly to the printer "whereby they may be mislaid or never returned" was condemned in 1787, and the clerks thereafter were required to deliver them to the secretary of state who was to make attested copies for the printer and "to take the necessary measures for the safe-keeping and preservation of the original acts. . . ."[62] In the same session, the comptroller's and treasurer's paid vouchers, warrants, orders, allowances, and drafts were ordered to be canceled by means of a punch a half inch in diameter.[63]

At the beginning of each session of the Assembly, the governor customarily laid before the legislature the important papers received by him since the last session. A comparison of the extant lists of such papers with the governors' papers now in the Archives indicates that not all of the records have been preserved.[64] The Assembly was so concerned over the preservation of the governors' correspondence that in 1782 it required his private secretary to enter into books all incoming letters of "considerable importance" as well as copies of all outgoing letters.[65] In 1787, a resolution, noting that "in many instances the official dispatches received by the late Governors may be necessary to establish the claims of this State against the United States or some of them, and as no steps have hitherto been taken to preserve them," required all

59. Clark, *State Records*, XX, 449 ff.
60. Clark, *State Records*, XX, 571.
61. Clark, *State Records*, XXIV, 966-67.
62. Clark, *State Records*, XXIV, 951.
63. Clark, *State Records*, XX, 282; XXIV, 951. These cancellation holes, about the size of a present-day penny, now cause great frustration in the State Archives because they often obliterate the name of the payee or other pertinent information.
64. For lists of governors' papers laid before the assemblies, see the following in Legislative Papers, State Archives: April, 1778; January, 1779; May, 1779; April, 1780. See also Clark, *State Records*, XVIII, 484-85, for an "inventory of public papers (put up in a chest) to be lodged in the Secretary's Office." The latter inventory contains "Letters and Public dispatches received by Governor Caswell," 1777-80, and other records, mostly of the period 1785-88.
65. Laws of 1782, c. 13, in Clark, *State Records*, XXIV, 445.

former governors or their representatives to lodge in the secretary of state's office "all official dispatches of every nature and kind which they may have received; also the journals of the Council of State, and books or copies of correspondence, during the time they were respectively in office." The clerks of the two houses also were required "after the rising of each session of the General Assembly, to lodge in the Secretary's office all such official dispatches as may remain in their respective offices or possession."[66]

A somewhat puzzling proposal was made in connection with the papers of former royal Governor Josiah Martin in 1782. An enemy landing force had previously "plundered" the possessions of one William Borden of Beaufort and made off with his papers consisting of "Accompts Books Deeds, Patents, Bonds, Notes of Lands, and other papers of Consequence." The privateers notified Borden that they would exchange his papers for those of the former Governor Martin. The papers of the royal governor were then in the admiralty office whose custodian would not release them. Borden petitioned the General Assembly which referred the matter to the governor and Council of State. Martin's papers were of no consequence to the State, Borden suggested; on the other hand, his were valuable to himself. The governor and Council, meeting at Nutbush, turned down Borden's request on the grounds that Governor Martin's papers contained "matters of great public importance" and should not be exchanged for "the papers of a private Individual of no importance but to himself."[67]

Efforts of the State to present its claims to the central government in connection with war expenditures were hampered by the loss or inaccessibility of wartime records. In 1777, a committee charged that the papers were "so blended" that it was impossible to determine all expenditures.[68] In 1789, Abishai

66. Clark, *State Records,* XX, 274; XXIV, 951.
67. Journal of the Council of State, June 7, 1782, in Governor's Papers, 1782, State Archives; petition dated April 29, 1782, in Legislative Papers, 1782, State Archives; Clark, *State Records,* XVI, 110. For the twentieth-century archivist, vitally concerned with the protection of public records as public property, this decision, and others like it, is reassuring evidence that the concept is not new.
68. Committee Report, April 22, 1777, in Legislative Papers, 1777, State Archives.

Thomas, North Carolina's agent to present its claims against the
United States, wrote that he had been unable to obtain copies of
all laws "for even in the Secretary's Office the Collection is not
compleated. . . ."[69] Three years later Hugh Williamson complained that the clerks of the Assembly "with their usual want
of attention to Duty" had failed to send him the necessary
records respecting a particular claim and charged that "patience
itself would be provoked at such execrable Neglect of Duty by
which so many People may be injured."[70]

No evidence has been found to indicate that the British
destroyed or carried off many public records.[71] The Treaty of
1783 ending the war with Great Britain provided that the King
should "order all archives, records, deeds and papers" belonging
to any of the states and which had been captured "to be forthwith restored and delivered to the proper States and persons to
whom they belong."[72] No evidence has come to light to indicate
that any such records were returned to North Carolina.

Except when the British occupied portions of the State, record
problems in the counties may not have been much greater than
in peacetime. True, the scarcity of paper, the absence of repairs
to courthouses, and the manpower shortage created unusual
problems. But the usual negligence, so pronounced in colonial
days, continued. Furthermore, some county officials were probably Tories, an affiliation that led to controversy and sometimes
to removal from office. In 1774, Maturin Colville, clerk of the
Court of Pleas and Quarter Sessions in Bladen County, refused
to turn over to his successor, Alfred Moore, the records of his
office including wills, indentures, and papers relating to settlements of estates. In 1777, the General Assembly directed that
the justices of the peace demand the papers from Colville and

69. Thomas to Governor Samuel Johnston, May 4, 1789, in Clark, *State Records,*
XXI, 554.
70. Hugh Williamson to Alexander Martin, February 17, 1792, in L. W. Smith
Collection, Morristown National Historical Park, Morristown, New Jersey (photocopy in State Archives).
71. In 1780, the papers of Thomas Bloodworth, commissioner of the specific
tax in New Hanover County, were placed aboard a ship in the Cape Fear River.
The British forces captured the ship and destroyed Bloodworth's records. Clark,
State Records, XXI, 694.
72. Clark, *State Records,* XVI, 880-81; XVII, 8.

anyone else having in their possession public records, upon threat of imprisonment. The county officers were directed to "make diligent search in all suspected places within the same county for the said Records and papers and for that purpose to break open doors and locks where they are suspected to be concealed."[73] Another bill the following year charged the same offense to James Sampson, former clerk in Duplin County, who refused to deliver his records to his successor, William Dickson. The justices of that county were directed to seek out the records and by force if necessary to return them to the clerk's office.[74] In the same year, a bill, later rejected, stated that "several Disputes have arisen between the County Courts & their Respective Clarkes who have been Discharg'd from their office & thereupon said Clarkes have Refused to Deliver the County Records when Demanded by order of the Court. . . ."[75] Another bill in 1783 complained that ". . . the frequent removal of County records from one place to another upon the alteration of Clerks and the inattention of Clerks of the County Courts with respect to conveying papers recording to the Secretaries office owing to the great distance the greater part of them live from the Secretaries office do frequently cause destruction of records and papers directed to be recorded in the Secretaries office. . . ." The ill-fated bill would have provided for a penalty for the removal of records from the courthouse and directed the clerk or his deputy to attend his office from 10:00 A.M. to 2:00 P.M. each day and to record within ten days after their receipt "in books by him to be kept for that purpose well bound" records so requiring to be entered.[76]

Courthouses lost during the period included Onslow, which had a second courthouse destroyed by storm in 1786;[77] Orange, where the courthouse burned about 1790 resulting in the use of

---

73. Clark, *State Records*, XXIV, 16-17. Colville's home had burned in 1768 and with it many of the Bladen County records. Lee, *Lower Cape Fear*, p. 141.

74. Laws of 1778, c. 24, in Clark, *State Records*, XXIV, 179. See also original bill in Legislative Papers, 1778, State Archives.

75. Original bill, dated April 18, 1778, in Legislative Papers, 1778, State Archives; Clark, *State Records*, XII, 561, 562, 671.

76. Original bill, dated April 25, 1783, in Legislative Papers, 1783, State Archives.

77. Crittenden and Lacy, *Historical Records*, III, 62. An earlier Onslow courthouse had been similarly destroyed in 1752.

a "private house" for office purposes;[78] New Hanover, whose courthouse in 1790 had to be "pulled down . . . to prevent the said town from being destroyed by fire" when an adjoining building burned;[79] and Hyde, whose courthouse burned at about the same time.[80] The toll of war may be seen in an act passed in 1788 noting that "the records of the registers office in the counties of Orange and Tyrrel [*sic*] are in a ruinous situation, occasioned by being removed at sundry times during the late war." It authorized the register to "transcribe in well bound books" those records requiring copying.[81]

As has been seen, the General Assembly at its 1787 session in Tarborough voted to hand the controversy over the location of the seat of government to a convention called to meet in Hillsborough in July, 1788, to consider ratification of the proposed Constitution of the United States. Willie Jones's resolution that the Convention should not fix the specific spot but rather to leave to the General Assembly the exact location of the capital provided it was within ten miles of the place chosen by the Convention was adopted. Six places were nominated—Smithfield, Fayetteville, Tarborough, Isaac Hunter's Tavern in Wake County, New Bern, and the Forks of the Haw and Deep Rivers. A first ballot was inconclusive. On second ballot, the Wake County site won a majority of votes. James Iredell then presented an ordinance which was adopted, but so strong was the opposition that it was agreed that those dissenting might be permitted to enter their protest in the journal. One hundred nineteen of the delegates did so, registering instead their preference of Fayetteville as the capital.[82]

Although the approximate site of the "unalterable" seat of government had been determined by the Convention, legislative action was necessary to implement the ordinance. But at Fayette-

78. Clark, *State Records,* XXV, 93.
79. Clark, *State Records,* XXV, 97.
80. Clark, *State Records,* XXV, 113. The Bladen County clerk's office burned about 1768. See above, p. 73, n. 73. See also 4 N.C. 410 (1817).
81. Clark, *State Records,* XXIV, 968. Some of the Orange County records had been buried in 1781 to escape capture by the British. See above, p. 63.
82. *Journal of the Convention [1788], passim.* See also Clark, *State Records,* XXII, 1-35.

ville in November, 1788, the House of Commons rejected a Senate-passed bill that would have carried it into effect.[83] The following year a similar bill was defeated by the tie-breaking vote of the presiding officer of the Senate.[84] It was not until January 5, 1792, that the Assembly finally appointed a commission of nine persons to determine the exact site of the capital city and another five persons to oversee the building of a state house at a cost not to exceed £10,000.[85] The new capital was to be named in memory of Sir Walter Raleigh.

The commissioners met at Isaac Hunter's residence on March 20, 1792, and ten days later voted to purchase 1,000 acres of Joel Lane's plantation for the sum of £1,378. William Christmas laid off the land into lots which were sold and the income used to construct the State House. Streets were named after the eight judicial districts of the State, the points of the compass, the commissioners themselves, and several other prominent citizens. The edifice was constructed on Union Square, one of five squares to be reserved for the public.[86]

The commissioners' actions were confirmed on December 15, 1792,[87] and the following year the Assembly directed that the July, 1794, session of the legislature convene in Raleigh and that all the public officers be directed to move to that city "with all the Publick Papers and Records of their Several offices by the first day of December next [1794]. . . ."[88] The State House was not ready for the summer session of the Assembly in 1794, how-

83. Kemp P. Battle, "Raleigh and the Old Town of Bloomsbury," *North Carolina Booklet*, II (November, 1902), 12. Cited hereafter as Battle, "Raleigh."

84. Battle, "Raleigh," p. 12.

85. Laws of 1791, c. 6, in Martin, *Public Acts*, II, 9; Dill, *Governor Tryon*, p. 256; Charles Earl Johnson, "History of the Capitol," *North Carolina Booklet*, V (October, 1905), 75. The site commissioners were Joseph McDowell, Sr., James Martin, Thomas Person, Thomas Blount, William Johnston Dawson, Frederick Hargett, Henry William Harrington, James Bloodworth, and Willie Jones. The building committee was made up of Richard Bennehan, John Macon, Robert Goodloe, Nathan Bryan, and Theophilus Hunter.

86. Report of the commissioners appointed to establish a place for the seat of government, in Secretary of State's Papers, Miscellaneous Papers, State Archives. It is interesting to note that Joel Lane was paid £30 for entertaining the commissioners. Was this a case of "lobbying"?

87. Laws of 1792, c. 14, in Martin, *Public Acts*, II, 28-29.

88. Resolution adopted December 26, 1793, in Legislative Papers, 1793, State Archives.

ever, and the legislators met for the last time in New Bern. Thus
not until December, 1794, did the Legislature finally convene in
the new "city." Most of the records were probably in Raleigh
by the time of the meeting of the Assembly. They came from
several directions—Hillsborough, Fayetteville, New Bern, and
Tarborough.[89]

Governor Alexander Martin noted with satisfaction that by
having the seat of government fixed, "the public offices will be
brought together, heretofore detached to too great distances—
archives of the state collected and preserved—and the different
departments of government conducted near each other, to the
quick dispatch of business and ease to the citizen."[90] A new era
began in both making and keeping the archives of North Carolina.

89. See various receipts and accounts in Treasurer's and Comptroller's Papers,
Executive Offices, State Archives.

90. Governor Martin's message to the General Assembly, 1792, in *Journal of
the House of Commons,* November 16, 1792. This is one of the earliest references
to the word "archives" in the North Carolina records.

IV

The Vicissitudes of the Records

1794-1903

THE STATE RECORDS IN RALEIGH, 1794-1861

Even before the General Assembly convened in the new "city" of Raleigh in December, 1794, the approximately fifteen full-time employees of the State—the secretary of state, comptroller, treasurer, attorney general, the Supreme Court, and their clerks—had already moved into the State House,[1] a two-story building designed, for all time, to accommodate the affairs of state government.[2] Records belonging to the State had been ordered moved to Raleigh, but it is doubtful if all of them—by then scattered about the State in various towns in which the legislatures had met and in which the officials had lived—were ferreted from their hiding places. Indeed, as late as 1826, some of the colonial rec-

---

1. The name "State House" was generally used rather than the term "capitol."
2. It is not clear whether the governor was permitted an office in the State House in 1794. From about 1802 until 1815, however, he had as his office a small building in the yard of the governor's house at the corner of Fayetteville and Hargett streets. In 1814, an office for the chief executive, to be of brick and 36 feet by 20 feet in dimensions, was ordered to be constructed on Union Square, and work commenced in 1815. In the latter year a new residence for the governor was ordered built at the south end of Fayetteville Street. *Raleigh Register*, December 23, 1814, and June 23, 1815; John L. Sanders, *Housing State Government: A Review, 1792-1957* (Chapel Hill: Institute of Government, 1958), p. 1; D. L. Swain, "Early Times in Raleigh," in W. J. Peele, *Lives of Distinguished North Carolinians with Illustrations and Speeches* (Raleigh: North Carolina Publishing Society, 1898), p. 258; Senate Resolution, adopted December 24, 1818, in Legislative Papers, 1818, State Archives.

ords belonging to the General Assembly were still in New Bern,[3] and later researches resulted in the location of many public records in private hands.[4]

Of the records placed in the new State House, four groups were both voluminous and important. The first of these comprised the original papers of the General Assembly—bills, resolutions, petitions, and the like—and the manuscript journals and laws. The responsibility for this group was placed upon the clerks of the two houses, but inasmuch as the clerks served only while the Assembly was in session, the legislative papers were probably stored in the second-floor offices of the State House between terms.[5] Consequently, the papers gradually became mixed and, as more room for recent records was required, the older ones were relegated to boxes, pigeon holes, or even to the floor.

The second group of records comprised the financial records, the bulk of them relating to the Revolutionary period. These records, belonging to both the treasurer and the comptroller, had been the subject of frequent attention from 1776 to 1792 because of their importance in the State's claims for the payment by the new federal government of the expenses incurred by North Carolina in the war. Even so, because of the confusion reigning in the offices of the various boards of auditors throughout the State, the records had been poorly kept—many not kept at all—and the State never was satisfied with the evidence supporting its claims upon the United States.

The papers of the governors comprised a third group. There were few surviving records for the colonial governors, and even during the Revolution the chief executives took many of their records with them when they left office. But beginning in 1782, the governor was required by law to appoint a private secretary

3. Resolution of the General Assembly in [North Carolina, General Assembly], *Acts Passed by the General Assembly of the State of North Carolina, at its Session Commencing on the 25th of December, 1826* (Raleigh: Lawrence and Lemay, 1827), p. 85. Because the exact title of the published laws varied from session to session, they will be cited hereafter as *Laws of [date of session]*. Where necessary, this short title will be preceded by the words public or private.

4. See below, chap. VI.

5. Later laws placed upon the secretary of state the responsibility for safekeeping the legislative records between sessions. See below, p. 81.

who was to copy into books all letters written by or to the governor as were official and important and any such other letters as the governor might think necessary. The book or books were to be laid before the next General Assembly, "and by the clerks carefully preserved in their offices."[6] It is doubtful, however, if the clerks exercised this responsibility since the governors continued to enter letters into the books after the meeting of the General Assembly. More than likely, the books were laid before the Assembly, perused by the committee assigned that responsibility, then returned to the governor's office for continued use. Too, there were the original incoming letters and other executive records which sometime were laid before the Assembly separately. These, presumably, were kept in the governor's office.[7]

The land grant books, comprising the fourth group and containing verbatim copies of all land grants issued since the beginning of the Colony, were kept by the secretary of state and, with their supporting papers, formed one of the most important bodies of records. Indeed, the granting of land was one of the more important functions of state government, and the secretary spent most of his time in that work.

Little is known about the records, their space assignments, and the conditions under which they were kept in the early years of the state government in Raleigh. The absence of complaints would suggest that the officials were reasonably well satisfied and that no major problems were involved. But within four years after the government was established in Raleigh, an armed guard had to be placed around the State House to protect the records.

John Armstrong, in charge of a land office in Nashville, Tennessee, conspired with one William Tyrrell, the clerk in Secretary of State James Glasgow's office in Raleigh, in the issuing and surveying of unlawful land grants in Tennessee. When the plot was discovered, Tyrrell fled, leaving behind the incriminating records, which were moved into the comptroller's office for protection. In 1798, Governor Samuel Ashe received information

6. Laws of 1782, c. 13, in Clark, *State Records*, XX, 45. See also Laws of 1784, c. 19, in Martin, *Public Acts*, I, 378.

7. At a later date it appears that the records of the early governors were placed in the keeping of the secretary of state. See below, p. 83.

from Nashville of another plot, allegedly inspired by the secretary of state himself, to burn the State House in order to destroy the evidence. For more than a month an armed guard was posted at the Capitol[8] and the conspiracy was thwarted. Glasgow, who had been one of the leaders of the State and who had held his office since the formation of the state government, was convicted.[9]

Two years later, the attention of the Assembly was again drawn to the land records. The first thirteen books, covering grants made from 1663 to 1767, were deteriorating so badly that the secretary of state was authorized to have them copied. He was to examine and compare the copies with the originals and to certify the accuracy of the copies, after which he was to "carefully pack up in a close chest or trunk, to be procured for that purpose, the original books, and deposit the same among the archives of the state. . . ."[10] He was also directed to require to be surrendered to him any records belonging to his office but in the hands of clerks of court or of other individuals, and the attorney general was ordered to prosecute anyone refusing to release to the secretary any such records. This cognizance of the importance of the original records, even after having been copied, is another encouraging bit of evidence that the Legislature was, at times, careful with the State's records. In 1813, the secretary was authorized to have copied the fourteenth book, covering grants from 1734 to 1769 (with similar provisions for preserving the original), to rebind "in his presence" the fifteenth book covering 1772-74, and to have the thirteenth book indexed.[11]

Additional duties were imposed upon the secretary of state in 1812 in a bill "more effectually to provide for the safe keeping of the Public Records. . . ." He was required to "collect all the

8. Instructions from Governor Samuel Ashe to Treasurer John Haywood to pay one Joshua Suggs £38 "being due himself & guard for guarding the State House with Wm. Tyrrell's Pa[pers] from the 20th of October 1798 to the 26th of November 1798," in Treasurer's and Comptroller's Papers, State Archives.

9. For the story of the fraud, see Samuel A. Ashe, *Biographical History of North Carolina from Colonial Times to the Present* (8 vols.; Greensboro: C. L. Van Noppen, 1905-17), VII, 115-21. Cited hereafter as Ashe, *Biographical History*. See also Samuel A. Ashe, *History of North Carolina* (2 vols.; Greensboro: C. L. Van Noppen, 1905-25), II, 152-53.

10. Laws of 1800, c. 26, in Martin, *Public Acts*, II, 158.

11. *Laws of 1813*, c. 16.

Books and Documents received, and intended for the use of the Legislature, . . . the Laws, Acts and Journals of the General Assembly, and all other Books and Documents, received and intended for the use of the Legislature. . . ."[12] Furthermore, he was to prepare a catalogue of all books, documents, laws, acts, and journals kept for use of the Assembly. He was, in effect, to take on some duties that previously had been the responsibility of the clerks of the Assembly and which later were to be carried on by the new office of state librarian.

After twenty years in Raleigh, the state government appeared to face no more than the usual problems in connection with record keeping. Officers were concentrated in one building with ample space for their clerical operations and for the preservation of their records. The General Assembly was within a few minutes of any record that it might command. The duties of officials were fairly well defined by law.

But a new threat to the archives of the State—fire—burst upon the scene in 1816. It was a threat that had not been an important factor in the loss of records during the first century and a half of North Carolina's history.

On the morning of June 11, 1816, a fire, thought to have been set by an incendiary, broke out in the back of William Shaw's store on Fayetteville Street. In the words of the *Raleigh Register:*

Large flakes of fire were wafted to a great distance—many of them fell on the State house: and had it not been for the prudent forethought and active zeal of the state officers who have charge of the house, this costly building had also been consumed. But fortunately they had the presence of mind to procure a quantity of rope, and a few proper characters to mount the roof, who by tying the rope to the Cupola and their own bodies, were capable of running in every direction, and of extinguishing the fire as soon as it fell.[13]

The State House was saved, but a block and a half of buildings on Fayetteville Street went up in flames.

The near-disaster frightened Secretary of State William Hill

12. *Laws of 1812,* c. 16.
13. *Raleigh Register,* June 14, 1816. See also petition of Wiley Sledge in Legislative Papers, 1816, State Archives, and receipt of Martin Adams in Treasurer's and Comptroller's Papers, Capital Buildings, State Archives.

into rushing a request to the General Assembly for the construction of a "Fire-Proof House for the safe keeping of the Books Papers and Records" of his office. The State House, with its roof of wood shingles, was not safe. A legislative committee agreed, "and as the cost will be inconsiderable when compared with the great security of the public records," recommended the construction of such a building on Union (Capitol) Square.[14] It was to be forty feet long, twenty-six feet wide, two stories high, and to contain four "apartments." One room was to be set aside as the State Library; the remainder was to be assigned to the secretary of state where "all the books, papers, and documents belonging to the Office of Secretary of State shall be constantly kept. . . ." The offices vacated by the secretary in the State House were to be set aside for the adjutant general and the committees and clerks of the Assembly.[15] The building was completed about 1819[16] and the secretary of state occupied it continuously until 1840.

The fire of 1816 also resulted in a demand for renovation of the State House. Between 1820 and 1822, both the treasurer and comptroller were moved out of the State House into rented office space while the building received a face lifting as well as a roof lifting. A third floor and north and south "projections" were added, providing more office space, and the chambers of the legislature were enlarged.[17] The officers, upon completion of the

14. Report of the committee in Legislative Papers, 1816, State Archives. See also resolution on the "Fire-Proof House" in *Laws of 1817,* p. 76.

15. Resolutions, dated December 20, 1817, and December 22, 1818, in Legislative Papers, 1817 and 1818, State Archives.

16. Order for payment from Treasurer John Haywood to Edmund Lane in Treasurer's and Comptroller's Papers, Capital Buildings, State Archives; statement of the comptroller for 1819, in Treasurer's and Comptroller's Papers, Accounts, State Archives.

17. The treasurer moved his office and records into John Scott's "Corner House" opposite the Eagle Hotel just north of the State House; the comptroller used space belonging to William Ruffin. Comptroller's statements in Treasurer's and Comptroller's Papers, Accounts, and receipt of Thomas Cobb, November 12, 1821, in Treasurer's and Comptroller's Papers, Capital Buildings, State Archives; report of "The Committee Who Were appointed to examine the State of the Public Buildings," December 25, 1818, and of "The Committee to Whom was referred that part of the Governor's Message, which relates to the Statue of the late General Washington, and the necessary preparations to be made for its reception, and permanent accommodation," December 7, 1819, in Legislative Papers, 1818

renovation, moved back into the Capitol.[18]

Whether for safety or for space—though the enlargement of the Capitol appears to question the need for the latter—the General Assembly of 1824 ordered the construction of another building on Union Square. This one, "for the security of the records, papers and money of Treasury Department," was to be a fireproof stone or brick building, with a vault, and was to be located on the southeast corner of the square.[19] Three years later the Assembly directed the erection of an arsenal[20] on the southwest corner of Union Square. Even earlier, in 1814, a small office near the State House had been ordered built for the governor.[21] Thus, by 1830, there were four outbuildings, in addition to the "necessary house" and woodshed, on the square.

Jared Sparks, the New England editor and historian, visited Raleigh in May, 1826, and recorded his impressions of the records of the state government. He spent four days, mainly in the secretary of state's office, and his journal furnishes evidence that most of the important manuscript materials not only of the secretary's office but also of both the General Assembly and the governor's office had been placed by that time in the "Fire-Proof House." Secretary of State William Hill[22] offered him "every facility in his power in examining the public documents." The manuscript journals of the Assembly and Council were well preserved

---

and 1819, State Archives. Unfortunately the drawings for the State House renovations, submitted by the superintendent of public buildings, William Nichols, and originally attached to the latter report, appear to have been lost. Although the crowded and dilapidated condition of the building had been the source of concern for several years, the prospective arrival of Canova's controversial statue of George Washington constituted the impetus for renovation.

18. Resolution in *Laws of 1828-1829*, p. 92.

19. *Laws of 1824*, c. 8. See also various papers in Treasurer's and Comptroller's Papers, Capital Buildings, State Archives. The same act provided for the secretary of state to make more secure the windows and doors of his building to protect his records against depredation and fire. All public offices were required to be open daily except Sunday and July 4 from 9:00 A.M. to noon and from 2:00 to 5:00 P.M.

20. *Laws of 1827-1828*, c. 17. This building, to be of stone or brick, forty-five by twenty-five feet with two stories, was later to figure significantly in the preservation of the public records. See below, pp. 113 ff.

21. See above, p. 77, n. 2.

22. William Hill served as secretary of state from 1811 to 1859—longer than any other occupant of that office.

from 1750 onward, Sparks wrote, but he was disappointed that there was not to be found in the state offices a copy of the early printed journals. He was impressed with the number of letters preserved from Governor Caswell's term of office during the Revolution, stating that "All are safely preserved, though not well arranged." He noted the absence of letters for 1781,[23] and the scarcity of original letters but the availability of the letter books of the governors after 1782. To the dismay of twentieth-century historians, Sparks candidly wrote: "By the politeness of Mr. Secretary Hill I have been permitted to take copies of several of the letters, which have been deposited in the files, & the originals he has given to me. . . . These original letters will assist in completing a collection for the purpose of a volume of the *fac simile* [*sic*] autographs of the revolutionary heroes & statesmen, which I may one day publish with suitable notices." In addition, Sparks arranged for the secretary to have copied for him all the other papers that he had "marked."[24] He also visited the State Library and commented on "the most remarkable instance of bibliomania, probably, which has occurred in this country"—the purchase by the State for sixty dollars of a first edition of John Lawson's history of Carolina.[25]

Jared Sparks may have been the first out-of-state historian to make direct use of the State's archives. Almost twenty years later he wrote, "I once spent a week in the State house in Raleigh

23. See above, pp. 61 ff., for a possible explanation of this absence. Sparks may not have known that the earliest journal published was that of the 1749 session.

24. These quotations were taken from Sparks's "Journal of a Southern Tour, 1826," as printed in John H. Moore, "Jared Sparks in North Carolina," *North Carolina Historical Review,* XL (July, 1963), 285-94. Sparks's visit to North Carolina was a part of a research trip to the state capitals in the various Southern states during March-July, 1826. John Spencer Bassett, *The Middle Group of American Historians* (New York: The Macmillan Company, 1917), p. 75. Cited hereafter as Bassett, *American Historians.*

25. Sparks was wrong about the price; the State actually paid $65.00 for the book. Although the State Library may have existed even earlier, a legislative resolution in 1817 directed a room in the "Fire-Proof House" to be set aside for the "Library of the State." The library, however, was back in the State House by 1824 when shelving for a "Libery" was installed. See claim of Giles Johnston, November 12, 1824, in Treasurer's and Comptroller's Papers, Capital Buildings, State Archives.

examining revolutionary papers, but they were in such extreme disorder, that my labor was not well rewarded."[26]

Fire, which shocked the State into providing security for its records in 1816, again struck the Capitol on January 6, 1831, when the roof caught fire. Through the "timely and energetic efforts of John B. Muse and Richard Roberts, at much personal hazard and risk," the building was saved.[27] But this second threat to the building prompted the Assembly to attempt to overcome the danger of fire resulting from the wood shingle roof. Both the Capitol and the "Fire-Proof House" containing the secretary of state's offices were ordered to be covered with copper, tin, or zinc, and the damage to the former was to be repaired.[28]

Work commenced soon thereafter and the final touches of soldering the zinc roof was about completed by mid-June. Early in the morning of June 21, 1831, as the final repairs were being made, a worker climbed the stairway with "a coal of fire, between two shingles." A draft supposedly wafted a spark from the fire to the ceiling and the dry wood caught fire. Within two hours, the State House was destroyed.[29]

Governor Montford Stokes took official notice of the loss of

26. Sparks to David L. Swain, March 5, 1845, in David Lowry Swain Papers, Southern Historical Collection, The University of North Carolina Library, Chapel Hill. This source will hereafter be cited as Swain Papers and the repository will be cited as Southern Historical Collection. Another distinguished researcher, Matthew St. Clair Clarke, clerk of the United States House of Representatives and partner of Peter Force, visited Raleigh during the summer of 1833 "collecting documents for the history of the States prior to the Revolution. . . ." John H. Bryan to his wife, June 25, 1833, in John Herritage Bryan Papers, State Archives. It is not known whether Clarke too was permitted to carry off originals.

27. Resolution in *Laws of 1830-1831,* p. 133. The Assembly was in session when the fire alarm was sounded, and a local editor wryly noted that the delegates did not wait for a formal motion for adjournment. *Raleigh Register, and North-Carolina Gazette,* January 13, 1831.

28. *Laws of 1830-1831,* c. 3. A trap door was ordered to be made in the ceiling of the office of secretary of state, another security precaution.

29. *Raleigh Register, and North-Carolina Gazette,* June 23, 30, 1831; *Star, and North Carolina State Gazette* (Raleigh), June 23, 30, 1831. The exact cause of the fire has never been ascertained, though it was generally accepted that it began as a result of the negligent workman as noted herein. The General Assembly, blaming the destruction upon Thomas Bragg, the contractor, ordered that he not be paid for the full sum specified in the contract for covering the State House, though he was authorized to be paid the full amount for the zinc roof that was simultaneously put over the secretary of state's "Fire-Proof House." Resolution in *Laws of 1831-1832,* p. 140.

the State House when the General Assembly convened in November. He lamented the loss of the structure which since its
remodeling in the early 1820's had become noted for its interior
beauty, but he called attention to the defective walls of the
original portion of the building. "Such were the defects in the
Construction of the old Walls erected in 1794, that it is very probable, that a part of the building would have fallen in a few years,
and perhaps caused the death of many of the assembled Representatives," he wrote.[30] Thus the State may have been lucky to
have suffered significant losses of neither archives nor assembly-
men.

Fortunately for the safety of the records, most of the archives
of the offices of the governor, secretary of state, and treasurer had
been kept in buildings on Union Square put up for those particular offices. The papers of the General Assembly (except those
in possession of the secretary of state), the comptroller, the adjutant general, the Supreme Court, and the State Library, however, were in the State House. There are conflicting contemporary reports as to what records were burned. The *Star* reported
two days after the fire that "all the furniture, with every thing
else, save the papers in the Comptroller's office, the office of the
Clerk of the Supreme Court, and the offices of the Clerks of the
two Houses of the Legislature, was consumed."[31] The competing
Raleigh Register said: "Considering the rapidity with which the
fire progressed, it is an alleviating circumstance that the public
papers were all secured. Besides the papers of the Clerks of the
two Houses of the Legislature, and those of the Comptroller, &
of the Clerk of the Supreme Court, a fine Copy of Stewart's Paint-
ing of the Father of our Country, and some articles of furniture
of the Legislative Chambers, were preserved from the flames."[32]
The following week the same editor wrote: "Our public Officers,
particularly the Secretary of State and Comptroller, have an
Herculean task to perform in reducing to order the chaotic confusion into which the papers have been thrown. The documents

30. Governor Montford Stokes's message to the General Assembly, November
22, 1831, in Governor's Letter Book, 1831 (G.L.B. 29), State Archives.
31. *Star, and North Carolina State Gazette,* June 23, 1831.
32. *Raleigh Register, and North-Carolina Gazette,* June 23, 1831.

belonging to the Clerks of the two Houses and some of the Comptroller's Papers are mixed with those of the Secretary of State; the attempt therefore, to hunt up at present any particular record would be nearly as hopeless a task, as to look for a needle in a hay-stack."[33] Finally, the editor of the *Star* wrote that the records were removed from all the public offices, but "the state of derangement into which they have been thus precipitated, will impose a task upon the Heads of Department[s] which will require many months of the most assiduous labor to accomplish."[34]

Available evidence indicates that few important records were lost in the fire. Even the comptroller's office, which was in the State House, lost remarkably few. A legislative committee reported that only eleven vouchers, amounting to $1,161.98, were lost or mislaid "in the bustle, hurry and confusion removing his books and papers from his office in the State House at its conflagration June last. So small a loss under the circumstances of this case, the committee think a most signal and fortunate occurrence; and has resulted in *no loss* or *injury* to the State. . . ."[35] Many years later, Charles Manly, secretary of the board of trustees of the University of North Carolina, wrote that a certain report "together with nearly all the other papers of the University prior to the year 1810 were in the Office of Treasr. Haywood & were destroyed in the State House."[36] Possibly Manly was correct, but if so, these must have been papers stored in an upper room in the State House. The treasurer had moved his office and records into a building constructed on the southeast corner of Union Square about 1826, though he may have left behind some noncurrent records. Besides, Haywood was not in office in 1831. Furthermore, an examination of the extant records of the secretary of state's correspondence and the papers of the treasurer's and comptroller's offices now deposited in the State Archives indicates no break in entries for the month of June, 1831. Ledgers and journals, for instance, continue from June 20 right on through the

33. *Raleigh Register, and North-Carolina Gazette,* June 30, 1831.
34. *Star, and North Carolina State Gazette,* June 23, 1831.
35. Report of committee of finance, *Laws of 1831-1832,* Appendix.
36. Cha[rle]s Manly to David L. Swain, October 16, 1844, in Swain Papers, Southern Historical Collection.

month, indicating that there was little interruption in either the records or daily activities of these offices as a result of the destruction of the State House.[37]

It will never be known just what records were destroyed in the fire.[38] It is likely that as many were lost in the confusion as were burned. Although there is no documentary evidence that some records were discarded rather than being arranged and placed in the proper offices, it is not difficult to suspect that in the ensuing months such destruction did take place. One thing is known: The papers of the treasurer and comptroller became so mixed that in the twentieth century the State Department of Archives and History was unable to separate the various records according to their provenance, and consequently the early records for these two offices are combined into one record group.

The Assembly directed that an agent be employed to arrange in proper order the papers that were saved from the fire and to deliver them to the proper offices.[39] The following year Governor Stokes reported that the task of sorting and arrangement had been completed, "but owing to the want of sufficient cases & shelves in the Government House to hold the papers belonging to the Senate and House of Commons, they have been carefully labelled and filed in a room in the office of the Secretary of State. . . ."[40] The Assembly also provided for the governor to have

37. See, for example, Secretary of State's Papers, Correspondence, 1831, and Treasurer's and Comptroller's Papers, Journals and Ledgers, State Archives.

38. That there were losses in the fire, however, was generally assumed, even though state officials five years later told a New England archivist that all had been saved. Richard G. Wood, "Richard Bartlett, Minor Archival Prophet," *American Archivist*, XVII (January, 1954), 13-18. Bartlett was one of the earliest writers on the subject of preservation of state archives. "To provide for the safe and perfect keeping of the Public Archives is so obviously one of the first and most imperative duties of a legislature, that no argument could make it plainer to a reflecting mind," he wrote. Everything that can be procured by money sinks into insignificance in comparison with original records of a state, he continued, and original records are "of so priceless a value, that no money could purchase them of the poorest state in the Union, or replace them when once destroyed."

39. Resolution in *Laws of 1831-1832*, p. 143.

40. Governor Montford Stokes's message to General Assembly, November 19, 1832, in Governor's Letter Book, 1832 (G.L.B. 29), State Archives. The "Government House" was the state-owned residence of the governor at the south end of Fayetteville Street, built about 1815. Prior to the latter date, the governor lived in a rented house at the corner of Fayetteville and Hargett streets. From 1831 to 1838, the Assembly met at the Government House.

all maps, drafts, and plans formerly in the possession of the state engineer placed in the executive office and for those needing it to be repaired.[41] This too was accomplished. In fact, the Assembly appeared unusually concerned with the records. It found defective the transcriptions made of the Cherokee land records which had been ordered copied by the previous session because they were "in a mutilated state and likely to become unintelligible." They were ordered to be copied again from the originals.[42] Finally, because the State Library had been burned, along with all printed copies of the journals and laws of the General Assembly, the governor was directed to appoint an agent to procure by gift or purchase one or more copies of these printed documents for the use of the State. It was noted that this could be done cheaper than "the expense of reprinting the said Journals [and laws] from the original manuscripts."[43] Joseph Gales, the publisher of the *Raleigh Register,* was appointed to carry out this resolution and, with the assistance of David L. Swain and others, was highly successful in replacing most of the lost volumes.[44] Former President James Madison, having read in the papers that the first edition of John Lawson's history had burned, sent his own copy of the 1714 edition as a gift to the State.[45]

From 1831 until the new capitol was completed in 1840, the papers of the offices of governor, secretary of state, and treasurer were in the outbuildings which had escaped the 1831 fire. The comptroller probably shared office space in one of these buildings, while the Supreme Court moved its offices into the session house of the Presbyterian Church. The General Assembly appreciatively declined an offer of the use of the Presbyterian Church and Session House and from 1831 to 1838 met instead in the Govern-

41. Resolution in *Laws of 1831-1832,* p. 143.

42. Resolution in *Laws of 1828-1829,* p. 93, and another in *Laws of 1831-1832,* p. 141.

43. Resolution in *Laws of 1831-1832,* p. 144.

44. Governor Montford Stokes's message to General Assembly, November 19, 1832, in Governor's Letter Book, 1832 (G.L.B. 29), State Archives. See also Carolyn Andrews Wallace, "David Lowry Swain, 1801-1835" (unpublished Ph.D. dissertation, The University of North Carolina, 1954), p. 312. The latter source is cited hereafter as Wallace, "Swain."

45. James Madison to Governor Montford Stokes, July 15, 1831, in Governor's Papers, State Series, 1831 (G.P. 62), p. 215. This was the book that the State had paid $65.00 for some years earlier. See above, p. 84, n. 25.

ment House, temporarily displacing the governor who moved into rented quarters. The 1838-39 session was held in a new building owned by Benjamin B. Smith at the corner of Market and Fayetteville streets.[46] At best, these temporary facilities meant that offices were cramped and the records of several departments probably were ill-kept. Some attention was given to the records, however. The secretary of state was directed to have rebound such old record books in his office as required it,[47] an agent was appointed to collect the books and papers furnished for use of the Legislature and to place them in the State Library,[48] and the committee on finance of the House of Commons expressed its "most entire satisfaction at the able, honest and business-like manner" in which the treasurer's and comptroller's books and accounts were kept.[49]

Upon completion of the new capitol in 1840 at a total cost of more than $530,000, all departments of government moved into it. The governor, secretary of state, comptroller, treasurer, and the Supreme Court were assigned main floor offices, and the adjutant general, State Library, and clerks of the Assembly were put on the upper floors. It appears that the records of the various departments were placed in or adjacent to their respective offices.

The Assembly then ordered that the old buildings on Union Square be sold and torn down.[50] The buildings housing the old offices of the governor and secretary of state were sold in 1849.[51] The date of the removal of the treasury office is not known, but the arsenal building was not removed until after 1907.[52] This latter

46. See resolution in *Laws of 1838-1839*, p. 181, which directed payment to Smith for use of his house for the General Assembly in 1838-39. See also *Raleigh Register*, November 5, 1838. The Convention of 1835, offered the facilities of both the Methodist and Presbyterian churches, met in the latter.

47. Resolution ratified January 21, 1837, in *Laws of 1836-1837*, p. 336.

48. Resolution in *Laws of 1838-1839*, p. 189.

49. Report of the committee of finance in *Laws of 1838-1839*, p. 197 (Appendix).

50. *Public Laws of 1842-1843*, c. 54. See also resolution ratified January 3, 1845, in *Laws of 1844-1845*, p. 136, and another ratified January 14, 1847, in *Laws of 1846-1847*, p. 246.

51. See report of the public treasurer in *Laws of 1850-1851*, p. 4 (Appendix), showing sale of these offices to William F. Collins for $550.12.

52. See [North Carolina, General Assembly], *Revisal of 1905 of North Carolina* (2 vols.; Raleigh: E. M. Uzzell & Co., 1905), II, sec. 5007, placing the building under the control of the keeper of the Capitol in 1905; and Governor Robert B.

building was to play a significant role in connection with the public records in later years.[53] Thus, about 1840, for the first time since 1816, not only all of the officers of the government, including the Legislature, but also all of the records of the State were safely housed in one building. Other buildings of convenience, including one for the storage of wood for the fireplaces and another for public toilets, remained for several decades, but it is to be hoped that no archives were relegated to them.

That some work continued on sorting and arranging records after their deposit in the Capitol was indicated in 1846 when Green Hill was paid for "assorting and filing away Legislative documents from 1749 to 1828," and in 1849 when Perrin Busbee, clerk of the House of Commons, was paid for "arranging and putting in order" the papers of his office.[54] In 1848, Governor William A. Graham urged the Assembly to exercise "a more strict supervision of the enrolment of the Acts which may receive their sanction." He said, "The wisest intentions may fail of effect by clerical omissions or inadvertaince & cases have occurred when the extremest license of construction was barely sufficient to effect the known purposes of the framers of the law."[55] Nine years later the Assembly directed the assistant clerks ". . . to collect and properly arrange, in the archives of the senate [and House], all the records and papers belonging thereto, which are now in the various rooms and departments of the capitol; and that he [they] be further requested to collect and have bound, or otherwise preserved, for the senate [and House] library, such laws, legislative documents and other papers, as have not already been obtained. . . ."[56] In 1859, the state librarian was appointed also to be the librarian of the Senate and House and he was

Glenn's message to the General Assembly, 1907, in Governor's Letter Book (G.L.B. 113), State Archives.

53. See below, pp. 113-14.

54. [North Carolina, General Assembly], *Report of the Comptroller's Department . . . for the Fiscal Year, Ending November 1st, 1845* (Raleigh: W. R. Gales, 1845), p. 10. See also private resolution in favor of Perrin Busbee, ratified January 29, 1849, in *Laws of 1848-1849*, p. 466.

55. Governor William A. Graham's message to General Assembly, November 21, 1848, in Governor's Letter Book, 1848 (G.L.B. 38), State Archives.

56. Resolution ratified February 2, 1857, in *Public Laws of 1856-1857*, p. 70.

charged with collecting and arranging in the archives of the two houses all records and papers belonging to the General Assembly. He was also directed to have cases and shelves constructed in the offices of the legislative clerks for the reception of the records.[57] In the same year the governor was assigned a room in the gallery of the Senate for the purpose of depositing any records for which he could not provide space in his offices. The other gallery room was assigned to the state librarian for records and books that no longer could be accommodated in the "Library Room."[58]

An act in 1850, had it been carried out, would have resulted in a valuable addition to the State's archives. A third-floor room was assigned for the reception of "maps, charts, documents and other material relating to the surveys which have been or may hereafter be made with reference to any work of public improvement in this State. . . ." All businesses incorporated were to be required to furnish the Bureau of Engineering "a correct map and profile of the contemplated improvement, drawn to an uniform horizontal scale of four hundred feet to an inch. . . ."[59] The duties were to be carried on by the state librarian until a state engineer was appointed. This act, if enforced at all, was soon ignored.

The cost of record keeping also was a source of concern. The Assembly asked for an accounting of all expenses paid for stationery and record-keeping materials. The comptroller, in an 1842 report, gave a detailed accounting, showing each purchase with description, quantity, and price. Such expenses, according to the report, totaled (in round figures) $700 in 1836, $245 in 1837, and $781 in 1838. The report reveals that paper, in particular, was selected for specific uses, indicating an eye for economy by the use of cheaper materials for records of little value. The twentieth-century records manager's concern with such matters is not new.[60]

57. *Public Laws of 1858-1859*, c. 41, pp. 83-85.
58. See both resolutions in *Public Laws of 1858-1859*, pp. 104-5.
59. Resolution in *Laws of 1850-1851*, p. 515.
60. Report of the comptroller, December 20, 1842, bound in [North Carolina, General Assembly], *Documents Printed By Order of the General Assembly . . . 1842-43* (Raleigh: Weston R. Gales, 1843). The title and printer of this series varied from time to time. The source is cited hereafter as *Public Documents,*

Thus it may be seen that the importance of records and record keeping was not only recognized by the State prior to the Civil War, but was indeed one of the prime considerations. Always a major argument in the efforts to fix the seat of government had been the need for a constant place of deposit for the records. Always the first thought when fire repeatedly struck the State House was salvaging the records. And both legislative and executive attention to the problems of making proper records and adequately preserving those already created was evident in numerous laws, resolutions, and directives. It is perhaps not surprising, therefore, that, as the Civil War approached, the State of North Carolina had lost relatively few records except as a result of the meanderings of the public offices in the eighteenth century. Although many of the records of the colonial existence of the Province had thus disappeared, fortunately copies of the more important ones had been sent to England. Then, with the exception of the loss of those records that had been removed by retiring officials and those that were never drawn from their hiding places upon the frequent removal of the seat of government up to 1794, there had been few significant losses up to the Civil War.

THE RECORDS AND THE WAR, 1861-1888

The Civil War brought another danger. For the first time since 1781, enemy troops threatened the seat of government. How great would be the damage to the archives of the State?

That question must have been uppermost in the minds of the members of the General Assembly when in secret session in 1863, just after the battles of Gettysburg and Vicksburg, they passed the following resolution:

WHEREAS, By reason of the frequent incursions of the enemy from his garrisons in the eastern part of the State towards the interior,

---

with the appropriate date. Record books were bought for about $12.00 each; governor's stationery for $5.00 per ream; foolscap paper for $4.25 per ream; and lamp oil for $2.00 per gallon. (The high price of lamp oil indicates that it may have been whale oil or possibly camphene). Other items included were tape, sealing wax, paper sand, candles, pens, quills, fountain pens (75 cents each), lead pencils, scrapers, and blotter paper. Several types of ink-stands were purchased: plain ones for a very low price, "fine cut glass" ones for $1.50, and pewter ink-stands for $6.00.

the public danger is increasing; and, whereas, by reason of these in-cursions, and the want of proper force for defence, the capitol of the State, with all the public papers and archives, money, bonds, army stores and all the effects of every kind connected with the State gov-ernment may be destroyed or put in peril of loss:

Resolved, That the Governor of the State be directed to have made or procure for the use of all the civil and military departments at the seat of government such boxes as may be needed for the removal of all the aforesaid government effects, as also to remove the same at his discretion, and he is authorized to draw upon the Treasury for such sum of money as may be needed for the execution of this purpose.[61]

Although hostile forces occupied much of the coastal area of the State throughout the war, the capital city was spared until towards the end of the conflict. The war, nevertheless, had its effect upon the archives of the State. Certainly the records no longer commanded the respect due them in the face of the more practical necessity of prosecuting a war. The Legislature was in session almost continuously during the war, and some confusion undoubtedly arose over the mass of legislation that was passed. It is perhaps not surprising, therefore, that the secretary of state reported that he was unable to locate several of the public docu-ments for the session of 1864-65, they having been "misplaced" before he came into office.[62] Even so, just as it was ironic that the State House in 1831 was destroyed by fire as a result of an effort to secure the building against such a catastrophe, it is also ironic that it was the end of the war that brought about the greatest threat to the records of the state government.

With General William T. Sherman marching into North Carolina from the south, Governor Zebulon B. Vance on March 13, 1865, called his Council of State together and with their ad-vice decided that the government should evacuate Raleigh in the event of imminent danger to the city. Treasurer Jonathan Worth had been placed in charge of preparations, and following the cap-ture of Fayetteville by Union forces, the governor advised state officials and the local banks to pack up their valuables in prepara-

61. Resolution ratified July 7, 1863, in *Laws of 1863* [*Secret Session*], pp. 73-74.
62. *Public Documents, 1864-1866,* p. 1 (Index).

tion for the move. Some of the "public moneys, papers, books &c. which had been previously packed, were put on board of a train of cars furnished by the State Quarter-Master, Maj. Devereux, & sent West on the N. C. Rail-Road" about the middle of March under the care of the clerks of the state offices and of the Bank of North Carolina and the Bank of Cape Fear.[63] While most of the boxes of papers and money appear to have been kept aboard the train at different points along the railway, some of them seem to have been deposited at Company Shops, Greensboro, and Salisbury.[64]

The materials moved about March 13, however, did not include the bulk of the records of the State. The latter, Treasurer Jonathan Worth wrote on March 20, were all packed and "ready to fly."[65] Then on March 23, with the enemy moving ever closer to the capital city, Worth took most of the remaining archives by train to Greensboro where he placed them in the Bank of Cape Fear in the care of his clerks.[66] Worth himself returned to Raleigh after five days, but upon hearing that Major General George Stoneman's cavalry was pushing eastward from the mountains, he rushed back to Greensboro. Stoneman, however, turned north, and the treasurer again on April 8 left for Raleigh.[67] The follow-

63. R[ichard] H. Battle to Cornelia P. Spencer, February 26, 1866, in Cornelia Phillips Spencer Papers, Southern Historical Collection. This source hereafter will be cited as Spencer Papers. The clerks included "Mr. Wiley" of the treasurer's office, "Mr. Bain" of the comptroller's office, "Mr. Bradley" of the governor's office, Colonel W. E. Anderson of the Bank of North Carolina, and W. H. Jones of the Cape Fear Bank.

64. R[ichard] H. Battle to Cornelia P. Spencer, February 26, 1866, in Spencer Papers, Southern Historical Collection. See also [North Carolina Historical Commission], *The North Carolina Historical Commission: General Information, 1911* (Raleigh: E. M. Uzzell, [1911]), p. 13. Cited hereafter as *Historical Commission, 1911*. See also Jonathan Worth to J. J. Jackson, March 13, 1865, in J. G. de Roulhac Hamilton (ed.), *The Correspondence of Jonathan Worth* (2 vols.; Raleigh: North Carolina Historical Commission, 1909), I, 366. The latter source hereafter will be cited as Hamilton, *Worth Correspondence*. Company Shops was at the present city of Burlington.

65. Worth to J. J. Jackson, March 20, 1865, in Hamilton, *Worth Correspondence*, I, 371. For Worth's role in protecting the archives during March and April, 1865, see Richard L. Zuber, *Jonathan Worth: A Biography of a Southern Unionist* (Chapel Hill: The University of North Carolina Press, 1965), pp. 185-91.

66. Worth to his wife, Martitia, March 25, 1865, in Jonathan Worth Papers, State Archives; Worth to J. J. Jackson, March 31, 1865, in Hamilton, *Worth Correspondence*, I, 373.

67. Worth to J. J. Jackson, April 3, 1865, and April 8, 1865, in Hamilton, *Worth Correspondence*, I, 376, 378.

ing day Stoneman again approached Greensboro[68] and a train carrying the stores and records was dispatched to Hillsborough, but returned toward Greensboro when Stoneman turned away for the second time.[69] On April 10, General P. G. T. Beauregard, then in Raleigh, ordered trains heading for Greensboro to proceed on to Salisbury. Evidence does not reveal if the records were actually unloaded at Greensboro, or whether they were aboard a train en route and consequently ordered on to Salisbury.[70] The records in this shipment were probably the bulk of the archives, but not those needed in the day-to-day operation of state government. The latter were required to be kept close at hand in Raleigh for current operations.

Back in Raleigh, former Governors William A. Graham and David L. Swain, as representatives of Governor Vance, were sent on April 11 to meet General Sherman who by then was only a few miles from the capital. The Union general promised safety for the remaining archives and to state officers as long as they remained within twelve miles of Raleigh.[71] This provision Vance would not accept on the grounds that he and the officers of the government would be virtual prisoners. Consequently, it was decided that the government and its records should be evacuated. The archives that had remained in Raleigh were undoubtedly those in daily use—i.e., the current records and those needed in the administration of the state government.

On the same day, with enemy forces only a few miles outside the city, wagons were hurriedly assembled. Treasurer Worth

68. R. N. Scott *et al.* (eds.) *The War of the Rebellion: A Compilation of the Official Records of the Union and Confederate Armies* (70 vols. [127 books, atlases, and index]; Washington, D. C.: Government Printing Office, 1880-1901), ser. I, XLVII, pt. III, p. 777. Cited hereafter as *Official Records.*

69. Worth to J. J. Jackson, April 21, 1865, in Hamilton, *Worth Correspondence,* I, 380.

70. See below, pp. 101-2.

71. Worth to J. J. Jackson, April 21, 1865, in Hamilton, *Worth Correspondence,* I, 380-81; Worth to Joseph A. Worth, April 22, 1865, in Hamilton, *Worth Correspondence,* II, 1288. Vance, in a note to Sherman, wrote, "The Capitol of the State with its Libraries, Museum and much of the public records is also left in your power. I can but entertain the hope that they may escape mutilation or destruction in as much as such evidences of learning and taste could advantage neither party in the prosecution of the war whether destroyed or preserved." Vance to General William T. Sherman, April 11, 1865, in Spencer Papers, Southern Historical Collection.

planned to take the papers and "valuables" to Morrisville, there to be placed aboard a railroad train to be taken into the country. But some of the wagoners "ran away" and replacements could not be obtained until Wednesday night. Consequently it was 9:00 P.M. before the wagon train left Raleigh. By then it was too late to meet the railroad train at Morrisville, so the wagons were ordered instead to Durham's Station. During the night they were caught among the army trains of the retreating Confederates and the progress was so slow that it was sundown Thursday before they finally reached Durham.[72] From there Worth telegraphed Confederate General Beauregard, "I am here in charge of the State funds and archives with the state wagon trains[.] Will you favor me with your opinion whether it will be safe to endeavor to carry off the effects by the wagon trains in the direction of Fayetteville or to fall back towards Greensboro and if you advise the latter at what point do you desire."[73] Whether upon Beauregard's orders or Worth's own decision, the wagons carrying the state records were ordered to proceed to Company Shops. Worth himself went on ahead and, after waiting for the wagons at the Shops until Friday afternoon, proceeded to Greensboro, leaving word for the wagons to follow as soon as possible.[74] The wagons probably reached Greensboro April 15, or possibly the

72. For the story of the evacuation of the officials and records from Raleigh on April 11, see Worth to J. J. Jackson, April 21, 1865, in Hamilton, *Worth Correspondence*, I, 380-81; Worth to Joseph A. Worth, April 22, 1865, in Hamilton, *Worth Correspondence*, II, 1288-91; R[ichard] H. Battle to Cornelia P. Spencer, February 26, 1866, and Zebulon B. Vance to Cornelia P. Spencer, April 7, [1866], in Spencer Papers, Southern Historical Collection; and Worth to the editor, *Daily Sentinel* (Raleigh), October 30, 1865. See also the report of the president of the Atlantic and North Carolina Railroad in *Public Documents, 1866-1867*, p. 201. Some records appear to have been hidden in Raleigh and not removed from the city. Secretary of State Henry J. Menninger in 1869 referred to records that had been moved into the city upon the approach of federal troops. Conceivably these were early records of the governor's office which soon after the turn of the century were found in a "leaky and dilapidated attic" of a building on Fayetteville Street which later was occupied by the insurance commissioner. *Historical Commission, 1911*, p. 13.

73. Telegram from Worth to General P. G. T. Beauregard, [April] 13, 1865, in P. G. T. Beauregard Papers, Duke University Library, Durham.

74. Worth to Joseph A. Worth, April 22, 1865, in Hamilton, *Worth Correspondence*, II, 1288. A reply to Worth's telegram has not been found. By Thursday night however, Union forces had occupied Raleigh and Morrisville, and Worth, thus faced with possible capture, may have decided to move on to Company Shops without waiting for a reply.

records were transferred to a railroad train at the Shops for transportation to Greensboro.

Negotiations meanwhile were opened between Confederate General Joseph E. Johnston and General Sherman, and presumably to protect the archives from depredation by Confederates who were looting other property at Greensboro, the records had been sent back to Company Shops where, upon suspension of hostilities on April 18, Worth joined them.[75] On April 19, Governor Vance, then at Greensboro, appealed to General Johnston for permission to accept Sherman's offer for safe passage in returning the archives to Raleigh. He asked that Treasurer Worth be permitted to take them to the capital city "in the cars now occupied by them." Such a move was necessary, he charged, because Confederate troops had already forcibly seized state property from Haw River to Greensboro and were then "threatening to sack the cars at the Shops in which are placed the archives and funds of the State treasury and State banks."[76]

General Johnston referred Vance's letter to Confederate Secretary of War John C. Breckinridge who endorsed it as follows: "Respectfully returned to General Johnston, with suggestion that it would be better, until the agreement of yesterday goes into effect, that the cars, archives, and other property of the State of North Carolina, now within our lines, be protected by our troops than sent for that purpose to the enemy."[77] Johnston thereupon refused Vance's request, but ordered a guard to be posted around the cars at the Shops.[78] For the time being, the archives at Company Shops presumably would be safe.

75. Worth to J. J. Jackson, April 21, 1865, in Hamilton, *Worth Correspondence,* I, 380-81.
76. Vance to General Joseph E. Johnston, April 19, 1865, in *Official Records,* ser. I, XLVII, pt. III, pp. 810-11. See also manuscript copy of this letter in Zebulon B. Vance Papers, State Archives. This source will be cited hereafter as Vance Papers. See also Worth to Vance, April 19, 1865, in Vance Papers, State Archives, in which the treasurer wrote, "The security of the valuables in my care [at Company Shops] imperatively requires that they be placed in the Capitol at the very earliest period possible. I need not state the reasons. In the midst of graver matters the importance of getting the State archives out of the way of marauders quickly may escape you & I therefore desire to impress on you the importance of procuring a permit to pass the lines as soon as possible."
77. Endorsement of Breckinridge on Vance's letter to General Johnston, April 19, 1865, in *Official Records,* ser. I, XLVII, pt. III, p. 811.
78. General Johnston to Vance, April 19, 1865, in Vance Papers, State Archives.

Worth, however, continued to press for a return of the archives to Raleigh. He wrote, "we ought to accept at once the permission to put our state archives in the Capitol. I can conceive of no one so obstinate and reckless as to refuse the privilege to us to return them except [Jefferson] Davis."[79] Then, upon learning of Washington's rejection of the terms of April 18, he wrote Vance, "It is believed here [at Company Shops] that hostilities are to be commenced [and] in this event what can I do with the State archieves [*sic*] [?] [M]ust I move west or remain where I am?"[80]

Following the signing of the formal armistice at the Bennett House on April 26, the governor yielded to Worth's insistence and sent him to Raleigh for an audience with General Sherman "in regard to the removal of the effects under his charge & belonging to the several departments of the state government." Vance wrote the Union general, "Under the circumstances attending the disbanding of an army it is considered highly important that these effects, most of which are records simply, should be returned to their usual place of deposit in the Capitol in Raleigh & your safe-guard Mr. Worth is authorized to solicit for this purpose."[81] Before Worth's arrival in Raleigh, Sherman had left the city, but Major General John M. Schofield, then in command, authorized the treasurer to return the records to Raleigh. Worth promised to go after them by the next available train,[82] and on the following day Schofield's assistant adjutant general gave written instructions for Worth to proceed to Greensboro and to bring to Raleigh "all public records and State property belonging to the several departments of the State Government in order that they may be deposited in the State House."[83]

79. Worth to Joseph A. Worth, April 22, 1865, in Hamilton, *Worth Correspondence*, II, 1291.

80. Worth to Vance, April 25, 1865, in Vance Papers, State Archives.

81. Vance to General Sherman, April 27, 1865, in Vance Papers, State Archives.

82. Worth to Vance (telegram), April 28, 1865, in *Official Records*, ser. I, XLVII, pt. III, p. 848; Vance to Cornelia P. Spencer, April 7, [1866], in Spencer Papers, Southern Historical Collection.

83. Lieutenant Colonel John A. Campbell to Worth, April 29, 1865, in Records of the United States Army Commands (Record Group 98), Headquarters, Department of North Carolina, Copybook of Letters Sent in the Field, March 7 to April 30, 1865, p. 97, National Archives, Washington, D. C. The trains containing

In accordance with Schofield's instructions, Worth appears to have brought these records back to Raleigh on May 1, on which date Vance wrote that the state officers were returning to the Capitol.[84] Vance himself remained in Greensboro and surrendered to General Schofield on May 2, at which time the latter authorized him to proceed to his home in Statesville.[85]

The governor, with foresight, had withheld from the records returned to Raleigh a box containing his two official letter books, the great seal of the State and the seal press, and the seals of the Literary Fund and Board of Internal Improvements.[86] This box,

---

the archives previously at Company Shops had been returned to Greensboro upon the signing of the armistice.

I had completed initial research for this study when I obtained leave, by a happy circumstance, to examine an unpublished manuscript by Dallas Irvine, senior specialist in the Office of Military Archives, National Archives, titled "What Happened to the Archives of North Carolina in 1865?" Irvine's excellent paper, based largely upon records of the War Department but supplemented by some of the printed sources that I had already located, has been of considerable assistance to me and I acknowledge my indebtedness to the author. In particular, Irvine's manuscript permitted me to identify and to obtain microfilm copies of pertinent materials from the National Archives, some of which are cited herein.

84. Vance to Captain Thomas White, May 1, 1865, in *Official Records*, ser. I, XLVII, pt. III, p. 860.

85. Clement Dowd, *Life of Zebulon B. Vance* (Charlotte: Observer Printing and Publishing House, 1897), p. 101.

86. Brigadier General S. P. Carter to Lieutenant Colonel Theodore Cox, May 29, 1865, in Records of United States Army Commands (Record Group 98), Headquarters, 3rd Division, 23rd Army Corps, Copybook of Letters Sent, September 10, 1864 to July 12, 1865, p. 200, National Archives. General Carter's letter did not specifically list the letter books as being in the box. Later reports, however, tended to establish that they were in the same box. See, for instance, Brigadier General Carter to Lieutenant Colonel Cox, May 26, 1865, in same source, p. 196; and A. M. McPheeters to Cornelia P. Spencer, April 11, 1866, in Spencer Papers, Southern Historical Collection. McPheeters, Vance's private secretary, wrote the following year that the box also contained some recent letters that had not been entered in the letter books. See Jonathan Worth to Governor Vance, August 12, 1865, in Hamilton, *Worth Correspondence*, I, 391.

As time passed, there were claims that other valuable documents had been in the box. Former Governor David L. Swain thought that it contained the letter book of Governor William Tryon that had been copied from the original at Harvard College a decade earlier, plus the journals of the Council of the Province from 1765 to 1771, and three volumes of Francois Xavier Martin's manuscripts purchased by the State in 1860. Francis Lieber to David L. Swain, February 15, 1867, and Swain to ———, December 9, 1867, in Swain Papers, Southern Historical Collection. Swain was in error because in 1868 Theophilus Hill, who was hired by Governor Worth to "search the closets and arrange documents," found them in the Capitol. Kemp P. Battle to Swain, May 12, 1868, in Spencer Papers, State Archives.

probably upon Vance's departure for Statesville or upon his arrest on May 13, was kept in the Greensboro branch of the Bank of Cape Fear. The whereabouts of the box containing Vance's letter books and the seals appears not to have come to the attention of the Union officials until mid-May. On May 19, an inquiry was made about a box marked "Executive Department No. 3" which had been "carried off by Governor Vance."[87] It was located in the bank on May 25, and the letter books were withheld in Greensboro, but the seals and some other contents were placed in a box and forwarded, with two boxes of Confederate records, to Raleigh.[88] Upon the arrival of the box at the depot in Raleigh it was broken open and the great seal of the State was stolen and never recovered.[89] The letter books were taken to Schofield's headquarters in Raleigh separately by a commissioned officer on May 29.[90] A few days later Schofield forwarded them to the War Department in Washington. They were not returned to North Carolina until ninety-seven years later.[91]

The odyssey of the records removed from Raleigh on April 11 has been described. These important current records—including the governor's letter books—appear to have been accounted for. But evidence points to the removal of some records about the middle of March and of a substantial quantity on March 23.[92] The former were said to have been deposited at various places

87. Lieutenant Colonel Campbell to Major General J. D. Cox, May 19, 1865, in Records of United States Army Commands (Record Group 98), Headquarters, Department of North Carolina, Copybook of Telegrams Sent, January 14, 1865 to January 13, 1866, p. 59, National Archives.

88. Endorsement of Major General Cox on Brigadier General Carter to Lieutenant Colonel Cox, May 25, 1865, in Records of United States Army Commands (Record Group 98), Headquarters, Department of North Carolina, Document File, 1865, irregularly registered item C, 16 (vol. 3), National Archives.

89. Major General Schofield to Major General Cox, May 28, 1865, in Records of United States Army Commands (Record Group 98), Headquarters, Department of North Carolina, Copybook of Telegrams Sent, January 14, 1865 to January 13, 1866, p. 73, National Archives.

90. Major General Cox to Major General Schofield, May 28, 1865, in Records of United States Army Commands (Record Group 98), Headquarters, Department of North Carolina, Copybook of Telegrams Sent, January 14, 1865 to January 13, 1866, p. 135, National Archives.

91. See below, p. 108.

92. See above, p. 95.

between Raleigh and Salisbury; the latter were being taken from Hillsborough to Greensboro on April 10.[93] What was their fate? The answer is not given in the sources found thus far. It might be conjectured that the train stopped at Greensboro and a few days later at least some of them were loaded in the cars containing the archives removed by Worth on April 11 to Company Shops and Greensboro and which were returned to Raleigh about May 1. But a more probable explanation is that the train carried them on to Salisbury, for on May 15, the Union commander there was ordered to send any state records in the city to Raleigh.[94] Union officials also received reports that Governor Vance had carried records with him to Statesville, and a search was ordered. Although no records were found there, the local Union general reported that they were at Salisbury, but upon arrival of the representative at the latter place, the records had been sent to Raleigh.[95] The communications imply that some records indeed had been at Statesville, but that they had been sent to Salisbury from where they were carried to Raleigh.

Thus the mystery of the State's archives remains partially unsolved. How many and what records were lost, pilfered, or otherwise not returned to Raleigh may never be known. At least one record taken westward in 1865 was not returned until the twentieth century. The letter book of the adjutant general for 1862-64 turned up many years later in Greensboro during the renovation of an old house. In 1924, it was delivered to the North Carolina Historical Commission (now the State Depart-

93. See above, p. 96.
94. Assistant Adjutant General J. A. Campbell to Major General Cox, May 15, 1865, in *Official Records,* ser. I, XLVII, pt. III, p. 504. Governor Vance wrote later that when he offered to surrender to Major General Schofield in Greensboro on May 2, he "told him of the quantity and whereabouts of the state property, records &c. and asked him to protect it from pillage & destruction. . . ." Inasmuch as Worth had already returned to Raleigh the records that had been at Company Shops, Vance apparently referred to records located elsewhere, probably Salisbury. Vance to Cornelia P. Spencer, April 7, [1866], in Spencer Papers, Southern Historical Collection.
95. Major General Cox to Major General J. Kilpatrick, May 19, 1865; Major General Kilpatrick to Lieutenant Colonel Campbell, May 20, 1865; Major General Cox to Lieutenant Colonel Campbell, May 22, 1865, in *Official Records,* ser. I, XLVII, pt. III, pp. 535, 545, 560.

ment of Archives and History).⁹⁶ From time to time other records, which give strong evidence of having once been among those carried by the wagons and railroad trains from Raleigh in 1865, have been found in private hands.⁹⁷

Records were also taken off by Union soldiers who occupied the Capitol in Raleigh. In August, 1865, Henry B. Dawson of Morrisania, New York, reported to Secretary of War Edwin M. Stanton that "the archives of the State of North Carolina have been recently pilfered, by soldiers belonging to General Sherman's army," and that "important papers belonging thereto" were in the possession of the Reverend Washington Gladden in that village.⁹⁸ The records, Dawson wrote, should be returned to North Carolina, and he offered his assistance toward that end. Thirty-two of the documents appear to have been returned to Raleigh the following October,⁹⁹ but others were reported in 1866 to have been seen "in a billiard saloon in the village, liable to be picked up and carried away by any body who happened to call there!"¹⁰⁰ Whether these papers were ever recovered is not known.

Union troops occupied both the Capitol and the Governor's Mansion during the spring and summer, and Treasurer Worth on several occasions objected to the carelessness of the troops and urged their removal. He wrote in July, 1865, that since the

96. See statement of J. B. Barnes, Sr., Rocky Mount, pasted in Adjutant General's Letter Book, 1862-64, State Archives. The book was given to the Historical Commission by Barnes in 1924.

97. Almost $100,000 in gold, belonging to the Commercial Bank of New Bern, was buried at Company Shops in April, 1865, but was found by troops of the Tenth Ohio Volunteer Cavalry and distributed among the finders. General Schofield heatedly demanded that the Union officers recover the money, and a portion of it was returned. Captain Henry Brown to Chief of Police, May 7, 1865, and endorsement of Major General Schofield on same; Major General Schofield to Major General Kilpatrick, May 16, 1865, in *Official Records*, ser. I, XLVII, pt. III, pp. 431, 512. See also references in the latter source, pp. 521, 522, 632.

98. Henry B. Dawson to Edwin M. Stanton, August 9, 1865, in Records of the Secretary of War (Record Group 107), Document File, National Archives.

99. Adjutant General E. D. Townsend to Governor William W. Holden, October 24, 1865, in Records of the Adjutant General's Office (Record Group 94), Copybook of Letters Sent, XLI, 307, National Archives. See also R. W. Best to D. L. Swain, March 6, 1866, filed with Jonathan Worth to President Andrew Johnson, March 6, 1866, in Records of the Adjutant General's Office (Record Group 94), Document File, 1866, A, 221, National Archives.

100. *The Sentinel* (daily edition, Raleigh), April 16, 1866.

occupation of the Capitol by the soldiers he could not find a copy of his last report nor that of the comptroller.[101]   A few months later the secretary of state referred to "the *archives* that were taken by the U.S. Officers and Soldiers from their place of deposit in the Capitol building."[102] Undoubtedly and perhaps inevitably other "souvenirs" were taken off by the soldiers and, just as likely, some records were either lost or disarranged by the moving of the public offices.

One of the most poignant stories in relation to public records concerned those of the University of North Carolina in the possession of former Governor Charles Manly, the secretary of the board of trustees. Just before Sherman's forces occupied Raleigh, Manly wrote his old friend David L. Swain:

> In regard to the University effects and my own, I concluded that no place was safe on *the top of the ground* & I have placed them in a thick wooden box & buried it, in the woods 3 miles from the City [Raleigh]. I performed the whole operation myself, digging the hole, toting off the dirt in a bag & throwing it in a branch and spreading over the locus in quo with the same sort of rubbins & leaves. It was a terrible job. I laid down on the ground perfectly exhausted before I could gain strength to mount my horse.
>
> And now after all my trouble I learn that the papers will soon become decomposed & rot. How is this? Is there any Philosopher in the Faculty that can tell me?[103]

The aging Manly a year later revealed the happy ending. He wrote:

> I had with the aid of my *trusty, confidential body servant* buried in the woods at my plantation sundry Boxes of Valuables and had myself at great personal labor alone buried a Box containing the Bonds & Money & valuable papers belonging to the University & also to myself. Learning that my confidant had betrayed me to the Bummers and fearing that they might find *the Box* in question I applied to Col. Poe (who was the Civil Engineer in Sherman's Staff

101. Worth to N. H. D. Wilson, July 26, 1865, in Hamilton, *Worth Correspondence,* I, 385.

102. R. W. Best to Secretary of War Edwin M. Stanton, February 17, 1866, in Records of the Secretary of War (Record Group 107), Document File, 1866, N, 26, National Archives.

103. Manly to Swain, April 8, 1865, in Swain Papers, Southern Historical Collection.

& who Occupied the dormitory of my Office) for assistance in exhuming & reclaiming the Box.

With great promptness & alacrity he ordered his carriage & 10 armed Cavalry & we rode out to the place recovered the Box & brought it home in triumph.[104]

Efforts to bring about the return of the Vance letter books began before the end of the year.[105] The State Senate in December asked North Carolina Secretary of State R. W. Best to report whether the letter books "and other public records . . . removed by military authority" had been returned, and if not, what steps had been taken to obtain them.[106] Best thereupon wrote the federal secretary of state in December and, receiving no reply, inquired again in April, 1866. Meanwhile, he had inquired directly of the War Department, but received no satisfaction. Worth, by now governor of the state, had already taken the matter to President Andrew Johnson, requesting that the records be delivered to former Governor David L. Swain who was then in Washington. Swain apparently delivered the Worth letter personally to the president. It, along with several other letters on the subject, was referred to the War Department, where Secretary of War Stanton, upon advice of Francis Lieber, chief of the Archive Office of the department, ordered that the letter books not be given up but that any other documentary materials that did not

104. Manly to Cornelia P. Spencer, April 25, 1866, in Spencer Papers, Southern Historical Collection.

105. The full story of these efforts is not appropriate for inclusion here. Dallas Irvine, senior specialist in the Office of Military Archives, the National Archives, has made available to me his unpublished manuscript, "The Story of Governor Vance's Confederate Letter Books," which admirably traces the subject from 1865 to 1888. Irvine has authorized Louis H. Manarin, editor of *North Carolina Troops: A Roster* (the first volume of which was published in 1966 by the State Department of Archives and History), to do further work on the manuscript, along with Irvine's article previously cited, "What Happened to the Archives of North Carolina in 1865?" with a view toward publication. I am indebted to Irvine for suggesting the various sources cited herein from the records in the National Archives, microfilm copies of which have been obtained for the State Department of Archives and History. The Irvine manuscript is hereafter cited as Irvine, "Letter Books."

106. A copy of the resolution, undated, is filed in a jacket dated December 6, 1865, in Records of United States Army Commands (Record Group 98), Headquarters, Department of North Carolina, Document File, 1865, S, 432, National Archives. The resolution has not been found in the printed resolutions of the General Assembly.

bear on the Civil War should be turned over to the State. No other records were found in the department, however.[107]

Swain returned to the State but asked John H. Wheeler, the North Carolina historian then employed in Washington by the Treasury Department, to continue to work for the return of the records.[108] Meanwhile, Governor Worth and Secretary of State Best had continued their correspondence with the federal officials to no avail. For the next twenty years the efforts were resumed, periodically, usually upon the appointment of a new secretary of war or upon the election of a new governor in North Carolina. On every occasion the department refused to give up the books, and even vacillated on the question of allowing a copy to be made of them.[109] The reason given was always the same (that is, when a reason was given—several letters were not answered and some others contained only curt replies with no justification): The books contained letters relating to the late "rebellion" and consequently were important to the federal government as evidence in protecting the United States against unjustified claims of the State and its citizens. In actual fact, the records were considered war trophies and the legitimate property of the federal government. To the archivist, they acquired a dual character: They had become a part of the federal archives without having ceased to be in origin a state record.[110]

In 1871, Vance, who had been elected to the United States Senate even though he was ineligible under the Fourteenth Amendment and consequently unable to take his seat, was given permission to peruse his letter books by Secretary of War Belknap.[111] This apparently was the first time that he had seen them since his departure from Greensboro on May 2, 1865. It is pos-

---

107. Irvine, "Letter Books," pp. 3-7. Swain had continued to claim that taken with the letter books of Governor Vance were the Tryon Letter Book, the Council minutes for 1765-71, and the three volumes of the Francois Xavier Martin manuscripts. Lieber, however, assured him that these records were not in the Archive Office. Lieber to Swain, February 15, 1867, in Swain Papers, Southern Historical Collection. See also above, p. 100, n. 86.

108. Governor Worth to Benjamin S. Hedrick, July 30, 1866, in Hamilton, *Worth Correspondence*, II, 709.

109. Irvine, "Letter Books," pp. 8 ff.

110. Irvine, "Letter Books," p. 10.

111. Irvine, "Letter Books," p. 18.

sible that Vance made copies of some portions bearing on the impeachment trial of Governor William W. Holden in May, 1871, because Belknap wrote the following year that copies of some portions of the records had already been permitted.[112]

Several years more of correspondence and personal interviews failed to produce results. Then, in 1876, the North Carolina delegation in Congress tried a new tactic—a congressional resolution. Such a resolution requiring the War Department to furnish copies of the two books passed the House but died in the Senate. Nevertheless, the opponents of Vance (who was successfully running for governor again) obtained copies of some of the letters for use in the campaign.[113] Upon taking office again, and armed with a legislative resolution,[114] Vance resumed his own efforts to recover the records through an intemperate exchange of letters with Secretary of War George W. McCrary. The latter argued that the records were valuable to the federal government as evidence against claims upon the treasury, but indicated that if the State would bear the expense, he would *consider* allowing copies to be made—but he doubted even the advisability of allowing a copy to be made.[115]

Vance became a United States Senator in 1879 and now he was able to carry on his efforts in the national capital. Early in 1880, he introduced a resolution directing the secretary of war to have made copies of the books for preservation in the War Department, the originals to be given to the State. The chairman of the committee to which the resolution was referred asked Secretary of War Alexander Ramsey for his opinion, and the latter expressed opposition to the proposal on the grounds that the originals, not the copies, should be retained by the depart-

112. Irvine, "Letter Books," p. 20.
113. Irvine, "Letter Books," pp. 22-23.
114. The General Assembly in 1877 had passed a resolution requesting the return of the books, or copies thereof if the originals were not released. "Resolution in Relation to the Letter-Books of the Executive of North Carolina," ratified February 16, 1877, in *Laws of 1876-1877*, pp. 593-94.
115. Vance to McCrary, September 10, 1877; McCrary to Vance, November 6, 1877; Vance to McCrary, November 22, 1877, in *Public Documents, 1879*, pp. 38-42 (Appendix). The Southern Claims Commission, established in 1871, was still in existence, and McCrary undoubtedly had in mind the numerous claims made upon the federal government in this connection. Irvine, "Letter Books," p. 25.

ment. The records, he wrote, had been "used before high judicial tribunals, where copies would not be admitted, in defeating large claims against the United States. They may be needed for this purpose again." The resolution was thereupon amended to direct copies to be made and presented to the State, and it passed the Senate only to be lost in the House. A similar fate met resolutions in the next two sessions.[116] Finally, in 1886, a congressional resolution was signed by President Grover Cleveland directing that copies be made, certified, and presented to the State.[117] It was not until March 12, 1888, that the copies were completed and certified, and the following day they were sent to North Carolina.[118]

The happy ending of the story of Governor Vance's letter books can be told briefly. The transcripts furnished in 1888 by the secretary of war were placed among the archives of the State and in the twentieth century were transferred to the North Carolina Historical Commission (now the State Department of Archives and History) where they have been used by numerous researchers. The original books, of course, remained in Washington. But they were not forgotten by North Carolinians. After 1934, the originals were transferred to the newly organized National Archives along with other War Department records. In 1962, Louis H. Manarin, then in the National Archives as the editor of a roster of North Carolina's Civil War troops and in the employ of the North Carolina Confederate Centennial Commission, made use of the volumes and casually mentioned the appropriateness of their return to North Carolina. His suggestion was received favorably, and upon the formal request of Christopher Crittenden, director of the North Carolina State Department of Archives and History, the books were returned to the State in 1962. Thus almost a hundred years after the nation was reunited, the return of the two manuscript volumes (plus a bound index) was effected in an entirely friendly atmosphere in stark contrast

116. Irvine, "Letter Books," pp. 27-31.
117. General Orders, No. 95, Headquarters of the Army, Adjutant General's Office, December 30, 1886 [containing a copy of the resolution] pasted in Governor's Letter Book, 1862-64 (G.L.B. 50.1) [certified copy], State Archives.
118. Irvine, "Letter Books," p. 34.

to the two decades of controversy that the records had evoked from 1865 to 1886. To dramatize the spirit of the return, Crittenden took the books to Asheville—in Vance's home county—for the official announcement at a special press conference.[119]

THE RECORDS IN THE POSTWAR PERIOD, 1865-1903

The reconstruction era probably brought about more confusion, if not losses, among the records than did the war years. Within a six-month period in 1865 the State had three different governors, and there were many changes among the holders of key offices for the next few years. The office of auditor, created in 1862, was abolished in 1866 and the duties of that office transferred to the comptroller. By the new constitution adopted in 1868, the latter office was abolished and the former re-established. Lesser offices were created and abolished, and both executive and legislative directives resulted in frequent exchanges of offices in the Capitol. But just as important were the temper of the politicians and the intrigues attending the relations between them. The reconstruction legislatures were dominated by men inexperienced in government and many with little education. Changes were easy; every problem could be solved by a law. Public records were of minor concern.

One incident serves to illustrate the dangers which faced the archives. The story, though told many years later by an aging Democrat with strong prejudices against the man to whom he referred, is supported by acts of the General Assembly of the time. In 1868, the Reverend S. S. Ashley, a native of Massachusetts and a virtual stranger to North Carolina, was elected superintendent of public instruction. Upon taking office, he was assigned a room far up on the third floor of the Capitol, away from the main activities of the building. Governor William W. Holden issued

119. For correspondence attending the return of the original books, see the following in the Correspondence of the State Archivist, State Archives: Christopher Crittenden to Wayne C. Grover, Archivist of the United States, June 7, 1962; Robert H. Bahmer, Acting Archivist of the United States, to Crittenden, August 17, 1962; H. G. Jones, North Carolina State Archivist, to Bahmer, August 21, 1962; and Crittenden to Grover, October 12, 1962. The transfer was made under provisions of G. S. A. Reg. 3-IV-201.01 of 1956.

an order for the Supreme Court to move into Ashley's attic office, for the secretary of state to move into the offices thus vacated by the Supreme Court, and for Ashley to take over the offices formerly used by the secretary of state on the main floor. The indignant justices sought to have the General Assembly override the executive order. While the matter was being argued heatedly on the floor of the legislature, Ashley was busy on the main floor moving into the rotunda and hall the records from one of the secretary of state's offices. In the end the Assembly passed the resolution, thus overruling Holden: all offices were to remain where they were. But the records, once in the rotunda and halls, offered too much of a temptation and, instead of their being put back in the secretary's office, they were carted off to the Arsenal located on the southwest corner of Union Square where they were piled among the tents, uniforms, blankets, arms, and other accoutrements of war that occupied the building.[120] There were to remain for many years some of the most valuable of the State's archives—including the original journal of the Provincial Congress which adopted the Constitution at Halifax in 1776.[121] By 1872, the building was reported to be "damp and full of moths and insects"—dangers perhaps as great to public records as careless and uninterested human beings.[122]

While the Constitution of 1868 did not radically alter the superstructure of state government it did make some significant

---

120. Thomas J. Jarvis, "North Carolina Must Preserve Its Historical Records," an address published in *Proceedings of the Eleventh and Twelfth Annual Meetings of the State Literary and Historical Association* (Raleigh: Edwards & Broughton, 1912), p. 21. Cited hereafter as Jarvis, "Historical Records." For legislative acts bearing on the controversy, see Resolutions No. 27, ratified August 11, 1868, and No. 40, ratified August 22, 1868, in *Public Laws of Special Session, July, 1868;* Resolution (unnumbered) ratified January 19, 1869, and c. 54 in *Public Laws of 1868-1869,* pp. 701, 128. The *status quo ante* adopted by the General Assembly provided for the Supreme Court to retain the rooms on the northeast wing and the secretary of state the rooms on the northwest wing of the main floor. Ashley had already raised the ire of Jonathan Worth by asking the former governor to turn over to him all records of the Literary Board that were still in his possession. Worth retorted that all such papers were left in their appropriate places in the Capitol, "methodically arranged." Worth to Ashley, July 16, 1868, in Hamilton, *Worth Correspondence,* II, 1231.

121. See below, p. 114.

122. Report of the keeper of the Capitol, January, 1872, Document No. 23, *Public Documents, 1871-1872.*

changes. The addition of the office of lieutenant governor had little effect insofar as the records were concerned. Neither did the creation of the office of superintendent of public works, because that office was abolished in 1872. The auditor replaced the comptroller, however, and the duties of the office of secretary of state were greatly broadened by legislative action. The offices of governor, lieutenant governor, secretary of state, auditor, treasurer, superintendent of public works, superintendent of public instruction, and attorney general were made elective for a term of four years. Thenceforth they would be subject to the electorate.

The General Assembly, in spelling out the duties of state officers, required the governor to maintain applications for pardons or commutations, a register of judges' reports of testimony in capital cases, and a variety of other records. His private secretary was not only to enter the governor's correspondence in his letter books, but also to keep the originals.[123] The secretary of state was charged with the custody of all statutes and joint resolutions, all documents that passed under the great seal, and all books, records, deeds, parchments, maps, and papers then deposited in his office or which thereafter might be deposited pursuant to law, and he was required "from time to time [to] make all necessary provisions for their arrangement and preservation."[124] The secretary's office, which in the colonial period had acquired considerable stature, again became the most important office insofar as the archives of the State were concerned. For the remainder of the century the secretary was to be viewed as the chief archival officer. Fortunately for history, most of the occupants of the office took their responsibility seriously.

The first secretary of state under the new constitution called attention to the conditions in which he found the records. Henry J. Menninger reported to the governor that he had found books, records, deeds, parchments, surveys, and other papers filed in "a manner lacking system and regularity," particularly the older records. Little had been done to arrange them since their return to the Capitol in 1865, he said, and they were neither secure nor

123. *Public Laws of 1868-1869*, c. 270, secs. 29-34.
124. *Public Laws of 1868-1869*, c. 270, sec. 41.

available for ready reference. He also reported that he had received a large quantity of ballots, books, and other papers from the headquarters of the Second Military District—many of which were of historical interest—but several tons of them were still in their boxes, his office lacking the clerical force to arrange them.[125] A year later he reported considerable progress towards "re-filing and placing in systematic order the records and papers of the State, which, through the changes incident to the late war, had become greatly neglected and disordered."[126]

Secretary of State William H. Howerton in 1873 called for a larger staff to carry on the same work. The indexes to the land grant books were defective, he said, and several of the books were in a very "dilapidated condition, and require transcribing." He also asked for a "large iron safe as a place of security" for valuable papers.[127] In the same year, Howerton had fourteen books rebound.[128]

Howerton appears to have been a conscientious officer in relation to historical records. Early in 1874, probably at his behest, the General Assembly adopted a resolution indicating that the original manuscripts of the public and private acts and resolutions and of the journals of the legislature "owing to the continued usage, the exposure to which they have been subjected (notwithstanding the care of the officer having them in charge), and to the destructability of the material of which they are composed, are now falling into rapid decay. . . ." Inasmuch as it was the duty of "every State to preserve such valuable manuscripts so long as it is possible to do," the resolution instructed the secretary of state to have these records "bound in some economical and durable manner and properly indexed. . . ."[129] Later

125. Report of the secretary of state, November 7, 1868, Legislative Document No. 9, *Public Documents, 1868-1869.* Governor Worth in 1868 hired Theophilus Hill "to search the closets and arrange documents" in the Capitol. It was Hill who rediscovered the Tryon Letter Book and Martin's manuscript notes. Kemp P. Battle to David L. Swain, May 12, 1868, in Spencer Papers, State Archives.

126. Report of the secretary of state, November 16, 1869, Document No. 2, *Public Documents, 1869-1870.*

127. Report of the secretary of state, November 4, 1873, Document No. 2, *Public Documents, 1873-1874.*

128. Receipt of W. T. Lee, September 24, 1873, in Secretary of State's Papers, Receipts, State Archives.

129. Resolution ratified February 10, 1874, in *Laws of 1873-1874,* pp. 494-95.

the same year, Howerton reported that he had rearranged "every paper in the office," and boasted that he could refer to any document on file in a very short time. He also had clerks copying the land grant books that were "almost in a complete state of decay," and had succeeded in having the original manuscript acts and journals of both houses from the earliest days arranged and bound. The iron safe for valuable records had also been installed, but he called for more office space in which to store the valuable records, including those in boxes housed in the Arsenal.[130] Two years later Governor Curtis H. Brogden reiterated the need for more space for the secretary of state and complimented Howerton on bringing order out of chaos among the records in his office.[131]

Joseph A. Engelhard, who succeeded Howerton, continued to request more space for the secretary's office, reporting that the records were "so crowded and insufficiently protected, that the wear and tear will, at no remote period, render them of little value." He continued, "I find in this office, and in those of the Secretary of the Senate and Clerk of the House of Representatives, stuck about in neglected pigeon holes and drawers, without labels, and without order, the most valuable papers connected with the early history of the State, the loss of which would prove a public calamity." Even those that he had arranged and bound were without a place for storage. The land grant books, numbering 169, the earliest dating from the seventeenth century, still were without good indexes, even though the mutilated ones had been copied under provisions of acts of the Assembly.[132]

Back in 1868, after Superintendent of Public Instruction Ashley had moved a portion of the secretary of state's records out into the hallway and rotunda, they had been carted off to the Arsenal.[133] This structure, used only for storage in 1879, caught the eye of Fred A. Olds, the quartermaster general of the State

130. Report of secretary of state, November 4, 1874, Document No. 2, *Public Documents, 1874-1875*.

131. Message of Governor Curtis H. Brogden to the General Assembly, Document No. 1, *Public Documents, 1874-1875*.

132. Report of secretary of state, January 1, 1879, Document No. 2, *Public Documents, 1879*.

133. See above, pp. 109-10.

Guard. He asked Governor Thomas J. Jarvis for permission to clean out the "debris"—old records, supplies, and leftovers from the war. William Laurence Saunders, who had succeeded to the office of secretary of state in February, 1879, following the death of his brother-in-law, Engelhard, was something of a student of history. After a personal visit to the Arsenal, the governor asked Saunders to go through the papers in the old building and destroy them if they were of no value. To his astonishment, among the rubble of decaying papers, Saunders found the State's most valuable archives—early legislative papers, records of colonial governors, and specifically the journal of the Provincial Congress that adopted the Constitution of 1776.[134] If Colonel Saunders had contributed nothing else to the preservation of the history of North Carolina, his quick action in salvaging the bulk of the manuscript materials of the early history of the State would have been a memorial to him. But the discovery of the old records which—since the death or removal from the State of such historians as David L. Swain, William A. Graham, and John H. Wheeler— had been virtually forgotten not only resulted in their preservation, but the event also stirred the imagination of the Civil War veteran. Late in 1880, he made an impassioned plea for the preservation of the history of the State. This could be done in two ways: First, the secretary of state must have more and secure space for the proper care of the original records; second, the State should at long last carry out the dreams of the late Governor Swain and publish the important documents. The great project that had "yielded to Bellona" in 1861 thus acquired a new patron.[135]

Saunders' concern for the records was supported by that of Governor Jarvis. The governor in his message a week later appealed for the Legislature to construct a new building for the Supreme Court on the southeast corner of Union Square, or on Nash Square, and an agricultural building on the latter square, thus allowing more offices for the agencies then squeezed in the

134. Jarvis, "Historical Records," pp. 20-21.
135. Report of secretary of state, December 31, 1880, Document No. 2, *Public Documents, 1881.* For the results of Colonel Saunders' suggestions, see chap. VII.

Capitol. He advocated an additional office for the secretary of state and an enlarged room for the State Library, leaving the old library room "as a repository of the old and valuable records of the state." He asked for a specific law requiring the deposit of the historical records in that room with a prohibition against their removal. He also supported Saunders' suggestion for the printing of important early documents "while it is yet possible to decipher them."[136] The General Assembly appropriated funds for the Agricultural Building, but not for the Supreme Court. The space problem, therefore, was not to be alleviated in the Capitol.[137] The governor was more successful in 1885, however, when the Legislature authorized an addition to the Agricultural Building which was to be designated the Supreme Court Building.[138] This plan was subsequently found impracticable, however, and instead a new building was constructed at the northeast corner of Edenton and Salisbury streets. When completed about 1888, the new Supreme Court Building housed not only the court with its clerk and library, but also the offices of the attorney general and superintendent of public instruction, and the State Library.[139]

Thus, by the end of the decade, the long-sought relief was available. For the first time since the occupation of the Capitol in 1840, there was, for a time, sufficient space for the keeping of the archives. At long last the records piled in the public cor-

136. Message of Governor Thomas J. Jarvis, January 5, 1881, Document No. 1, *Public Documents, 1881.*

137. *Public Laws of 1881,* c. 373. Instead of putting up a new building, the State purchased the old National (formerly the Eagle) Hotel on the northwest corner of Edenton and Halifax streets, facing Capitol Square, and converted it into an agricultural building. It housed the offices of the commissioner of agriculture, state geologist, state chemist, and the State Museum. Later, it also housed the commissioner of corporations. Message of Governor Thomas J. Jarvis, 1883, Document No. 1, *Public Documents, 1883.* The State Museum was at that time largely a mineralogical, geological, and agricultural museum. It was not concerned with historical papers. The "Agricultural Building" was demolished in 1919 to make way for the present Agriculture Building.

138. *Public Laws of 1885,* c. 121.

139. *Public Laws of 1885,* c. 121; *Public Laws of 1887,* c. 225, c. 258. See also Message of Governor A. M. Scales, January 1, 1887, Document No. 1, *Public Documents, 1887.* This original Supreme Court Building is now identified as the Labor Building.

ridors of the Capitol[140] and those rotting in the upper story of
the old Arsenal were moved into a room in the Capitol formerly
housing the State Library, and adequate space was available for
the preservation of the records of the various departments of
government. So helpful was the additional space to the secretary
of state that ten years later the occupant of that office, C. M.
Cooke, proudly announced that a project, begun under his deceased predecessors, Saunders and Octavius Coke, had been completed, thus ". . . placing the papers in relation to land grants,
according to counties and dates, in suitable paper boxes, properly
stamped and labeled . . . and it is so now that a few minutes would
be sufficient to procure any paper touching a land grant in this
office from Earl Granville's time to the present date."[141]

The Library, too, with its new quarters, had space for its
holdings. For the state librarian, though, more duties were
added in 1887 when the legislature made him custodian of the
record rooms and libraries of the two houses in the Capitol. He
was directed to have the records in the clerks' offices of the Senate and House of Representatives removed to the rooms to be
vacated by the superintendent of public instruction and the
State Library, and properly classified, arranged, and labeled.[142]

Thus, by the end of the nineteenth century, state government
had provided reasonably adequate facilities for the preservation
of its records. There existed, however, no over-all direction, no
over-all responsibility for the records of the State. The records
of the Legislature, for instance, were from time to time in three
different charges—the clerks of the two houses during the sessions
and the secretary of state and/or the state librarian between
sessions. The records of the other departments were under the
supervision of each, resulting in an uneven interest and attention
being given the papers. Except for the earlier records which had
been placed in the "record room" in the attic of the Capitol and

140. Report of Secretary of State W. L. Saunders, December 1, 1884, Public
Document No. 3, *Public Documents, 1885.*

141. Report of Secretary of State C. M. Cooke, 1897, Document No. 2, *Public
Documents, 1897.*

142. *Public Laws of 1887,* c. 258. The superintendent and State Library the
following year moved into the new Supreme Court Building.

which had been put under the general supervision of the secretary of state, there was no central archives. The location of particular records was difficult, in that no one state officer had jurisdiction over all of the records of the government. The need for an agency with specific responsibility over the archives of the State was evident. It is not at all surprising, therefore, that at the turn of the century a successful movement was launched for such an archival agency.[143]

One other problem encountered in the nineteenth century—but certainly not limited to that period—was the removal of records by outgoing officials or their executors. The willingness of Secretary of State William Hill to permit Jared Sparks to take original letters from his office (substituting therefor copies) was indicative of the laxness with which original documents were guarded. Even after a law of 1787 required governors to deliver their papers to their successors there appears to have been little enforcement as is evidenced by the varying quantities of papers of the governors for the period following that date. But perhaps the most striking case of the removal of public records involved Secretary of State William L. Saunders who died in office in 1891 soon after the publication of the tenth volume of *The Colonial Records of North Carolina,* which he edited.[144] In his dual capacity as secretary of state and as editor, Saunders had in his possession or at his command the official records of the State. Upon his death, a number of manuscript journals of the Legislature and at least one original land grant book were taken by his heirs. Journals for one or both houses for either all or portions of several sessions of the colonial legislature found their way to the Southern Historical Collection in the University of North Carolina Library where they comprise a part of the Wil-

143. See below, chap. VIII. Even though there was no official archival agency prior to 1903, modern historians can find encouragement in the attitudes of some of the public officials such as that of State Librarian James C. Birdsong who wrote, in response to an inquiry concerning autographs, ". . . if there are any autographs of Hooper, Caswell and others in the Clerk's office of the Senate they are quite likely to remain there as I am not engaged in the sale of documentary records belonging to the State, and therefore have not taken the trouble to make the search." Birdsong to Edward Cantwell, May 24, 1887, in State Librarian's Letter Book, State Archives.

144. See below, chap. VII.

liam Laurence Saunders Papers. Many of the letters written to Saunders by W. Noel Sainsbury, the agent who copied records for the State in London, are also among the papers in the Southern Historical Collection. The original manuscript copy of Land Grant Book 23, on the other hand, is now found among the William Laurence Saunders Papers in the Manuscript Department of the Duke University Library where, until identified during this study, it was erroneously labeled as "Volume XXIII" of the *Colonial Records*.[145]

THE RECORDS OF COUNTIES AND MUNICIPALITIES, 1794-1903

The records of the various counties and municipalities from 1794 to 1900 fared at an uneven rate. The four chief enemies were fire, neglect, normal deterioration, and the insistence of some county officials on keeping their offices in places other than the courthouses.

An auspicious beginning of the period insofar as the records were concerned was provided by the General Assembly when, in 1795, it ordered that there be kept "and maintained in good and sufficient repair, in each and every county in this state, a court house and common gaol: the whole expense of building whereof when there shall be occasion, as well as repairing such as are already built, shall be defrayed by the county. . . ."[146] The office of treasurer of public buildings was provided for in each of the counties. In many cases, however, the determination of what constituted "good and sufficient repair" was left to the counties themselves with the result that some counties provided substantial and fireproof courthouses, while others continued to utilize inadequate and unsafe public buildings or even private dwellings.

Many officials preferred to keep their offices and records in

145. Land Grant Books 20 and 23 were copied about 1881, and the copies are in the secretary of state's office. The law authorizing the copying directed that upon their being copied, the original books were to be packed up in "a close chest or trunk, to be procured for that purpose, . . . and deposit[ed] . . . among the archives of the state." The discovery of Book 23 raises the interesting question of what happened to the other original volumes that were copied from time to time, beginning in 1800. See *Public Laws of 1881*, c. 56.

146. *Public Laws of 1795*, c. 4.

their homes, places of business, or in locations other than the county buildings. From 1795 to 1835, one or more officials (usually the register and/or clerk of court) of no fewer than thirty-three counties were ordered by the General Assembly to move their offices to the courthouses, to the county seats, or to within a specified distance of the seat.[147] The register and clerk of Tyrrell County had even been keeping their offices outside the county![148] These laws became so frequent that the Assembly delegated specific authority to the County Court of Pleas and Quarter Sessions to fix the place where the register was to keep his office and records and made failure to comply a misdemeanor.[149] Even this law failed to meet the needs, and, in 1849, the legislature took back the responsibility and ordered all registers, entry takers, and clerks to keep their records and offices in the courthouse in their respective counties or within a mile thereof. Failure to comply made the official liable to a fine of $100 and forefeiture of office.[150] This itinerant nature of many of the county offices inevitably resulted in both the loss and disarrangement of public records. All told, it probably resulted in the loss of more records than any other single factor.

Fire, the ever-present danger, also contributed heavily to the loss of county records. From 1794 to 1900, no fewer (and probably many more) than forty separate fires in either courthouses or other buildings housing public records are known to have occurred, many of which resulted in serious losses of records. In addition, some records from at least four other counties were "taken off" or destroyed by invading Union troops.[151]

147. Laws requiring the register, clerk, or other officials to keep their offices in or near the courthouse were passed for the following counties: Bladen in 1795; Anson and Beaufort in 1799; Caswell in 1800; Ashe, Granville, Rockingham, and Tyrrell in 1801; Surry in 1802 and 1804; Bertie, Hyde, and Robeson in 1805; Iredell in 1810; Mecklenburg and Warren in 1820; Martin, Mecklenburg, and Surry in 1821; Davidson in 1824; Rowan in 1825; Lincoln and Wilkes in 1826; Hyde, Orange, and Sampson in 1827; Chatham and Nash in 1828; Caswell and Gates in 1829; Buncombe in 1832; Camden in 1833; and Guilford in 1834. This compilation was made from the published laws of the various sessions.

148. *Laws of 1801,* c. 121.

149. *Laws of 1840-1841,* c. 35.

150. *Laws of 1848-1849,* c. 68.

151. Fires occurred between 1794 and 1903 in courthouses or other buildings

Most of the fires occurred as a result of the flimsy construction of many of the public buildings. But at least two of the losses of county records resulted from arson. In Hertford County in 1830, one Wright Allen, having been indicted for forgery, set fire to the courthouse in Winton. Allen's caprice was to no avail— Clerk of Court Lewis M. Cowper, by violating the intent if not the letter of the law by keeping many of his records at his home in Murfreesboro, had the incriminating evidence in his possession. Allen was convicted and publicly whipped.[152] But no punishment for an "evil disposed person" served to bring back the records that had been burned in the courthouse. The General Assembly, enraged by the arson and perhaps remembering the unsuccessful efforts to burn the State House in 1798, passed a stringent law providing the death penalty without benefit of clergy for ". . . any person or persons [who] shall wilfully and maliciously burn

housing records in the following counties: Anson, 1868; Ashe, 1865; Bladen, 1800 and 1893; Buncombe, 1830, 1835, and 1865; Burke, about 1799; Cabarrus, 1874; Camden, date unknown; Cherokee, 1865 and 1895; Clay, 1870; Davidson, 1865; Gaston, 1874; Granville, 1886; Greene, 1876; Guilford, 1872; Harnett, 1892 and 1894; Hertford, 1830 and 1862; Hyde, about 1827; Iredell, 1854; Jones, 1862; Lenoir, 1878 and 1880; Lincoln, about 1797; Martin, 1884; Montgomery, 1840 and 1886; Moore, 1889; New Hanover, 1798, 1819, and 1840; Pitt, 1857; Swain, 1879 and 1900; Wake, 1831; Washington, 1862 and 1873; and Watauga, 1873.

Counties in which records were said to have been carried off or destroyed by Union troops were Alexander, Burke, Sampson, and Watauga, all in 1865. This compilation was made from the laws of the various sessions, from information contained in Crittenden and Lacy, *Historical Records*, I-III, *passim*, and Olds, *Story of the Counties, passim*. In addition, J. G. de Roulhac Hamilton, in his article, "The Preservation of North Carolina History," *North Carolina Historical Review*, IV (1927), 3-21, stated that fires also occurred, destroying records, in Duplin, Gates, Pasquotank, and Richmond counties. Fred A. Olds, in his *Story of the Counties of North Carolina with Other Data* (Oxford: Oxford Orphanage Press, 1921), said that the Pasquotank fire was in 1862 and that two others, in 1869 and 1881, occurred in Washington County. Olds stated that some records were destroyed by federal troops in Henderson and Rowan counties.

The Crittenden-Lacy work omits several fires indicated in the laws, and contains some incorrect dates for others. It is, nevertheless, accurate in general, though undoubtedly additional fires occurred for which documentary evidence is absent. Even the reading of all extant minutes of the Courts of Pleas and Quarter Sessions for the various counties will leave the list incomplete because of the subsequent loss of many of these minutes.

152. *Laws of 1830-1831*, c. 68; Benjamin B. Winborne, *The Colonial and State Political History of Hertford County, N. C.* ([Raleigh]: Edwards & Broughton for the Author, 1906), p. 146. Most of the records that Clerk of Court Cowper saved in 1830 by disobeying the law were destroyed in 1862 when Union troops burned the Hertford County Courthouse.

the State House or any of the public offices of this State, or any court house, jail, arsenal, clerk's office, register's office, or any house belonging to any incorporated town in this State, in which the archives, documents or public papers of such town are kept. . . ."[153] The law, however, did not deter one Benjamin F. Seaborn from burning many of the deed books of Wake County in 1832. The register, Richard Smith, elected to maintain his office in his store on Fayetteville Street instead of in the court-house. Seaborn, a clerk in his store, set fire to the building to cover up evidence of his theft of money from his employer. His punishment was public hanging.[154]

Depredations of unknown extent were suffered by counties at the hands of Union troops in 1865. Evidence, however, points to records being taken or destroyed by troops in Alexander, Burke, Sampson, and Watauga, and courthouse burnings by the troops in Hertford and Washington.[155] Other losses undoubtedly occurred, because in 1866 the General Assembly provided for the reregistration of records, noting that "during the late war . . . the courthouse records and other papers of many of our counties of this State were destroyed. . . ."[156] Two years later, another act referred to the "casualties of war"[157] and, in 1870, an act provided for admission of written evidence executed prior to May 1, 1865, in those counties where "the records of the several courts of law and equity were destroyed by the burning of the court-houses and by other causes during the late war. . . ."[158] It was a common practice for the Legislature to authorize the reregistra-

153. *Laws of 1830-1831*, c. 41. This act was passed before the burning of the State House in June, 1831.

154. [William Perry Johnson], "Wake County Deeds, 1771-1832," *The North Carolinian*, IV (September, 1958), 455. At least fifteen deed books were destroyed in the fire.

155. The records of Hyde County "were removed from the courthouse, and then taken from place to place in the county" until they were lost sight of. J. R. Stubbs to David M. Carter, December 23, 1867, in David Miller Carter Papers, Southern Historical Collection. "Ten Boxes and one Valise" containing Hyde records were returned in 1866. H. D. Teel to Carter, May 30, 1866, in same collection.

156. *Public Laws of 1866*, c. 41. During the war—probably early in 1865—the records of New Hanover County were temporarily stored in Lumberton. Olds, *Story of the Counties*, p. 46.

157. *Public Laws of 1868-1869*, c. 160.

158. *Public Laws of 1870-1871*, c. 86.

tion of uncontested original documents upon the loss of will, deed, and other books in the counties.

Although in general both papers and inks in use prior to the Civil War were of a superior quality when contrasted with those in use in the twentieth century, paper records constantly deteriorated from various causes. Particularly deed books, the most frequently referred to of the courthouse records, were subjected to heavy wear and tear. Will books and some other court records also required repair or copying. The General Assembly frequently passed laws authorizing county courts to have certain records copied. Once the books had been copied, and the new copy properly certified, the original books were often relegated to a storeroom or destroyed outright. In 1798, as a result of the petition of the register of Chowan County, a committee investigated and reported that several old books were "much worn and Torn to pieces" and that some were missing entirely and others had paper covers and different sizes of pages.[159] An act providing for Onslow to have its real estate records copied in 1804 noted that "a considerable part of the records . . . [are] much obliterated, owing to time and use. . . ," and one for Mecklenburg in 1805 noted that many records were in "insecure condition" and "written with very bad ink, and such an indifferent handwritting [*sic*] . . . ." So frequent were the special acts for authority to copy records that the Assembly in 1814 passed a blanket law authorizing the county courts to have transcribed registers' books which "as from decay or other causes may require to be transcribed and indexed. . . ."[160] But the special acts continued.[161]

159. Report on the records in the register's office, September, 1798, in Chowan County Records, State Archives.
160. *Laws of 1814,* c. 19.
161. Records of the register or entry taker were authorized to be copied in the following counties: Burke, New Hanover, and Orange, 1794; Bertie and Montgomery, 1795; Moore, 1796; Chowan and Surry, 1797; Cumberland and Currituck, 1798; Bladen, 1799; Franklin, 1801; Wayne, 1802; Johnston, Lincoln, and Northampton, 1803; Anson and Onslow, 1804; Carteret, Hertford, Mecklenburg, and Nash, 1805; Craven, Granville, Iredell, and Rutherford, 1807; Bertie, 1809; Jones, 1811; Pasquotank, 1812; Halifax, 1813; Bladen, 1816; Burke, 1820; Wake, 1822; Burke, 1875; Greene, 1876; Lenoir, 1881; and Cabarrus, 1883. Records unspecified, or in general, were authorized to be copied in the following counties: Beaufort and Onslow, 1800; Greene, Johnston, Lenoir, Perquimans, and Wayne,

In spite of frequent examples of copying deteriorating records an unknown quantity of vital records were lost by failure of officials to keep them in repair. So concerned was the Legislature in 1844 that it required the solicitor at each session of the county court to examine the offices of the registers and clerks of the county and superior courts, for the purpose of ascertaining whether records were being properly registered and preserved,[162] and, in 1876, registers and clerks were directed to provide indexes and cross-indexes to all records in their keeping.[163]

Competency of the various county officials was perhaps no greater a problem in the nineteenth century than in the twentieth. There were good officials and bad ones; there were those who recognized the value of and cared for their records and there were those who indiscriminately destroyed them. But perhaps a greater villain than outright destruction was lack of concern on the part of many registers and clerks. Chowan County, which earlier had provided for the copying of deteriorating records in the register's office, in 1829 received a report that the records in its clerk's office had been in a "deranged state for many years, so much so that it is with difficulty than any records, or papers filed of long standing can be found. . . ."[164] From Pasquotank, a leading citizen wrote in 1849: "I have searched our archives here but I can find nothing earlier than 1730, and that very unimportant. The fact is, . . . every thing is getting into confusion through neglect, and in many cases, through the utter incapacity of some of them [the county officials], to perform the simplest duties connected with their offices. If things continue in this state much longer, and I see no prospect of a change, the antiquities of most of the counties of North Carolina will date back

---

1801; Buncombe, 1820; Hyde, 1827; Northampton, 1830; Hertford, New Hanover, and Richmond, 1831; Gates, 1832; Montgomery, 1840; Pitt, 1859; Hertford, 1862; Burke, 1865; Washington, 1866; Anson, 1868; Clay, 1870; Watauga, 1865 and 1874; Washington, 1873; and Bladen, 1895. This compilation is taken from the laws of the various sessions of the General Assembly, 1794-1900, *passim*.

162. *Laws of 1844-1845*, c. 5.

163. *Public Laws of 1876-1877*, c. 93.

164. Document appointing commissioners to arrange the Superior Court Clerk's office, June, 1829, in Chowan County Records, State Archives.

but four years."[165] In 1854, it was stated that the "former clerk" at Edenton had destroyed "several barrels full" of the older records of his office.[166] Three years later, from the same place, another citizen wrote to David L. Swain: "A large number of very interesting papers were destroyed in 1848 by the person then acting as clerk of the Superior Court of this County. They comprised the journals and proceedings of the Provincial Legislatures which met in this place, custom house books, and fragmentary papers of various kinds. If you should write the history of the State I hope you will consign him to an immortality of infamy for such a piece of vandallism."[167]

The citation of these examples of losses and destruction of records of the counties should not be construed as evidence that few records survived in the courthouses. Indeed, a surprising quantity and variety of county records not only survived but are being used in the twentieth century for both administrative and historical purposes. Many of them, no longer needed for administrative purposes in the county courthouses, have been transferred to the State Archives.[168] The losses, nevertheless, were serious, and the very nature of county records—the records that most closely affect the citizen's family, property, and rights—caused the losses to be more heavily felt by the populace than even the loss of important state records.

Records of municipalities fared as badly as or worse than

165. William B. Shepard to David L. Swain, March 15, 1849, in Swain Papers, Southern Historical Collection. Shepard may not have searched carefully. A considerable number of records dating prior to 1730 have been preserved for Pasquotank County.

166. T. L. Skinner to David L. Swain, January 18, 1854, in Swain Papers, State Archives.

167. E. C. Hines to David L. Swain, February 15, 1857, in Swain Papers, Southern Historical Collection.

168. For an account of the State Department of Archives and History's county records program inaugurated in 1959 (which contains a brief historical sketch of the county records), see H. G. Jones, "North Carolina's County Records Program," *American Archivist,* XXIV (January, 1961), 25-41. See also John Alexander McMahon, "The Local Records Program in North Carolina," *North Carolina Historical Review,* XXXIX (Spring, 1962), 165-74; John Alexander McMahon, "A County Official Looks at a State-Supervised County Records Program," *American Archivist,* XXV (April, 1962), 211-18; and [A. M. Patterson], *North Carolina's Local Records Program* [a leaflet] (Raleigh: State Department of Archives and History, 1964).

the records of the counties. The very nature of municipal records, however, made their loss less damaging than corresponding losses of those of the counties. North Carolina's structure of government—both under the 1776 and the 1868 constitutions— placed upon the county the responsibility for maintaining records relating to vital statistics, property, and to a large extent, regulation of the daily lives of the people. Cities and towns, of course, also had regulatory powers, but this authority extended largely to taxes, business licenses, streets, livestock, and public behavior. Except for the minutes of the governing body of a municipality, the records of cities and towns were of a routine nature which generally had little value except for short-term administrative purposes. Consequently, there were relatively few municipal records that warranted long-term preservation. Unfortunately for the historian, however, the minutes of the governing bodies have survived for but few municipalities. Other geographical divisions such as the early "captain's districts" and later the townships were creatures of the county, and as such kept no records of consequence.

PART TWO

THE NINETEENTH-CENTURY HISTORIANS

1780-1907

V

The Collection and Publication of the Records

1780-1838

Chalmers, Williamson, Martin, Murphey, and Jones

By 1903, two hundred forty years after the granting of the Carolina Charter, the public offices of North Carolina—both state and local—had created a wide variety of records, the quantity of which cannot be estimated. Many of those records, however, were no longer in existence. Some had been purposely destroyed as having no further value, and included among those were records that should have been preserved for historical purposes. Others had been lost by neglect, theft, disaster, or normal deterioration. Still others had been lost in the movements of the public offices. Yet, a surprising proportion of the records of continuing value were still extant. All of the record fatalities had been, in comparison to the whole, quite small.

Upon the publication of the colonial and state records to 1790, the State had in its possession either the original records or copies of those in England sufficient to reveal a fairly comprehensive story of its colonial existence. Historians could at last begin their stream of monographs on various aspects of the early history of the State. The publications that flowed after 1900 from the pens of historians—professional and amateur—struck a responsive chord. Governor Charles B. Aycock, elected in that year on a platform of improved educational opportunities, captured the spirit of the times. History, perhaps the basic ingredient of any educational process, began to play an increasingly significant role in the interests of the people. A new era had dawned.

This heightened interest in North Carolina history did not come about by accident. At its root lay almost a hundred years of efforts by an impressive roster of officials and historians who sought—by collecting source materials, writing letters and articles, and promoting legislative action—to encourage their fellow North Carolinians to learn more about their heritage.

Throughout the nineteenth century there were individual attempts to collect, preserve, copy, and publish the historical records of North Carolina. These efforts were carried on by many different persons, first privately, then with state aid. The story of their activities reveals that they all recognized that the manuscript records in the public offices of Great Britain were indispensable to any comprehensive history of the Colony.

In fact, the State itself soon recognized the importance of the records available only in London, and North Carolina appears to have been the first state in the Union to obtain copies of colonial records from the British offices. In March, 1806, during the controversy over the boundary line between North and South Carolina, John Steele, formerly a congressman, comptroller of the currency, and then a commissioner to fix the boundary, asked Senator James Turner to obtain through James Monroe, United States minister to Great Britain, authenticated copies of various documents in the public offices of that country that would support North Carolina's claims in relation to the boundary dispute.[1] Senator Turner, not knowing Monroe personally, referred the request to Nathaniel Macon[2] of North Carolina, then Speaker of the United States House of Representatives, and Macon, on April 2, 1806, wrote Monroe as follows: "The papers wanted

1. Steele to Turner, March 6, 1806, in Secretary of State's Papers, Boundary Commissioners (S.S. 1036), State Archives.

2. Turner explained the following year how he had handled the request. Turner to Governor Nathaniel Alexander, January 12, 1807, in Governor's Letter Book, 1805-8 (G. L. B. 16), State Archives.

are the order of King in Council for dividing Carolina into two seperate [*sic*] provinces, that of North & South, also copies of all orders of the King in Council concerning the dividing line between the two Carolinas and all orders of any of the Lords Commissioners of trade concerning the said dividing line. Indeed every paper relating to the division of Carolina into two provinces, and the line which divides North from South Carolina."[3]

Monroe appears to have had no difficulty in obtaining the desired copies, for on November 20, 1806, George Chalmers, chief clerk of the Privy Council, certified to the accuracy of a series of copies.[4] Monroe, however, had failed to inform Macon and Turner of the progress toward procuring the copies,[5] and it was not until April, 1807, that they were received by Senator Turner who carried them from Washington to his home at Warrenton.[6] By April 22, two maps with "many" accompanying documents, "all handsomely executed and no doubt valuable to the State," had reached the governor's office in Raleigh; they were then forwarded to Steele in Salisbury.[7]

The parcel contained the following copies of documents: (1) two maps "in a tin case annexed together, called 'A Plan of the temporary boundary line between the Provinces of North & South Carolina'" prepared in 1764; (2) documents from the

3. Macon to [James Monroe, the principal diplomatic representative of the United States in London], April 2, 1806, in General Records of the Department of State, (Record Group 59), Diplomatic Despatches, Great Britain, Vol. 13 [spine reads "13, England, James Monroe, August 5, 1805, May 25, 1812, Department of State"], National Archives. I am indebted to Philip M. Hamer, former director of the National Historical Publications Commission, for furnishing me with a copy of this letter.

4. "A Plan of the Temporary Boundary Line between the Provinces of North and South Carolina run agreeable to the Instructions given us by His Excellency Arthur Dobbs Esqr. Governor of North Carolina, and His Honour William Bull Esqr. Lieut. Governor of South Carolina and finished as Witness our Hands this 24th. Sepr. 1764," [a copy], in Map Collection (M.C. 53-C), State Archives.

5. Alexander to Turner, January 6, 1807, and Turner to Alexander, January 12, 1807, in Governor's Letter Book, 1805-8 (G.L.B. 16), State Archives.

6. Turner to Alexander, April 19, 1807, in Governor's Letter Book, 1805-8 (G.L.B. 16), State Archives.

7. John Haywood to Major General John Steele, April 22, 1807, and John M. Guion to Steele, June 2, 1807, in Secretary of State's Papers, Boundary Commissioners (S.S. 1036), State Archives; Steele to Alexander, May 16, 1807, and July 16, 1807, in Governor's Letter Book, 1805-8 (G.L.B. 16), State Archives.

Board of Trade; (3) documents "from the Books of the Privy
Council"; (4) "Order of his Majesty in Council respecting the
Boundaries of N. & S.C. dated 30th March 1763"; and (5) an
extract from instructions to Governor Gabriel Johnston, August
3, 1733. In addition, there were nine items identified as "Letters,
billets & accounts."[8] These documents played an important role
in the settlement of the boundary controversy.[9]

This first apparent instance of copying English records for
an American state was, of course, done for a specific administrative purpose and not for historical purposes per se. It was an
important step, however, for at least two reasons: First, it indicated the common knowledge among public officials that the
records sent to England or created there in connection with the
administration of the Colony could be of value in proving the
State's claims in a particular matter; and second, the ease with
which the copies were obtained gave indication that British officials would permit copying for legitimate purposes.

Attention now may be turned to the men who, for the sake
of history, sought to collect, copy, publish, and/or make use of
the public records. Some of them—Chalmers, Williamson, Martin,
Murphey, Jones, Wheeler, and Hawks—were interested primarily
in incorporating documentary materials within their own narratives. Others—Swain, Saunders, and Clark—were less interested
in writing a narrative history than in the publication of the
sources themselves. All, however, contributed to the evolution
of historical writing in North Carolina by stimulating interest
which in some instances led to state financial assistance and in
all instances to the encouragement of the study of the history of
the State. Each, therefore, deserves his recognition.

8. "List of the Several Documents from London," an undated inventory of
documents copied in London and containing the bill for cost of copying (£18
5s. 2d.) and postage from New York to Washington ($20.40), in Secretary of
State's Papers, Boundary Commissioners (S.S. 1037), State Archives.

9. For the story of the settlement of the issue, see H. M. Wagstaff (ed.), *The
Papers of John Steele* (2 vols.; Raleigh: North Carolina Historical Commission,
1924), II, 798 ff. Cited hereafter as Wagstaff, *Steele Papers*. See also Marvin
Lucian Skaggs, *North Carolina Boundary Disputes Involving Her Southern Line*
("The James Sprunt Studies in History and Political Science," Vol. XXV, No. 1
[Chapel Hill: The University of North Carolina Press, 1941]).

GEORGE CHALMERS

The first historian to make extensive use of documentary sources relative to the history of North Carolina was George Chalmers, a Scottish historian and lawyer who resided in Maryland for a decade before the American Revolution, returned to England in 1775, and took a government position which gave him access to the records of the Board of Trade.

His book, *Political Annals of the Present United Colonies . . .* ,[10] was a running narrative, interspersed with copies of official records, of the early history of the American colonies. Chapter XVIII was devoted to Carolina,[11] but it carried the history of the Colony only through the seventeenth century. A second volume was never published.[12]

In his preface, Chalmers indicated the difficulty of his task. He was restricted to the use of the records available in London; he thus faced the exact reverse of those problems encountered by later historians of North Carolina who had access only to the records within the United States. "The records and state-papers were discovered to be on different sides of the Atlantic," he wrote; "no regular collection of their [the colonists'] laws had been yet published; the other materials were found of a nature dry and dissatisfactory. . . ."[13] By incorporating official records, he believed himself to be the first historian to use them for historical purposes. Chalmers made liberal use of documents. And, unlike many of his contemporaries, he generally identified his sources in footnotes at the end of the chapters,[14] even including volume

10. The full title is *Political Annals of the Present United Colonies From Their Settlement to the Peace of 1763: Compiled Chiefly from Records, and authorised often by the Insertion of State-Papers* (London: The Author, 1780). Cited hereafter as Chalmers, *Political Annals*.

11. Chalmers, *Political Annals*, pp. 512-66.

12. Actually an introduction to a second volume was printed but never published. The whole edition was sold for waste paper and only two copies were known to have been saved. Henry Baxter Adams, *The Life and Writings of Jared Sparks Comprising Selections from His Journals and Correspondence* (2 vols.; Boston and New York: Houghton, Mifflin and Co., 1893), II, 383.

13. Chalmers, *Political Annals*, Preface [unpaged].

14. For references used in his chapter on Carolina, see Chalmers, *Political Annals*, pp. 552-66.

and page numbers. But, as was the vogue, his work reflected his
own bias against the colonies and their cause.

Its faults notwithstanding, Chalmers' volume stands as a
landmark in the history of North Carolina. The quotation of
original sources within a narrative was henceforth to be a common practice of historians. Furthermore, he accumulated a
rather substantial body of materials from the British public
offices, a collection that was sought after by later historians. Six
volumes of his papers were purchased in 1843 by Jared Sparks
and placed at Harvard College, and two more volumes of his
notes and transcripts were obtained by George Bancroft at a
later date.[15] Chalmers, however, refused to allow the use of his
materials by Americans during his lifetime,[16] perhaps accentu-
ating his ill-feeling toward the Americans who had received his
book with something less than enthusiasm at a time when the
wounds of war had not yet healed. Bancroft, decades later, cau-
tioned fellow historians to use the Chalmers collection "with
great hesitancy" because "the coloring is always wrong; the facts
usually perverted. He writes like a lawyer and disappointed politician, not like a calm inquirer."[17]

HUGH WILLIAMSON

For only about one-fifth of his life Hugh Williamson lived in
North Carolina, but in those seventeen years he played a significant role in the establishment of the new State under its own
constitution and an equally important part in the first four
years under the Constitution of the United States which he
helped to frame. Then, long after he left the State, he wrote the

15. John Beverley Riggs, "The Acquisition of Foreign Archival Sources for
American History to the Year 1940" (unpublished Ph.D. dissertation, Yale University, 1955), p. 46. Cited hereafter as Riggs, "Acquisition."

16. See below, p. 136. Interestingly enough, however, was the fact that in
1806, Chalmers, as clerk to the Privy Council, certified to the accuracy of copies
made in London for the State of North Carolina. See above, p. 131.

17. Quoted in Stephen B. Weeks, "Historical Review of the Colonial and
State Records of North Carolina," in Stephen B. Weeks (comp.), *Index to The
Colonial and State Records of North Carolina Covering Volumes I-XXV* (4 vols.;
Raleigh: State of North Carolina, 1914 [comprising vols. XXVII-XXX of the
combined series]), XXX, 12. Cited hereafter as Weeks, "Historical Review."

first full-length history of North Carolina to be based upon documentary sources.

Contemporary opinion of this post-revolutionary leader ranged from high praise to denunciation. But his critics and supporters alike agreed that he was a remarkable man. Born of an Irish immigrant father and a mother who once was captured by the pirate Blackbeard, he too was destined to view the excitement of history in the making, ranging from observation of the Boston Tea Party to the capture by the British of the ship on which he was sailing. He became noted in the fields of theology, philosophy, mathematics, medicine, general science, mercantilism, and history. His writings in the various fields were voluminous, ranging from serpents and lightning rods to the history of North Carolina.

Born in 1735 in West Nottingham, Pennsylvania, Williamson later studied and taught mathematics and theology, preached in the Presbyterian Church, then went to Holland and obtained a degree of doctor of medicine, a subject which he taught upon his return to Philadelphia. He was sent on a scientific expedition to Europe, but before his ship sailed, he witnessed the Boston Tea Party, a firsthand account of which he took to Benjamin Franklin in London. He was in Holland when news of the declaration of independence reached him, and, upon his return trip, the ship upon which he was sailing was captured by the British off Delaware. Williamson, however, escaped in a small boat. Soon thereafter he moved briefly to Charleston, South Carolina, and thence to Edenton, North Carolina, where he settled in 1776.

At Edenton, Williamson successfully entered the mercantile and shipping business. During the war he ministered to both the souls and bodies of North Carolina troops, and from 1779 to 1782 he was surgeon general of the State's forces. In the latter year he was sent to the House of Commons which in turn elected him a delegate to the Continental Congress where he served until 1785, then again in 1787 and 1788. He was a delegate to the convention which framed the Federal Constitution and returned to North Carolina to participate in the State Convention which ratified it. He represented North Carolina in the first and second Congresses from 1789 to 1793 and upon the expiration of his last term moved to New York City where he spent the remainder of his life. He died in 1819.[18]

During his residence in North Carolina, Williamson developed a strong attachment to the State and determined to write a history based upon documentary evidence. He searched the early records among the State's archives, borrowed private papers from such families as the Pollocks and Waddells and "some of the most ancient and respectable citizens of the state," and obtained some materials from abroad. From Switzerland he procured "a large file of letters, in a corrupt German language, written by the Baron de Graffenried"; and a friend in London copied from several publications not available in the United States. His effort to fill the "chasms" in the records by gaining access to George Chalmers' papers, however, was unsuccessful. Not only would Chalmers not allow him to see his collection, but he threatened to "interfere" if Williamson made application for permission to obtain copies of records from the public offices in London.[19]

The result of Williamson's research was a two-volume, first-person-plural narrative of the history of the Colony from the explorations to the Revolution. Each of these small volumes contained at the end a section called "Proofs and Explanations" incorporating matter which a century later would have been relegated to footnotes. But in addition to such explanatory notes, full documents were often quoted with varying accuracy. Included, for example, were the "second charter" granted by Charles II in 1665, letters to and from the Lords Proprietors, extracts of Council journals, dockets of the General Court, and documents relating to the North Carolina-Virginia boundary. Many of the documents appeared to have been copied from originals in the

18. Allen Johnson and Dumas Malone (eds.), *Dictionary of American Biography* (20 vols.; New York: Charles Scribner's Sons, 1943), XX, 298-300. Hereafter cited as Johnson and Malone, *D.A.B.* See also *Biographical Directory of the American Congress 1774-1927* (Washington: Government Printing Office, 1928), p. 1709. Cited hereafter as *Biographical Directory of Congress.* For a contemporary evaluation of Williamson, see Delbert Harold Gilpatrick, "Contemporary Opinion of Hugh Williamson," *North Carolina Historical Review,* XVII (January, 1940), 26-36.

19. Hugh Williamson, *The History of North Carolina* (2 vols.; Philadelphia: Thomas Dobson, 1812), I, v-xiv.

state offices, but others were obtained abroad, including several from the "Carolina Papers" in London.

Williamson's *History of North Carolina* is of little literary or historical merit, and it contains the pronounced prejudices evident in most writing of the times. Judged by twentieth-century methodology and alleged objectivity, it is a travesty. But it is nevertheless significant. It was the first attempt at a full history of the colonial period. The author did make use of official and private manuscript sources—even if for ulterior motives. And the narrative, with all its shortcomings, served to stimulate others to write better histories. Finally, his insertion, at the end of each volume, of extensive quotations from original sources, even though sometimes unfaithful, indicated Williamson's willingness in many instances to let the past speak for itself. It is perhaps to his credit that he did not carry his story through the period in which he played an important role, though such an extension would have been useful as a contemporary account of the most eventful time in the history of the State.[20]

Following Williamson's death in New York in 1819, historians began to exaggerate the value and extent of the papers that he had collected. In 1833, Joseph Seawell Jones, then preparing his own "history," was told by Williamson's executor, David Hosack, that he knew of no such papers except a few which were to be deposited in the New-York Historical Society of which Williamson had been a member.[21] Fifteen years later David L. Swain received word that the Williamson papers were still in existence, but upon the opening of the boxes in which they were thought to be preserved, Hosack's son reported that his supposition had been wrong.[22] The fate of the Williamson collection may never be known.

20. Among historians, Jared Sparks was perhaps the most critical of Williamson. He wrote in 1826, "Twice have I read his [Williamson's] history; it is dull & meagre beyond description. . . . Again I repeat, his history is the most inane of all human compositions." Jared Sparks, "Journal of a Southern Tour, 1826," p. 292.

21. Hosack to Jones, February 6, 1833, in Swain Papers, Southern Historical Collection. The executor, however, indicated that Williamson may have given his papers to a relative in Pennsylvania.

22. Pliny Miles to Swain, November 8, 12, December 14, 1847, in Swain Papers, Southern Historical Collection. In Miles's first letter, he wrote that Hosack's son

FRANCOIS XAVIER MARTIN

The author of the second published history of North Carolina, like Williamson, was not a native of the State and also was to spend only a small portion of his life in the State about which he was to write. In fact, he was not even a native American. Francois Xavier Martin, born in Marseilles, France, in 1762, settled in New Bern, North Carolina, about 1783. He taught French and learned English, delivered mail, and worked in and later purchased a local print shop. In 1785, he founded a weekly newspaper, *The No^th. Carolina Gazette, Or New-Bern Advertiser,* which he published under various titles until 1798.[23] Meanwhile, he studied law and was admitted to the bar in 1789. In addition to his paper, he published a variety of pamphlets, almanacs, books, and acts of assembly, and edited and published several volumes of laws. In 1803, the General Assembly employed Martin to publish a revisal of the public acts and the work appeared the following year.[24]

His revisal of the laws impressed upon Martin the need for a history of the State. He immediately began collecting materials, and when in 1806 he was elected to represent the borough of New Bern in the House of Commons, he requested and was granted permission to make extracts from executive and legislative records. He also was given access to private papers. Among the

---

remembered his father's nailing up in large boxes papers believed to contain those of Williamson. He later revealed his disappointment. He thought, however, that they might have been left in the hands of a "Mr. McIvers" in Pennsylvania. No further word came to Swain on the subject. Secretary of State William L. Saunders in 1883 wrote that "no one knows what has become of this collection." Report of trustees of the State Library, Document No. 21, *Public Documents, 1883.*

23. The earliest extant issue of the title is that of November 3, 1785. Between that date and July 11, 1787, the title was changed to *Martin's North-Carolina Gazette,* but his name was dropped from the masthead sometime thereafter. The issue of February 24, 1798, is the last to carry his name as printer. H. G. Jones and Julius H. Avant (eds.), *Union List of North Carolina Newspapers 1751-1900* (Raleigh: State Department of Archives and History, 1963), p. 72.

24. Francois-Xavier Martin (reviser), *The Public Acts of the General Assembly of North-Carolina* (2 vols. in 1; Newbern: Martin & Ogden, 1804). For biographical sketches of Martin, see Ashe, *Biographical History,* IV, 306-15; Johnson and Malone, *D.A.B.,* XII, 335-36; and W. B. Yearns, "Francois X. Martin and His History of North Carolina," *North Carolina Historical Review,* XXXVI (January, 1959), 17-27. The latter article will hereafter be cited as Yearns, "Martin."

latter were the letter book of Acting Governor Thomas Pollock (which Williamson had previously made use of), the surviving papers of Governor Gabriel Johnston (whose name Martin habitually misspelled), those of Council President Matthew Rowan and the Ashe family, and early records of the Quakers in the Albemarle region and of the Moravians at Salem. He also copied extensively from "magazines" and "gazettes," as well as from other printed sources.[25]

By 1809, Martin had compiled the makings of a history, but before he could publish it President James Madison appointed him to a judgeship in the Superior Court of the Territory of Mississippi. A year later he was given a similar appointment at New Orleans. Upon the admission of Louisiana to the Union, Martin became its first attorney general and, in 1815, he was appointed to the Louisiana Supreme Court where he served the remainder of his life, becoming chief justice in 1836.[26]

Upon his departure from North Carolina, Martin shipped his historical papers by way of New York to New Orleans. When many years later he finally published his history, he wrote: "In their circuitous way the sea water found its way to them: since their arrival, the mice, worms, and the variety of insects of a humid and warm climate, have made great ravages among them. The ink of several very ancient documents has grown pale, as to render them nearly illegible, and notes hastily taken on a journey, are in so cramped a hand, that they are not to be deciphered by any person but him who made them."[27]

Judge Martin might never have published his work had not Archibald Debow Murphey applied to him for permission to use his collection. Upon learning of Murphey's ambitious plans for writing and publishing a history, Martin not only refused to permit the use of his collection, but set about to complete his own history. As if trying to get his own work into print ahead of Murphey's (though in his preface Martin indicated his well-

25. Francois-Xavier Martin, *The History of North Carolina, from the Earliest Period* (2 vols.; New-Orleans: A. T. Penniman & Co., 1829), I, vii-viii. Cited hereafter as Martin, *History of North Carolina.*
26. Johnson and Malone, *D.A.B.,* XII, 335.
27. Martin, *History of North Carolina,* I, xi.

founded doubt that Murphey would succeed in his own plan), the judge published his two volumes in 1829 without revision. Thus, twenty years after he left North Carolina, Martin put into print a compilation of materials that he had made between 1803 and 1809. He had not even seen Williamson's volumes which had been published in 1812.[28] Under such a dubious procedure, Martin's history suffered not only from lack of proper editing but also from a lack of sources that would have been available to him had he taken the time and effort to co-operate with Murphey and others who had, by 1829, become vitally interested in the writing of a good state history.

Martin's two-volume history was an improvement over Williamson's in that he exhibited little bias, though this very attribute made for a dry, straightforward listing of fact after fact with neither feeling nor judgment. His use of sources was perhaps no better or worse than that of other historians of the times, and he copied carelessly, interspersed sources with his own writing without differentiating between the two, and seldom gave full citations. As an example of the latter, his sources for the chapter dealing with the Regulator revolt were simply listed as "Records—Magazines—Gazettes."[29] Few authors have written about the Regulators without taking sides. In recording Edmund Fanning's conviction for extortion, Martin noted that he was fined one penny on each count.[30] The reader is left only with his imagination to determine Martin's sympathies. "He presented his dry and factual account without defending, accusing, or exterpolating," wrote one twentieth-century historian.[31]

In his first volume, Martin copied unashamedly from earlier printed works, particularly those relating to Virginia and South Carolina. In the second volume, he quoted extensively from original documents for the period immediately preceding the Revolution; these documents presumably came from the secretary of state's office and from private sources. This material was "merely dumped . . . on the printed page, the result resembling

28. Martin, *History of North Carolina*, I, xi.
29. Martin, *History of North Carolina*, II, 285.
30. Martin, *History of North Carolina*, II, 243.
31. Yearns, "Martin," p. 25.

an almanac as much as history." While no better or worse than the histories of his contemporaries, "it exceeded them in information and was inferior to them in inspiration."[32] Upon publication it received no reviews and was barely mentioned in *Debow's Review*, published in the city in which the history was printed.

Although the printed history terminated with events of the summer of 1776, Martin had collected materials for the period from 1776 to 1809 and had "ample notes" for a volume on the Revolution and another for the postwar period. He pledged to publish these volumes if his health improved.[33] But the judge, who had for several years suffered from failing eyesight, gradually became virtually blind, and as his health deteriorated he grew more eccentric and miserly. He never again turned his attention to the State of his former residence. He died in 1846 at the age of eighty-four, a lonely and crotchety bachelor. His estate was valued at nearly a half million dollars—an amount less characteristic of a historian than of the penurious life that the old judge had lived.[34]

After the publication of Martin's history, others became intrigued with his reference to "very ancient documents" which he had indicated were among his collection.[35] His reference also to materials on the war and postwar periods interested historians. As the years passed, young historians like David L. Swain came to suspect that Martin had carried off public records, and the extent of his collection grew in the minds of North Carolinians. Swain, then president of the University of North Carolina and founder of the North Carolina Historical Society, persuaded his friend, Governor William A. Graham, to write the aging judge immediately upon Graham's inauguration in 1845, requesting the return of "any of our public documents . . . which may be under your controll. . . ."[36] The old chief justice, irritated by

32. Yearns, "Martin," pp. 22, 26, 27.
33. Martin, *History of North Carolina*, I, xii.
34. Johnson and Malone, *D.A.B.*, XII, 336.
35. Martin, *History of North Carolina*, I, xi.
36. Graham to Martin, February 8, 1845, in Governor's Letter Book, 1845 (G.L.B. 36), State Archives. See also J. G. de R. Hamilton (ed.), *The Papers of William Alexander Graham* (4 vols.; Raleigh: State Department of Archives and History, 1957-61), III, 25. Cited hereafter as Hamilton, *Graham Papers*.

the implication that he had taken off public records, replied that his printed history had ended with the beginning of the Revolution and that "documents relative to that time have been collected by me, and it is with regret that I find us not able to sadisfy [*sic*] you, as I would have been desirous to do."[37] As stingy with words as he was noted to be with his money, Martin gave no hint of having papers of the post-1776 period to which he had referred earlier.

Governor Graham was not satisfied with Martin's reply. Following the judge's death, he wrote to Martin's executor, Robert Nash Ogden, that he believed Martin had carried with him "a large mass of material for the History, and that a considerable portion consists of public documents."[38] He wanted them back. Ogden replied that the late judge's brother and sole heir, Paul B. Martin, had, according to the author's wishes, turned over to him all the papers, but that a search of them failed to locate any that were identifiable as public records. In fact, he wrote, he had questioned Judge Martin about the matter just prior to his death and had received assurance that he had no materials belonging to the State. Ogden suggested, however, that if Graham would designate any missing items believed to be in the collection, he would look for them and return them if found to be public records. Furthermore, he wrote, Martin had requested Ogden himself to prepare the third volume for the press and that he was "very anxious to see the unfinished history completed" if he could find time to do it.[39] The matter appears to have been dropped for more than a decade.

Then, in 1858, came exciting news. Bishop William Mercer Green wrote Swain, "I had the pleasure of seeing what, if I mistake not, you would like to feast your eyes upon, *The Manuscript History of N. Carolina by Judge F. X. Martin.*" It was in the possession of Colonel John Francis Hamtramck Claiborne at Shieldsboro, Mississippi, and consisted of five volumes covering the following periods: 1584-1729, 1730-65, 1765-75, 1776-80, and

37. Martin to Graham, March 29, 1845, in Hamilton, *Graham Papers*, III, 35.
38. Graham to Ogden, June 21, 1847, in Hamilton, *Graham Papers*, III, 199. Ogden was an attorney and a descendant of the Nash family of Hillsborough, Governor Graham's residence.
39. Ogden to Graham, July 8, 1847, in Hamilton, *Graham Papers*, III, 201-2.

1780-81. The manuscripts had "an unfinished appearance" and each volume was about seven by sixteen inches with three-fifths of an inch thickness.[40]

Indefatigable Swain lost no time in attempting to obtain the manuscripts. Rather than contacting Claiborne directly, Swain requested the intercession of Secretary of the Interior Jacob Thompson, a native of Caswell County, North Carolina, who had earlier moved to Mississippi. Thompson in turn forwarded Swain's request to Claiborne, who replied that he would not only be glad for the papers to come to North Carolina, but that he would bring them to Chapel Hill on an anticipated trip northward.[41] Swain, impressed by this generosity, suggested in a letter to the Mississippian that he, Claiborne, prepare an additional volume on North Carolina for publication, to be based upon the Martin manuscripts and upon sources which would be furnished from the Historical Society's collection at Chapel Hill.[42] Claiborne clarified his offer in his reply. He had not meant to donate the papers. In fact, they belonged to Ogden, Martin's executor and "a North Carolinian of a distinguished lineage, but in narrow circumstances." Claiborne wanted to sell them, the money to be turned over to Ogden. Furthermore, he wrote, he was too busy to write a history of North Carolina, and instead urged Swain to do it.[43] Swain, realizing now that he had misinterpreted Claiborne's earlier letter, offered to buy the papers if he could examine them and satisfy himself as to their value.[44]

Finally, on February 11, 1860, the papers reached Chapel Hill, though by express rather than by hand. One look at them resulted in Swain's disappointment. There were only three

40. Green to Swain, December 22, 1858, in Swain Papers, Southern Historical Collection. Claiborne was a noted historian of Mississippi. Green was consecrated a bishop in the Episcopal Church in 1849. Dunbar Rowland, *History of Mississippi, The Heart of the South* (2 vols.; Chicago-Jackson: S. J. Clarke Publishing Co., 1925), II, 596-97.

41. Claiborne to Thompson, June 19, 1859, in Swain Papers, Southern Historical Collection.

42. Swain to Claiborne, July 4, 1859, in Swain Papers, Southern Historical Collection.

43. Claiborne to Swain, July 18, 1859, in Swain Papers, Southern Historical Collection.

44. Swain to Claiborne, December 26, 1859, in Swain Papers, Southern Historical Collection.

volumes, one being the draft used by Martin in Volume II for
the period 1765-76, another consisting of notes for a history
covering the period from 1776-80, and a third consisting of notes
preparatory to the completion of a narrative for the year 1780.
The first two volumes, seen by Bishop Green earlier, were not
among them. Nor were there any "ancient documents." Thinking that Claiborne had overlooked sending the first two volumes,
Swain again wrote to the Mississippian.[45] Getting no immediate
reply, he wrote again, asking about the first two volumes and
expressing the reluctant view that the papers received were of
so little value that he should not even suggest a price on the
grounds that it might offend Claiborne.[46] The latter made another search and replied that he could not find the papers to
which Bishop Green had referred. He also pointed out that
neither he nor Ogden's heirs (who were "foreigners" to North
Carolina) had any interest in the papers, and that he would,
on the latter's behalf, accept whatever Swain wanted to pay for
them.[47] Shortly thereafter Swain apologetically offered $100, and
Claiborne accepted.[48] The payment was made from state funds.
Swain's disappointment in the papers was not as great as he had
first indicated to Claiborne. In fact, he wrote the Reverend
Francis L. Hawks that "they are indispensable nevertheless, and
I have purchased them for the State."[49]

   The Martin manuscripts were retained by Swain for a time
and he intended for them to be utilized in the publication of a
documentary history being compiled by himself and Francis
Lister Hawks.[50] They were, however, later deposited in the
Capitol in Raleigh, for Swain after the war charged that Union
officials had sent to Washington, along with the Vance letter

45. Swain to Claiborne, February 13, 1860, in Swain Papers, Southern Historical
Collection.
   46. Claiborne to Swain, April 16, 1860, in Swain Papers, Southern Historical
Collection.
   47. Claiborne to Swain, April 30, 1860, in Swain Papers, Southern Historical
Collection.
   48. Claiborne to Swain, July 10, 1860, in Swain Papers, Southern Historical
Collection.
   49. Swain to Hawks, September 13, 1860, in Swain Papers, Southern Historical
Collection.
   50. See below, chap. VI.

books, "the manuscript continuation of Francis Xavier Martins History of North Carolina purchased by me for the State from his representatives in Louisiana just before the beginning of the war."[51] The charge was groundless.[52]

Thus, the Martin manuscripts dropped from sight except for a brief resurrection in 1868.[53] In 1883, Secretary of State William L. Saunders reported that their location was not known.[54] Yet, Saunders had at least two of the three volumes in his possession all the while, but did not recognize them as the Martin manuscripts. This fact was revealed when in 1964 these two volumes were found among the William Laurence Saunders Papers in the Southern Historical Collection, where they were designated as "unidentified." One volume, labeled "Chapter 3," comprised notes incorporated into Chapters 7-11 of Volume II of Martin's published work, and the other, "Chapter 4," comprised rough notes and abstracts for the period 1776-80.[55] The last of the three volumes purchased by Swain in 1860 has not been located but, even if found, it will be of little significance except to the antiquarian. Obviously Martin vastly exaggerated the extent of his "collection," and the intriguing mystery that surrounded it for more than 130 years has turned out to be almost as great a hoax to North Carolina historians as did some of the antics of Martin's young contemporary, Joseph Seawell Jones.[56]

ARCHIBALD DEBOW MURPHEY

The man who contributed most to the stimulation of historical interest in the first half of the nineteenth century never

51. Swain to ——, December 9, 1867, in Swain Papers, Southern Historical Collection.

52. For a denial that the records ever were in the War Department, see Francis Lieber to Swain, February 15, 1867, in Swain Papers, Southern Historical Collection.

53. See above, p. 100, n. 86.

54. Report of the trustees of the State Library, Document No. 21, *Public Documents, 1883.*

55. I did not locate and identify the two volumes of Martin's manuscripts in the Southern Historical Collection until after I had written the first draft of this book. In that draft I had concluded the section on the Martin papers with the editorial statement that "There are slim hopes that they may yet be identified among large collections of official or private papers. Greater miracles have occurred."

56. See below, pp. 157 ff.

wrote a history. In fact, he failed at almost everything that he set out to accomplish, but his ideas and his work laid the foundation upon which others were to build. He was plagued by illness, financial ruin, and the scorn of his less farsighted colleagues; yet he ranks today as one of the intellectual giants of the State. He simply had the misfortune of living many decades before the public was ready to accept his ideas. He was, indeed, a "prophet of a new era."

Archibald Debow Murphey was born in Caswell County about 1777, studied in David Caldwell's log college, was graduated from the University of North Carolina in 1799, and became a teacher at the latter institution. Three years later he was admitted to the bar at Hillsborough and earned a reputation as an able lawyer. He served in the State Senate from Orange County from 1812 to 1818, and in the latter year he was appointed a judge of the Superior Court.[57]

Archibald Murphey was the most remarkable North Carolinian of his day. He combined a love of the past with a vision of the future. Of his vision, perhaps his most lasting contribution was his advocacy of a state-wide system of public education and internal improvements. While in the State Senate he submitted a report on education which has been called the first definite plan for public education to be presented in North Carolina. But North Carolina was not ready for such notions, and it was many years before the State took effective steps to implement the idea. In 1819, Murphey submitted his memoir on internal improvements which advocated a vast network of roads, canals, and navigable streams. Little was done in this connection until the advent of the railroad. He urged judicial reform, an improvement that came only piecemeal and is still in progress. Ironically, one of his recommendations was the abolition of imprisonment

57. Johnson and Malone, *D.A.B.*, XIII, 345-46. See also William A. Graham, "Memoir of Hon. Archibald D. Murphey, Late a Judge of the Superior Court of North Carolina," in William H. Hoyt (ed.), *The Papers of Archibald D. Murphey* (2 vols.; Raleigh: North Carolina Historical Commission, 1914), I, xix-xxxiv. This source hereafter is cited as Hoyt, *Murphey Papers*. See also Margaret E. Lerche, "The Life and Public Career of Archibald D. Murphey (unpublished doctoral dissertation, The University of North Carolina, 1948). I have followed Hoyt, great-grandson of the historian, in using "Debow" in preference to "De-Bow" as Murphey's middle name.

for debt—ironically, because Murphey himself was to go to jail for that offense some years later.[58]

Murphey's influence on the writing of the history of North Carolina was almost as important as his other contributions. As early as 1819, he began urging his elders to write their recollections of the Revolution while they yet lived.[59] Finding no one willing to do the job alone, he urged such men as General Joseph Graham, General William Lenoir, and Colonel William Polk to submit their articles to him. He in turn edited them and offered them to the newspapers of the State. Only the *Hillsborough Recorder,* however, appears to have used the articles extensively.[60] The narratives only whetted Murphey's interest, and, by 1820, he was speaking of devoting much of his own time to history. His enthusiasm grew, and the following year he wrote, "I feel some zeal upon the subject, for a large portion of our history now lives only in the recollections of a few survivors of the Revolution. We must soon embody it, or it will be entirely lost."[61] Two months later he divulged his idea of his own role—that of collector. "I shall never have time to write such a History," he said, "but I feel anxious that before the Memory of events passes away, all the information respecting them which now remains should be collected and embodied, that some Man of competent Talents and who has leisure, may write the History of the State. . . ."[62]

By midsummer, his enthusiasm growing, Murphey had abandoned his role as collector only and decided to become a writer of history himself. Not only that, but he had also expanded his plan. His idea of a history of the Revolution had given way to a proposed full history of North Carolina, which he promised to

58. Hoyt, *Murphey Papers,* I, 385.

59. Murphey to Colonel William Polk, July 16, 1819, in Hoyt, *Murphey Papers,* I, 147.

60. William A. Graham, *General Joseph Graham and His Papers on North Carolina Revolutionary History* (Raleigh: Edwards and Broughton, 1904), p. 189; Murphey to Colonel Charles D. Conner, January 10, 1821, and Murphey to General Joseph Graham, July 20, 1821, in Hoyt, *Murphey Papers,* I, 187, 211.

61. Murphey to General Joseph Graham, January 10, 1821, in Hoyt, *Murphey Papers,* I, 193-94.

62. Murphey to Colonel Ransom Sutherland, March 8, 1821, in Hoyt, *Murphey Papers,* I, 194.

write. "It is a work on the history, soil, climate, legislation, civil institutions, literature, etc., of this State," he wrote.[63] The work would be "in a style worthy of its subject. . . ."[64]

Already Murphey was being afflicted by his three nemeses. Yet only forty-five years of age, he suffered from rheumatism which, for long periods, prevented his doing any work at all. Though a prominent and leading citizen, he invested his own funds in visionary internal improvements projects, investments that brought him financial ruin. And his notions on educational and moral matters elicited little favorable response from those in a position to see them put into action.

In 1823, he turned to his friend and fellow Caswell native, Senate Speaker Bartlett Yancey. His proposed history would cost a great deal, Murphey wrote Yancey, and booksellers had informed him that little or no profit could be expected from the quality of history that he envisioned because of "the Fashion and Taste of the Times being for Compilations, Epitome, and Abridgements." Such a "Catch-penny production," he said, would do honor to neither the State nor the writer, and he was not willing to write something so unworthy. He was too poor to spare the expense and time required to collect and arrange the materials and to write the history unless he could obtain financial assistance. He proposed to purchase the collection of Judge Martin, copy the public records in Raleigh, travel over the State, and visit other states to gather material and interview emigrant North Carolinians. "The Money and time which I have heretofore spent in the public Service, have contributed in a considerable degree to my ruin, and Prudence forbids my again embarking in it without a Certainty that I would not Sustain a Loss," he wrote. Murphey proposed that the State lend him $10,000 for eight or ten years, interest free, the mortgage to be secured by his real estate. The State also should agree to pay for engravings and to give him access to the public records. With his letter he sent

63. Murphey to General Joseph Graham, July 20, 1821, and Murphey to General William Lenoir, August 18, 1821, in Hoyt, *Murphey Papers,* I, 211, 231.

64. Murphey to General Joseph Graham, November 27, 1822, in Hoyt, *Murphey Papers,* I, 273.

a resolution for the consideration of the General Assembly.[65] His effort to obtain the loan was unsuccessful.

Discouraged by the Assembly's failure to support him, Murphey appears to have done little further work on his history for two years. By mid-1825, however, he reported that his health had improved and that he was "engaged in Arranging the plan and Details of our Colonial History."[66] The "plan" to which he referred evolved into a printed pamphlet comprising a memorial to the General Assembly and a remarkably comprehensive outline of his proposed history.[67] In the memorial he proposed to devote most of his time to the production of his history and solicited "such aid in the prosecution of this work, as will enable him to complete it."[68] The "plan" was divided into seven parts: the discovery, aboriginal history, colonial period, general history since 1776, geography, geology, and botany. That he expected little from the General Assembly was revealed in a letter written to Willie P. Mangum: "As to the Memorial, it is presented; but I have no Idea that any such Aid will be given as my Work will require. I thought, however, public Notice might be thereby drawn to the Subject, and some Men be induced rather to send me their old Papers, and Pamphlets, than to cast them into the Fire."[69]

Representative John Scott, a neighbor of Murphey's in Hillsborough, presented the memorial to the General Assembly. It was referred to a joint committee which reported favorably a bill to authorize Murphey to conduct a $25,000 lottery and to give him access to the public records. The bill passed the House but in the Senate it ran into opposition. Lotteries, formerly an acceptable method of raising money, were becoming less popular on moral grounds. Murphey's personal appearance in Raleigh to plead his cause may have turned the tide, and the bill finally

65. Murphey to Yancey, December 8, 1823, in Hoyt, *Murphey Papers*, I, 398-99.

66. Murphey to Colonel William Polk, July 13, 1825, in Hoyt, *Murphey Papers*, I, 310.

67. The pamphlet, containing no title page but printed by Dennis Heartt in Hillsborough in 1825, is printed in Hoyt, *Murphey Papers*, II, 333-40.

68. Hoyt, *Murphey Papers*, II, 334. What appears to be Murphey's introduction to his proposed history is printed in Hoyt, *Murphey Papers*, II, 363 ff.

69. Murphey to Mangum, December 20, 1825, in Hoyt, *Murphey Papers*, I, 323.

passed on January 4, 1826, with the amount reduced to $15,000.[70] It also authorized access to the records of the offices of the governor, secretary of state, comptroller, and of the General Assembly.

Murphey was disappointed that the amount had been reduced and that only three classes of drawings were authorized, but he set out immediately to make the lottery a success. He was doomed to disappointment. In August, 1826, his son reported the "dull prospect" for selling tickets in Murphey's own Orange County,[71] and in Caswell County the sales were "not brisk."[72] Newspapers, however, appeared to be generally favorable to the lottery and its purpose. Murphey, again incapacitated by rheumatism and doctoring himself with the waters of Rockingham Springs at Lenox Castle, carried on a spirited correspondence both in support of the lottery and of the collection of historical materials. During the year he was cheered by the promise of the papers of, among others, Governors William R. Davie[73] and Benjamin Smith.[74]

But the lottery went badly. He offered to turn it over to "Northern Brokers"; they declined because the sum was not sufficient to justify their concern.[75] As a result, the General Assembly at its next session authorized the Literary Board to conduct a lottery for $50,000, half of which was to go to Murphey's history project.[76] But no action was taken to carry the act into effect.

The new lottery act did, however, encourage the ailing Murphey. He appeared ready to begin putting his materials into

70. *Laws of 1825-1826*, c. 35. See also John D. Delacy to Murphey, December 30, 1825, and John P. Carter to Murphey, January 1, 1826, in Hoyt, *Murphey Papers*, I, 324, 326.

71. Victor M. Murphey to Archibald D. Murphey, August 12, 1826, in Hoyt, *Murphey Papers*, I, 338.

72. John McAden to Murphey, September 28, 1826, in Hoyt, *Murphey Papers*, I, 341.

73. Allen J. Davie to Murphey, January 17, July 25, August 9, November 17, 1826, in Hoyt, *Murphey Papers*, I, 327, 332, 337, 344.

74. Junius A. Moore to Murphey, March 2, 1826, in Hoyt, *Murphey Papers*, I, 329.

75. Murphey to Theodore Shulz, November 30, 1831, in Hoyt, *Murphey Papers*, I, 395.

76. *Laws of 1826-1827*, c. 16. See also Hoyt, *Murphey Papers*, I, 347n.

shape for publication[77] when he noted the absence of many important colonial documents that might be found only in the British offices in London. He therefore prepared, and in February, 1827, Representative John Scott introduced, a resolution requesting the governor "to make a respectful application to the British government for liberty to procure, for the use of the State, from the office of the Board of Trade and Plantations, in London, copies of such papers and documents as relate to the colonial history of North-Carolina." The resolution further requested the aid of the American minister in London in obtaining an agent for copying the records. It passed without recorded opposition on February 9, 1827.[78] Murphey's desire to obtain copies of colonial records from England may have been encouraged by Congressman Edward Everett of Massachusetts who asked him, "Would it not be worth while, with a view toward a revision of our early colonial History, to endeavor to have the Records of the Plantation office at London examined?"[79]

Governor Hutchins G. Burton forwarded a copy of the February 9 resolution to Albert Gallatin, the American minister in London, on April 19. Gallatin lost no time in applying to the British government for permission to obtain copies of records relating to North Carolina. He was informed that papers of interest were located in several offices and he found the "most liberal disposition to grant the request and to afford the necessary facilities of procuring the copies asked for." In order that the desired documents might be designated for copying, a list or "index" of records relating to the Province was prepared. Both Lord Dudley, the principal secretary of state for foreign affairs, and the members of the Board of Trade informed Gallatin that they would issue instructions that an authorized agent be permitted to make copies of the papers designated by Governor

77. Murphey to Colonel William Polk, December 14, 1826, in Hoyt, *Murphey Papers*, I, 347-48.

78. The resolution is printed in *Laws of 1826-1827*, p. 85. The Assembly also authorized Murphey to borrow books from the State Library. Resolution in *Laws of 1826-1827*, p. 88. See also John Scott to Murphey, February 14, 1827, in Hoyt, *Murphey Papers*, I, 350.

79. Edward Everett to Murphey, December 4, 1826, in Hoyt, *Murphey Papers*, I, 346. Everett was formerly editor of the *North American Review*.

Burton from the list. The minister sent the list to the governor on August 25, along with his cover letter and his correspondence with British officials.[80]

No action was taken to carry out the plans for obtaining copies from London because of the General Assembly's reluctance to appropriate the necessary funds. What had been an auspicious beginning for filling in the "chasms" in the documentation of North Carolina history ended as quickly as it began.

Meanwhile, Murphey's financial condition became even more precarious. But he clung to his plans. In 1827, he engaged an agent to procure subscriptions for his proposed history and had hopes of getting 3,000 advance orders. He wanted to pay off his debts and then devote himself exclusively to the compilation of his history.[81] But the agent failed to live up to his promises, and Murphey's health continued to deteriorate. Despite sporadic efforts to revive it, the lottery was unsuccessful. The crowning blow came in 1829 when, while attending court in Greensboro, Murphey was sentenced to twenty days in prison for a debt that he could not pay. Upon completion of his sentence, he took the insolvent debtor's oath.[82] Broken in health and in spirit and out of work, the former judge spent the next two years in an effort to make a living.

Then, in 1831, his health seemingly improved and his financial condition ameliorated but not solved, Murphey resumed his plan. A New York brokerage firm offered to take over the lottery authorized in 1826 and to draw it upon commission. The drawing was scheduled to begin in the spring, but in the meantime Murphey agreed to ask the General Assembly to enlarge the

80. Both the letters and list are bound in an unpaged volume titled "Calendar North Carolina Papers at London Board of Trade 1729-1775" in the State Archives. The list was printed in 1843 by State Treasurer John Hill Wheeler, by authorization of the General Assembly, with the title *Indexes to Documents Relative to North Carolina During the Colonial Existence of Said State: Now on File in the Offices of the Board of Trade and State Paper Offices in London: Transmitted in 1827: By Mr. Gallatin, Then the American Minister in London, and Now Published By Resolution of the Legislature of 1842-43: Under the Direction of the Public Treasurer* (Raleigh: T. Loring, 1843). The document was reprinted in the *North Carolina University Magazine*, I (December, 1844), 1-120.

81. Murphey to Colonel William Polk, February 25, 1827, in Hoyt, *Murphey Papers*, I, 351.

82. Hoyt, *Murphey Papers*, I, 385n, and II, 434-35.

amount.[83] His last memorial was dated November 29, 1831. In it Murphey reviewed his efforts and adversities for more than ten years. No man could write a history such as he planned without pecuniary aid from the State, and the small amount and restricted number of drawings had resulted in his inability to carry off successfully the lottery previously authorized, he argued. That, coupled with his confinement with rheumatism and the refusal of the Assembly to take action to obtain copies of the records listed in the "index" prepared in 1827, had resulted in no further accomplishments. If the Assembly would grant him further aid, he wrote, he himself would "proceed to London, or send an agent of Intelligence to procure copies of the papers and documents," and after writing the history, he would present the transcripts to the General Assembly to be deposited in the Public Library. "They will fill up many large volumes in manuscript," he continued. He promised also to present to the General Assembly several volumes of manuscripts containing copies of such documents and papers relating to North Carolina's history as he was able to collect in the United States. In view of the fact that Murphey was asking for not one cent from the treasury, this perhaps stands as the greatest bargain ever offered the State of North Carolina.

Murphey asked for authorization for a new lottery in the amount of fifty thousand dollars, but implied that he could succeed with $20,000, provided the number of drawings not be limited. He also asked again to have access to the public records in Raleigh for the purpose of temporary withdrawal for the making of copies. To his memorial he appended a proposed bill incorporating his requests.

The memorial was referred to a committee whose report effectually ended for more than a decade the State's efforts to encourage the preparation of a history. It read: "That however anxious they are to see a correct History of North Carolina, yet a failure of a similar attempt made by the petitioners, not many years since, connected with the system of hazard, contemplated

83. Murphey to the Reverend Theodore Shulz, November 30, 1831, in Hoyt, *Murphey Papers*, I, 395.

in the Memorial, upon the morality of the community, induces
your Committee to return the Bill and Memorial to the House
and recommend its rejection."[84] Archibald Murphey's last hope
for his proposed monumental history was thus filed away among
the archives of the State.

Though the judgment of time is against the men comprising
"Rip van Winkle's" legislature, justice requires that Murphey
himself share the blame. A visionary—perhaps more than any
other man he foresaw the potential greatness of North Carolina—
and a believer in his dreams, he staked his own material possessions upon the success or failure of schemes for internal improvements. When they failed, he became a virtual pauper in worldly
possessions.[85] Without funds, he could do little. The failure
of the authorized lottery Murphey always blamed on legislative
restrictions on the amount and drawings. Even so, a better
manager probably could have made a success of the lottery. But
regardless of where the blame lay, the State was deprived of what
might have been its first good history. Nevertheless, Murphey's
efforts inspired others, and the materials that he collected, though
years later scattered into unidentifiable units in various repositories, provided valuable sources for later and better historians.

Archibald Murphey died on February 1, 1832,[86] leaving behind the largest and most valuable collection of manuscript North
Caroliniana extant at that time. The following year his son,
Victor, offered the materials for sale, and young Governor David
L. Swain, probably not yet aware that Murphey's mantle as the
leading historical figure of the State would soon fall upon his
own shoulders, made overtures to "some gentlemen" engaged in
historical writing who expressed interest in the collection.[87] The

84. The memorial and committee report are printed in Charles L. Coon, *The
Beginnings of Public Education in North Carolina: A Documentary History
1790-1840* (2 vols.; Raleigh: North Carolina Historical Commission, 1908), I,
529-31.

85. Murphey's continuing financial crises need not be recorded here. It is
sufficient to note that his friends, particularly his former student, Judge Thomas
Ruffin, were generous and patient in assisting him. See Hoyt, *Murphey Papers*,
I, 287, and *passim*.

86. *Fayetteville Observer*, February 4, 1832.

87. Victor Murphey to Swain, September 25, 1833, in Swain Epistolary Correspondence, North Carolina Collection.

"some gentlemen" probably referred to Joseph Seawell Jones, who was writing a history of the State, and to William A. Graham who was encouraging Jones in his research. Jones already had obtained some of the papers.[88] A large portion of the Murphey collection went into the hands of Graham[89] who took from them letters of his father, General Joseph Graham, and allowed Jones to take some others.[90] The bulk of these papers, however, were kept intact by Graham. As early as 1836, Swain, by then president of the University of North Carolina, inquired of Graham about the possibility of purchasing the papers for the university.[91] Nothing appears to have come of the idea at the time, though Swain continued his efforts.[92]

Graham became governor in 1845 and left his collection in the hands of John Umstead Kirkland in Hillsborough.[93] Graham had already prepared—or was soon to prepare—a descriptive list of his Murphey papers which revealed their great significance.[94] Among the original manuscripts were letters of Gabriel Johnston, William Hooper, Joseph Hewes, John Penn, Samuel Johnston, Richard Caswell, Thomas Burke, Cornelius Harnett, Alexander Martin, Jethro Sumner, Joseph Graham, William Gaston, and James Saunders. Included also were proceedings of the Wilmington Committee of Safety, the Cumberland Association, and other "public records." Printed matter included pamphlets, newspapers, and journals of legislative bodies. There were also transcripts from records that could have been obtained only from London—among them a Lords Proprietors' Minute Book. "On the subject of the Revolution, the materials were most ample," Graham noted.

Finally, in 1848, the Murphey papers then owned by Graham

88. Jones to Graham, June 4, November 30, 1832, in Hamilton, *Graham Papers,* I, 235-36, 241; Hoyt, *Murphey Papers,* II, 213n; Swain to James J. Iredell, August 8, 1856, in Swain Papers, Southern Historical Collection.

89. It is not known whether Graham purchased them or simply took them over when Victor Murphey moved westward.

90. Jones to Graham, June 4, 1832, in Hamilton, *Graham Papers,* I, 235-36; Hoyt, *Murphey Papers,* II, 213n.

91. Swain to Graham, September 28, 1836, in Hamilton, *Graham Papers,* I, 440.

92. Swain to Graham, May 13, 1848, in Hamilton, *Graham Papers,* III, 223 ff.

93. Graham to Swain, July 2, 1845, in Swain Papers, Southern Historical Collection.

94. The catalogue is printed in Hoyt, *Murphey Papers,* II, 419-20. The original is in the William A. Graham Papers, State Archives.

were procured by Swain for the Historical Society of the University of North Carolina at Chapel Hill. Upon examination, Swain found significant materials not included in Graham's inventory. "The largest and most valuable portion of the collection, are public property," he wrote, "and ought, I suppose, to be deposited in your [the governor's] office." Among them were official letters and papers of Governors Abner Nash and Thomas Burke, the location of which had been the source of inquiry for many years.[95] These papers helped fill important gaps for the last years of the Revolution. Among other significant items not included in Graham's inventory were papers of Jesse Franklin, James Iredell, Sr.,[96] Archibald Maclaine, William Lenoir, and Waightstill Avery.

Thus, by the middle of the century, many of Murphey's papers had been placed in the Historical Society at Chapel Hill. A few remained in the hands of Graham and Jones, but these two groups later found their way to the Swain collection also. Upon Swain's death, they joined the odyssey of his collection.[97]

In the meantime, for almost sixty years another portion of Murphey's papers remained hidden in a garret just outside of Hillsborough, where they presumably had been left by Victor Murphey upon his removal to Mississippi in 1835. It was not until around 1890 that the aging John Umstead Kirkland found them and sold them for a "trifling sum" to Walter R. Benjamin, a well-known autograph dealer. Among them were not only Murphey's personal papers but many letters collected for his proposed North Carolina history. Benjamin sold most of the letters and documents relating to the Revolution to autograph collectors, including Thomas Addis Emmet of New York and

95. Swain to Graham, May 13, 1848, in Hamilton, *Graham Papers*, III, 223-26. Miss Mary Burke, the late governor's daughter, had already given the State a valuable collection of the papers of Governor Burke.

96. A controversy arose in 1856 over the James Iredell, Sr., and Samuel Johnston papers in the Murphey collection. Iredell's grandson claimed that the manuscripts had only been loaned to Murphey and he demanded them back. Swain contended, however, that their deposit had been with the approval of Governor James Iredell, Jr., and that he, Swain, had been permitted to take other materials to add to the collection. James J. Iredell to Swain, August 5, 1856, and Swain to Iredell, August 8, 1856, in Swain Papers, Southern Historical Collection.

97. For the story of the dispersal of Swain's papers, see below, chap. VIII.

Zachary T. Hollingsworth of Boston. Those purchased by the former are now in the Emmet collection in the New York Public Library. Those purchased by Hollingsworth were scattered after being sold at auction in New York in 1927, some of them—particularly those of General Jethro Sumner which Murphey had borrowed from the general's daughter—going to the William L. Clements Library in Ann Arbor, Michigan. Meanwhile, the bulk of the private papers of Murphey remained in Benjamin's hands for about fifteen years. In 1904, William Henry Hoyt, the young great-grandson of Murphey, accidentally learned of their being in Benjamin's hands. He immediately bought them. His acquisition so excited the young man that he spent the remainder of his life collecting historical materials relating to North Carolina in general, his ancestor in particular. His manuscripts have in recent years been given to the State Department of Archives and History and to the Southern Historical Collection.[98]

Archibald Murphey, a "failure" when measured by his immediate accomplishments, may be credited with the preservation of valuable historical sources which, had it not been for his zeal and foresight, might have been lost to posterity. The man who never wrote a history provided many of the sources for his successors.

JOSEPH SEAWELL ("SHOCCO") JONES

Joseph Seawell Jones won his rank among the historians of the nineteenth century not because of the quality of his writings but rather because he was a collector who left behind, and thereby saved from possible loss, a considerable quantity of manuscript and printed materials. Besides, he was one of the most intriguing —and tragic—figures in North Carolina history.

Born in Warren County about 1806, Jones acquired the nickname "Shocco"—after Shocco Creek near his place of birth—

98. For his story of the discovery and subsequent trail of the Murphey papers that remained unknown until about 1890, see Hoyt's "Reminiscences of a Collector of Books and Manuscripts," *The Bookmark* [a publication of the University of North Carolina Library], No. 23 (June, 1955). For a partial version, see the preface to his *Murphey Papers*, I, iv. See also William H. Hoyt to R. D. W. Connor, January 7, 1908, and October 23, 1909, in North Carolina Historical Commission Records, Correspondence of the Secretary, State Archives.

while a student at the University of North Carolina. Expelled from the University for his erratic class attendance, Jones later went to Harvard Law School, where, after dropping out three times, he obtained a law degree in 1833.[99] There he met and became acquainted with young men of future influence and there, too, he began his work on a book to refute what he considered "aspersions" upon North Carolina by Thomas Jefferson who had expressed doubts of the authenticity of the "Mecklenburg Declaration on Independence."

Jones had conceived the idea of his book by early 1832. He wrote his friend William A. Graham to see if the late Judge Murphey's papers were for sale. He presumed that Murphey had done much toward arranging his history and that the work might now be completed and published by someone else.[100] Upon learning from Graham that Murphey had actually done little toward "arranging" his history, Jones visited Hillsborough and went through the collection, making copies and taking some originals.[101] Meanwhile Judge David L. Swain, another friend from Jones's Chapel Hill days, visited him at Warrenton and was impressed by his materials and enthusiasm. Swain wrote in his diary that young Jones "seems to have taken more pains, to obtain information with regard to the early history of the state, than any individual with whom I have met. . . ."[102] Swain was so impressed that he chose Jones as one of the incorporators of the North Carolina Historical Society in 1833.[103]

Meanwhile Jones had been in touch with Historian Jared Sparks, who informed him that a great deal of material relating to the early history of North Carolina was available in London.

99. For a biographical sketch of Jones, see Edwin A. Miles, "Joseph Seawell Jones of Shocco—Historian and Humbug," *North Carolina Historical Review*, XXXIV (October, 1957), 483-506. Cited hereafter as Miles, "Joseph Seawell Jones."

100. Jones to Graham, February 20, 1832, in Hamilton, *Graham Papers*, I, 231.

101. Jones to Graham, June 4, November 30, 1832, in Hamilton, *Graham Papers*, I, 235, 241; Jones to David L. Swain, August 24, 1833, in Swain Epistolary Correspondence, North Carolina Collection. In the latter letter, Jones stated that he had obtained a large number of letters of the Henderson family, relating to the settlement of Kentucky. These were probably from Murphey's collection.

102. David L. Swain Diary, July 3, 1832, State Archives. Jones apparently had taken from the Murphey papers some copies of the papers of Samuel Johnston, Thomas Burke, Abner Nash, and others.

103. See below, chap. VIII.

Jones wrote, "I hope I shall go to London in a few years—and if so I intend to bring home all that industry and curiosity can gather." He lamented the "degredation" of North Carolina, a plight that he blamed upon the fact that the people did not know their history. He wrote, "If our ancestors ever did any thing praiseworthy their deeds are buried in manuscripts and unpublished and timeworn journals. We have no history—we have no books in the way of biographies or essays. . . . Our own young men . . . are more ignorant of the history of their Fathers than of the Kings of Britain or France. . . ."[104] Jones was particularly desirous of establishing North Carolina's claim to greatness in connection with the Revolution and suggested that the General Assembly provide for the publication of the journals of the congresses and legislatures during that period.

Jones gave no pretense of planning an objective history. He wrote Graham, "I shall treat of the Regulation and I shall endeavour to give it a better name than Martin or public opinion."[105] Two weeks later he wrote that he was "leaping on like an antelope with my book and think of scarcely any thing else save its advancement. . . . I espouse the cause of the Regulators—vindicate them—and sanctify them with the title of real Fire Worshippers."[106] To Swain he wrote, ". . . I shall be obliged to state in my work many facts without giving authority."[107] In another letter, he wrote that "I draw heavily upon the papers which my friend . . . Iredell gave or rather lent me and shall take the occasion to celebrate the virtue of the Father of that gentleman."[108] Neither did Jones lay claim to literary quality,

104. Flipp [Joseph Seawell] Jones to Daniel M. Barringer, November 24, 1832, in Daniel Moreau Barringer Papers, Southern Historical Collection.

105. Jones to Graham, December 31, 1832, in Hamilton, *Graham Papers*, I, 244. In this letter Jones referred to Martin as "that old sloth."

106. Jones to Graham, January 12, 1833, in Hamilton, *Graham Papers*, I, 247. Jones noted that he planned the following week to go to New York "to see that creature, Doct. Hosack about old Williamson's papers, having an order on him from Hugh Waddell for his quarters [papers?]" It does not appear, however, that he was any more successful than others in locating the Williamson collection.

107. Jones to Swain, August 24, 1833, in Swain Epistolary Correspondence, North Carolina Collection.

108. Jones to Swain, October 26, 1833, in Swain Epistolary Correspondence, North Carolina Collection.

intending that the book "shall be more elegant in its Mechanical than in its literary execution."[109]

During the summer of 1833, Jones examined the public records in the office of Secretary of State William Hill who gave him altogether too much assistance and co-operation. Wrote Jones, ". . . the old gentleman who is extremely ignorant of the proper use of the papers in his office, was not at all disposed to permit me to search for myself, and would *squire* me about from Shelf to Shelf and say, 'here are the patents for the year 80,' and so on." Jones confided that he wanted the Assembly to give him free access to the records in the secretary's office so he could "give those papers a thorough overhauling and see what is in them of historical value." He expected to bring with him three "assistants," including Peter Force, "to go through those papers and see what is in them and I should take great pleasure and pride in returning them to order and a better State of preservation."[110] In compliance with his request, Graham, who was then in the House of Commons, obtained passage of an act authorizing Jones to inspect the public records and to make extracts in the offices of the executive and legislative branches so long as he did not interfere with the regular duties of the officers.[111]

Jones sent his book to the printer in 1833, but the high cost

109. Jones to Graham, November 18, 1833, in Hamilton, *Graham Papers*, I, 269. In this letter Jones referred to North Carolina as "the Rip-Van-Winkle of the South." Jones has been given credit by some for coining the nickname "Old North State" for North Carolina. Ashe, *Biographical History*, VI, 331.

110. Jones to Graham, November 18, 1833, in Hamilton, *Graham Papers*, I, 269-70. Jones accused Francois X. Martin of carrying off the journal of the legislative branch for 1765 inasmuch as Martin quoted from it and Jones could not locate it in the offices in Raleigh.

Peter Force's partner, Matthew St. Clair Clarke (who was clerk of the United States House of Representatives), visited Raleigh in June, 1833, "collecting documents for the history of the States prior to the Revolution. . . ." John Herritage Bryan to his wife, June 25, 1833, in John Herritage Bryan Papers, State Archives. Force himself visited New England capitals in the fall of 1833 for the same purpose. Bassett, *American Historians*, p. 252. Jones may have met him at that time.

111. *Laws of 1833-1834*, c. 135. The latter provision may have been Jones's way of insisting that the secretary of state give him no further unrequested help. Jones sought election by the General Assembly as secretary of state to succeed Hill who, he said, had a "sick wife and really has no curiosity in the contents of the papers on his shelves." Jones to Daniel M. Barringer, November 3, 1834, and November 12, 1835, in Barringer Papers, Southern Historical Collection.

of publication forced him to eliminate much material and to sell his copyright to a "Mr. Patterson" of Boston.[112] It was finally published jointly in 1834 by Charles Bowen of Boston and Turner and Hughes of Raleigh under the title of *A Defence of the Revolutionary History of the State of North Carolina From the Aspersions of Mr. Jefferson.* In his introduction, Jones indicated the use of a variety of sources—public records from the offices in Raleigh, private correspondence of Revolutionary leaders such as James Iredell, Sr., and, in Jones's words, interviews with "every old man and old woman from Cape Hatteras to the Blue Ridge."[113] It contained at least some materials obtained from Murphey as well as manuscripts obtained from other sources, though his infrequent footnotes made it impossible for the reader to determine their origins.

The book was largely a glamorized history of the State to 1776, a defense of the "Mecklenburg Declaration of Independence" supposedly drawn up on May 20, 1775, and of the loyalty of William Hooper whom Jefferson had called a Tory. The attack on Jefferson and his views was vehement. Jefferson's party, wrote Jones, "was a paralysis upon the vitals of the State. It cramped the nerves, stupified the brain, obscured the vision, and almost arrested the pulsation of the heart."[114] Thomas Jefferson, not George III, was the chief villain, one historian has written.[115] The book received a mixed reception in North Carolina, many of its readers objecting to Jones's harsh treatment of Jefferson, the spiritual father of the new Democratic party.

Not long after the appearance of his *Defence*, Jones announced that he had in the press a new book entitled *Curiosities of North Carolina*.[116] In connection with his research for the book, he claimed to have copied records in the federal departments in Washington and boasted that "I have by the favour of the Presi-

112. Jones to Swain, February 12, 1834, in Swain Epistolary Correspondence, North Carolina Collection.

113. Jo[seph] Seawell Jones, *A Defence of the Revolutionary History of North Carolina From the Aspersions of Mr. Jefferson* (Boston: Charles Bowen, and Raleigh: Turner and Hughes, 1834), p. 6. Cited hereafter as Jones, *Defence.*

114. Jones, *Defence*, p. viii.

115. Miles, "Joseph Seawell Jones," p. 490.

116. Jones to Graham, November 21, 1834, in Hamilton, *Graham Papers*, I, 331.

dent [Jackson] . . . got an insight into the Colonial office at London." Jackson had, Jones wrote, permitted him to order copies
of records in Great Britain in the president's name. He said that
he had already received an invoice in the amount of £187 for copies which he had ordered and expected to receive the copies soon.
Having learned that the "index" obtained by Gallatin in 1827
was very incomplete, Jones said that "I am determined if I can
by any means arrange my private affairs to go to London during
the next spring—to study in the aforesaid [Colonial] office."[117]
He never went.

The volume did not appear within the next year as promised,
and, late in 1835, Jones wrote that he had changed the title of
the proposed book to *A Picturesque History of North Carolina.*
But neither *Curiosities* nor *Picturesque* ever appeared. In the
light of Jones's subsequent behavior, it appears that either the
proposed book was one of his earlier hoaxes, or possibly he
planned to publish such a work from the articles on North Carolina that he provided for the *New-York Mirror* and the *Raleigh
Register.*[118]

Little was heard of Jones's historical interests for several
years. Having switched his political loyalties from Whig to Democrat, he appears to have maneuvered himself into the company
of the administration in Washington. Early in 1837, the *New
York Courier* carried a rumor that Lewis Cass was to be recalled
from his mission to France and that Shocco Jones was to be his
successor, adding that the appointment would be highly accept-
able to the people.[119] In the fall, a visitor to Washington wrote
that Jones was at Gadsby's Hotel where "he lives in high stile
and keeps a private or rather public Parlour, and *sees everybody!*
He seems quite familiar with all parties and I suspect he is
looking for an office."[120]

In 1838 appeared Jones's little 87-page volume titled *Memo-*

117. Jones to Swain, October 23, 1834, in Swain Epistolary Correspondence,
North Carolina Collection.
118. Miles, "Joseph Seawell Jones," p. 496.
119. Paraphrased in Susan Washington to William A. Graham, February 17,
1837, in Hamilton, *Graham Papers,* I, 485.
120. James Graham to William A. Graham, September 17, 1837, in Hamilton,
Graham Papers, I, 526.

rials of North Carolina.[121] It contained chapters on the Roanoke colony, Flora Macdonald, the "Mecklenburg Declaration of Independence," an "Extract from 'Picturesque History of North Carolina,'"[122] and a long section in which he defended his previous claims for North Carolina. Some of the material had previously been published in the *Mirror*.

By 1839, Shocco Jones was becoming famous—not because of his scholarly activities, but because of his inexplicable behavior. Unmasked as a perpetrator of a mammoth hoax in which he claimed to have killed a man in a duel near Portsmouth, Virginia, he fled to Mississippi. In Columbus, he ceremoniously deposited in a bank several packages labeled "Cape Fear Money" and "Public Documents" and announced that he had come as an agent for the Bank of Cape Fear and for the United States Treasury Department. For the bank, he sought to make loans, and for the Treasury Department, he was supposedly to force a Natchez bank to repay the government deposits that had been placed there prior to the suspension of specie payments. He exulted in the hospitality shown him: Politicians and bankers wined and dined him; one bank, anxious to obtain a loan from the North Carolina bank, elected Jones's stepfather as its president; Shocco was treated with great deference when he moved his parcels from one bank to another.

Before the end of the year, a federal marshal exposed Jones as a fraud. In slipping away, Shocco did not take time to pick up his "Cape Fear Money" and "Public Documents." When the parcels were opened, the "money" turned out to be blank pieces of paper; the "documents" were newspapers neatly wrapped.[123]

Joseph Seawell Jones's career as a respected citizen was over. He returned to Mississippi, however, and remained there until his death in 1855. The *Columbus Democrat* carried this parting evaluation: "He was a remarkable man in many respects—possessed a vigorous well cultivated intellect and fine social qualities,

121. Published in New York by Scatcherd & Adams, 1838.
122. No book by this title appears to have been published.
123. Jones's Mississippi venture is described in Miles, "Joseph Seawell Jones," pp. 499-506.

but unfortunately, he yielded to the tempting seduction of the Epicurain [*sic*] philosophy and buried a talent which, if properly used might have raised him to distinction. . . . But there was no malice, ill-feeling or selfishness in his hoaxes and humbugs. It was all done for the humor and fun of the thing. . . . ALAS! POOR SHOCCO!!''[124]

It had been supposed that Jones had taken his manuscript collection with him to Mississippi. But such was not the case. When he fled to the Southwest, Jones left a trunk of papers in the possession of a relative, who, upon his own removal from the State, gave them to a third party for safekeeping. The latter custodian was unaware of the nature of the contents of the trunk, but, thinking them valuable, deposited it in the vault of the Raleigh branch of the Bank of Cape Fear. There they remained for more than fifteen years. Meanwhile, in 1845, Governor William A. Graham had been unsuccessful in attempting to persuade Jones to give his collection to the State. Jones notified the governor that the papers were in North Carolina, but he refused to indicate their repository. He also indicated that he had no notion of returning to his native State.[125]

Following Jones's death in 1855, the search was renewed. A note on the question in the *University Magazine* caught the eye of the man who had placed the trunk in the bank and he enlisted the aid of Graham and Swain in persuading the bank to allow an inspection of the trunk. Its contents bared, the bank officials agreed to turn the collection over to the Historical Society at Chapel Hill.[126] Swain, exuberant over having traced

124. Quoted in Miles, "Joseph Seawell Jones," p. 506. Jones himself wrote a glamorized account of his own folly, titled *The Mammoth Humbug; or, The Adventures of Shocco Jones, in Mississippi, in the Summer of 1839, including the History of His Visit to Alabama and "the way he come it over" Certain Members of its Legislature, &c., &c.* (Memphis: No publisher, 1842).

125. Richard T. Brownrigg to Graham, March 20, 1845, in Hamilton, *Graham Papers*, III, 34. Brownrigg, a native and former legislator of North Carolina, had moved to Mississippi. Lyman C. Draper, noted collector, also unsuccessfully sought to locate the Jones papers. See A. E. Henderson to Draper, May 23, 1847, and June 30 and August 12, 1850; T. W. Brown to B. G. Sneed, July 22, 1850; and F. M. Hubbard to Draper, October 19, 1850, in Draper Collection, Kentucky Papers, State Historical Society of Wisconsin, Madison, Wisconsin (microfilm copy in State Archives). This source will be cited hereafter as Draper Collection.

126. Kemp P. Battle, *History of the University of North Carolina* (2 vols.;

the papers to their hiding place, wrote, "It has cost me much labor to make an approximation towards an arrangement of them. . . . The trunk containing them had been opened, and the papers seem to have been thrust in originally in the most careless manner."[127] After a more thorough examination, he found the collection "meager in number and in details in comparison with what Jones descrit [*sic*] of it" had led his readers to believe.[128] Even so, there were varying quantities of manuscripts of or relating to Joseph Graham, Richard Henderson, John Williams, James Iredell, Sr., and Samuel Johnston.[129] Among them were papers which Jones had borrowed from Archibald D. Murphey before the latter's death and never returned.

Though Swain loaned some papers from the Jones collection, at least some were returned to Chapel Hill.[130] Thus the Shocco Jones papers, after being hidden in a bank vault for nearly two decades, joined the Swain collection in their circuitous route during the last half of the nineteenth century.

Raleigh: Edwards & Broughton, 1907-12), I, 487. Cited hereafter as Battle, *History of the University.* See also *North Carolina University Magazine,* V (February, 1856), 1.

127. Swain to Benson J. Lossing, July 4, 1855, in Draper Collection, Kentucky Papers. See also Swain to Lyman C. Draper, June 10, 1855, in same collection.

128. Swain to Draper, July 20, 1855, in Draper Collection, Kentucky Papers.

129. Swain to James J. Iredell, August 8, 1856, in Swain Papers, Southern Historical Collection. See also Lyman C. Draper to Swain, June 20, 1855, and Benson J. Lossing to Swain, August 27, 1855, in same collection.

130. Swain loaned Benson J. Lossing a package of letters of Richard Henderson and John Williams relating to Transylvania. Swain to Lossing, July 4, 1855, and Swain to Draper, July 20, 1855, in Draper Collection, Kentucky Papers. At least some of the letters loaned to Lossing were never returned to Swain, and several of them are now in the Duke University Manuscript Department. Unfortunately the Duke accession records do not reveal from what source they were acquired, thus making impossible a tracing of the letters from 1855 until their acquisition after 1930. Mattie Russell to H. G. Jones, November 16, 1965, in author's possession. The Iredell papers were sent by Swain to Griffith J. McRee who used them in his *Life and Correspondence of James Iredell, One of the Associate Justices of the Supreme Court of the United States* (2 vols.; New York: D. Appleton and Co., 1857-58), cited hereafter as McRee, *James Iredell.* Swain, during a controversy over the ownership of the Iredell papers, made the shortsighted statement that after the McRee publication had been issued, the manuscripts themselves would "be a matter of comparatively little importance. . . ." Swain to James J. Iredell, August 8, 1856, in Swain Papers, Southern Historical Collection. McRee returned the papers to Swain upon publication of his volumes. See also Griffith J. McRee to Swain, March 12, 1857, in Swain Papers, Southern Historical Collection.

VI

The Collection and Publication of the Records

1843-1868

Wheeler, Swain, and Hawks

By 1840, notwithstanding the works of Williamson, Martin, and Jones, North Carolina still had no published history worthy of the name. The defects of their books were so great that it is perhaps fortunate that few North Carolinians read them. Furthermore, Williamson's manuscripts had been lost for all time; Martin's were jealously guarded by the old judge in Louisiana; Jones's were hidden in a bank vault in Raleigh unknown to historians; and Murphey's were partially in the possession of a caretaker in Hillsborough and the remainder piled away in a garret where they were not to be found for fifty years.

Renewed interest developed in the following decade, however, largely through the energetic—and sometimes competing— activities of John Hill Wheeler and David Lowry Swain. They, with the aid of William A. Graham and Francis L. Hawks, were to make lasting contributions to the preservation and dissemination of the history of the State.

JOHN HILL WHEELER

North Carolina historians of the nineteenth century were all interesting characters. John Hill Wheeler was no exception.

He was a legislator, state treasurer, minister to Nicaragua, and the only American historian, north or south, who braved an enemy blockade to go to England and copy the public records in the midst of the Civil War. His history probably still holds the distinction of having perpetuated more errors than any other; but even so, it stands as a forerunner to later and often little improved reference works, and its influence was greater than any other secondary history published in the nineteenth century.

Wheeler was born in 1806 at Murfreesboro, the son of a prosperous shipping merchant. After attending a local academy he graduated from Columbian College[1] in the national capital in 1826 and later attended the University of North Carolina. He studied law and was admitted to the bar in 1827. The same year, at twenty-one years of age, he was elected to the House of Commons from his native Hertford County. He served four terms, then ran unsuccessfully for a seat in Congress. In 1832, President Jackson appointed him clerk of the French spoliation claims commission, and from 1837 to 1841, he was superintendent of the Charlotte branch of the United States Mint. The following year he became a resident of Lincoln County and was elected state treasurer.[2]

It was as state treasurer that Wheeler made his first important contribution to the history of the State. Recalling that the index furnished by Albert Gallatin in 1827 had been relegated to the shelf and that no action had been taken to procure copies of Carolina records in London, Wheeler obtained passage of a legislative resolution on January 26, 1843, authorizing the treasurer to print the index and to deposit the original manuscript and ten copies of the printed volume in the State Library.[3] Publication of the *Indexes to Documents Relative to North Carolina*[4] excited no one more than it did Wheeler himself. He was already gathering historical materials for a proposed book, and now he broadened his plan to include records from England. By mid-1843,

1. Now George Washington University.
2. For biographical sketches of Wheeler, see Johnson and Malone, *D.A.B.*, XX, 50; Ashe, *Biographical History*, VII, 472-78.
3. The resolution is printed in *Laws of 1842-1843*, p. 112.
4. See above, p. 152, n. 80.

he was writing sketches of leading North Carolinians.[5] The following year he wrote the United States Minister to England, Edward Everett, about the colonial documents, and the diplomat appears to have expressed the belief that permission for making copies could be obtained.[6]

Likely at the behest of Wheeler, Governor John M. Morehead suggested in 1844 that the General Assembly provide for the copying the records listed in the *Indexes*. "It is believed that an agent, well qualified for the purpose, can be found who will proceed to England and procure such copies as may be deemed useful, for a sum but little exceeding the expenses of the trip and pay to clerks for making the copies," he said.[7] The agent mentioned may have been Wheeler, who had just been defeated for re-election as treasurer.

Exactly one week later, however, Governor Morehead sent a special message to the Assembly withdrawing his former recommendation. On subsequent reflection, he said, and upon examining into the condition of the public records in the state agencies, he had determined that "we have a work to perform at home, of deeper interest, and of more immediate necessity, than that contemplated by the foreign agency which has been commended to your consideration." He reviewed the eighteenth-century act which required the governor's private secretary to enter into letter books both incoming and outgoing letters of importance. Except for Alexander Martin's manuscripts, Morehead continued, there were few papers of the governors dating prior to 1784. He proposed, therefore, that the Assembly authorize his successor to collect, arrange, and copy such papers as might be needed to complete the series of letter books back to the beginning of the Revolution. "These memorials are now scattered over the state, and gradually disappearing; and like the leaves of the Sibyl, they rise in value as their numbers decrease,"

5. Wheeler to David L. Swain, July 9, 1843, in Swain Papers, State Archives.
6. Everett's reply is mentioned in Wheeler to Swain, August 13, 1844, in Swain Papers, State Archives.
7. Message of Governor John M. Morehead to the General Assembly, November 14, 1844, in Governor's Letter Book, 1844 (G.L.B. 35), State Archives. This message was also printed as Document No. 1, *Public Documents, 1844-1845*.

he said.[8] The Legislature on January 10, 1845, ratified a resolution incorporating the governor's latest suggestion and authorizing an expenditure of $500.[9]

Morehead's change of mind may indeed have been occasioned by his own examination of the records of his office, but it would not be unreasonable to suspect that William A. Graham, who had just been elected to succeed him, and Graham's good friend and fellow Whig, David L. Swain, suggested the importance of first collecting the records at home. The Graham-Swain duo began work in earnest following the new governor's inauguration. Wheeler went back to his home at Beattie's Ford and continued his writing. But, in his words, "conscious of the importance of these papers [listed in the *Indexes*], and their vital connection with the State, I sent a distinguished friend, then in London, a list of such as seemed to me of the most importance, and they have been procured."[10] The friend was George Bancroft, the new minister to England. Thus at his own expense Wheeler procured an unknown number of copies from England which the State had been urged to obtain for twenty years. The copies furnished with Bancroft's assistance were said to have filled 500 manuscript pages and the volume was in existence as recently as 1900.[11] Its present location is not known.

That Wheeler knew that great quantities of uncopied North Carolina materials were still in London was indicated by his

8. Message of Governor John M. Morehead to the General Assembly, November 21, 1844, in Governor's Letter Book, 1844 (G.L.B. 35), State Archives. Printed as Document No. 47, *Public Documents, 1844-1845*.

9. The resolution, ratified January 10, 1845, is printed in *Laws of 1844-1845*, p. 140. The resolution also authorized the governor to collect the original papers or copies of the proceedings of the various town, county, and district committees of safety and the provincial congresses. The collection of the papers of the governors was carried out under Governor Graham with the aid of Swain. See below, p. 186.

10. John H. Wheeler, *Historical Sketches of North Carolina, From 1584 to 1851. Compiled from Original Records, Official Documents, and Traditional Statements. With Biographical Sketches of Her Distinguished Statesmen, Jurists, Lawyers, Soldiers, Divines, Etc.* (2 vols. bound as 1; Philadelphia: Lippincott, Grambo and Company, 1851), I, xviii. Cited hereafter as Wheeler, *Sketches of North Carolina*. See also Riggs, "Acquisition," p. 70.

11. Weeks, in his "Historical Review," p. 36, said, "This volume of transcripts, a folio of some 500 pages, was in existence some 15 years since and was seen by this writer." The material it contained was presumably recopied by Sainsbury and printed in Saunders, *Colonial Records*.

petition to Governor Graham in 1848 in which he renewed his proposal that the State obtain copies of the remaining papers. The governor transmitted the petition to the Assembly which in turn referred it to a special committee. Supporting the petition was a letter from Bancroft in London, addressed to Swain, urging the State to spend a few hundred dollars to copy the Carolina papers.[12] The committee reported that the records of the early history of North Carolina could only be procured in England and that "from this fact it has arisen, that no historian who has hitherto undertaken to write the history of North Carolina, has ever had it in his power to present the truths of history in such a manner as to render justice to the State." It recommended that the assistance of Bancroft be obtained and it proposed a resolution authorizing the governor to procure the needed copies for the archives of the State.[13] Up to $1,000 was authorized for the purpose. The resolution was ratified early in 1849.[14]

Governor Charles Manly in 1849 appointed Swain rather than Wheeler as the agent to go to England under provisions of the resolution, but the university president decided to delay his trip until he could ascertain more accurately what records were in Raleigh.[15] Circumstantial evidence points to a strong suspicion that Wheeler and Swain were working at odds with each other, even though their infrequent correspondence was friendly. For whatever the reason, no action was taken to obtain the copies for several years.

As Wheeler was nearing completion of the manuscript for his history, he sought legislative approval for borrowing books from the library and for using the public records. This simple request was referred to the library committee which examined his unfinished manuscript and gave a glowing report of Wheeler's "patriotic and praiseworthy effort to rescue from oblivion important facts in our early history, and to elevate the character

12. Bancroft to Swain, July 4, 1848, printed in the report of the committee, Senate Document No. 11, *Public Documents, 1848-1849.*

13. Senate Document No. 11, *Public Documents, 1848-1849.*

14. The resolution, ratified January 27, 1849, is printed in *Laws of 1848-1849,* pp. 234-35.

15. Message of Governor Charles Manly to the General Assembly, November 18, 1850, Document No. 1, *Public Documents, 1850-1851.*

and standing of his native State. . . ." The report continued,
". . . the archives of the State and the desks of ancient families
now bury the story of the rise and progress of the State of North
Carolina. Ignorance and wickedness may misrepresent the character of her history, if efforts are not made to break away from
the darkness that surrounds it."[16] The committee recommended
adoption of the resolution to grant his request for access to the
library and public records, and also recommended the purchase
by the State of a number of copies for the State Library upon
publication of the book. The resolution, limited to one year,
was passed, but without reference to the purchase of copies.[17]

Wheeler's *Historical Sketches of North Carolina* was published
in 1851.[18] It was profusely dedicated to George Bancroft ("whose
writings have marked the age in which he lives, and the only
historian who has done justice to North Carolina"), Peter Force
("whose patient labor and indefatigable research have proved
her early patriotism"), David L. Swain ("whose native worth,
whose services and whose talents, are alike her pride and orna-
ment"), and "the Young Men of the State of North Carolina."
Incorporated in the front matter was a full page of testimonials
for the work, including a quotation from the report of the library
committee.

Historical Sketches, comprising two volumes bound as one,
was less a narrative history than a collection of sources. "Series I,"
comprising the narrative for 1584 to 1776, occupied but 83 pages,
and "Series II," for the period 1776 to 1851, filled only 54 pages,
most of the latter being a directory of members of the various
Revolutionary committees of safety and congresses, state officials,
and graduates of the degree-granting colleges. Volume II comprised the greater bulk of the work—480 pages—and contained
county-by-county historical sketches. Each county was given a
brief narrative, often including quotations from other sources,

16. "Report of the Committee on the Library," Senate Document No. 82,
Public Documents, 1850-1851.

17. The resolution, ratified January 24, 1851, is printed in *Laws of 1850-1851,*
p. 826.

18. Volume I comprised 138 pages; Volume II comprised 480 pages, including
the index.

biographical sketches of its important leaders, and, in most cases, a roster of the county's senators and representatives from 1777. The account for Beaufort, one of the older counties, occupied only two full pages, one of which was the list of legislators. Alamance, on the other hand, formed only two years before the work was published, was given 10½ pages, most of which was devoted to documents relating to the Regulator revolt.

Wheeler presented his work with both pride and modesty. In his preface, he confessed his inadequacy for the task, but his efforts, he felt, might "have one effect: they may assist and inspire some abler hand to undertake and complete this work, now so hesitatingly commenced." He continued: "I do not aspire to the position of an historian; that niche in the temple of fame can be occupied by some more worthy person. All that I hope is to present a fair and truthful record of facts, illustrative of the early times of our beloved and venerable State; the names of those who have done her service in the field and senate; and valuable statistical information of her resources and products; thus affording data to other and abler hands to occupy the historic field. . . ."[19] He gave an appraisal of his predecessors who had written on the history of the State. He lightly dismissed Williamson as one "whose labors terminated by an elaborated dissertation on fevers." Martin was referred to as a "foreigner by birth, and the citizen of another State by adoption" who wrote "heavy pages." Jones was dismissed, except for a few of his documents, as a man with a "misplaced temper."[20]

Wheeler gave an account of the State's procurement of the Gallatin list in 1827, of his printing of them in 1843, and of the legislative resolution of 1849 empowering the governor to obtain copies of the documents in London. After describing his own successful efforts to procure through Bancroft copies of certain records in London, he continued:

Aided by these, and by printed works of rare merit, procured from abroad at much labor and expense, as well as by the records of the State Department, to which, by resolution of the last General Assembly (1850), and the courtesy of the present venerable Secretary of State

19. Wheeler, *Sketches of North Carolina*, I, xvii, xix, xx.
20. Wheeler, *Sketches of North Carolina*, I, xvii.

(Wm. Hill), free access was obtained; aided, also, by gentlemen not only of our own State, but of other States, with copies of official documents, and faithful traditional statements, important and interesting, this work, "with all its imperfections on its head," is committed to the press.[21]

In addition to the manuscripts that Bancroft had copied for him in Britain, Wheeler also probably obtained copies from Bancroft's own collection in the United States. His acknowledgment of the aid of Peter Force and David L. Swain also indicates use of the materials collected by them. In a letter accompanying his book, he wrote Force, "your god-child, for whom at the baptismal font you are made to stand, is before you."[22] But much of his materials came from the earlier printed works of Hakluyt, Archdale, Lawson, Chalmers, Williamson, Martin, and Jones. Even so, more meticulously than any previous North Carolina historian, though by no means satisfactorily, Wheeler quoted extensively from unpublished records in the public offices in London and in Raleigh and from private manuscripts, usually identifying sources—sometimes including volume and page numbers—from which he had copied.

The work made no claim to being a great historical product. Its shortcomings were in the main recognized by its author. Coming as it did at a time when political partisanship was a paramount consideration, it is perhaps to be expected that Wheeler's prejudices would show up—so much so that his political opponents dubbed the volume "The Democratic Stud-Book."[23] That the Democratic-controlled General Assembly approved the book, however, may be seen in the report of a legislative committee which in 1852 recommended that the State purchase 150 copies of the work, one copy to go to each executive office, to each clerk of court, and the remaining copies to the State Library.[24] The

21. Wheeler, *Sketches of North Carolina*, I, xviii-xix.

22. Wheeler to Force, July 3, 1851, in Peter Force Manuscripts, Library of Congress, quoted in Bassett, *American Historians*, p. 278. Two months later Wheeler wrote of Force, Bancroft, and Swain as "having stood at the fount as sponsors for my bantling." Wheeler to Force, September 13, 1851, in same source, p. 279.

23. Johnson and Malone, *D.A.B.*, XX, 50.

24. "Report and Resolution in Relation to Wheelers [sic] History of North Carolina," Senate Document No. 31, *Public Documents, 1852.*

Assembly, perhaps more concerned with economy than history, authorized the purchase of only 50 copies for the executive offices and State Library.[25]

Wheeler, his history published, turned again to politics and was elected to the House of Commons from Lincoln County.[26] The following year President Franklin Pierce appointed him as his assistant secretary and Wheeler commenced his duties on May 30, 1854.[27] This appointment probably came through the influence of North Carolina's James C. Dobbin, secretary of the navy. On August 2 of the same year, Pierce appointed Wheeler resident minister of the United States to the Republic of Nicaragua where he served until 1856 when he was recalled because of his alleged involvement in internal political matters.[28] While in Nicaragua, he turned his historical bent toward the history of that country and gathered a mass of information.[29]

After a brief period at his home in Beattie's Ford, Wheeler returned to Washington where Secretary of Interior Jacob

25. The resolution, ratified December 27, 1852, is printed in *Laws of 1852*, p. 647. Fourteen years later the General Assembly was considerably more liberal toward the work of a Virginian who had fired the first shot at Fort Sumter. The Assembly appropriated $143 for the binding of 2,000 copies of Edmund Ruffin's *Sketches of Lower North Carolina*, all but 140 of the copies to be distributed by members of the Legislature. Resolution ratified March 3, 1866, in *Laws of 1866*, p. 137.

From time to time, the State authorized public expenditures for the printing of books relating to North Carolina troops in the various wars. These publications, however, were probably more the result of patriotism and genealogical interest than of purely historical interest. The following volumes were published: Adjutant-General's Department, *Muster Rolls of the Soldiers of the War of 1812: Detached from the Militia of North Carolina, in 1812 and 1814* (1851 and revised edition, 1873); Adjutant-General's Department, *Roster of North Carolina Troops, in the War with Mexico* . . . (1887 and undated supplement); John W. Moore (ed.), *Roster of North Carolina Troops in the War Between the States* (1882, 4 vols.); General Assembly, *Brief Sketches of the North Carolina State Troops in the War Between the States* (1894); Adjutant-General's Department, *Roster of the North Carolina Volunteers in the Spanish-American War, 1898-1899* (1900). In addition, William L. Saunders issued two separate booklets titled *North Carolina Troops in the Continental Line, 1776-1782* and *Abstracts of Records and Documents, Relating to the Colonial History of North Carolina, During the Proprietary Government*, while he was editing the *Colonial Records*.

26. Wheeler was a member of the General Assembly which agreed to purchase his books.

27. John H. Wheeler Diary, May 30, 1854, Library of Congress.

28. Wheeler Diary, August 2, 1854, and *passim*, Library of Congress; Johnson and Malone, *D.A.B.*, XX, 50.

29. His Nicaraguan documents are in the Library of Congress.

Thompson of Mississippi, a native of Caswell County, North Carolina, appointed him superintendent of documents for his department. He accompanied Thompson and President James Buchanan on an official visit to North Carolina in June, 1859.[30]

Wheeler began in 1859 a concerted but unsuccessful effort to obtain an appointment to the faculty of the University of North Carolina at Chapel Hill.[31] As the Civil War approached, he became even more anxious to return to North Carolina. Early in 1861, he wrote Chief Justice Thomas Ruffin: "I wish to return to N.C. You can, my dear Judge, aid me. The Chair of History is vacant at the University. . . . I wish to issue another edition of my History of N.C. and render it more complete and more worthy of public attention. It certainly received a kind reception, far beyond its merits—for an edition of 10,000 copies was sold."[32] Soon after Lincoln's call for troops, Wheeler rushed to Swain a recommendation from former President Buchanan and confided that he needed Swain's help and advice which he could best obtain by being on the faculty at Chapel Hill.[33] But no appointment was forthcoming.

Wheeler was in Washington in the early days of the war, but in August he returned to North Carolina. He brought with him

30. Wheeler Diary, June, 1854, Library of Congress.

31. George Bancroft to David L. Swain, September 12, 1859, in Swain Papers, Southern Historical Collection.

32. Wheeler to Thomas Ruffin, March 24, 1861, in J. G. de R. Hamilton (ed.), *The Papers of Thomas Ruffin* (4 vols.; Raleigh: North Carolina Historical Commission, 1918-20), III, 141. Cited hereafter as Hamilton, *Ruffin Papers*.

Weeks and Henderson claimed that 2,700 copies of *Historical Sketches* were ultimately consigned to a paper mill. They appear to have been mistaken, however, because Wheeler in 1866 wrote that his book "ran through an edition of 10,000 copies in one year" and that he planned to issue a new edition illustrated with steel or copper engravings. Weeks and Henderson may have meant to refer to the posthumous edition of Wheeler's *Reminiscences and Memoirs of North Carolinians*. Stephen B. Weeks, "The North Carolina Historians," *Proceedings and Addresses of the Fifteenth Annual Session of the State Literary and Historical Association [December 1-2, 1914]* (Raleigh: North Carolina Historical Commission, 1915), p. 79; Archibald Henderson, *North Carolina: The Old North State and the New* (2 vols.; Chicago: Lewis Publishing Company, 1941), II, 678; Wheeler to Daniel M. Barringer, November 17, 1866, in Barringer Papers, Southern Historical Collection.

33. Wheeler to Swain, April 19, 1861, in Swain Papers, Southern Historical Collection. Buchanan's letter to Wheeler, dated April 8, 1861, is in Miscellaneous Papers, State Archives.

the manuscript narrative of Colonel David Fanning, a noted Tory during the Revolution. This document may have been obtained from Fanning's descendants in Nova Scotia, because as early as 1855 George Bancroft had suggested to Swain that he inquire about the Fanning papers,[34] and, in 1857, Jared Sparks transmitted a letter confirming that the papers were in Nova Scotia.[35] Bancroft had seen the document and pronounced it genuine and interesting,[36] and, in 1861, Wheeler obtained it from a "Mr. Bliss" of New York.[37] On December 18, 1861, Wheeler sent a copy of the printed "treasure trove" to Swain.[38]

For the next two years Wheeler played no important role in government, but he continued his historical interests. Then, in 1863, at the age of fifty-seven and in the midst of a Civil War, he made a bold decision. Recalling the earlier legislative authorizations, he decided to volunteer to be the State's agent to go to England to copy the remaining colonial records. He preferred an official appointment, but he would be a self-appointed agent if necessary. On July 30, 1863, he recorded in his diary: "Mett at Treasurer's Office Govr Swain and Judge Ruffin; Examined with the latter the resolutions of the Legislature as regards an Agent for Colonial Documents, and then conversed with the Governor, who is willing to give me authority to examine the offices of the Board of Trade in London, and look to the General Assembly for my expenses; if any are incurred."[39] Governor Vance gave him a letter of introduction addressed to James M. Mason, the Confederate agent in London, saying, ". . . any aid you can extend him in furtherance of his [Wheeler's] object will

34. Bancroft to Swain, August 30, 1855, in Swain Papers, Southern Historical Collection.

35. Jared Sparks to Swain, January 23, 1857, in Swain Papers, Southern Historical Collection.

36. Bancroft to Wheeler, April 11, 1861, accompanying Wheeler to Swain, April 19, 1861, in Swain Papers, Southern Historical Collection.

37. Wheeler to Swain, September 17, 1861, in Swain Papers, Southern Historical Collection.

38. Wheeler to Swain, December 18, 1861, in Swain Papers, Southern Historical Collection. The little volume of 86 pages was printed as John H. Wheeler, *The Narrative of Colonel David Fanning* . . . (Richmond: "Printed for Private Distribution Only," 1861). Only fifty copies were issued.

39. Wheeler Diary, July 30, 1863, Library of Congress.

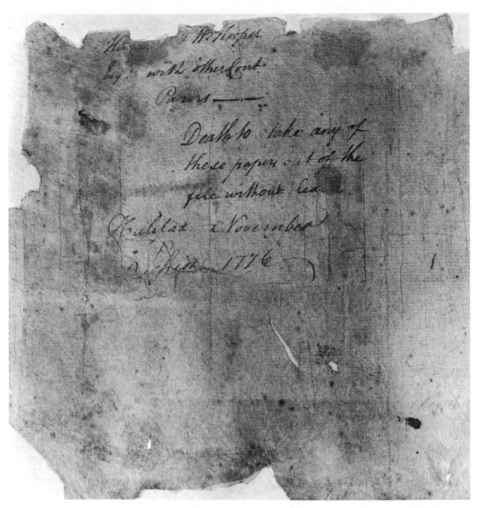

That public officials took seriously the preservation of public records during the Revolution is indicated by this manuscript found among the records of the Provincial Congresses, 1774-1776, in the State Archives. It apparently was used as a wrapper for a packet of papers. It reads: "Hancock & W. Hooper Esqrs. with other Cont. Papers—.—Death to take any of these papers out of the file without leave. Halifax November Session 1776."

Archibald D. Murphey
(c. 1777-1832)

David L. Swain
(1801-1868)

Hugh Williamson
(1735-1819)

Courtesy State Department of Archives and History

be thankfully received and worthily bestowed."[40] Wheeler immediately set out for Wilmington from where the "Ad-Vance" was to sail for Bermuda. From there he wrote Vance thanking him for his letter of introduction and requesting permission to take aboard twenty bales of cotton which he would sell in Bermuda or Nova Scotia to finance his trip.[41] The governor refused the request, however, on grounds that the cotton was needed in North Carolina.[42] Learning that he would need a passport from the Confederate government, Wheeler then rushed to Richmond where he also sought funds for the trip. He decided the best way was to try to sell a North Carolina bond at Halifax, Nova Scotia. If he failed, he would have to return to North Carolina and await action by the General Assembly.[43]

On September 23, 1863, with Wheeler on board, the "Ad-Vance" slipped through the federal blockade off Fort Fisher and three days later arrived in Bermuda. From there Wheeler took passage to Nova Scotia, arriving at Halifax on October 23. In that province he visited relatives and awaited passage to England.[44] From Halifax, Wheeler wrote Governor Vance again, giving a review of past efforts to obtain copies of the English records and requesting the governor to ask the General Assembly at its new session to provide financial assistance for the project.[45] He finally found space on the steamer "Asia" and sailed on November 27, arriving at Liverpool on December 5 and London six days later.

Wheeler took a room at Tavistock Hotel and lost no time in trying to locate Mason. To his dismay, he learned that Mason was in Paris. When Wheeler requested access to the public

40. Vance to Mason, July 30, 1863, original pasted in manuscript volume titled "State Papers on file in Public Rolls of England," in Wheeler Papers, Library of Congress.

41. Wheeler to Vance, August 24, 1863, in Governor's Papers, 1863 (G.P. 168), State Archives.

42. Wheeler Diary, September 2, 1863, Library of Congress.

43. Wheeler to Vance, September 5, 1863, in Governor's Papers, 1863 (G.P. 169), State Archives.

44. Wheeler Diary, September 23 and 26, October 23, and *passim*, 1863, Library of Congress.

45. Wheeler to Vance, November 9, 1863, in Governor's Papers, 1863 (G.P. 169), State Archives.

records, to make matters worse, he was instructed to apply through the United States minister, Charles Francis Adams. As a citizen of the Confederacy, Wheeler would not accept this indignity.[46] He then went to the office of the colonial secretary, the Duke of Newcastle, whom he had met in Washington, but the Duke was away also. Wheeler was advised to apply to Sir Frederic Rogers, under secretary of state for the colonial department, and he wrote to Rogers on December 16, enclosing a copy of Vance's letter to Mason.[47] On the same day he visited Louis Mallet, chief clerk of the Board of Trade, who was polite and indicated his sympathy for Wheeler's request.[48]

Receiving no immediate reply from Rogers, Wheeler decided to sail to France. He located Mason in Paris and visited him on Christmas Day. Mason wrote a note of introduction on the reverse of Governor Vance's letter and requested the assistance of the Foreign Office in Wheeler's mission.[49] While in Paris, Wheeler was entertained by several old friends, including former Governor John M. Morehead.[50]

By January 10, Wheeler was back in London and found a reply waiting for him from the under secretary which indicated a further delay. It was not until January 18 that Rogers finally wrote that the Duke of Newcastle had instructed the master of the rolls to allow Wheeler to make copies of records relating to Carolina as contained in the list furnished by Gallatin in 1827.[51]

The length of time spent by Wheeler in the public offices is not known.[52] He was still researching on February 2 when he wrote Governor Vance that he had "been most assiduous in examining and in some instances having copies taken" of items of value. Many of the records had never been examined before,

46. Wheeler Diary, December 5, 11, 12, 1863, Library of Congress.

47. Wheeler to Sir Frederic Rogers, December 16, 1863, pasted in manuscript volume titled "State Papers," Wheeler Papers, Library of Congress.

48. Wheeler Diary, December 16, 1863, Library of Congress.

49. This letter, bearing Mason's endorsement of January 8, 1864, is pasted in the manuscript volume titled "State Papers," Wheeler Papers, Library of Congress.

50. Wheeler Diary, December 21-31, 1863, Library of Congress.

51. Sir Frederic Rogers to Wheeler, December 29, 1863, and January 18, 1864, pasted in manuscript volume titled "State Papers," Wheeler Papers, Library of Congress.

52. His diary is so badly mutilated that many entries are unreadable.

he stated, and inasmuch as his private funds were exhausted, he expressed the hope that Vance might "feel it a duty to the country to direct me to continue my researches and forward an order to meet the necessary expenses of copying."[53]   Vance, valiantly trying to rally the State behind the ill-fated war effort, appears not to have replied.

Upon completion of Wheeler's research, Alfred Kingston, senior clerk in the Public Record Office, wrote the following testimonial:

Col. Wheeler has been through the Board of Trade Collection relating to North Carolina & has made copious extracts & some copies from some:—The collection consists of 42. Volumes—

Col. Wheeler has also examined all relating to North Carolina in the Collection designated under the Title of "America & West Indies," & has made copious extracts & some copies from same:— These consist of 18 Volumes.

Col. Wheeler has in addition cursorily examined the Board of Trade collections under the Titles of "Proprieties & Plantations General," to see if any paper of importance touching North Carolina might be found in those collections:—These consist of 95 Volumes—

I have much pleasure in bearing testimony to your having (as far as my opportunities of observation would permit) examined the papers above described thoroughly, with a view to correcting—as writer of the History of North Carolina—any inaccuracies or wants in the history of that State which the original papers alone would supply—

I can only add that I have experienced much gratification in being of help to you in an undertaking of so much interest to your State & of such importance to your History.[54]

The manuscript volume prepared by Wheeler in London comprised a combination of indexes, extracts, and copies.   The

53. Wheeler to Vance, February 2, 1864, in Governor's Papers, 1864 (G.P. 174), State Archives. This letter was forwarded to the governor by Woodbury Wheeler, the historian's son, from Fort Caswell. Wheeler was obviously in error when he recorded in his diary under date of January 15, 1865, that "Today year I left England for America." The departure date for Nova Scotia or Bermuda was perhaps March 15, because he arrived in Bermuda on April 12. Woodbury Wheeler to Vance, May 2, 1864, in Governor's Papers, 1864 (G.P. 174), State Archives. See also Wheeler Diary, April 13, 1865, Library of Congress.

54. Alfred Kingston to Wheeler, February 26, 1864, pasted in manuscript volume titled "State Papers," Wheeler Papers, Library of Congress. In his preface Wheeler gave profuse acknowledgments to Kingston and to T. L. Moore of the Rolls House.

compilation was indeed significant. Though some of the documents had already been published, Wheeler's copies were made directly from the manuscripts. He listed such items as the letter patent from Queen Elizabeth to Walter Raleigh, March 26, 1584, "to search, find out and view, any remote heathen Lands, not possessed by any Christian Prince nor inhabited by Christian people," to which Wheeler gave the exact citation: "Domestic State Papers, Elizabeth, March 1584, Vol. 169, No. 37." Among the other materials were copies of documents relating to the Culpeper Rebellion, instructions from the Lords Proprietors, appointments of landgraves, the journal of the commissioners appointed to fix the dividing line between North Carolina and Virginia in 1728, reports of the governors, tax lists of counties, and facsimile signatures of various famous personages. Included also were a number of letters of the last royal governor, Josiah Martin. Some of the copies were made by persons other than Wheeler.

Wheeler arrived back in Bermuda on April 12, 1864.[55] Where he went from there is not known. Then, on January 1, 1865, he turned up in Washington[56] where he became an intimate of Vice-President Andrew Johnson, a native of North Carolina, and other high officials. His diary indicates that he accepted the inevitability of a southern defeat, and, in fact, he was greatly relieved when it came. Soon after the war ended he asked Governor William W. Holden for a testimonial for delivery to Johnson, by then president of the United States. "My condition and the support of my family demands this of me," he wrote.[57] Soon thereafter he was employed by the Treasury Department.[58]

Wheeler spent most of the remainder of his life in Washington engaged in government work and journalism. He continued his historical interests, however, delivering occasional addresses

55. See Wheeler Diary, April 13, 1865, Library of Congress, in which he says he arrived back in Bermuda a year from the previous day.

56. Wheeler Diary, January 1, 1865, Library of Congress. It is not known how Wheeler got to the national capital in the midst of the war. He may have sailed from Bermuda on a Union ship, or perhaps he came back to North Carolina, then went through enemy lines to Washington.

57. Wheeler to Governor William W. Holden, June 24, 1865, in Governor's Papers, 1865 (G.P. 185), State Archives.

58. Irvine, "Letter Books," p. 8.

and writing essays. He gave the commencement address at the University of North Carolina on June 8, 1870, and was elected president of the Historical Society there.[59] Five years later he journeyed to Raleigh for the organization of a new Historical Society.[60] He died December 7, 1882, and two years later his final "essay" on the early history of the State, along with a potpourri of other articles, genealogies, county sketches, and miscellany, was published under the title *Reminiscences and Memoirs of North Carolina and Eminent North Carolinians.*[61]

Before Wheeler's death his library, containing a goodly quantity of North Carolina printed works, including some rare pamphlets,[62] had been sold through a New York auction house. Following his death, it was rumored that his manuscripts were to be given to the State,[63] but the hope was dissipated when word was received that Major Woodbury Wheeler, the historian's son, declined to donate them. The collection was then split, much of it going to the Library of Congress and the remainder being sold in 1899 to Stephen B. Weeks.[64] The Library of Congress has the bulk of these papers now, including Wheeler's diaries, many letters, and much of the historical material and copies that he accumulated.

59. Alexander McIver to Wheeler, June 13, 1870, Document No. 2, *Public Documents, 1870-1871.* For the story of his election as president of the Historical Society, see *North Carolina Standard* (Raleigh, weekly edition), June 22, 1870. Among Wheeler's postwar publications were *The Early Times and Men of Albemarle; An Oration Delivered at Elizabeth City, N.C., on 7th of August, 1877, at request of the Albemarle Historical Society* ([Elizabeth City?], 1877); *The Lives and Characters of the Signers of the Mecklenburg Declaration of Independence, on the 20th of May, 1775; delivered at Charlotte, N.C., on the 24th day of May, 1875, at the request of the Mecklenburg Historical Society* (Charlotte: Observer Book and Job Power Press Print, 1875); and *Sketch of the Life of Richard Dobbs Spaight of North Carolina* (Baltimore: W. K. Boyle, pr., 1880).

60. W. C. Kerr to Cornelia Phillips Spencer, May 6, 1875, in Cornelia Phillips Spencer Papers, State Archives.

61. Published in Columbus, Ohio, by the Columbus Printing Works, 1884.

62. John Hill Wheeler, *Catalogue of the Library of John H. Wheeler, the Historian of North Carolina . . . to be Sold at Auction, Monday Afternoon, April 24, 1882, by Bangs and Co.* (n.p., n.d.).

63. "Report of the Trustees of the Library," February 3, 1883, Document No. 21, *Public Documents, 1883.*

64. Weeks, "Historical Review," 71n.

DAVID LOWRY SWAIN AND FRANCIS LISTER HAWKS

David Lowry Swain heads the list of men who contributed significantly toward preserving North Carolina history during the first three quarters of the nineteenth century. Though he never wrote a history book, he collected the sources that otherwise might have been lost to posterity. He died a disappointed man, but he blazed the trail for others who, through the use of his materials and encouraged by his unfulfilled plans, were to do better what he might have done poorly. His apparent failure may have been one of the good fortunes of history.

Swain was born in Buncombe County, North Carolina, in 1801. His father, a hatter by trade, had migrated from Massachusetts to Georgia where he became a state legislator before moving on to the mountains of North Carolina. Young David was educated locally, spent four months at the University of North Carolina, studied law in Raleigh, and became an ardent Whig. From 1824 to 1826 and from 1828 to 1829, he represented Buncombe County in the General Assembly. For the next three years he was successively a solicitor and judge of the Superior Court, and, in 1832, he was elected governor—the youngest man to hold that position in North Carolina. He was chief executive until 1835 when he was elected president of the University of North Carolina, a position he held until a few months before his death in 1868.[65]

While serving on the bench Swain became involved in his first important historical endeavor. The General Assembly of 1830-31 provided for the publication of the alleged "Mecklenburg Declaration of Independence" and papers pertaining thereto, and Swain was called upon to compile the material and to write the preface. The result was an official state pamphlet unequivocally

65. Among biographical sketches of Swain are the following: Malone, *D.A.B.,* XVIII, 230-31; Ashe, *Biographical History,* I, 447-58; and Zebulon B. Vance, "The Life and Character of Hon. David L. Swain," *North Carolina University Magazine,* I (May, 1878), 73-93. For a scholarly treatment of his early life, see Carolyn A. Wallace, "David Lowry Swain 1801-1835" (unpublished Ph.D. dissertation, The University of North Carolina, 1954). The latter source is cited hereafter as Wallace, "Swain."

endorsing the disputed document.[66] The publication, an answer to Thomas Jefferson's contention that the declaration was a myth, laid the groundwork for a controversy that still rages, but which, happily, is not a fit subject for treatment here.

The following year, while on the judicial circuit, Swain spent his spare time searching the records in county courthouses, roaming the countryside copying tombstone inscriptions, and interviewing local antiquarians. In Perquimans County, he recorded in his diary that "many ancient records, formerly deposited there [in the courthouse] have I understand been either carried of[f] by antiquarians or lost by carelessness & inattention."[67] The concern expressed in that entry was to occupy the attention and energy of David L. Swain for the remainder of his life. In Warren County he visited another young man, Joseph Seawell Jones, whom Swain characterized as having "taken more pains, to obtain information with regard to the early history of the state, than any individual with whom I have met. . . ."[68] A short time later he was eagerly searching the early records in the secretary of state's office in Raleigh,[69] and he entered into a correspondence with Jones, Francis L. Hawks, and others mutually interested in the collection of documentary materials.[70]

Although his gubernatorial administration was primarily concerned with the promotion of education, internal improvements, and other progressive legislation, Swain maintained an active historical interest and was largely responsible for the formation of the North Carolina Historical Society, chartered by the General Assembly early in 1833.[71] The society was never active. At the request of Edward Livingston, the federal secretary of state, Swain attempted to gather historical and statistical data on North

66. Wallace, "Swain," pp. 178 ff. The pamphlet appeared as *The Declaration of Independence by the Citizens of Mecklenburg County, on the Twentieth Day of May, 1775, with Accompanying Documents, and the Proceedings of the Cumberland Association. Published by the governor, Under the authority and direction of the General Assembly of the State of North Carolina* (Raleigh: Lawrence & Lemay, 1831).

67. David Lowry Swain Diary, March 14, 23, 1832, State Archives.

68. Swain Diary, July 3, 1832, State Archives.

69. Swain Diary, no date [p. 77], State Archives.

70. Wallace, "Swain," p. 298.

71. *Private Laws of 1832-1833*, c. 63; Wallace, "Swain," p. 297.

Carolina, but many county court clerks did not return his questionnaire and his tabular study was incomplete.[72]

After assuming the presidency of the University of North Carolina, Swain grew even more interested in the history of the State. In 1836, he inquired about purchasing the Archibald D. Murphey collection of documents,[73] and, in 1841, he was a leader in forming the North Carolina Literary and Historical Society,[74] which, like the Historical Society of eight years earlier, failed to hold a single formal meeting. It did, however, serve as the germ from which was organized in 1844 the State's first active historical association, the Historical Society of the University of North Carolina.[75] Swain not only was the prime organizer of the group; he was also the dominant figure in its activities. Its purposes were to induce the General Assembly to make provision for obtaining copies of records in England relating to North Carolina's colonial history and to collect, arrange, and preserve historical materials.[76] Swain was instrumental in the birth of a literary and historical publication, the *North Carolina University Magazine,* which appeared first in March, 1844, and which became the organ of the senior class and of Swain himself.[77]

Already Swain was collecting historical materials. He corresponded with descendants of Revolutionary War leaders and particularly sought to locate the papers of Richard Caswell and William R. Davie.[78] One of his earliest and most exciting acquisitions was an orderly book of General Hugh Waddell's detachment of forces sent against the Regulators in 1771.[79]

72. Wallace, "Swain," pp. 292 ff.

73. See above, p. 155.

74. Will[iam] H. Haywood, Jr., to Swain, October 25, 1841, in Swain Papers, Southern Historical Collection. See also below, chap. VIII.

75. For a discussion of the formation of this association, see below, chap. VIII.

76. *First Report of the Historical Society of the University of North Carolina, June 4, 1845* (Hillsborough: Dennis Heartt, 1845), p. 1.

77. The magazine, published monthly, was initially printed in Raleigh by Thomas Loring.

78. Richard Washington to Swain, July 23, 1841, and Allen J. Davie to Swain, December 1, 1843, in Swain Papers, Southern Historical Collection.

79. G[riffith] J. McRee to Swain, December 16, 1844, in Swain Papers, State Archives. McRee enclosed a letter from A. A. Brown to Swain, December 16, 1844, in which it was revealed that the orderly book had been preserved in the family of General Thomas Brown, an aide to Waddell in 1771. The volume is now in the War of the Regulation Collection, State Archives.

Swain probably played no direct part in the publication in 1843 of the list of documents furnished by Albert Gallatin in 1827,[80] but he certainly was interested in the turn of events and he was probably influential in persuading Governor Morehead to reverse his previous proposal that an agent be appointed to go to England. As has been pointed out, Morehead in 1844 withdrew that proposal and suggested instead that the correspondence of Governors Caswell, Nash, Burke, and Martin be brought together, arranged, and copied into letter books.[81] The General Assembly adopted a resolution on January 10, 1845, to carry out the latter suggestion. Swain's emphasis on collecting the early records received the encouragement of Jared Sparks who wrote him: "Till the public papers shall be collected & arranged in a suitable order for inspection, it will be impossible for any writer to do justice to the history of any of the States. They are all negligent in this respect. Men are so much absorbed in the vortex of the present, that they forget the past; and yet it is only from the deeds of those who have gone before us, that we have any character as a nation. Take away the history of a people, and what is left but a name?"[82]

William A. Graham, who succeeded Morehead as governor early in 1845, was the son of a famous revolutionary general. He too had exhibited a keen interest in history as early as 1832.[83] As a resident of Hillsborough, a graduate of the University of North Carolina, a fellow Whig, and a member of the General Assembly while Swain was governor, he and Swain had much in common.[84] Their historical comradeship ended only with Swain's death.

80. See above, p. 152, n. 80.
81. See above, p. 168.
82. Jared Sparks to Swain, March 5, 1845, in Swain Papers, Southern Historical Collection.
83. See above, p. 158.
84. For biographical sketches of Graham, see Johnson and Malone, *D.A.B.*, VII, 480-81; and Montford McGehee, *Life and Character of the Hon. William A. Graham. A Memorial Oration* (Raleigh: News Job Office and Book Bindery, 1877). Graham served as United States Senator from 1840 to 1843 and as governor from 1845 to 1849. He was secretary of the navy under President Millard Fillmore and in 1852 was the Whig nominee for vice-president. An opponent of secession, he nevertheless supported the Confederacy following North Carolina's withdrawal from the Union and in 1864 was elected to the Confederate Senate. He died in 1875, shortly after he had been elected president of the new Historical Society.

Governor Graham gratefully accepted Swain's offer of assistance in carrying out the legislative resolution to collect and copy the papers of the revolutionary governors. A succession of letters moved to and from Chapel Hill, and the two friends met frequently to boast of their discoveries. The governor, of course, had access to the records of the executive offices in Raleigh; Swain met with considerable success in acquiring papers in private hands. Many of the governor's hours were spent in the office of "Old Sec"—William Hill, the secretary of state since 1811.[85] There he found the manuscript journals of the provincial congresses, including the one that met in Halifax in April, 1776, and authorized North Carolina's delegates to the Continental Congress to concur in a declaration of independence from Great Britain—the first official action of that nature by any colony.[86] He was delighted with the richness of the State's archives, but found disappointment in the scarcity of records of the district, county, and committees of safety and in the secretary of state's lack of familiarity with his records.

Meanwhile, efforts to acquire materials from private hands were highly successful. It had been assumed that Caswell's papers in the hands of his descendants, but Swain acquired a memorandum in Caswell's handwriting which indicated that he had, in accordance with a legislative resolution, deposited his papers in the office of the secretary of state. Swain immediately communicated with Graham and the governor, after a more thorough search, located them in the secretary's office.[87] Thus a significant group of papers, long sought by historians, was all the while filed away in the public offices in Raleigh. With the Caswell papers were found a few of Governor Burke's. The main body of the Burke papers, however, was indeed in private hands. They belonged to the governor's daughter, Miss Mary Burke, but

85. Graham to Swain, February 8, 1845, in Swain Papers, Southern Historical Collection.

86. This volume is now in the State Archives. Graham also located the manuscript journal of the Provincial Congress of November, 1776, which adopted the first constitution of the State. Hamilton, *Graham Papers*, III, 32.

87. Swain to Graham, January 31, 1845, and Graham to Swain, February 8, September 2, 1845, in Hamilton, *Graham Papers*, III, 21-22, 26-28, 72-73; and Richard Washington to Swain, January 31, 1845, in Swain Papers, Southern Historical Collection. Swain's wife was a granddaughter of Caswell.

were in the custody of Dr. James Webb in Hillsborough. Upon Graham's request, Miss Burke graciously gave them to the State.[88] This collection was one of the most valuable ever to be acquired by the State. Included were many official records removed from the governor's office by Burke, and so rich was the collection that Graham decided to have them (and some others located in Raleigh) entered into two bound letter books without delay. The task was carried on by James G. Scott under Swain's supervision during the summer of 1845.[89] Graham found additional Burke papers in the secretary of state's office, but because the discovery was made too late for them to be copied in the proper chronological sequence in the Burke letter books, they were copied later when Caswell's papers were entered.[90] Thus a reasonably complete story of the administrations of Governors Caswell and Burke resulted from arranging and copying their papers.[91] Few papers of Governor Nash were located until Swain came into possession of a portion of the Archibald D. Murphey collection in 1848. These papers also appeared to have been taken from the governor's office by Burke and possibly were obtained by Murphey from Miss Burke around 1830.[92] The Nash papers were not entered into letter books. A few additional papers of Alexander Martin were found also, but they were not copied inasmuch as Martin's letter book had begun in April, 1782.

Thus Graham and Swain succeeded in a few years in resurrecting many of the papers of the governors and some records of the legislative bodies of the Revolution. These accomplishments were the result of the legislative resolution of 1845, but there also was a valuable by-product of the efforts because through

88. Graham to Miss Mary Burke, February 6, 1845, and Miss Burke to Graham, May 12, 1845, in Hamilton, *Graham Papers,* III, 23-25, 45-46.

89. Swain to Graham, August 22, 1845, in Swain Papers, Southern Historical Collection. Scott was paid $225 for preparing the two volumes. Hamilton, *Graham Papers,* III, 169.

90. Graham to Swain, September 2, 1845, in Swain Papers, Southern Historical Collection. See also Hamilton, *Graham Papers,* III, 169. The Caswell letter books were copied in a handwriting other than Scott's.

91. The letter books and many of the original papers are now in the State Archives. Some of the originals, however, went the way of other materials in the Swain collection. See below, chap. VIII.

92. Swain to Graham, May 13, 1848, in Hamilton, *Graham Papers,* III, 223.

the campaign to locate the papers of the governors many other significant historical materials were acquired. Among the Burke papers Swain discovered one of the most significant documents ever to find its way to North Carolina. It was the very first draft of John Adams' four versions of a manuscript prepared in March, 1776, entitled "Thoughts on Government" upon whose principles the constitutions of most of the original states were based. William Hooper and John Penn, two of North Carolina's delegates to the Continental Congress, preparing to return to Halifax for a meeting of the Provincial Congress, asked Adams for his advice on a state constitution. Adams "concluded to borrow a little Time from his Sleep and accordingly wrote with his own Hand, a Sketch, which he copied, giving the original to Mr. Hooper and a Copy to Mr. Penn, which they carried to Carolina."[93] The original manuscript[94] was probably given to Burke by Hooper upon their return to North Carolina and it had reposed among Burke's papers thereafter.[95] Thus Graham and Swain acquired for the State one of the most valuable historical documents in American history.

93. Lyman H. Butterfield (ed.), *The Adams Papers: Series I, Diary and Autobiography of John Adams* (4 vols.; Cambridge: Belknap Press of Harvard University Press, 1961), III, 331n. Cited hereafter as Butterfield, *Adams Diary*.

94. Adams later made two other copies from memory, one for George Wythe of Virginia and one for Jonathan Dickinson Sergeant of New Jersey. The Penn copy —the only one made directly from the original given to Hooper—is now in the Massachusetts Historical Society. The Wythe version was printed; the Sergeant copy has been lost.

95. Butterfield, *Adams Diary*, III, 331-32n; Swain to Graham, June 9, August 22, 1845, and Graham to Swain, August 26, 1845, in Hamilton, *Graham Papers*, III, 47, 65-66, 68. The Adams document, unsigned, undated, and not addressed, was copied into the Burke letter book. The original document of six pages remained in Swain's possession until his death and eventually came into the possession of the North Carolina Historical Commission (now the State Department of Archives and History) where it formed a part of the David L. Swain Papers. Scholars used the letter book copy, but for many years the original was not recognized for its significance. In 1961, during the publication of the Adams papers, correspondence between the State Department of Archives and History, the Southern Historical Collection, and Lyman H. Butterfield, editor of the project, resulted in the recognition of the document as the "very first version of John Adams' influential plan and the germ of his first important publication on constitutional law. . . ." Lyman H. Butterfield to H. G. Jones, November 8, 1961, in State Archivist's Files, State Archives. For a brief story of the rediscovery, see Lyman H. Butterfield, "Documentary Enterprises: Guidance by Remote Control," *American Archivist*, XXV (July, 1962), 393-94.

Another rare record was extracted by Swain from an old house in Hillsborough. It was a British orderly book covering military operations in 1780-81 in New York, Virginia, and South Carolina, and including Cornwallis' march through South Carolina and North Carolina to and including the battle of Guilford Courthouse.[96] The discovery of a British military document was an exciting find, and Graham speculated that it may have been at one time in the possession of Edmund Fanning, a Loyalist leader who had earlier been a target of the ire of the Regulators at Hillsborough.[97]

Some of the long-sought papers of Archibald D. Murphey were finally acquired for the Historical Society at Chapel Hill in 1848,[98] but Graham and Swain were unsuccessful at the time in obtaining the papers of Judge Martin[99] and of Joseph S. Jones.[100] These two failures, however, were offset by greater successes in acquiring other significant acquisitions which were added to the Historical Society's collection.[101] The interests of the society, therefore, benefited greatly from the official encouragement of the legislative resolution of 1845 and from the interest and activity of Swain's friend in the governor's office. But the collection of source materials and the preparation of the letter books did not end their interest. For instance, the discovery in 1845 by William H. Foote of an "old manuscript" purporting to give

96. Swain to Graham, January 24, 1845, in Hamilton, *Graham Papers*, III, 17. The volume was found among the papers of Mrs. Joseph Watters in Hillsborough. Graham to Miss Mary Burke, February 6, 1845, in Hamilton, *Graham Papers*, III, 24. It probably had once been among William Hooper's papers.

97. Graham to Swain, February 8, 1845, in Swain Papers, Southern Historical Collection. The volume is now in the State Archives. It was edited by A. R. Newsome and printed as "A British Orderly Book, 1780-1781," in the *North Carolina Historical Review*, IX (January, 1932), 57-78; IX (April, 1932), 163-86; IX (July, 1932), 273-98; and IX (October, 1932), 366-92. Newsome was not aware of its origin.

98. Swain to Graham, May 13, 1848, in Hamilton, *Graham Papers*, III, 223-26. See also above, pp. 155-56.

99. Francois Xavier Martin to Graham, March 29, 1845, Graham to Robert Nash Ogden, June 21, 1847, and Nash to Graham, July 8, 1847, in Hamilton, *Graham Papers*, III, 35, 199-200, 201-2.

100. Richard T. Brownrigg to Graham, March 20, 1845, in Hamilton, *Graham Papers*, III, 34-35.

101. The Martin and Jones collections were later acquired by Swain. See above, pp. 143, 164.

more proof of the "Mecklenburg Declaration of Independence"[102] resulted in an appropriation of $600 by the General Assembly for a revised edition of the pamphlet on that subject previously published in 1831, along with the journals of the Revolutionary congresses and other documents relating to the early history of the State.[103] No publication, however, was issued.

Meanwhile, Swain gave serious consideration to going to England to copy records in the public offices. He made inquiries in Washington and was informed that he might be given an honorary commission as a bearer of dispatches to provide his passage.[104] Nothing came of the idea.

But Swain certainly intended that someone should go. He corresponded with George Bancroft, then American minister to Great Britain, who wrote that copies of the most important materials in the State Paper Office could be made for a few hundred dollars.[105] Swain permitted his friend, John H. Wheeler, to attach Bancroft's letter to Wheeler's petition to the governor, who transmitted it to the General Assembly.[106] As has already been noted, the Assembly adopted a resolution early in 1849 authorizing the governor to obtain Bancroft's assistance in acquiring copies of materials in London pertaining to North Carolina, and authorizing an expenditure of up to $1,000 for the purpose.[107]

Charles Manly, a close friend of Swain's who succeeded Graham as governor in January, 1849, immediately appointed the university president as historical agent to carry out the provisions of the latest resolution. Swain, however, still vacillating, decided again that it was more important first to ascertain what materials

---

102. Graham to Swain, November 10, 1845, in Governor's Letter Book, 1845 (G.L.B. 36), State Archives. Foote, a clergyman, wrote *Sketches of North Carolina, Historical and Biographical* (New York: Robert Carter, 1846), largely a history of the Presbyterians in North Carolina.

103. The resolution, ratified January 18, 1847, is printed in *Laws of 1846-1847*, p. 244.

104. T. L. Clingman to Swain, September 2, 1847, in Swain Papers, State Archives.

105. Bancroft to Swain, July 4, 1848, in Swain Papers, Southern Historical Collection.

106. Message of Governor Graham to the General Assembly, December 19, 1848, in Governor's Letter Book, 1848 (G.L.B. 38), State Archives.

107. The resolution, ratified January 27, 1849, is printed in *Laws of 1848-1849*, 234-35. See also above, p. 170.

were already available in North Carolina.[108] That he had earlier considered the plan for procuring copies from England a priority item was indicated in an exchange of letters between Swain and C. Frank Powell in 1849. Powell wrote from Washington that he had had experience in copying records in the British offices and would spend several months in London on his way to Muscat, where he was to become a United States consul. He offered to make the copies of all records designated by Swain or Bancroft for £175 (about $800).[109] Swain replied that the price was too high, and Powell offered to bargain.[110] A further exchange of letters merely confused the negotiations, particularly when Swain indicated that he himself would probably go to London.[111] Swain appears to have wanted to go abroad himself, just as Wheeler wanted to go, and he was reluctant to permit another copyist to do the work. With Manly as governor, he assumed that the General Assembly would continue the authorization.

Whatever the reason for his indecision, Swain energetically began his work to determine just what materials were within the bounds of the State. He pulled from his own papers his diary written in 1832 when on the judicial circuit and noted that he had seen in the courthouses of the counties of the Albemarle area records of the General Court dating back to the seventeenth century. Inasmuch as the General Court was actually a body of the entire Province rather than merely of the old precincts—now counties—Swain argued that these records should be placed in the secretary of state's office. He also urged the rescue of neglected precinct and county records.[112] Late in 1850, Governor Manly, in explaining the delay in carrying out the 1849 resolution, told

108. Swain to R. R. Heath, August Moore, and Robert T. Paine, February 6, 1849, in Governor's Letter Book, 1849 (G.L.B. 39), State Archives.

109. C. Frank Powell to Swain, January 26, 1849, in Swain Papers, State Archives.

110. Powell to Swain, March 31, 1849, in Swain Papers, State Archives. Swain's letter of March 1, referred to by Powell, has not been found.

111. Powell to Swain, April 10, 1849, in Swain Papers, State Archives.

112. Swain to R. R. Heath, August Moore, and Robert T. Paine, February 6, 1849, in Governor's Letter Book, 1849 (G.L.B. 39), State Archives. It is interesting to note that the records of the General Court and other provincial courts were not turned over to the State until the twentieth century. The last large quantity of these records was acquired by the State Archives from a bank vault in Edenton in 1961.

the Assembly, "Considerable, and not unsuccessful, attention has been devoted to domestic research, and the materials thus obtained will be preserved for the use of our future historian. The agent [Swain] informs me that he has acquired such knowledge of the sources which exist in our own country as will enable him to examine with proper intelligence the archives of the Mother Country; and that he will very cheerfully enter upon the duty at an early day if such shall be the pleasure of the General Assembly."[113]

Early in 1851, the library committee, chaired by Calvin H. Wiley, appears to have reviewed Swain's work and made a personal examination of the records in the secretary of state's office. The committee reported that it found the colonial records "in an unsafe condition—the manuscripts are becoming illegible, are liable to be so destroyed by mice and moths, by fire and other possible accidents." It recommended that Secretary of State William Hill and State Librarian James F. Taylor be instructed to have printed the journals of the general assemblies and congresses for the colonial and revolutionary periods.[114] The Assembly partially followed the recommendation and instructed the governor, secretary of state, treasurer, and comptroller to contract for the printing and binding of 150 copies of the journals and authorized an expenditure of up to $1,000.[115]

The 1849 resolution with its appropriation remained in effect, but Swain believed that the amount was insufficient to permit him to go to England. He still was unwilling to have someone else do the job, however. During 1851 and 1852, he concentrated his efforts on acquiring materials for the Historical Society at Chapel Hill and carried on a frequent correspondence with Benson J. Lossing, the author, to whom Swain furnished materials relating to North Carolina. David Reid succeeded Manly as governor in 1851 and, concerned primarily with non-historical

113. Governor Manly's message to the General Assembly, November 18, 1850, in Governor's Letter Book, 1850 (G.L.B. 39), State Archives.

114. "Report from the Committee on the Library," House Document No. 90, *House and Senate Documents, 1850-1851.*

115. The resolution, ratified January 29, 1851, is printed in *Laws of 1850-1851,* pp. 508-9.

William L. Saunders
(1835-1891)

Walter Clark
(1846-1924)

John H. Wheeler
(1806-1882)

Courtesy State Department of Archives and History

"Preface" to the volume of transcripts entitled "State Papers on
File in Public Rolls of England, relative to Colonial History of
North-Carolina, collected by J. H. Wheeler," Wheeler Papers in
the Manuscripts Division, Library of Congress.

matters, was apparently relieved when he explained to the General Assembly that he had declined to appoint an agent to procure copies from England because the $1,000 appropriated in 1849 was insufficient. He left the decision of whether to enlarge and continue the appropriation up to the Assembly.[116] No further official action was taken until the final days of Reid's term when, apparently without the governor's recommendation, the General Assembly made a magnanimous gesture toward the efforts to obtain copies from England. It authorized the agent to receive payment for traveling and other expenses, including clerk hire, should he decide to go to England. Here, at last, was virtually a carte blanche for procuring the early records of North Carolina. No previous legislative body had been so generous.[117]

Thomas Bragg, who succeeded Reid as governor soon after the resolution was ratified in 1855, reappointed Swain as the historical agent.[118] Bancroft continued to recommend that the copies be procured through a clerk in the British offices,[119] but Swain again expressed his indecision as to the necessity of obtaining copies from London at all. He wrote the governor: "I am taking the requisite pains to render myself familiar with the materials for history at my command, so as to be able in due time to form a satisfactory opinion, whether it will be indispensable to the accomplishment of the liberal purposes of the legislature that an agent shall visit the mother country and search the ample and well arranged repositories there, public and private, for records, books and manuscripts, not to be obtained on this side of the Atlantic."[120] Two days later, however, he wrote to Secretary of the Navy James C. Dobbin, a North Carolinian, asking how he should proceed in obtaining access to the English

116. Governor Reid's special message to the General Assembly, December 17, 1852, in Governor's Letter Book, 1852 (G.L.B. 40), State Archives.

117. The resolution, ratified January 9, 1855, is printed in *Public Laws of 1854-1855*, p. 127.

118. Bragg to Swain, May 14, 1855, in Governor's Letter Book, 1855 (G.L.B. 43), State Archives.

119. Bancroft to Swain, June 25, 1855, in Swain Papers, Southern Historical Collection.

120. Swain to Governor Bragg, November 20, 1855, in Governor's Letter Book, 1855 (G.L.B. 43), State Archives.

records,[121] and the very next day he sent a lengthy letter to Peter Force for similar advice.[122] Dobbin replied that he would be happy to assist in the laudable enterprise, but that the time was not propitious for opening the subject with Sir John Crampton, the British minister to the United States, because of tension between the two countries.[123] Swain renewed his inquiry early in 1856, but Dobbin replied that relations with Crampton still were not good enough to ask a favor of him. He suggested that Swain communicate with George M. Dallas, newly appointed United States minister to England,[124] and Swain wrote Dallas a few days later, enclosing a letter of introduction furnished by Dobbin. Again Swain indicated that he wanted to study further the materials at home and that even if he went to England, it would not be before May, 1857.[125] Meanwhile, Dobbin had written Dallas on the subject and Dallas' reply in August was somewhat noncommittal, noting that a clerk would be reluctant to make a private search without assurances of compensation.[126] A few days later, however, Dallas wrote that he had induced Horatio Gates Somerby, who had been engaged in copying early records for the State of Maine, to examine the State Paper Office and some other repositories and that Somerby had reported that there were many records relating to North Carolina not listed in the index obtained by Albert Gallatin in 1827, that South Carolina had already obtained copies of many of the Carolina papers and Swain might be able to copy those without going to England, and that papers could be obtained from the British offices but

121. Swain to Dobbin, November 22, 1855, in David Lowry Swain Papers, Manuscript Department, Duke University Library, Durham. This source is cited hereafter as Swain Papers and the repository as Duke University.

122. Swain to Force, November 23, 1855, in Hamilton, *Ruffin Papers*, II, 501-4.

123. Dobbin to Swain, December 4, 1855, in Swain Papers, Southern Historical Collection.

124. Dobbin to Swain, February 26, 1856, printed in *Report of Hon. David L. Swain, LL.D., on the Historical Agency for Procuring Documentary Evidence of the History of North-Carolina* (Raleigh: Holden & Wilson, 1857), p. 9. Cited hereafter as *Swain Report, 1856*.

125. Swain to Dallas, March 1, 1856, in Swain Papers, Southern Historical Collection.

126. Dallas to Dobbin, August 18, 1856, printed in *Swain Report, 1856*, pp. 13-14.

that the cost would be high. Somerby also suggested that, if Swain could not come to England, he might have a copyist paid £100 in advance and placed under his, Somerby's, supervision.[127]

Meanwhile, Peter Force had been brought into the discussion and he urged that the purposes of the legislative resolution be carried out. He wrote, ". . . it will be a proud day for North Carolina when his [Swain's] suggestions are carried into full effect. Every public paper in England that relates to the State should be obtained . . . and this can only be done in the employment of an intelligent and Faithful Agent."[128] If Swain could not go to England himself, then Force recommended that Henry Stevens, an American who was rapidly gaining a reputation for procuring copies for both public and private interests, be employed. No other person, Force felt, would be as satisfactory. Earlier, Jared Sparks had strongly recommended that Swain himself go to England. He wrote, ". . . I deem it absolutely essential that you, or some other agent from this country, should make a personal research in the offices, and I am sure that no instructions to any person there, however precise, will secure a thorough and complete examination."[129] Francis L. Hawks also continued to urge that the copies be obtained, noting that his own researches in 1836 proved to him that vast numbers of North Carolina materials were available in London.[130]

Late in 1856, Swain prepared a detailed report of his accomplishments which Governor Bragg submitted to the General Assembly.[131] In addition to reporting on materials collected, Swain suggested a continuation of the agency and asked for authority to visit the public offices and historical societies of neigh-

127. Dallas to Dobbin, August 22, 1856, printed in *Swain Report, 1856*, pp. 14-15.

128. [Peter Force] to [J. C. Dobbin], August 22, 1856, in Swain Papers, Duke University.

129. Sparks to Swain, February 1, 1856, printed in *Swain Report, 1856*, p. 16. Sparks offered to allow Swain to copy six volumes of the papers of George Chalmers which he had purchased in London.

130. Hawks to Swain, October 25, 1856, printed in *Swain Report, 1856*, pp. 18-19.

131. Swain dated his report December 1, 1856, but the governor's cover letter was dated November 21, 1856. Governor's Letter Book, 1856 (G.L.B. 43), State Archives; *Swain Report, 1856*, p. 4.

boring states.[132] Swain appeared before a special committee appointed to study his report,[133] and upon recommendation of the committee, the Assembly adopted a resolution allowing him to examine the records in other states as well as in the mother country, with his expenses to be taken care of by the State, and directing him to report to the Assembly at an early date.[134]

With this added endorsement, Swain now prepared and printed a circular letter which he sent to selected "historiographers" around the State. In it he called attention to the resolution which gave him authority to obtain copies of materials relating to North Carolina history in other states and in England, and asked for assistance in locating other documentary evidence within North Carolina. He listed a variety of topics on which materials were desired, ranging from accounts of Indian tribes to church records, in addition to private and public records. He also urged each addressee to prepare a historical sketch of his own county, using Wheeler's *Sketches* as a starter, correcting and adding as necessary.[135]

Even before sending out his printed circular, Swain continued to be successful in acquiring documents. He drew from "their hiding place" the collection of Joseph Seawell Jones which contained papers obtained from, among others, the Iredells, Hendersons, and Archibald D. Murphey.[136] He also acquired some of the Harnett family papers (probably from the Jones collection

132. *Swain Report, 1856*, p. 8. Swain corresponded with officials in South Carolina and Virginia. He sought permission to copy the records that South Carolina had already obtained from England. He was first refused permission, but later was told that he could copy them if British authorities had no objection. See R. W. Gibbes to Swain, October 6, 1856, and William J. Rivers to Swain, April 11, 1857, November 6, 1858, in Swain Papers, Southern Historical Collection. See also Swain to Conway Robinson, February 2, 1857, in the same source.

133. Swain to Governor Bragg, January 1, 1857, in Governor's Letter Book, 1857 (G.L.B. 43), State Archives.

134. The resolution, ratified January 8, 1857, is printed in *Public Laws of 1856-1857*, p. 71.

135. There are extant at least two circulars, quite similar. One, dated January 20, 1857, is in Hamilton, *Ruffin Papers*, II, 541-42; another, dated February [10], 1857, is in Henry T. Shanks, *The Papers of Willie Person Mangum* (5 vols.; Raleigh: State Department of Archives and History, 1950-56), V, 331-32. The latter source will be cited hereafter as Shanks, *Mangum Papers*.

136. Lyman C. Draper to Swain, June 20, 1855, in Swain Papers, Southern Historical Collection.

also) which he loaned to Sparks and Bancroft;[137] a copy of the letter book to Thomas Pollock, from Thomas P. Devereux;[138] a manuscript copy of the laws of 1715 from William B. Rodman;[139] and additional Iredell papers from Griffith John McRee, to whom Swain had loaned other Iredell papers from the Jones and Murphey collections.[140] He also obtained some official records from the county courthouses, including the proceedings of the Pitt County Committee of Safety from Greenville.[141] But with his success Swain also received reports of the disappearance of valuable papers. From Edenton he heard of the destruction of some of the revolutionary period papers by a former clerk of the county court;[142] from New Bern came the painful story that George E. Badger, prominent North Carolinian who served as secretary of the navy in 1841, had in his youth made kites out of the correspondence of several leading revolutionary figures, that the early records of the Episcopal church in New Bern had been used for wrapping paper "& other vile purposes," and that the second wife of James Davis, the colony's first printer, "in one of her fits . . . consigned the whole of them [Davis' papers] to the flames."[143]

In 1856, Swain obtained for the State a copy of another valuable record. During a visit to Harvard College, William A. Wright, a resident of Wilmington, North Carolina, discovered

137. Bancroft to Swain, December 5, 1855, in Swain Papers, Southern Historical Collection.

138. *Swain Report, 1856*, p. 6.

139. *Swain Report, 1856*, p. 7.

140. Griffith John McRee to Swain, January [n.d.], 1856, in Swain Papers, Southern Historical Collection. McRee and Swain corresponded frequently. Of interest is McRee's statement that he sent some original manuscripts directly to the printer rather than having them copied for that purpose. This appears not to have been an uncommon practice in the nineteenth century. No wonder so many errors in transcriptions occurred! See McRee to Swain, February 8, 1856, and March 12, 1857, in Swain Papers, Southern Historical Collection.

141. E. C. Yellowly to Swain, April 17, 1857, in Swain Papers, Southern Historical Collection. A fragment of the cover of this document has been found in the Swain Epistolary Correspondence in the North Carolina Collection. The remainder of the volume is in the State Archives.

142. E. C. Hines to Swain, February 15, 1857, in Swain Papers, Southern Historical Collection. See above, p. 124.

143. James W. Bryan to Swain, February 26, 1857, in Swain Papers, Southern Historical Collection.

that Jared Sparks had purchased from Henry Stevens, the London bookseller, the original letter book of Colonial Governor William Tryon.[144] Originally two volumes—one containing letters and another the minutes of the Council—the documents had been bound together by Stevens and the combined volume totaling 523 pages was placed by Sparks in the Harvard College Library.[145] Both Wright and Swain enlisted George Bancroft's aid in seeking permission from Sparks to have a copy made,[146] and Sparks not only gave the permission but supervised the copying by James W. Harris.[147] The General Assembly quickly appropriated $150 for the purpose,[148] and the bound copy was ready for Swain late in 1855.[149] It was delivered to Governor Bragg with Swain's report in November, 1856.[150] Thus through the generosity of a New England historian, North Carolina came into possession of a copy of one of its most significant colonial documents.

Another of Swain's efforts appears to have failed. In 1856, he urged Governor Bragg to direct his private secretary and the heads of state agencies to collect, to arrange in chronological order, and to prepare descriptive guides to the public records in their possession.[151] Though no proof has been found to indicate widespread compliance, the fact that Quentin Busbee was compensated for collecting and arranging "in the archives of the senate, all the records and papers belonging thereto" may indicate that Bragg made a halfhearted attempt to carry out the suggestion.[152]

Swain's plans for going himself or sending an agent to England

144. William A. Wright to Swain, January 30, 1854, in Swain Papers, Southern Historical Collection.

145. Sparks to Swain, June 6, 1855, in Swain Papers, Southern Historical Collection.

146. Swain's letters have not been found, but Bancroft's replies, dated October 27 and November 18, 1854, are in Swain Papers, Southern Historical Collection.

147. Sparks to Swain, May 25, June 6, 1855, in Swain Papers, Southern Historical Collection.

148. The resolution, ratified January 9, 1855, is printed in *Public Laws of 1854-1855*, p. 127.

149. Sparks to Swain, October 1, November 4, 28, 1855, in Swain Papers, Southern Historical Collection. Harris was paid $100.00 for making the copy and the cost of the binding was $8.00.

150. *Swain Report, 1856*, p. 51. The volume is now in the State Archives.

151. Swain to Bragg, January 1, 1857, in Governor's Letter Book, 1857 (G.L.B. 43), State Archives.

152. Weeks, "Historical Review," p. 60n.

for copies were abruptly reversed in 1858. This reversal was caused by Francis Lister Hawks, a lawyer-clergyman-historian who published in that year the second volume of his *History of North Carolina*.[153] Whereas Swain and Governor William A. Graham had teamed up to breathe new life into the movement to collect documentary materials in 1845, Swain now entered into an agreement with Hawks to bring out a publication to be entitled *Documentary History of North Carolina*.

Hawks was a native of New Bern and a graduate of the University of North Carolina. He studied law, served as reporter for the North Carolina Supreme Court, edited a series of volumes of reports of court decisions, and represented the borough of New Bern in the House of Commons in 1821. He gave up the practice of law to enter the Episcopal ministry. He served in various cities of the North, declined election as bishop in two different states, helped found the predecessor institution to Tulane University in New Orleans, and became a famed orator, writer, and church historian.[154]

In 1835, the General Convention of the Episcopal Church appointed Hawks to go to England to obtain copies of records relating to the Anglican Church in America. His mission was given a friendly reception by the Bishop of London, who helped him to gain access to the archiepiscopal library of manuscripts at Lambeth Palace, the records at Fulham Palace belonging to the See of London, and the documents in the office of the Society for Propagation of the Gospel in Foreign Parts. He also was admitted to the public offices, and he returned with seventeen folio volumes of manuscripts, mostly relating to the early ecclesiastical affairs of the eastern seaboard.[155] Among them were many letters and reports sent to England by government officials and Anglican clergymen in North Carolina. His trip was made during a period when little interest was being shown in North Carolina concern-

153. Francis L. Hawks, *History of North Carolina: With Maps and Illustrations* (2 vols.; Fayetteville: E. J. Hale & Son, 1857-58). Cited hereafter as Hawks, *History of North Carolina*.

154. For a biographical sketch of Hawks, see Evert A. Duyckinck, *A Memorial of Francis L. Hawks, D.D., LL.D.* (New York: [n.p.], 1871). Cited hereafter as Duyckinck, *Memorial*. See also Johnson and Malone, *D.A.B.*, VIII, 416-17.

155. Duyckinck, *Memorial*, p. 17.

ing its history, but at least one citizen suggested that the State purchase the copies relating to North Carolina.[156]

Hawks lost no time in making use of the manuscripts, publishing within the year the first of his proposed state-by-state ecclesiastical histories.[157] Hawks was diverted from his plan and his North Carolina manuscripts remained unused for twenty years. These North Carolina papers consisted of about 650 pages, and, though most of them related to the Anglican Church, Hawks had copied some letters of Royal Governors Tryon and Martin, and, in addition to the copies obtained in England, he had come into possession of original materials on North Carolina history from various sources, including some papers found among those of his grandfather.[158] As his collection grew, Hawks determined to write a full-scale history of his native state, rather than just an ecclesiastical history. Even more than Chalmers and others before him, Hawks determined to allow the documents themselves to tell the history insofar as possible. His first volume, published in 1857, consisted largely of reprints of documents, mostly from Hakluyt, relating to exploration and settlement in the sixteenth century. Interspersed in the reprints by means of brackets were Hawks's commentaries.

Upon publication of his first volume, Hawks turned his attention to the second. He encouraged Swain to obtain the copies from London which he recalled seeing when he was there in 1836.[159] By special resolution of the General Assembly, the public records and State Library were opened to him, and he spent some time in Raleigh for that purpose.[160] While Hawks was in North

156. *Raleigh Register and North Carolina Gazette* (weekly edition), February 12, 1838.

157. His *Contributions to the Ecclesiastical History of the United States: Virginia* appeared in 1836.

158. Hawks to Swain, December 31, 1856, in Swain Papers, Southern Historical Collection. Years earlier, Hawks had found among his grandfather's papers the original letter book of Governor Martin, which he deposited in the office of the secretary of state in Raleigh, retaining a copy of it. Hawks's grandfather, John Hawks, architect of Tryon Palace, came to the Province with William Tryon.

159. Hawks to Swain, October 25, 1856, in Swain Papers, Southern Historical Collection.

160. The resolution, ratified December 23, 1856, is printed in *Public Laws of 1856-1857*, p. 73.

Carolina, he and Swain had ample opportunity to discuss their historical interests, each presumably encouraging the other. Hawks returned to New York and in 1858 his second volume was published. Unlike the earlier volume, this one made use of many previously unpublished manuscript sources, including various records found in the State's executive offices and others copied in England, as well as some of Chalmers' papers then in the hands of Bancroft, who loaned them to Hawks. The volume, covering the period from 1663 to 1729, was superior to any history thus far published. Swain read the copy and approved it prior to publication.[161]

Notwithstanding Hawks's prominent position and fame, he never attained financial affluence due partially to several short-lived ventures into publication and education. He was in particularly bad financial condition in the mid-1850's when he offered to sell his private library (which he called "one of the most valuable private libraries of American History") to the Historical Society of the University of North Carolina for $5,000.[162] The expense of his two volumes on North Carolina impoverished him even more. Now, his proposed third volume would have to depend heavily upon the materials in Raleigh and at Chapel Hill, and Hawks sought means of combining his research with an occupation. In 1858, he offered his services to the University of North Carolina so that he could make use of the materials in the State. Otherwise, he said, he would not continue his volumes. He wrote, "It is better that the story should remain untold, than that it should be told defectively. I can write *a book now,* and call it the 3d. Vol. of N. Carolina's History; but will it be? No one knows better than you do how much care must be taken in the examination of original authorities. . . ."[163]

During the year, Hawks and Swain determined to combine their efforts toward producing a monumental documentary history of the State. As early as 1856, Hawks had alluded to the

161. Hawks, *History of North Carolina,* II, 8-9.
162. Hawks to Swain, December 31, 1856, in Swain Papers, Southern Historical Collection. The Historical Society was financially unable to accept the offer.
163. Hawks to Swain, August 16, 1858, in Swain Papers, Southern Historical Collection.

desirability of their collaboration.[164] The association of the two men had a decided effect upon the previous plans of each individually. Hawks, for his part, gave up his plan to continue his own history series. And Swain, now with access to the materials collected by Hawks and the permission of George Bancroft to copy his great collection relating to North Carolina,[165] began to doubt the necessity of going to England at all. By late summer a plan was agreed upon,[166] and in November they submitted an ambitious proposal to the Legislature.[167]

In the joint memorial, Hawks and Swain traced their independent interests and efforts to preserve North Carolina's history and paid tribute to the General Assembly's encouragement in the past. As further background, they wrote: "In the examination of those [records] in the public offices of the state, your memorialists have seen, with deep regret, that many of our earlier archives have been so injured by time, that portions of them are already illegible, and that unless means be speedily taken to preserve the contents of those that can yet be decyphered, there is reason to fear that ere long, the historic evidence they afford will be completely lost."[168]

They proposed to publish, under authority and auspices of the State, a chronologically arranged series to be titled the *Documentary History of North Carolina* to consist of public records and private papers found within the United States and of documents from England. The latter would not require a trip to London, they wrote, because of George Bancroft's offer to allow the copying of his materials. Any other necessary documents might be copied through arrangements with the London offices inasmuch as the 1827 index would permit identification of the

164. Hawks to Swain, October 25, 1856, in Swain Papers, Southern Historical Collection.

165. Bancroft to Hawks, April 12, 1858, quoted in Weeks, "Historical Review," p. 64.

166. William A. Graham to Swain, August 17, 1858, in Swain Papers, Southern Historical Collection.

167. "Memorial of D. L. Swain and Francis L. Hawks," November, 1858, Document No. 49, *Public Documents, 1858-1859.* Cited hereafter as "Swain-Hawks Memorial."

168. "Swain-Hawks Memorial."

desired items.[169] They proposed to extend publication over a long period and the volumes, when published, would belong to the State. They offered to prepare and edit the work, giving explanatory notes where needed, on two conditions: first, that the work be carried through to completion, and second, that their work be accepted without remuneration. Finally, they suggested the publication of the North Carolina statutes-at-large and offered to edit those on the same conditions. They concluded that "with these two publications completed, North-Carolina could point to her authentic history, even should no narrative of it ever be written."[170]

The memorial was referred to a special committee in each house which in turn recommended approval of the proposal. The Assembly on February 16, 1859, adopted a resolution authorizing the governor to enter into an agreement with Hawks and Swain to edit and publish "within the next two years, two volumes of the 'Documentary History of North-Carolina or of the Statutes at Large,' of this State, upon the plan and conditions set forth in their memorial to this General Assembly. . . ." Not more than 1,000 copies of each volume were to be printed.[171]

The limitations imposed by the Legislature as to time and the number of volumes were to result in still another failure for North Carolina's efforts to preserve and disseminate her history. From the beginning, Hawks chafed under the restriction. Nine months after the Assembly had authorized the project, Hawks wrote Swain, "I am ready to do my part as soon as the State complies to your satisfaction with the conditions we proposed in our memorial, one of which was that they would publish *all*, & not leave the work incomplete." He continued, "I do not think that either of us should be found doing a miserable piece of imperfect, fragmentary patch work."[172] Swain asked Governor John W. Ellis

169. Swain and Hawks inexplicably described the indexes obtained by Gallatin as "complete," despite warnings of both Bancroft and Sparks that they were by no means exhaustive.

170. "Swain-Hawks Memorial."

171. The resolution, ratified February 16, 1859, is printed in *Public Laws of 1858-1859*, p. 106.

172. Hawks to Swain, October 27, 1859, in Swain Papers, Southern Historical Collection.

for an interpretation of the intentions of the General Assembly. The governor agreed that the Legislature was pledged to the publication of a full documentary history, but that it authorized him to contract for only two volumes between sessions.[173]

Thus, almost a year passed before Hawks and Swain really began work. In 1859, Hawks turned down an offer of a professorship at the University of North Carolina on the grounds that he could not live on the salary. Instead, he asked for *two* professorships![174] But early in 1860, apparently mollified, Hawks examined the Bancroft collection and reported that the papers relating to North Carolina would fill a thousand pages. Bancroft suggested a chronological work beginning in 1748 and offered to lend his volumes to Hawks for copying. Hawks agreed and asked Swain to begin copying the records in the Raleigh offices starting with those for 1748.[175] Swain replied that this procedure would lead to expensive duplication and asked instead that Hawks copy the Bancroft manuscripts from 1748 to 1783, then let him fill in the gaps from the public archives and private collections in North Carolina. Upon completion, they then could sit down and jointly annotate the work.[176] Swain sent Hawks's previous letter to Governor Ellis for his comments,[177] and Ellis, with an eye to economy, suggested that the printing be done in North Carolina and that Swain select a university senior to do the copying—thus providing historical research training and also saving money.[178] A few days later, Swain and Hawks submitted to the governor their formal plan. They had determined to concentrate first on the period from 1748 to 1783, "To so shape our labours as to present *finally* in chronological order every Document worth pre-

173. Swain to Hawks, December 26, 1859, in Swain Papers, Southern Historical Collection.

174. Hawks to Swain, October 27, December 9, 1859, in Swain Papers, Southern Historical Collection.

175. Hawks to Swain, January 3, 1860, in Swain Papers, Southern Historical Collection.

176. Swain to Hawks, January 13, 1860, in Swain Papers, Southern Historical Collection.

177. Swain to Governor John W. Ellis, January 14, 1860, in Governor's Papers, 1860 (G.P. 148), State Archives.

178. Governor Ellis to Swain, January 18, 1860, in Swain Papers, Southern Historical Collection.

serving in our history from *the first settlement of the State.* We should therefore, after the volumes first published, *go back* and bring the past up to 1748." Hawks would supervise copying in New York, Swain in North Carolina.[179] Ellis approved the plan and authorized the necessary expenses.[180] Hawks, however, continued to procrastinate. Swain's suggestion that Bancroft's North Carolina documents be purchased by the State turned out to be impracticable because all of Bancroft's manuscripts were bound chronologically regardless of the colony to which they pertained. Bancroft did, however, offer to let Hawks use his volumes in the latter's own study.[181]

It was not until May, 1860, that Hawks informed Swain that he had made a list of the Bancroft collection for the period 1748-83 and that now it appeared that his (Bancroft's) manuscripts would amount to more than three volumes of 500 pages each. But Hawks did not enclose the list, and a pessimistic tone appeared in his letter. First, he expressed concern over Swain's health. Second, he expressed doubt that they could, because of their age, complete the task, but that "if we did no more, we should at least collect, arrange, and leave behind us, all procurable materials for those who are to come after us." Third, he was worried about the political situation.[182] Earlier he had expressed the fear that "the State will have need to husband her money for other purposes than that of preserving her past history. It almost kills me to think she may be obliged to use it in making a bloody chapter in her future history."[183]

Hawks's letter of May 1, 1860, was followed by a silence of almost a year. He had planned to go to Chapel Hill for commencement, and when he failed to show up, Swain reminded

179. Hawks and Swain to Governor Ellis, January 26, 1860, in Governor's Papers, 1860 (G.P. 148), State Archives.

180. Governor Ellis to Swain and Hawks, January 28, 1860, in Swain Papers, Southern Historical Collection.

181. Hawks to Swain, February 4, 1860, in Swain Papers, Southern Historical Collection.

182. Hawks to Swain, May 1, 1860, in Swain Papers, Southern Historical Collection.

183. Hawks to Swain, December 9, 1859, in Swain Papers, Southern Historical Collection.

him that he was still waiting for the list of Bancroft's papers.[184] Receiving no answer, Swain wrote again in September saying that he could do nothing on the project until he received the list.[185] There was still no answer. The following month, E. J. Hale of Fayetteville, who had published Hawks's two-volume *History of North Carolina,* confided to Swain that he also was unable to get a reply. Hale told of Hawks's mortification over the failure of his history to win the acclaim of either the Legislature or the people and expressed the belief that this had caused Hawks to determine to write no more.[186]

The inaction of Hawks and Swain was the source of considerable irritation to the General Assembly and brought to Swain numerous embarrassing questions as to the cause. Swain wrote again in April, 1861, urging Hawks to break his silence and telling of his own plan to visit him in New York in May if Hawks did not come South.[187] At last—almost a year after his previous letter—Hawks wrote to Swain. He described the torment that he had endured as a result of his sympathy for the South in the sectional controversy. "In the contemplation of the horrors which threaten my country, I am utterly unfitted for work of any kind," he wrote; "If I attempt to read or write, my mind will not fasten to my occupation, but wander away . . . to my country & the scenes passing around me." As for the list of Bancroft papers, he had mislaid it the previous year when his papers were thrown into confusion upon the moving of his study, but he promised to have it ready when Swain visited New York in May. He concluded, "But my dear Govr. are you sure you *can* come in May? Troops by the thousands are mustering in this latitude, to fill up

184. Swain to Hawks, June 13, 1860, in Swain Papers, Southern Historical Collection.

185. Swain to Hawks, September 13, 1860, in Swain Papers, Southern Historical Collection.

186. E. J. Hale to Swain, October 17, 1860, in Swain Papers, Southern Historical Collection. The General Assembly at its 1858-59 session had rejected a bill that would have directed the purchase of Hawks's history for use in the public schools. Hale urged Swain to prevent former Governor Morehead, who had sponsored the previous bill, from reintroducing it in the new session "because he knows it will not do it and this would only hurt Dr. Hawks more."

187. Swain to Hawks, April 16, 1861, in Swain Papers, Southern Historical Collection.

the intervening country, and actual hostilities may be existing in May."[188] Hawks was never more correct. Thus ended the most ambitious publishing plan to that time.

The blame for the failure of the Hawks-Swain plans is too easily placed on the Civil War. One historiographer has passed it off with the statement that "Clio had yielded to Bellona."[189] The fact remains, however, that had the two men entered into their duties promptly and energetically, there would have been ample time to have published the two volumes authorized by the General Assembly. Furthermore, Hawks and Swain were both burdened by their occupations and other activities. Hawks's carelessness in failing to send the list of Bancroft's papers appears to have been characteristic, and Swain had vacillated for many years over the question of obtaining copies of records from London. Both men, as great as were their contributions to the history of the State, failed their friends and supporters in the most ambitious of all their plans.[190]

188. Hawks to Swain, April 19, 1861, in Swain Papers, Southern Historical Collection.

189. Weeks, "Historical Review," p. 67.

190. Hawks resigned his pastorate at Calvary Church in New York in 1861 when he was accused of sympathy for the South. He served a pastorate in Baltimore during the war and later returned to New York where he died in 1866. His manuscripts were placed in the Church Missions House in New York City. They later were deposited in the New-York Historical Society, but about 1960 were transferred with other Episcopal records to the Church Historical Society, Austin, Texas. Weeks, "Historical Review," pp. 72n, 160; Library of Congress, *The National Union Catalog of Manuscript Collections 1959-1961* (Ann Arbor: J. W. Edwards, 1962), pp. 251, 297; Nelle Bellamy to H. G. Jones, March 4, 1964, in State Archivist's Files, State Archives. A microfilm copy of the Hawks Papers relating to North Carolina is now in the State Archives and in the Southern Historical Collection. The papers include a variety of copies and originals. Among the copies are letters relating to North Carolina copied from the papers of Governor Alexander Spotswood of Virginia, instructions to colonial governors, and records of the Quakers in the Albemarle area. Among the originals are a rough draft of the journal of the House of Commons for 1773 and correspondence between John Stanly and Richard Dobbs Spaight and letters and statements relating to their duel.

Weeks appears to have been in error when he stated that Hawks's manuscripts "went to North Carolina before the war for the purpose of becoming a part of the Documentary History which he and Governor Swain had in mind to edit." I have found no evidence that Hawks sent materials to Swain. Some of the records copied by Hawks in London were published in his *History of North Carolina* and in Saunders' *Colonial Records*. Hawks's library was placed in the New-York Historical Society in 1871. The catalogue is given in Duyckinck, *Memorial*, pp. 47-166.

There was one more historical effort on the part of the State before the war put an end to it all. To Swain's surprise, the Assembly on February 23, 1861, resolved that the secretary of state and state librarian be directed to contract for the printing of 100 copies of the manuscript journals of the pre-revolutionary legislative sessions, of the provincial congresses of 1774-76, and of the legislative sessions to 1800 which had not previously been printed.[191] Evidently an effort was made to carry out this resolution because payment was made later in the year "for copying colonial records under resolution of general assembly authorizing the publication thereof. . . ."[192] But on December 12, 1861, the State Convention resolved that the publication "be suspended until further order from the Convention, or of the General Assembly of the State."[193]

The war ended virtually all historical efforts within the State.[194] Now those who would have recorded North Carolina's history turned to making it. The loss of certain records to Federal authorities stirred anew the interest in 1865, however, and Swain participated in efforts to repossess them for the State.[195] He continued his collecting zeal at the university, but the repeated stories of losses of valuable documents by war and neglect must have tormented him.[196]

191. The resolution, adopted February 23, 1861, is printed in *Public Laws of 1860-1861*, pp. 80-81.

192. Quoted in Weeks, "Historical Review," p. 67.

193. Resolution No. 21, *Ordinances and Resolutions Passed by the State Convention of North Carolina. First Session in May and June, 1861* (Raleigh: John W. Syme, 1862), p. 73.

194. Except that of the indomitable Wheeler. See above, pp. 176 ff.

195. See above, pp. 105 ff.

196. See, for instance, William B. Rodman to Swain, December 19, 1867, in Swain Papers, Southern Historical Collection. Rodman had written Swain ten years earlier about a mass of manuscripts in the Blount homestead near Washington, North Carolina, but in 1867 he wrote that "some of these were destroyed or lost during the late war: some of them—the oldest and probably the most interesting—were burned by an accidental fire some 20 years ago. I procured one trunk full since the war." They were mostly letters on private business beginning in 1774 and some of them were letters of Thomas Blount while in Congress; but Rodman with characteristic public shortsightedness wrote, ". . . they are too late in date to contain any thing not well known." Furthermore, he wrote, "Many of them . . . I burned last winter after examination."

James A. Bryan wrote from New Bern that his father's papers, "like most of our treasures . . . have fallen prey to the 'Trophy finders' of the U.S. Army, or

His old colleague Hawks dead, and old age creeping up on him, Swain on July 11, 1868, attempted to revive his dreams of a documentary history. He sent to Governor William W. Holden a copy of his and Hawks's report of 1856 and called the governor's attention to the correspondence in the executive letter books concerning the historical agency with which he had so long been connected. He wrote: "The troubles through which our country has been called to pass, greatly impeded but did not entirely suspend my researches. It will afford me pleasure to submit the result to the consideration of your Excellency, or to a Committee of the General Assembly at such time as may be convenient, for you or for them to afford me an opportunity." He concluded, "I am prepared to close or to continue my agency upon the plan, and on the terms originally proposed, as the General Assembly may be pleased to direct."[197] Within seven weeks North Carolina's greatest collector of the nineteenth century was dead, the victim of injuries sustained from a fall from his carriage. His last conversation before losing consciousness was on his favorite topic—North Carolina history.[198]

The passing of David L. Swain was keenly felt by those interested in the history of the State, and the Historical Society of the University of North Carolina summed up the general sentiments that his loss was "not only sorrowful but irreparable."[199] For the university, his death brought another loss—the temporary loss of some of the Swain papers and the permanent loss of others. That story belongs with that of the Historical Society below. It

---

been swept away by some unlettered hand as the worthless rubbish of a Rebel's house. When my father left Newberne in /62, the top shelf of his office was filled with papers containing information in regard to the early history of our state sufficient in itself to have made a most valuable & interesting record; these fell into the possession of the Yankees, & were no doubt destroyed. Mrs. Shepard informs me that the papers in her father's possession of a like nature, shared the same fate." Bryan to Swain, February 2, 1868, in Walter Clark Papers, State Archives.

197. Swain to Governor Holden, July 11, 1868, in Walter Clark Papers, State Archives. Holden's reply, if he made one, has not been found.

198. Rev. Charles Phillips to ———, August 27, 1868, in Walter Clark Papers, State Archives. Swain died in Phillips' presence on August 27, 1868.

199. Resolution of the Historical Society of the University of North Carolina, August 31, 1868, in Walter Clark Papers, State Archives.

is sufficient here to note that the scattering of Swain's life's collection of historical materials may have served history in the long run. Swain, a prodigious letter writer who did not write a single book, became the guiding light for historical source collectors in North Carolina.

VII

The Collection and Publication of the Records

1879-1907

Saunders and Clark

The death of David L. Swain in 1868 marked the end of another era in the efforts of North Carolina historians to collect and publish the documentary sources. For more than twenty years Swain had been the focal point of practically all historical endeavors. Now, his leadership gone, his manuscript collection locked in a bank vault, and the people struggling to recover from the effects of the war, no one came forward to assume the role that he had played.[1] The few who did write concentrated on one subject: the glorification of the lost cause.

The hiatus lasted for more than a decade. Not until 1880 did a full-length history of the State appear and its author did little more than draw upon the earlier historians for the period prior to the Civil War. John Wheeler Moore, a kinsman of his namesake, did furnish some original sources for the Civil War and the reconstruction era and, in fact, was the first North Carolinian to

---

1. Former Governor Henry Toole Clark sought in vain to persuade Daniel M. Barringer and William H. Battle to take over where Swain left off and to edit and publish the colonial records. It was a "shame and slur" that the State had never published its early records "thru down-right stinginess," he wrote. Clark to Battle, March 25, 1872, in Battle Family Papers, Southern Historical Collection; Clark to Barringer, March 26, 1869, in Barringer Papers, Southern Historical Collection.

make considerable use of documentary sources in a history of those troubled times.[2] He does not, however, merit inclusion among the historians who contributed significantly to the collection and publication of documentary materials.

WILLIAM LAURENCE SAUNDERS AND *The Colonial Records of North Carolina*, 1879-1891

Swain's mantle fell accidentally upon a lawyer-journalist who had distinguished himself on the field of battle as well as in the political life of the State. With no formal training in history, he accomplished what Murphey, Hawks, and Swain had sought unsuccessfully to do. His published work laid the foundation for the first really professional studies of the early history of the Colony, and his name became a byword for researchers in colonial history. No individual even to the present day has contributed more to North Carolina history.

William Laurence Saunders was born in Raleigh in 1835, the son of an Episcopal minister. He attended the Raleigh Academy and in 1854 was graduated from the University of North Carolina. Four years later he received a law degree from the same institution. Until 1861, he practiced law and wrote for the *Salisbury Banner,* but soon after the outbreak of war he volunteered as a private in the Rowan Rifle Guards. He rose rapidly in rank and by 1864 was a colonel commanding the Forty-Sixth Regiment, North Carolina Troops. At Fredericksburg he was wounded three times—once in the forehead, once in the foot, and then, while he laughed off these wounds, a ball entered his open mouth, knocked out a tooth, and exited through his cheek,

2. Moore's history was titled *History of North Carolina from the Earliest Discoveries to the Present Time* (2 vols.; Raleigh: Alfred Williams & Co., 1880). The year previous, he had published his *School History of North Carolina* (Raleigh: Alfred Williams & Co., 1879), written on the grade school level. For a commentary on Moore's work, see Stephen B. Weeks, "The North Carolina Historians," in *Proceedings and Addresses of the Fifteenth Annual Session of the State Literary and Historical Association* (Raleigh: Edwards and Broughton, 1915), pp. 81-82. For the story of Moore's preparation of his *Roster of North Carolina Troops in the War Between the States* (4 vols.; Raleigh: State of North Carolina, 1882), see entries in the Minutes of the Meetings of the Trustees of the Public Libraries of North Carolina for various dates in 1881-82.

leaving, as he said, a "beautiful dimple." Two years later at the Battle of the Wilderness there was less humor when another ball entered his open mouth and crashed through the back of his neck—a near-fatal wound that left him with impaired speech and which ended his practice of law. As a result of his war suffering, he also contracted rheumatism, an affliction which crippled him while yet a young man and caused him to spend much of his remaining life in a wheel chair or in bed.

Following the war he lived briefly in Florida where he suffered still another misfortune in the death of his bride of only seventeen months. Just a few weeks earlier their only child had been stillborn. He returned to North Carolina and divided his time between Chapel Hill and Grimes' Landing in Pitt County. He soon became the "director" of the Ku Klux Klans in North Carolina, though it is said that he never was a member of the organization. His participation in the activities of that group led to his appearance in 1871 before a congressional committee where he refused to divulge information about his co-workers. Meanwhile, in 1870, he became chief clerk of the State Senate, a seasonal position that he held for four years. In 1872, he joined his brother-in-law, Joseph A. Engelhard, in editing the *Wilmington Journal*. Engelhard in 1876 became secretary of state and Saunders followed him to Raleigh where he and Peter M. Hale established the *Observer*. He was one of the leaders in the reopening of the University of North Carolina in 1875 and was a member of the Board of Trustees for the remainder of his life. All the while he was becoming an increasingly prominent leader of the conservatives and upon the death in 1879 of his brother-in-law, Engelhard, Saunders was appointed secretary of state.[3]

Saunders was only forty-four years of age when he took

3. For biographical sketches of Saunders, see the following: Alfred Moore Waddell, *The Life and Character of William L. Saunders, LL.D., An Oration Delivered before the Alumni Association of the University of North Carolina, Tuesday, May 31st, 1892* (Wilmington: Jackson and Bell, Steam Power Presses, 1892); Ashe, *Biographical History*, IV, 381-89; Johnson and Malone, *D.A.B.*, XVI, 384-85; Peter Michel Wilson, *Southern Exposure* (Chapel Hill: The University of North Carolina Press, 1927), pp. 125-30; and H. G. Jones, "William Laurence Saunders and the Publication of *The Colonial Records of North Carolina*," unpublished manuscript delivered before the Historical Society of North Carolina, April 9, 1965, a copy of which is in the society's files.

office, but he already was an invalid. For long periods it was necessary for him to ease his pain from rheumatism with the waters of the various springs so popular in those days. Neither his confinement to a wheel chair, nor to his bed, nor his grotesque speech resulting from his war wound, daunted him. He entered office the same year in which his close friend and political ally, Thomas J. Jarvis, assumed the governorship. Judging from their later correspondence, one man may never have had more influence over a governor than Saunders did over Jarvis. The relationship was fortunate for the preservation of the history of the State.

Soon after Saunders entered the office of secretary of state, he was called upon by Governor Jarvis to examine a mass of old records found by Quartermaster General Fred A. Olds in the Arsenal on Capitol Square.[4] The papers, Saunders found, included many of the most valuable early records of the Colony and State. Only a nod of assent by Governor Jarvis would have resulted in their destruction by Olds. This shocking possibility must have had its effect upon the secretary of state, for he asked the governor, "Isn't there some way that can be devised to enable me to collect the Colonial Records of the Colony of North Carolina and get them together so as to preserve them?" Replied the governor noncommittally, "I don't know, Saunders, but I will think about it. Come tomorrow and we will talk this matter over."[5] The conference the following day resulted in Jarvis' suggestion that Saunders draw up a simple resolution authorizing the trustees of the State Library to collect and publish the colonial records. The resolution would be submitted to the next General Assembly in 1881.

In the meantime, Saunders paid particular attention to the public archives. His report to the governor in December, 1880, gave primary emphasis to the crowded and scattered conditions of the records. He wrote,

Old papers that have been handled as carelessly and as roughly as have the records of this office have necessarily suffered; indeed, it is

4. For the story of how the records came to be in the Arsenal, see above, pp. 109-10.
5. Jarvis, "Historical Records," p. 22.

painful to see the condition in which the early records of the State now are. It may be said that under any circumstances it is a duty a State owes to itself to preserve its records, but when those records reflect as much honor upon a people as do the records of North Carolina, their preservation would seem to be a matter of pride and boast as well as a suggestion of duty.

He then reviewed earlier legislative attempts to collect and publish the records. "Unforeseen events rendered the execution of these resolutions impossible, though the lapse of twenty years and experience in the fortunes of war show that what was important then is now absolutely imperative," he wrote. The prediction of Swain and Hawks that "ere long the historic evidence they [the records] afford will be completely lost" if not published was indeed almost an accomplished fact, he continued. Saunders recommended that the General Assembly appoint a committee to make a personal inspection of the records and that it authorize the library trustees to "select such as may be worthy of such preservation, in order to their proper printing and binding in suitable volumes by the State Printer." After having been printed, the original records "should then be put away secure from further accidents, from further rough usage or careless handling."[6]

Governor Jarvis, in his accompanying message to the General Assembly, strongly supported the secretary of state's request for more space for the records and for authorization to collect and print them. "Some of them are now so mutilated that it is absolutely necessary that they be printed while it is yet possible to decipher them," he said.[7]

A resolution, originally prepared by Saunders and introduced by Senator Theodore F. Davidson of Buncombe County, was ratified on February 17, 1881. It read in part, ". . . the trustees of the public library are hereby authorized to publish such number of volumes of suitable size, of the records, papers, documents and manuscripts as they may deem proper, bearing date prior to the year 1781, belonging to the state of North Carolina. . . ."[8]

6. Saunders' report is printed as Document No. 2, *Public Documents, 1881.*
7. The governor's message, dated January 5, 1881, is printed as Document No. 1, *Public Documents, 1881.* See above, p. 115, for the governor's recommendation concerning space for housing the records.
8. *Laws of 1881,* c. 88; Saunders, *Colonial Records,* I, vi.

It required the printing and binding to be done by the public printer and authorized the trustees to sell copies not reserved for public libraries. The cost was to be paid from the regular appropriation to the library. The resolution, so simple and innocent, failed to evoke from the legislators the question of magnitude of the work or its total cost. Wrote Governor Jarvis later, ". . . a little resolution it is, in length, but no man can tell how much it cost to carry it out, or the intrinsic, the eternal, the everlasting value of the work. . . ."[9]

Responsibility for carrying out the legislation was placed upon Jarvis, Saunders, and Superintendent of Public Instruction John C. Scarborough, who were the trustees of the State Library. The actual work fell to Saunders to whom the governor said, "I have plenty of my own work to do. You look after this and when you want a meeting of the trustees call it, and understand you always have two votes, yours and mine."[10]

Thus was launched the most ambitious historical collection and publication program in the history of the State. Its success was by no means assured. That it succeeded at all is surprising. William L. Saunders, in the first place, was a politician with a full-time job in administering the office of secretary of state. Second, he was a soldier, lawyer, and strongly-opinionated journalist, with no special training for impartial historical research. But even more foreboding was his health. Not only was he usually unable to walk—even after spending months at a time soaking in the waters of medicinal springs—but his ambitious project took on the appearance of a race against disease. Disease was to win in the end, but not until after Saunders had completed his monument in the form of ten published volumes of colonial records.

Early in 1883, Saunders, in the name of the trustees, submitted a detailed report of the accomplishments since passage of the 1881 act. In it he reviewed the decision to print nothing until he could complete a detailed inventory of the records of his office, using as a terminal date December 18, 1776—the day on which the

9. Jarvis, "Historical Records," p. 22.
10. Jarvis, "Historical Records," p. 22.

State's first constitution was adopted. Working from that date backwards, he had gained familiarity with what was available from 1776 to 1711. Unfortunately, except for the Tryon Letter Book which had been copied from the original at Harvard in 1856 and for journals for some of the later sessions of the General Assembly, there were relatively few complete series of records in the Capitol for the colonial period. The secretary of state thereupon turned attention to private collections. Just prior to the death of John H. Wheeler, Saunders obtained transcripts of the papers of Royal Governor Josiah Martin which the aging historian had obtained from London. Saunders reported that he could find no information on the location of the collections of Hugh Williamson, Francois X. Martin, and Francis L. Hawks, even though, as has already been seen, he had in his office all the while the Martin "collection" purchased by David L. Swain for the State in 1860.[11] Of great significance, however, was his report that Mrs. Swain had donated the papers of her late husband to the State and that he had them in his possession.

Even the combination of the archives in Raleigh and the Swain collection, however, left important gaps in the records. Saunders recalled earlier efforts to obtain copies of the records in London and wrote, "For over fifty years the General Assembly has been authorizing this thing to be done. Let it now be done, done well and done for all time." If the legislators failed to give such authorization, though, the trustees would proceed "to publish the fragments of records they now have."[12] Governor Jarvis, in transmitting the report to the General Assembly, paid tribute to Saunders' efforts and urged the adoption of the recommendation to obtain needed copies from London.[13]

A resolution prepared by Saunders and championed in the Assembly by Lieutenant Governor James L. Robinson and by Samuel McDowell Tate, member of the House of Representatives from Burke County, was ratified on March 12. Whereas the 1881 act authorized the publication of colonial records "belong-

11. See above, p. 145.
12. The report is published as a part of Document No. 21, *Public Documents, 1883.*
13. Message of Governor Jarvis to the General Assembly, February 16, 1883, in Governor's Letter Book, 1879-83 (G.L.B. 67), State Archives.

ing to the state," the cost of which was to be defrayed out of the
State Library appropriation, the new act authorized the procurement and publication of all colonial records "as may be missing
from the archives of the state" and further provided that "in
case the library fund shall prove to be insufficient to meet the
expenses incurred in carrying out this resolution, the auditor is
directed to draw his warrant for such sums as the trustees" should
need.[14]

Thus armed with virtually a carte blanche both as to authority
and funds, Saunders lost no time in initiating the task of collecting and copying the colonial records. The project developed
into three directions: arranging and copying the records in the
Capitol, procuring copies in private hands and in other repositories, and copying records in London and other European repositories.

Most of the transcribing of records in the Capitol was done
by the clerks in the secretary of state's office or by temporary
copyists.[15] But to the despair of later historians, Saunders arranged many original documents, marked the portions to be
copied, and sent them directly to the printer. Some appear never
to have been returned.[16]

Saunders made a concerted effort to locate other early records
within the State. He circularized county officials about the records
in the courthouses and in all too many instances heard the refrain that records had been destroyed by fire or neglect.[17] Nevertheless he did find valuable contributions to colonial history in
such counties as Chowan, Craven, and Perquimans; and the sec-

14. The resolution is printed in *Laws of 1883*, pp. 619-20. See also Saunders,
Colonial Records, I, vi. An original draft of the resolution, in Saunders' handwriting, is found in the William Laurence Saunders Papers, Southern Historical
Collection. Cited hereafter as Saunders Papers. A later hand has incorrectly
dated the paper 1885.

15. Part-time copyists, including his nieces Rosabelle Engelhard and Frances S.
Saunders, produced an estimated 15,000 handwritten pages in the Capitol at
rates of from ten to sixteen cents per sheet. See various vouchers in the Secretary of State's Records, State Archives, and the Saunders Papers in the Southern
Historical Collection and the State Archives.

16. Many original documents now in the State Archives retain Saunders' penciled marks and notes.

17. See, for example, H. B. Ansell to Saunders, September 17, 1883, in Saunders
Papers, Southern Historical Collection; and Walter L. Parsons to Saunders, September 28, 1887, in Saunders Papers, State Archives.

retary of state, in spite of his infirmities, visited several court-houses to examine the records.[18] Among private papers, too, he found useful materials. Two clergymen—Fordyce M. Hubbard and Lachlan C. Vass—were particularly helpful in locating private papers.[19] Among the papers volunteered were those in possession of Congressman John S. Henderson of Salisbury; three copyists transcribed them.[20]

For other domestic copying, Saunders engaged a number of prominent citizens, perhaps the most helpful of whom were Graham Daves, member of a prominent North Carolina family, and the Reverend Joseph Blount Cheshire, later a bishop in the Episcopal Church. Daves, then living in South Carolina, was commissioned to survey the holdings of the South Carolina Historical Society in Charleston and the University of South Carolina and the state offices in Columbia, and he served as a contact between Saunders and others believed to possess papers of value.[21] Cheshire was instrumental in gathering and copying materials relating to the Anglican Church in North Carolina. He obtained on loan from Bishop William Stevens Perry of Iowa, historiographer of the Episcopal Church in the United States, the Francis L. Hawks manuscripts which Cheshire studied while attending the general convention of the denomination in Philadelphia in 1883.[22] The manuscripts were later sent to Cheshire in Charlotte where he and his family copied them.[23] Cheshire also searched the Quaker records in Philadelphia repositories.[24]

18. Saunders to Governor Jarvis, March 28, 1888, in Saunders Papers, Southern Historical Collection.

19. Saunders, *Colonial Records,* I, viii; L. C. Vass, "North Carolina Colonial History," *Daily Journal* (New Bern), June 19, 1886.

20. Henderson to Saunders, September 12, 1887; J. M. Horah, H. N. Woodson, and Charles D. Crawford to Saunders, December 9, 1887, in Saunders Papers, State Archives.

21. The Saunders Papers in both the State Archives and the Southern Historical Collection contain many letters from Daves.

22. Cheshire to Saunders, September 19, October 9, 11, 17, 24, 29, 1883, in Saunders Papers, Southern Historical Collection. He was paid $90.00 for his notes.

23. Saunders paid Cheshire $135.75 for the copies, including express charges from and to Davenport, Iowa. Cheshire to Saunders, December 3, 15, 1885, in Secretary of State's Papers, Correspondence, State Archives; Cheshire to Saunders, February 10, 18, 1886, in Saunders Papers, State Archives. For a description of these papers, see above, p. 200.

24. Lawrence F. London, *Bishop Joseph Blount Cheshire* (Chapel Hill: The University of North Carolina Press, 1941), p. 89.

Others who assisted in locating materials outside of the State but within the country included William J. Rivers, a South Carolina historian then living in Maryland;[25] Charles C. Jones, Jr., a Georgia lawyer and historian;[26] S. F. Phillips, solicitor general of the United States;[27] Charles De F. Burns, a New York book and autograph dealer;[28] and R. A. Brock, secretary of the Virginia Historical Society.[29]

Copies of records in foreign repositories were procured from at least two sources. Alfred DuFour, a native of France who had settled in North Carolina, obtained a copy of the de Graffenried manuscripts from the library at Yverdon, Switzerland, where he had previously worked. The copy, in French, was translated for Saunders by DuFour.[30]

By far the most important project, however, was the copying of records in London. Soon after passage of the 1883 resolution Saunders approached Cheshire about the latter's going to England to transcribe the records, and Cheshire tentatively accepted.[31] But it was to the senior clerk of the British Public Record Office, W. Noel Sainsbury, that Saunders turned for the task which the State, after previous failures, finally undertook. Remarkably enough, it was Sainsbury who 23 years previously had offered to furnish copies to David L. Swain.[32] Sainsbury, first employed as a temporary clerk in the State Paper Office in 1848, had been absorbed into the Public Record Office in 1854 where, eight years

25. Rivers to Saunders, August 29, 1884; November 2, 1885; March 13, 1886, in Saunders Papers, State Archives; Saunders, *Colonial Records,* I, viii.

26. Jones to Saunders, March 16, 1883; December 15, 1884, in Saunders Papers, State Archives.

27. Phillips to Saunders, December 28, 1885, in Saunders Papers, State Archives; Saunders, *Colonial Records,* I, viii.

28. Burns to Saunders, February 24, March 6, September 14, 1883, in Saunders Papers, State Archives.

29. Brock to Saunders, July 20, August 3, 1886, in Secretary of State's Papers, Correspondence, State Archives.

30. DuFour to Saunders, June 8, October 9, 1885, in Secretary of State's Papers, Correspondence, State Archives; DuFour to Saunders, August 18, September 25, 1885, in Saunders Papers, State Archives. The cost to the State of the copy and translation was approximately $40.00.

31. Cheshire to Saunders, May 16, 21, 1883, in Saunders Papers, State Archives.

32. Sainsbury to "Sir," May 8, 1860; Sainsbury to Saunders, May 21, 1883, in Saunders Papers, Southern Historical Collection.

later, he became senior clerk.[33] He was well-known to American historians, having edited various calendars of papers relating to the colonies and having provided copies of English records for several states and individuals, including George Bancroft, who wrote, "I have known him for nearly forty years, have employed him very frequently during that time, and have always found him intelligent, accurate, and in every way trustworthy. My own collection of documents is full of copies of State papers which he has made for me."[34] No man in England could have been obtained with finer credentials. Sainsbury's familiarity with the records was greatly enhanced by his preparation of calendars of papers relating to the North American continent.

Saunders first wrote Sainsbury on May 1, 1883, and received a prompt reply.[35] "It is somewhat strange that I should have your letter *at last*," Sainsbury wrote, recalling that Bancroft had approached him a quarter of a century earlier about copying records for Swain and Hawks. Thus began a unique relationship between an editor and his copyist. It was a relationship which grew in both warmth and enthusiasm for the next eight years and ended only with the death of the secretary of state.

In answer to Saunders' inquiry about Sainsbury's estimate of the cost of copies, the latter replied, after considerable review of the hundreds of volumes and bundles that would need to be surveyed, that he could give no estimate. He suggested, however, that Saunders send an advance payment against which charges would be made until it was used up, at which time a new payment would be made. He proposed to deliver the copies to the American embassy to be sent through the despatch bag.[36] Saunders accepted both proposals and on July 2 sent the first deposit of £50.[37] Sainsbury's first parcel of transcripts was delivered to

---

33. For a biographical sketch of Sainsbury, see Sidney Lee (ed.), *Dictionary of National Biography* (63 vols.; New York: The Macmillan Co., 1897), L, 117.

34. Bancroft to Saunders, November 17, 1884, in Saunders Papers, Southern Historical Collection.

35. Sainsbury to Saunders, May 21, 1883, in Saunders Papers, Southern Historical Collection.

36. Sainsbury to Saunders, June 9, 1883, in Saunders Papers, Southern Historical Collection.

37. Citizens National Bank of Raleigh to Saunders, July 5, 1883, in Saunders

the embassy on July 27,[38] and was followed by five other parcels before the end of the year.

Sainsbury hired "several" copyists to transcribe the documents, beginning with the Board of Trade records, then going into other groups such as those of the Colonial Office and of the Lords Proprietors. Although Saunders left to Sainsbury most of the decisions of what to copy, the latter frequently sent lists so that the secretary of state could determine if particular documents were needed. By April, 1885, the copying of records up to 1729 was completed except for a few strays that inevitably turned up later. Sainsbury proudly wrote that he had searched 154 volumes.[39] A year later he had furnished copies of what he believed to be all the records up to 1750,[40] and by the end of 1887 the copying had been completed through Tryon's administration.[41] Finally, with his work almost finished and with the first four volumes of Saunders' "Magnificent Work" in his hands, Sainsbury totaled up his contributions: "I find I have had the pleasure of sending you Forty parcels of transcripts which have contained upwards of Ten Reams of Paper and that I have examined upwards of 350. Volumes of our Colonial Records to make this Collection as complete as possible."[42] He suggested to Saunders, ". . . if you are of opinion that my Services have been valuable & useful would it be improper for me respectfully to suggest that an Honorarium be awarded to me[?]"[43] Saunders, answering the question in the same spirit in which it was asked, replied, "While I appreciate fully not only the value of your services but the cordial way in which they have been tendered,

---

Papers, Southern Historical Collection. The total charge for the draft, including the bank charge, was $246.25.

38. Sainsbury to Saunders, July 27, 1883, in Saunders Papers, Southern Historical Collection.

39. Sainsbury to Saunders, April 10, 1885, in Saunders Papers, Southern Historical Collection.

40. Sainsbury to Saunders, May 12, 1886, in Secretary of State's Papers, Correspondence, State Archives.

41. Sainsbury to Saunders, September 14, 1887, in Secretary of State's Papers, Correspondence, State Archives.

42. Sainsbury to Saunders, January 30, 1888, in Secretary of State's Papers, Correspondence, State Archives.

43. Sainsbury to Saunders, November 3, 1887, in Secretary of State's Papers, Correspondence, State Archives.

and appreciating especially the assistance you have given me individually, it would give me great pleasure to respond to your suggestion about the honorarium." But, he noted, the legislative act authorized only the necessary expenditures and made no provision for payment even of himself. His own reward, he wrote, was simply "the honor of the thing."[44] While the main work of copying had been completed, Saunders continued from 1888 to 1890 to call upon Sainsbury for transcripts of missing records, particularly those relating to the Indians, and for copies of maps and newspapers.

The seven years of correspondence between Saunders and Sainsbury reveals more than just an editor-copyist relationship.[45] Each became warmly interested in the activities, health, and progress of the other. They exchanged photographs; Sainsbury became interested in Saunders' political campaigns and eagerly received newspaper clippings; each comforted the other upon the death of members of the family; but of most concern to Sainsbury was the deterioration of Saunders' health. After about 1881, Saunders was confined almost continually to his wheel chair or to his bed in the Yarborough House in Raleigh or at Cleveland Springs near Shelby. Indeed, he was unable to write legibly much of the time.[46] Saunders in 1886 wrote, "I send you two photo-

44. Saunders to Sainsbury, February 12, 1888, in Secretary of State's Papers, Correspondence, State Archives.

45. The extant Sainsbury-Saunders correspondence is found in three places—in the Saunders Papers both in the State Archives and in the Southern Historical Collection and in the Secretary of State's Papers in the State Archives. Most of Sainbury's letters have been preserved except for the periods September 24, 1884-February 3, 1885 and December 16, 1886-June 8, 1887. In the course of this study I have obtained Xerox copies of these letters and filed them together in the State Archives. In spite of the fact that there are few of Saunders' letters to Sainsbury—and those mostly penciled drafts—the correspondence would be valuable in a study of this significant copying-publishing project. The British Public Record Office indicates that the whereabouts of the Sainsbury correspondence is not known or whether it exists at all.

46. In 1882, Saunders spent at least 37 days at Cleveland Mineral Springs where he took warm baths for his rheumatism. See bill from Cleveland Mineral Springs, dated October 16, 1882, in Saunders Papers, State Archives. In September, 1883, he was at Warm Springs. See Graham Daves to Saunders, September 13, 1883, in Saunders Papers, Southern Historical Collection. In 1884, he was not only ill but in extreme financial straits. See, for instance, E. R. Stamps to Saunders, July 21, 1884, in Saunders Papers, State Archives. In the same year he was again at one of the springs at which place Governor Jarvis wrote him, "I am so glad

graphs, one as I was twenty years ago and more. . . . The other
is as I now am. I have not walked for 3 or 4 years."[47] Replied
the Englishman, ". . . the later one [photograph] shows unmis-
takeably traces of pain & suffering with firm courageous endur-
ance."[48]

It is remarkable that Saunders was able to produce the ten
volumes of *The Colonial Records of North Carolina*. He held
a full-time job as secretary of state; he had to run for re-election
three times; and his health prevented him from carrying on the
activities of a normal body. Yet he read untold thousands of
pages of manuscripts and edited them, wrote hundreds of pages
of introductory notes, and arranged the entire bulk and saw it
through the press. His method was fairly simple and generally
lacking in scholarship. In spite of frequent warnings from Sainsbury, the editor was anxious to get his copies into print. Consequently, he set the materials in type and ran a number of
proofs which he distributed for comments from others interested
in the history of North Carolina. Some of these readers objected to or disagreed with various documents and, basing history on their own opinion rather than on contemporary evidence,
urged that it be "corrected."[49] His prefatory notes, too, he sent
to readers who challenged his interpretations and facts.[50] He
also issued as separate pamphlets several portions of the materials, including his prefatory notes, a roster of North Carolina
troops in the Continental Line, and a booklet titled *Abstracts*

---

to hear that the *water* has struck you and that you feel better from it. Stick
to the water while you are there and reserve the other liquid till you return and
I will find help for you in disposing of that." See Jarvis to Saunders, August 16,
1884, in Saunders Papers, State Archives. In 1888, his drug bill included such
assorted remedies as lithia water, castalian water, quinine capsules, liniment, and
"headache cure." See bill of Lee, Johnson & Company, to Saunders, March 21,
1888, in Saunders Papers, State Archives.

47. Saunders to Sainsbury, February 17, 1886, in Secretary of State's Papers,
Correspondence, State Archives.

48. Sainsbury to Saunders, March 3, 1886, in Secretary of State's Papers, Correspondence, State Archives.

49. See, for instance, L. C. Vass to Saunders, November 4, December 8, 1886, in
Secretary of State's Papers, Correspondence, State Archives.

50. See, for instance, Joseph B. Cheshire to Saunders, July 9, 1886, and B. F.
Grady to Saunders, July 16, 1886, in Secretary of State's Papers, Correspondence,
State Archives.

of Records and Documents Relating to the Colonial History of North Carolina During the Proprietary Government.

Perhaps Saunders himself conveyed the most vivid picture of his work and the conditions under which it was carried on. In 1888, he wrote former Governor Jarvis:

Last August I began printing the 5th and 6th Volumes of the Colonial Records, one volume in Edwards & Broughton's office, and the other in Uzzell's office, and it proved a job that I never intend to undertake again, for night and day it kept me busy. As soon as I got through printing the volumes proper, I went to Charlotte, Salisbury and Hillsboro' to examine the County Records there, for matter to put in an Appendix, then I went to Pitt for a quiet time in which to prepare the Prefatory Notes to the two volumes. I staid there nearly three weeks hard at work every day Sundays included and then found I had hardly begun but I was in for it and you know I don't give up easy. I came back here and continued the work, sometimes in bed and sometimes out and got through only about ten days ago. I send you herewith a copy of the notes but of course they don't show the amount of labor required to get them up. I think as a general rule anyway that the better a paper of that sort is prepared the less the ear-marks of work stick out. The paper is the result of near four months hard, tedious, and I may say disagreeable work. To vary the monotony of it however, while in Charlotte I had a violent attack of gravel, and on my way down to Pitt two more attacks in Raleigh and one in Tarboro', all in less than a month, so you see I've been busy, and very naturally did not realize how the time was flying. . . .[51]

When, in 1890, the last of the ten volumes of *The Colonial Records of North Carolina* was published,[52] Saunders laid down

51. Saunders to Governor Jarvis, March 28, 1888, in Saunders Papers, Southern Historical Collection.

52. The contract for the first four volumes was given in 1886 to Peter M. Hale, who farmed out the actual printing to E. M. Uzzell. These volumes covered the following periods: I, 1662-1712; II, 1713-28; III, 1728-34; and IV, 1734-52. The remaining six volumes carried the name of Josephus Daniels, printer to the State, though the actual printing of Volume V was done by Uzzell and Volumes VI-X by Edwards and Broughton. Volume V, covering 1752-59, appeared in 1887 and Volume VI, covering 1759-65, was published in 1888. The final four volumes were printed in 1890 and covered the following periods: VII, 1765-68; VIII, 1769-71; IX, 1771-75; and X, 1775-76.

It should be noted that the State of North Carolina was actually the publisher of both the Saunders and Clark series, but, as was the vogue, the printing contractor put his name on the title page. All printing was contracted with the

his pen—or rather pencil, because his rheumatism often prevented him from writing at all and usually prevented him from using a sharp pen. The legislative act authorized the publication of the records down to 1781, but the continuing deterioration of Saunders' health led to the termination of the project. The General Assembly, by a rising vote, adopted a resolution expressing that the "thanks of the people of the state are due and are hereby tendered to Col. William L. Saunders for the valuable service he has rendered the state of North Carolina in the accomplishment of this laborious work and in the preparation of the prefatory notes, the excellence of which entitle them to the admiration of our patriotic people.[53] The resolution was delivered to Saunders on February 28, 1891.[54] Within five weeks he was dead.

WALTER CLARK AND *The State Records of North Carolina,* 1893-1907

The task of continuing the collection and publication of the records fell to another state official. Like his predecessor, he was a war hero, an attorney, and a popular political leader. But with those attributes the similarities between the old and the new editor ended.

Walter Clark, born August 19, 1846, in Halifax County, was

---

state printer who, if he chose, could sublet the work. The cost of printing each volume of 750 copies averaged about $1,250.

The exact cost of copying, arranging, editing, publishing, and distributing the ten volumes will never be known. I estimate the total cost, exclusive of Saunders' salary, at $25,000. Saunders contributed his time without remuneration except for the $1,000 annual salary he received as secretary of state. Many other individuals volunteered their services. A study of the Sainsbury-Saunders correspondence indicates that Sainsbury was paid at least £1,065 (or more than $5,100) for the copies obtained from London. A compilation—probably prepared by either R. D. W. Connor or Walter Clark in 1907—indicates that the total cost was $6,340.50 exclusive of printing. See typescript "Cost of Compiling the Colonial and State Records" in North Carolina Historical Commission Records, Correspondence of the Secretary, 1907, State Archives. This figure, however, is probably low and, even if accurate, covers only the cost of copying and certain incidental expenses. It certainly does not cover the cost of clerical assistance to Saunders or any salaries or printing charges.

53. The resolution, ratified February 12, 1891, is printed in *Laws of 1891*, p. 655.

54. Lieutenant Governor Thomas M. Holt to Saunders, February 28, 1891, in Saunders Papers, Southern Historical Collection.

a member of a prominent family which traced its ancestry to many illustrious names of the colonial period. His father, a man of wealth and learning, served as a brigadier general of the militia during the Civil War and engendered in his young son not only an appreciation of learning but also of military glory. At the age of fourteen young Walter, fresh out of a military academy in Hillsborough, entered the Confederate army as a drillmaster. At sixteen years of age he was first lieutenant and adjutant of the Thirty-Fifth Regiment, North Carolina Troops. A year later he was a major (lieutenant colonel temporarily) in the Seventieth Regiment—the youngest officer in either army—and held that rank until the end of the war. Meanwhile he participated in numerous skirmishes and took time off to graduate from the University of North Carolina after only sixteen months of study. His remarkable record as a youth was a portent of things to come. Upon his discharge in 1865, he studied law in Chapel Hill, New York City, and the District of Columbia, and he was a practicing attorney at the age of twenty-one. He first located at Scotland Neck, then at Halifax, but, in 1873, he opened law practice in Raleigh where he also became editorial director of the Raleigh *News.* He married the daughter of William A. Graham, the former governor and secretary of the navy who contributed significantly to the preservation of the State's history.

Clark built up in Raleigh an extensive law practice and occupied a high place in the political and social life of the State. His interests were diverse: he was a leader in Methodism; he wrote prolifically on several subjects; he fostered what at that time were radical ideas concerning government regulation of big business; and he participated actively in Democratic party politics. In 1885, he was appointed a judge of the Superior Court. As his reward for declining to run for governor in 1888, he was appointed to the position of associate justice on the Supreme Court, a position that he held until his elevation to the chief justiceship in 1902. He remained in the highest judicial post until his death in 1924, though, in the meantime, he was on several occasions supported by his friends for a vacancy on the United States Supreme Court and for the Democratic nomination for vice-president of the nation. In fact, no less a man than William Jennings Bryan suggested him for the presidency of the United States in 1904.[55]

From the standpoint of education, ability, and interest, Walter Clark was eminently qualified to succeed Saunders in the great task of publishing the records. As a justice (later chief justice) of the Supreme Court, however, he faced a handicap of sharing his time with his judicial duties. Like Saunders, he overcame this problem by carefully budgeting his time. He took part in his church and Masonic affairs as well as in politics, but he declined to use his time in "mixing" with the public, preferring instead to work far into the night on his editing chores. It is estimated that, including his numerous volumes of Supreme Court reports, Clark wrote or edited more than two hundred books in his lifetime.

It will be recalled that the act of 1881 authorized publication of the early records to January 1, 1781, but that Saunders had been forced by ill health to stop at the end of 1776. Legislation, therefore, was still in force to provide for publication of the records for five additional years. The series could have been continued by the simple act of appointment of a new editor by the library trustees. This was not done immediately, the reason for which is not clear.

Inaction on the part of the trustees appears to have resulted in plans for a new bill, the nature of which is not known but which might have included a specific appropriation for the work with possible remuneration to the editor. The year following Saunders' death, Clark discussed the matter with David Schenck, a Greensboro attorney, at which time the justice indicated his willingness to take on the responsibility. At Schenck's suggestion,

55. For biographical sketches of Clark, see Ashe, *Biographical History*, VII, 67-76, and Johnson and Malone, *D.A.B.*, IV, 140-41. For a full-length biography which fails to do more than mention Clark's work on the *State Records*, see Aubrey Lee Brooks, *Walter Clark, Fighting Judge* (Chapel Hill: The University of North Carolina Press, 1944). Selections from Clark's papers have been published in Aubrey Lee Brooks and Hugh Talmage Lefler, *The Papers of Walter Clark* (2 vols.; Chapel Hill: The University of North Carolina Press, 1948), cited hereafter as Brooks and Lefler, *Clark Papers*. Unfortunately, few of Clark's papers relating to the collection, copying, and publication of the records have been preserved.

Clark drew up a bill. At the same time, however, Edwin A. Alderman, then a member of the faculty of the State Normal School at Greensboro, began a movement to establish a new state historical society with the aim of continuing the publication of the records. The new organization, called the William L. Saunders Historical Society of North Carolina, was informally established in the summer of 1892. Clark and Alderman apparently had contrary plans, but through the intercession of Schenck and others they appear to have reached an accord.[56]

Clark seems to have accepted Alderman's plan for the publication of the records under the direction of the proposed historical society. The Alderman bill, introduced "by request" by Senator J. L. King of Guilford, called for the incorporation of the William L. Saunders Historical Society of North Carolina with an annual appropriation of $1,000 and authority "to take proper steps to diffuse and publish information concerning the history of the state and to print and publish such records as they may be directed to do by the Trustees of the Public Library of North Carolina. . . ." The Assembly amended the bill by striking out the appropriation and then passed it on February 28, 1893.[57] Without funds, the Historical Society faded into obscurity.[58]

The failure of the Alderman plan, however, did not prevent the resumption of the publication of the records. In fact, it may have facilitated the matter because the library trustees were not hampered by what in effect would have been an advisory com-

56. Schenck to Clark, December 14, 1892; January 14, 17, 1893, in Brooks and Lefler, *Clark Papers*, I, 257-59; Martin H. Holt to Clark, January 27, 1893, in Brooks and Lefler, *Clark Papers*, I, 260. Schenck wrote, "This legislature is a liberal one and we must not lose the opportunity to do all we can for the State during its session." He suggested the appointment of a legislative committee to study all historical matters.

57. *Private Laws of 1893*, c. 131. The original bill, S.B. 204, first introduced January 20, is in Legislative Papers, 1893 (L.P. 1331), State Archives.

The Assembly appointed a joint committee on colonial records (H.R. 134, S.B. 45) to which were referred bills to direct the trustees to have prepared an index to the ten volumes of *Colonial Records* (H.R. 275, S.B. 347), to direct the secretary of state to deliver one complete set of the volumes to each member of the General Assembly (S.R. 91), and to authorize each member of the legislative body to select one college, high school, or public library to which a complete set would be given (S.R. 658). All of these measures were rejected. The original bills and resolutions are in Legislative Papers, 1893 (L.P. 1325), State Archives.

58. For a more detailed discussion of the society, see below, chap. VIII.

mittee on publications. The interest that had been aroused resulted in the trustees' decision, soon after the legislative session ended, to call upon Clark "to carry on Col. Saunders' Colonial Records from 1776 where he left off work down to 1781. . . ."[59] The new editor thus worked directly under the trustees which, as in the case of Saunders, meant that he had virtually a free hand.

Justice Clark began his work energetically. He first circularized prominent citizens around the State, as follows: "There is no compensation whatever attached to the labor except the consciousness of endeavoring to aid in the vindication of our past and our heroic dead. Knowing your feelings and services in that respect I beg that you will aid me with your advice, suggestions and information as to what should be published and the best means of procuring materials."[60]

Next, he arranged and had copied the remaining records to 1781 in the state offices in Raleigh. Thinking that additional materials might be located in England, he called upon the aging Sainsbury for a further search. His suspicion was correct. Some papers were located which had not been copied previously, and these Sainsbury and his daughter furnished under the same financial arrangements used by Saunders.[61] B. F. Stevens, a bibliographer and purchasing agent in London for many American libraries and individuals, also lent assistance.[62] Having been an executor of the estate of the late Mrs. David L. Swain, Clark had previously returned to the University of North Carolina a portion of the Swain collection. His request that the papers be transferred back to Raleigh for copying was at first rejected[63]

59. Clark to "Friends," May 24, 1893, in Brooks and Lefler, *Clark Papers*, I, 265.
60. Clark to "Friends," May 24, 1893, in Brooks and Lefler, *Clark Papers*, I, 265.
61. Sainsbury to Clark, August 10, October 14, 1893, in Brooks and Lefler, *Clark Papers*, I, 272. Most of the pre-1777 material located by Sainsbury was published as the first part of Vol. XI of *The State Records of North Carolina*. The laws, however, were withheld and published in Vol. XXIII.
62. Stevens to Clark, July 19, 1893, in Brooks and Lefler, *Clark Papers*, I, 270-72.
63. Kemp P. Battle to Clark, May 30, 1893, in Brooks and Lefler, *Clark Papers*, I, 266. Battle, then a professor but previously president of the university, suggested that Clark authorize him to supervise the copying by students in Chapel Hill.

but later granted on the grounds that Clark had, "in fact, secured much of it for us."[64]

Clark approached Stephen B. Weeks, a former Trinity College professor, about assisting him. A collector in his own right, Weeks energetically aided the judge, searching for materials both within the State and in Maryland and Pennsylvania.[65] Graham Daves, who had been of significant help to Saunders, was employed to gather materials for several years.[66] Clark also sought out the late John H. Wheeler's transcripts of records in London[67] and investigated various other sources to determine if Saunders might have overlooked colonial records.

The judge traveled extensively. In Washington, he searched for revolutionary materials among the records of the state, war, and other departments. In Madison, Wisconsin, he also found valuable materials relating to the Colony and State, these papers having been collected by Lyman C. Draper and deposited with the State Historical Society of Wisconsin. He located additional papers in the libraries of New York City, including the correspondence of General Horatio Gates relating to the military campaigns in North Carolina.[68]

Two years after Clark began his arduous task, he suggested that the terminal date for the publication be extended to November, 1789, the date of North Carolina's entry into the federal union. He based the proposal upon the fact that January 1, 1781, was an arbitrary date without any special meaning in the history of the State, and that he had found an abundance of materials on the confederation period. Governor Elias Carr recommended the extension[69] and the Assembly went even further

64. George T. Winston to Clark, June 15, 1893, in Brooks and Lefler, *Clark Papers*, I, 269. Winston was president of the institution.

65. George T. Winston to Clark, June 15, 1893, in Brooks and Lefler, *Clark Papers*, I, 269; Weeks to Clark, July 19, October 21, 1893, January 1, 1895, in Brooks and Lefler, *Clark Papers*, I, 270, 273, 277.

66. S. F. Telfair to Clark, May 22, 1895, in Brooks and Lefler, *Clark Papers*, I, 279.

67. Robert D. Graham to Clark, June 8, 1893, in Brooks and Lefler, *Clark Papers*, I, 267.

68. Clark, *State Records*, XI, iv-v.

69. Message of Governor Elias Carr to the General Assembly, [1895], printed as Public Document No. 1, *Public Documents*, 1895.

and directed the printing of the records down to January 1, 1790.[70] But of equal importance was the action by the General Assembly to direct the library trustees to have prepared and published an index to the combined Saunders-Clark series.[71] Weeks, by then employed by the Department of the Interior in Washington, was appointed to prepare the index for the entire series for $1,200.[72]

In a sense Clark's feat of gathering, copying, editing, and seeing through the press sixteen volumes of state records was more remarkable than Saunders' had been. Although he was not troubled with ill health as the secretary of state had been, he was burdened with other responsibilities. His judicial duties could have occupied all his time. But he assumed other tasks without hesitation. He wrote scores of articles—both legal and historical—and edited the reports of the Supreme Court while, at the same time, playing an important role in the political activities not only of the State but of the entire country. As if he did not already have enough to do, Clark, at the request of the Confederate Veterans Association and the General Assembly, supervised the writing of and edited the five-volume work, *Histories of the Several Regiments and Battalions from North Carolina in the Great War 1861-'65.*[73] This work, written by members of the

70. *Laws of 1895,* c. 464, s. 2. The 1901 General Assembly further extended the terminal date to January 1, 1791. *Laws of 1901,* c. 632.

71. *Laws of 1895,* c. 464, s. 3. A bill to authorize an index had been rejected in the 1893 session.

72. Weeks to Governor Elias Carr [April, 1895], Superintendent of Public Instruction Records, State Archives, hereinafter cited as Superintendent of Public Instruction Records. Subsequent negotiations resulted in an increase in the amount paid Weeks for work on the series. Including $375 for indexing the 1790 census and $500 for salvaging a portion of the index damaged by water while in possession of the printer, Weeks had received by 1913 a total of $2,955 (some of it in books), and he asked for an additional $427.50. Weeks to Clark, November 11, 1913, Walter Clark Papers, State Archives. For other references to the prolonged negotiations, see S. F. Telfair to Clark, March 22, 1895, Brooks and Lefler, *Clark Papers,* I, 279; Weeks to Governor Elias Carr [April, 1895], and Weeks to John C. Scarborough, June 1, 1895, Superintendent of Public Instruction Records; Weeks to M. O. Sherrill, December 31, 1906, and September 23, 1912, Correspondence of the State Librarian, North Carolina State Library Records, State Archives; and the following in Minutes of the Trustees of the Public Library of North Carolina, State Archives: minutes of meetings of November 18, 1901, March 22, 1909, and July 1, 1909, and letters from John C. Scarborough to Weeks, May 27, 1895, and Clark to Sherrill, January 30, 1906, copied in the minutes.

73. 5 vols.; Raleigh: E. M. Uzzell, 1901, and Goldsboro: Nash Brothers, 1901.

various military units, remains to the present time a standard work on North Carolina's military role in the Civil War.

The preparation of the materials for the years 1777 and 1778 —and the additional unpublished papers for the period from 1730 through 1776—was completed within two years after Clark began his work. Thus, in 1895, appeared from the presses of M. I. and J. C. Stewart in Winston the initial two volumes of the Clark series. The first volume included the newly-found colonial records plus the general papers for 1777; the second included largely the legislative journals for 1777 and 1778. In numbering his volumes, Clark made a decision that has caused untold anguish to researchers since. Instead of beginning with a new series of volume numbers, *The State Records of North Carolina* began with Volume XI. While it is true that this plan facilitated the indexing for the combined Saunders-Clark series, it has for three-quarters of a century plagued historians in their bibliographical citations.

Two more volumes, covering 1778-80, appeared in 1896 from the same press. Thereafter the printing was transferred to Nash Brothers in Goldsboro, but the general format was followed with the result that the entire Clark series physically and typographically matched the Saunders work. Clark attempted to follow a chronological arrangement of the documents, but the temptation to hasten publication resulted in the placement of many items out of their proper sequence and in several volumes of overlapping years. His arrangement, to say the least, was less satisfactory than that of Saunders. Documents of 1781, for example, are found in four different volumes. Fortunately for the researcher, however, Clark did withhold the laws, which he printed in a distinct series—though even with the laws there was an overlapping of dates in two volumes. Wise, too, was his decision to include an index with the three volumes of laws. Volume XXVI was devoted to the printing of the Census of 1790, indexed by Weeks, and names contained in that volume were not included in the master index for the series. Miscellaneous items, including many received too late to be included in their proper sequence, were withheld and published as Volume XXII in 1907—

the last Clark volume to appear.[74] Thus it was fourteen years
from the time Judge Clark began his work until his final volume
of the *State Records* appeared.

In the meantime, Stephen B. Weeks, under authorization of
the 1895 act, had been assiduously at work compiling an index
to the ten volumes edited by Saunders and fifteen volumes edited
by Clark, as well as the indexing of the census volume. Weeks
sought to include "every proper name and every proper adjec-
tive every time it occurs and in each different connection; to index under each heading to which it can properly be assigned
every historical fact that is sufficiently full in itself without the
necessity of cross references."[75] His tedious work took almost as
long as it required Clark to edit and publish his sixteen volumes,
and the fourth volume of the index did not appear until 1914.[76]
The delay in publishing the final volume—Volume IV under
Weeks's name but Volume XXX under the title of the full
series—resulted from the preparation of Weeks's narrative survey of historical activities in the State and his analysis of materials included in the Saunders-Clark work. His study remained
for many years the best and most thorough study of the State's
efforts to preserve its history. Unlike Saunders and Clark who

74. The printer, date of publication, and inclusive dates of the contents of
each volume were as follows: M. I. and J. C. Stewart, Winston—1895: Vol. XI,
1777 and Supplement, 1730-76; Vol. XII, 1777-78; 1896: Vol. XIII, 1778-79; Vol.
XIV, 1779-80. Nash Brothers, Goldsboro—1898: Vol. XV, 1780-81; 1899: Vol. XVI,
1782-83; Vol. XVII, 1781-85; Vol. XVIII, 1786 and Supplement, 1779; 1901: Vol.
XIX, 1782-84 and Supplement, 1771-82; 1902: Vol. XX, 1785-88; 1903: Vol. XXI,
1788-90; 1904: Vol. XXIII, Laws, 1715-76; 1905: Vol. XXIV, Laws, 1777-88; Vol.
XXVI, Census of 1790; 1906: Vol. XXV, Laws, 1789-90; Omitted Laws, 1669-1783,
and Index to Vols. XXIII-V; 1907: Vol. XXII, Miscellaneous. A thorough bibli-
ographic description is included by Weeks in Vol. XXX.

75. Stephen B. Weeks, *Index to the Colonial and State Records of North
Carolina, Covering Volumes I-XXV* (4 vols.; Goldsboro, Charlotte, and Raleigh:
State of North Carolina, 1909-14), I, preface (unnumbered). These four volumes
comprise, respectively, vols. XXVII-XXX, of the combined Saunders-Clark series.
The volume number on the spine of the volume being cited, therefore, is XXVII.

For the story of Weeks's preparation of the index, see H. G. Jones, "Stephen
Beauregard Weeks: North Carolina's First 'Professional' Historian," *North Carolina Historical Review*, XLII (Autumn, 1965), 410-23.

76. Vol. I, A-E, was printed in Goldsboro by Nash Brothers in 1909; Vol. II,
F-L, and Vol. III, M-R, in Charlotte by Observer Printing House in 1910 and
1911, respectively; and Vol. IV, S-Z, and "Historical Review," in Raleigh by
E. M. Uzzell in 1914.

received no monetary remuneration, Weeks was paid for his preparation of the index. But the approximately $3,000 paid him undoubtedly was one of the most worthwhile expenditures ever made by the State of North Carolina.[77]

The completion of the project of publishing the records relating to the history of North Carolina through the year 1790 marked the most significant achievement in almost a century of efforts on the part of many historians and state officials. Almost a hundred years passed between the publication of Hugh Williamson's *History of North Carolina* and the completion of Walter Clark's *State Records*. During that time historians criticized their fellow citizens and excoriated their detractors on the grounds that the history of North Carolina had been neglected. Many of these persons only complained. But there emerged in almost every decade a determined individual bent on uncovering and disseminating the documentary evidence of the State's history. Among these individuals six merit singular recognition: Archibald D. Murphey for his collecting zeal and his ambitious but unfulfilled plans to write the first true history of North Carolina; David L. Swain for ferreting out a great accumulation of manuscript materials and for stirring the pride and interest of the citizenry in their history; William A. Graham for championing the cause of Swain and all others intent upon preserving the State's records; John H. Wheeler for his perspicacity in collecting materials and in writing of the past and for his courage in braving an enemy blockade in the course of his research; and William L. Saunders and Walter Clark for bringing to fruition the efforts and hopes of all the others.

As the nineteenth century gave way to the twentieth, by a fortunate coincidence, a new school of historians emerged—men trained to search for facts rather than myths and to distinguish between the two. Men like John Spencer Bassett, William K. Boyd, Robert D. W. Connor,[78] J. G. de Roulhac Hamilton, and Stephen B. Weeks, indoctrinated in a new methodology in re-

77. See above, p. 232, n. 72.
78. Though Connor had only an earned bachelor's degree, he merits inclusion with his more degree-laden colleagues because he used their methodology.

search, came on the scene at the very time that, for the first time, the mass of source materials contained in the colonial and state records became available. Without these sources, they too might have faltered under the same frustrations that prevented Archibald Murphey or David Swain from writing the history of which they were so proud. But their good fortune was to be the good fortune of North Carolina. They, their contemporaries, and their students, finding thrown open for them the recorded history of North Carolina as it happened, eagerly delved into it. The edited works of Saunders and Clark, the collected manuscripts of Murphey and Wheeler and Hawks and Swain, and, yes, even of Shocco Jones, having lain fallow so long, finally came to life through the pages of countless articles and books that flowed from the pens of the new historians. The groundwork laid by Murphey, Swain, and all the rest had not been in vain.

PART THREE

CARETAKERS FOR CLIO

1833-1907

VIII

The Formation of Historical Societies and the Establishment of a State Archival-Historical Agency

1833-1907

No fewer than seven identifiable historical societies—all purporting to be state-wide in activities—were formed in North Carolina prior to 1900. Yet at the end of the century only one of them was still in existence and that one was largely a faculty-student club at the University of North Carolina. The fact that these societies foundered is not evidence that they were of little importance to the historical activities of the period. Indeed, several of them made lasting contributions. Not until late in the year 1900, however, was there organized a society which has survived and which has had considerable impact upon the twentieth century; and it was not until 1903 that the State finally established a tax-supported historical agency designed to preserve and disseminate the written history of North Carolina.

SIX EARLY HISTORICAL SOCIETIES, 1833-1887

The first North Carolina Historical Society began auspiciously with formal incorporation by the General Assembly in 1833. The society appears to have originated in the minds of David L. Swain and Joseph Seawell Jones during the Superior Court judge's visit with Jones in 1832.[1] Upon his return to Raleigh, Swain prepared a bill which the Assembly passed early in 1833 providing that he, Jones, James Iredell, Jr., Alfred Moore, Louis D. Henry, Isaac T. Avery, Joseph A. Hill, William D. Mosely, and Richmond Pearson be incorporated into "a body politic and corporate, to be known and distinguished by the name and style of the North Carolina Historical Society." The act stipulated that ". . . the said society shall have free access to all the public records of this State, and shall be permitted at their own costs and charges, to transcribe or cause to be transcribed any of the said records, it being understood that such transcription is to be made in the offices respectively, in which such records now are for safe custody, and without interruption to the duties of the officers having charge of the same."[2]

Meanwhile Swain had been elected governor of the State. It may be assumed that his high office occupied all of his time, but it is nevertheless strange that he failed to call a meeting of the incorporators during the following year. Finally, on October 16, 1834, Jones placed a notice in the *Raleigh Register* calling attention to the incorporation of the "Historical Society of North-Carolina" the previous year and proposing that the corporators and "other Gentlemen who may be curious as to the Annals of the State" meet in Raleigh on the first Monday in December to organize the society.[3] No record of such a meeting has been found.

Seven years later a notice signed by "Several Citizens" appeared in the same newspaper expressing the regret that Raleigh had no "Literary or Scientific Association." It urged that some citizen take the lead in establishing something more than a "debating club." The editor of the paper added his opinion that such a society was certainly needed but that "we have no one among us better calculated to give the Association a start, than

1. Swain Diary, July 3, 1832, and Swain to Jones, December 20, 1832, in Swain Papers, State Archives; Jones to Daniel M. Barringer, December 11, 1832, in Barringer Papers, Southern Historical Collection.
2. *Private Laws of 1832-1833*, c. 63.
3. *Raleigh Register* (weekly edition), November 18, 1834.

the writer of the above."[4] The "writer of the above" was probably William H. Haywood, Jr., a former speaker of the House of Representatives, who the following month wrote Swain, by then president of the University of North Carolina, "The Ex Com: of our Lity. & His: Socy did not meet 1st week in October as had been appointed. . . ." Swain, he said, had been named "Chairman to the Committee" and a meeting was proposed to be held November 13, 1841, in Raleigh. He continued, "Unless we mean to see this effort of ours share the fate of all similar exertions in N. C. we must move in some such way & at an *early* day and *inter nos* if you and I dont do it nobody will do it. It can be carried through—it is worthy of the labor it costs us and I feel sure you share with me in anxiety for our success. . . ."[5] Haywood, the following month, indicated that the meeting had not been held. He wrote Swain,

What shall be done? is a question upon which much depends in regard to our Society and as your duties at C. Hill will be suspended soon for a few weeks I hope you will visit Raleigh where we can have the advantage of a conference and if resolved upon it as I believe *we are something can be done*. At present I incline to the notion that our annual meeting should be postponed & hereafter fixed at a period of the year more convenient to all, at all events in those years when our Assembly does not convene. How would it do to start with the Lectures at C. Hill 20 May?

He discussed current politics, but added, "Avoiding even all appearances of party politics I have hoped that our Society can be made an efficient instrument for good. And why may it not be the means of producing reformation where it is so much required. Much very much may be done by two or three persons engaged in the work heartily. . . ." He concluded, "I think you will agree with me that most persons unite in all our first movements to a literary or State object in N. C. from mere fashion & hardly

4. *Raleigh Register, and North-Carolina Gazette* (semiweekly edition), September 3, 1841.

5. Haywood to Swain, October 25, 1841, in Swain Papers, Southern Historical Collection. Members of the "Executive Committee" in addition to Haywood and Swain were Bishop Levi S. Ives, Judge Frederick Nash, and Judge William B. Shepherd. Archibald Henderson, "Historical Society of North Carolina," *Asheville Citizen*, August 10, 1956.

recollect a week after it the engagement they entered upon at the outset."[6]

The association—or perhaps Haywood himself—determined to hold a meeting at Chapel Hill during the commencement exercises the following year. In March, Haywood again asked Swain to come to Raleigh "on the subject of Historical Society." Bishop Levi Silliman Ives, he wrote, had been invited to deliver the address and Swain was asked to notify the bishop of the exact date.[7] The university president did not carry out the request and it was not until two days before the date proposed for the meeting that the bishop was informed of the time and place. In a pointed reference to the oversight, Ives wrote that inasmuch as he did not carry speeches "in *my pocket* 'ready made' for such occasions, & as I cannot consent to disgrace myself & help to break down the 'Historical & Literary Society of No. Ca.,'" he was forced to decline the invitation.[8] Without a speaker, the embryo of a society was never born.

The failure of the Literary and Historical Association may have resulted from the lack of support by Swain who wanted to establish a historical society at Chapel Hill. This he accomplished in January, 1844, with the organization of the Historical Society of the University of North Carolina. The entire faculty comprised the executive committee, and, as might be expected, Swain was its president. Ashbel G. Brown was named secretary and Ralph H. Graves was appointed treasurer and librarian.[9] Announcement of the fledgling society was made by Swain in the *Raleigh Register*. Its purposes were

first . . . to excite such interest in the public mind, in regard to the history of the State, as may induce the Legislature to adopt early and efficient measures, to obtain from England the most interesting documents in relation to the Royal Government, together with such papers

6. Haywood to Swain, November 23, 1841, in Swain Papers, Southern Historical Collection.

7. Haywood to Swain, March 28, 1842, in Swain Papers, Southern Historical Collection.

8. Ives to Swain, May 31, 1842, in Swain Papers, Southern Historical Collection.

9. [David L. Swain], "The Historical Society of the University of North Carolina," *North Carolina University Magazine*, I (April, 1844), 82-84.

as may be found to reflect light on the obscure history of the Proprietary Government of North Carolina; and, secondly, to collect, arrange and preserve at the University, *as nearly as may be possible,* one or more copies of every book, pamphlet and newspaper published in this State . . . and, especially, all the records, documents and papers to be found within the State, that may tend to elucidate the history of the American Revolution.[10]

The article also reported that a constitution had been adopted and that Bishop Ives had accepted an invitation to speak at the first annual meeting of the society during commencement exercises. This time, with adequate prior notice, the bishop did deliver his address and it was published in an early issue of the *North Carolina University Magazine,* another Swain brainchild, which was first issued almost simultaneously with the founding of the new society and which he used partially as an organ of the society.[11]

At the society's first anniversary meeting in June, 1845, an ambitious report, ostensibly written by Secretary Charles Phillips but almost surely from Swain's pen, was delivered. It showed the chief concern of the organization: the filling of the "deficiencies" in the records of the State relating principally to the American Revolution. The Historical Society, it stated, had determined "that although it cannot consider itself at all committed to the labor of preparing such a stable record of Revolutionary events as is understood by the term history, yet the simplest form of its duty will be to render accessible to the historian, whoever he may be, as far as possible, *all* the facts which may be connected with the war in North Carolina." Already the society had been at work, "and the amount of material already contributed, may

10. *Raleigh Register, and North Carolina Gazette* (semiweekly edition), January 26, 1844.

11. "Bishop Ives' Introductory Address: Delivered before the Historical Society of the University of North Carolina, June 5, 1844," *North Carolina University Magazine,* I (July, 1844), 201-16. An accompanying letter indicated that Charles Phillips was then secretary of the society. The magazine, begun in March, 1844, ceased and resumed publication from time to time and continued into the twentieth century. Its title was changed periodically, as was the habit of newspapers and journals of the nineteenth century. It served mainly as a means of publication of articles by the students and faculty—and Swain in particular—but occasionally the writings of outsiders were included.

well be assumed as a fair precursor of a greater degree of success than had been anticipated" in its organization, the report stated.

Indeed Swain had been at work. Three pages of the report were devoted to a description of printed and manuscript materials acquired. The printed works included session laws, journals of the legislative branch, and newspapers. But of more significance were the manuscripts. Among them were an orderly book kept during the War of the Regulation and another kept by British forces during the American Revolution; a "large collection" of the papers of John Steele and Thomas Burke; more modest collections of papers of James Hogg, Richard Caswell, William Hill, Charles W. Harris, and others; a "most interesting, extensive, and valuable collection of papers" relating to the Revolution; and several biographical sketches.

After detailing the first year's accomplishments, the report turned to the future. As a means of extending the influence of the society beyond the university community, a number of branch associations were proposed, the members of which would be "appointed by the parent Society, or by its President." The aim of interesting more people could be "best attained by incorporating them into our members, and in this way, clothing them with an *ex officio* authority to make collections in our name; at the same time, it is believed that a membership will inspire them with a peculiar interest in the welfare of the Historical Society." Another proposal was the publication of historical pamphlets and addresses which would be exchanged with similar organizations throughout the country.[12] The report was circulated widely and was well received. John H. Wheeler wrote that "had such an institution earlier existed, conjecture tradition and error had not covered so completely much of our early *History*."[13] Others offered to co-operate and wished success to the new organization.[14]

12. Historical Society of the University of North Carolina, *First Report of the Historical Society of the University of North Carolina, June 4, 1845* (Hillsborough: Dennis Heartt, 1845), pp. 1-8.

13. Wheeler to Swain, June 20, 1845, in Swain Papers, Southern Historical Collection.

14. See, for example, George Bancroft to Swain, May 2, 1845, in Swain Papers, Southern Historical Collection; Walter L. Steele to Swain, September 27, 1845, in Swain Papers, State Archives.

In spite of its auspicious beginnings, the society remained largely a one-man association. The proposal for broadening its membership was forgotten, and even the faculty members lost interest except when Swain called upon them for special tasks. No business meeting of the group seems to have been held after 1845, although eminent men continued to deliver addresses to the "membership" during commencements. The society was little more than David L. Swain, whose primary interest—a highly creditable one—was in obtaining historical source materials. In the words of a young student of Swain's who was later to follow in his steps to the presidency of the University of North Carolina, "On the belief that the Society was an entity, a live organization, valuable books and documents were presented to it. . . . The President was active and successful in procuring letters of prominent men in the State. When he could not obtain gifts of such he solicited loans, which were seldom returned."[15] But the society, in name, maintained an existence at least until the outbreak of the Civil War. In 1851, the Reverend Fordyce M. Hubbard delivered a paper on the subject of the earlier historians of the State,[16] and, in 1852, the *University Magazine* was revived with the help of the society.[17] Bishop Thomas Atkinson addressed the society in 1855,[18] and Francis L. Hawks, distinguished theologian and historian, delivered the address in 1858.[19]

In the meantime Swain had pursued vigorously the acquisition of books and manuscripts. The collection, nominally the

15. Battle, *History of the University*, I, 486.
16. Battle, *History of the University*, I, 624.
17. Archibald Henderson, "Buncombe's D. L. Swain, Founder of Historical Society of North Carolina," *Durham Morning Herald*, April 13, 1956; *North Carolina University Magazine*, I [second series] (February, 1852), 1.
A correspondent in 1853 wrote Swain, "May I suggest again, the resuscitation of the Historical Society?—or if it is breathing, its invigoration?—Much would be gained, I think, by keeping it more prominently before the eye of the publick. Would it not be well to hold publick meetings of the Society, either once in two years in Raleigh, during the meeting of the Legislature, or once every year at the University, during Commencement-week?" Drury Lacy to Swain, April 15, 1853, in Swain Papers, Southern Historical Collection. No copy of Swain's reply has been found.
18. Thomas Atkinson, *Address Delivered Before the Historical Society of the University of North-Carolina, June 6, 1855, By Rt. Rev. Bishop Atkinson* (Raleigh: Holden & Wilson, 1855).
19. Battle, *History of the University*, I, 685.

property of the Historical Society but always in the custody of Swain, grew year by year.[20] Some of the manuscripts he displayed in a cabinet, and he perhaps allowed researchers access to them. By 1854, the university library had grown to 3,600 volumes—meager even at that date—but it is not known if these included the historical volumes collected by Swain.[21]

Little is known of the Historical Society of the University of North Carolina from 1858 until 1868, but it is supposed to have remained alive on paper only, with the traditional address being delivered before it during commencement activities. Inasmuch as Swain had remained its dominant force, it might have been expected to disappear completely with his death on August 27, 1868. Soon after notification of his passing, the society met and adopted the following resolution: "That in addition to other causes of sorrow for his death, this Society would commemorate his love for his native state, his indefatigable zeal in collecting the memorials of its history, his minute, extensive, and most accurate knowledge of men and events connected with it, and his unfailing readiness to communicate to all inquirers his ample stores of information—which make his loss not only sorrowful but irreparable."[22] The resolution was signed by Charles Phillips, secretary. Inasmuch as Phillips had been secretary of the society in 1845, he may have remained in that capacity through the years. The society, in fact, probably had only two continuously-active members—Swain and Phillips. Without its president, the society ceased to exist in 1868.

In June, 1870, John H. Wheeler came from Washington to deliver the commencement address to the senior class. The memories of Swain's work of collecting historical materials and the news of Mrs. Swain's removal of the collection upon her husband's death aroused renewed interest. Consequently "several members of the Historical Society of North Carolina met in the University Library for the purpose of reorganizing the So-

20. For a review of the materials collected by Swain, see above, pp. 186 ff.

21. Archibald Henderson, *The Campus of the First State University* (Chapel Hill: The University of North Carolina Press, 1949), p. 147.

22. The resolution, dated August 31, 1868, is in the Walter Clark Papers, State Archives. Cited hereafter as Clark Papers.

ciety. . . ." Professor Alexander McIver, the temporary chairman, turned the gavel over to Wheeler, who was elected president. McIver thereupon was named secretary and treasurer. Thirteen prominent North Carolinians, including Governor William W. Holden, were elected vice-presidents, and all university trustees were made ex officio members. Thirteen prominent persons were made honorary members, among whom was George Bancroft. Then the society turned to its real purpose: "Superintendent Ashley, Hon. Curtis H. Brogden, and James F. Taylor were appointed a committee to procure from Mrs. Eleanor H. Swain the books and manuscripts claimed by the society."[23] But it was too late. A few months afterward the university closed its doors. The fourth historical society formed within a span of 38 years ceased to exist.

During the political turmoil of reconstruction, Swain was in effect suspended from the office of president of the university though he continued to claim the title. He remained president of the Historical Society in the absence of elections, however, and therein lies an interesting complication which figured in later controversy over the Swain collection. Was the Historical Society of the University of North Carolina legally a part of the university, or was it simply a private organization of individuals, the majority of whom were connected with the university? It was never incorporated by the General Assembly. What was its legal status? If it were a legal part of the university, then the materials given to it belonged to the university. On the other hand, if it were a private organization, the university could not lay claim to the collection. Furthermore, if membership had been discontinued and only Swain—and possibly Charles Phillips—had been active, would the materials not belong to Swain who collected them?[24]

23. *North Carolina Standard* (Raleigh, weekly edition), June 22, 1870; Battle, *History of the University*, II, 36. Three months after the meeting the librarian of the university issued a circular reporting the removal of the library to "the building designed for it." In the library, he wrote, "should be preserved a copy of every book and pamphlet printed in North Carolina or connected with her history. Every such publication, however trifling, will be welcomed." Fisk P. Brewer, "Library Circular," (Chapel Hill: The University of North Carolina, 1870).

24. While not attempting to answer these questions, I am of the opinion that

Swain omitted any reference to the historical collection in his will.[25] But he named his wife executrix and William H. Battle and William A. Graham executors. Both Battle and Graham had active historical interests, and if Swain did consider the collection as his own, he may have thought that his friends would settle the matter properly. On the other hand, the fact that he made no mention of the materials in his will (which was written in 1858 when the Historical Society was still supposedly active) would seem to indicate that he did not think of them as his private possessions. Mrs. Swain, however, had no thought but that her husband personally had been responsible for the collection and that it was a personal possession. This attitude was strengthened in view of her opinion that he had been wronged by the trustees and that she was due her husband's back salary and other considerations by the State. Consequently, when she found the historical papers "in his library alongside his own, and mixed with letters of her grandfather, Governor Caswell, [she] naturally thought that they were vested in her as executrix." The new president of the university made no claim for them and Mrs. Swain instructed the executors to take them to Raleigh where they were placed in a tin box in the vault of the Citizens National Bank.[26]

Swain never thought otherwise than that his collection would be left to the Historical Society which he considered a part of the university—if not legally, then certainly spiritually. In his arguments for donations of materials, he repeatedly intimated that they would be cared for by the university, an agency of the State. Former Governor Henry Toole Clark in 1872 wrote, ". . . I am under the impression that the almost entire lot with very few exceptions belong to the Historical Society and that persons were induced to part with these papers for the Society and for no other purpose. . . . Govr. S. always solicited these as contributions to the H. Society after the institution of the Society. Everything collected was *for it*. And he certainly intended & so said, that all his own collection previously made [i.e., prior to 1844], were to go to it." Clark to William H. Battle, March 25, 1872, in Battle Family Papers, Southern Historical Collection. Charles Phillips, Swain's co-worker in the earlier Historical Society, wrote that it was difficult to determine which of the papers Swain owned and which ones "he merely was guard[ing]." Phillips to Lyman C. Draper, October 18, 1881, Draper Manuscripts, Kings Mountain Papers.

25. Swain's will is recorded in Will Book G, pp. 539-42, Office of the Clerk of Superior Court, Orange County Courthouse, Hillsborough.

26. Battle, *History of the University*, II, 107; William H. Battle to Mrs. Swain, August 25, 1873, in Clark Papers, State Archives. It should be remembered that beginning in 1868 the university was governed by a new board of trustees dom-

The committee appointed by the reconstituted Historical Society of North Carolina[27] was unsuccessful in its attempt to persuade Mrs. Swain to give up the collection. In 1873, Battle transmitted to her a request for permission to consult a particular document in the vault. From Freeport, Illinois, where she was living with her daughter, Mrs. Swain wrote, "To preserve the value of the work, I must not permit the removal, or use made, of any important paper among the collection. I consider this labor of my husband, a sacred trust, not to be intermeddled with, without the advice of some friend interested & competent to decide for me." She promised to bequeath "to the State of N.C. or the *University*," all of the papers that her daughter did not choose to retain.[28] Fifteen months later, however, she did allow Graham to borrow the journal of the Provincial Congress that met at Hillsborough in 1775.[29]

With the university no longer open, the society reorganized in 1870 appears not to have held another meeting. But the manuscripts, hidden in the Raleigh bank, remained a choice prize. It is not surprising therefore that early in 1875 a group of citizens interested in extracting the collection from the bank vault where it was supposed to be "liable to damage from insects in its present condition"[30] began a movement to organize a new society to lay claim to it. In order to establish its legal basis, the

inated by Republicans. The membership of the society as reorganized in June, 1870, included the trustees and others whose political views ran counter to members of the university administration that was suspended from office in 1868. Mrs. Swain and many of her friends might legitimately have feared that the papers would not be properly cared for if turned over to the university at that time. In fact, R. H. Morrison wrote that "the Libraries & Archives of the University have fallen into the hands of the Vandals," who, he feared, had "Swept them . . . into oblivion." Morrison to Lyman C. Draper, November 27, 1871, Draper Manuscripts, Kings Mountain Papers.

27. It is perhaps significant that the words "the University of" were omitted from the title of the reorganized society. The names chosen for officers indicate plainly that the new group was not to be limited to the university.

28. Eleanor H. Swain to William H. Battle, October 27, 1873, in Clark Papers, State Archives.

29. Notation of Kemp P. Battle, January 27, 1875, on Graham to Battle, January 22, 1874 [1875], in Miscellaneous Papers, State Archives. Graham noted, "The first copy of it I ever saw, was among the Murphey papers which passed into the hands of Govr. Swain."

30. Graham to Cornelia Phillips Spencer, May 7, 1875, in Spencer Papers, State Archives.

new Historical Society of North Carolina (the fifth such society with varying titles to be organized since 1833 but only the second to be chartered) was incorporated by the General Assembly. The act, ratified March 22, 1875, named among the incorporators Graham, William H. Battle and his son Kemp P. Battle, John H. Wheeler, and Cornelia Phillips Spencer, all of whom were anxious to see the collection opened again. The fourth section of the act read,

The said corporation shall have authority to acquire and hold such real and personal property as may be proper for carrying out the objects of its creation, especially books, manuscripts, documents, papers, and memorials of whatever kind relating to the history of this State, *particularly those possessed by the late Historical Society of North Carolina* [italics mine]. It shall likewise be authorized to accept donations of money or property for the purpose of enabling it to prosecute researches into said history and make publication relating thereto.[31]

Shortly after passage of the act Graham sent out a card calling for a meeting of the incorporators at the Yarborough House in Raleigh on May 4, 1875. Present for this first meeting were Graham, the Battles, Washington C. Kerr, Stephen D. Pool, and Wheeler (who had come all the way from Washington). Several others sent letters regretting their inability to attend but promising to support the society. Graham was elected president and Pool secretary. The aging Graham pointed out "the necessity that existed for the Society and what material was still wanting to complete the early history of the State." Following the appointment of a committee to draw up a constitution and bylaws, the incorporators turned to their chief interest. After a discussion of the controversy over the Swain collection, a committee composed of Graham, former Governor Vance, and Mrs. Spencer was appointed "to see Mrs. Swain, or to correspond with her relative to the historical documents in the possession of her late

31. *Private Laws of 1874-1875*, c. 127, s. 4. As early as 1873, Former Governor Clark had proposed the establishment of a new historical society "the great object of which should be to collect, preserve, and publish" materials relating to North Carolina history. He suggested that the headquarters be in Raleigh and that the society publish a monthly "Historical Register." Clark to Kemp P. Battle, May 28, 1873, in Battle Family Papers, Southern Historical Collection.

husband, Gov. Swain." The group then adjourned to meet again on call of the chairman.[32]

Another significant provision of the act creating the society was that the keeper of the Capitol was authorized "to furnish said society a room in said building for the safe keeping of the books, papers and effects of the society. . . ."[33] Thus the 1875 organization was the first of the societies since the one chartered in 1833 that was to be considered a truly state-wide group with headquarters in the capital city. This provision supports the theory that it was the intention of the organizers to establish a repository for historical papers in the Capitol and that they did not propose to return the Swain collection to the University. This theory cannot be proved, however, because the university's doors were still closed when the legislation was passed, and the skeptic might suspect that the plan for an office in the Capitol was to be only a temporary expedient until the reopening of the university. Only a few months after the organization of the new society, the university did reopen.

Graham began immediately to carry out the society's instructions. A letter in the name of the committee was addressed to Mrs. Swain beseeching her to put the entire collection into the possession of the new society "for preservation, & future use." In doing so, it said, she would be carrying out Swain's wishes, "knowing so well as we do how dear to his heart were the good name & fame & history of his native State, & how his last thoughts were occupied with plans for employing, this collection of material for History, in her service."[34] It fell to Mrs. Spencer—a warm friend of the Swains—to forward the letter. In her accompanying note, she wrote, "It seems to me the Historical Society is very cooly asking you to make them a very valuable present. Yet I suppose it has always been your intention to let the State possess the material for History."[35] In a formal reply to the com-

32. "Official Proceedings of the First Meeting of the North Carolina Historical Society," *Our Living and Our Dead,* III (July, 1875), 62-64. The incorporators also elected to membership ten additional persons.

33. *Private Laws of 1874-1875,* c. 127, s. 5.

34. Graham, Vance, and Mrs. Spencer to Eleanor H. Swain, May 13, 1875, in Clark Papers, State Archives.

35. Mrs. Spencer to Mrs. Swain, May 13, 1875, in Spencer Papers, State Archives.

mittee, Mrs. Swain declined "at present, at least" to give up the papers. She continued, "I cannot indicate at this moment, what disposition I will eventually make of that collection. They shall be carefully preserved, and disposition will be made of them in the future as will, in my judgment, the most nearly comply with the intentions and desires of my late Husband."[36] Graham, upon receipt of the letter, wrote, "I think Mrs. Swain has made a *mistake* in supposing the Historical Society and the Trustees of the University to be the same corporation and secondly, in thinking that her late husband considered the Historical matter . . . which was so freely yielded to him, as *individual* property."[37]

Later in the summer Mrs. Spencer told the widow that in her previous letter she had assumed that she was asking for the donation of private property. But she had discussed the matter with Judge Battle and others at the reopening of the university and all had the opinion that "Gov. Swain did never at any time consider the Hist. papers he was collecting with such zeal & diligence, as *private property.*" She said that there had never been a question on the issue and that the only reason that they were not called for immediately after Swain's death was that his friends "refused to give such a crew [as the 'Carpetbag regime' at the university] any aid; & I was delighted to be able to say that *you* possessed all the papers of any value. Those who knew better than I were very willing the papers sh^d. be sheltered by such alleged private ownership for the time."[38]

Mrs. Swain, still refusing to give up the collection, wrote: "It seems strange to me, that after the lapse of seven years, any one should question the right of my lamented husband to the historical collection which he had been so 'curious' in obtaining— The claiments refer^d. to in your letter, & all other contributors who desire it can have returned their papers, which they con-

36. Mrs. Swain to Graham, Vance, and Mrs. Spencer, May 19, 1875, in Clark Papers, State Archives.
37. Graham to Mrs. Spencer, June 7, 1875, in Spencer Papers, State Archives.
38. Mrs. Spencer to Mrs. Swain, undated letter in Spencer Papers, State Archives. Mrs. Spencer probably referred to a meeting of the trustees on June 16 at which time a faculty was elected for the reopening of the university on September 4. Battle, *History of the University*, II, 77.

sider so val^ble[.] I have no objection to this, & have no disposition to withhold them. But the *demand* is for the *whole,* as
property belonging to the State." She protested that Governor
Graham and Judge Battle, if they thought the materials possessions of the State, should have told her so when she was making
out her will. She curtly suggested that any future correspondence
on the matter should be directed to her daughter, Ella, who, she
said, had "no thought, of letting this favorite work of her Father
slip from her so easily." She concluded, "The reason for my
connecting the debt due Mr Swain from the Uni. with his history,
was simply I regard^d the Uni. & Historical Soc. as Institutions of
the State, & I saw no justice in adding one obligation to another,
when considering the prob^le loss in one case, & the value of the
other."[39]

The Society's president, Graham, died on August 11, 1875,
and William Hooper of the University of North Carolina faculty
was elected to succeed him. Then, in June, 1876, Mrs. Spencer
was elected corresponding secretary, with the result that the
"office" of the society—still little more than a paper organization—
became centered at Chapel Hill. By then the controversy over
the Swain collection had been well publicized and Mrs. Spencer
wrote that "sundry persons who made donations of valuable
papers to that collection, are moving now to reclaim their papers—
saying they were donated to the *Society*—& not to the Gov."
Among those demanding the return of their donations were the
Avery and Henderson families, the former claiming that they
had offers of purchase. She urged Mrs. Swain to change her mind
and to give them to the Historical Society. She concluded, "There
is misunderstanding about it, & likely to be misrepresentation.
The Hist. Soc. of N.C. has no papers but those—& has not them
if you say No."[40] Kemp Battle reasoned that if she would turn
them over to the society, it in turn would persuade these and
other donors to relinquish their claims to the papers. He referred
to "the paper Father has showing that Gov. Swain held these

39. Mrs. Swain to Mrs. Spencer, [September 2, 1875], in Spencer Papers, State
Archives.

40. Mrs. Spencer to Mrs. Swain, August 11, 1876, in Spencer Papers, State
Archives.

documents as Trustee for an imaginary 'Historical Society.' "[41] But the pleas went unheeded.[42]

William Hooper, who had succeeded to the presidency of the Historical Society in 1875, died a year later, and at the annual meeting during commencement activities in 1877 Judge John Kerr was elected to the office.[43] The only other order of business appears to have been the assessment of a one dollar membership fee to replenish the empty treasury. The following year considerable progress was reported, all pointing toward centering the society at the university. An article in the *University Magazine* (which had been revived in March, 1878) noted that President Battle had set apart an alcove in the old Dialectic Society Hall for use of the society and that Mrs. Swain had turned over to it "50 or 60 books" formerly in her husband's possession.[44] All members were exhorted to collect materials and turn them over to the society. Officers, in addition to Judge Kerr, were R. H. Graves, recording secretary; Mrs. Spencer, corresponding secretary; and C. D. Grandy, treasurer.[45]

On June 2, 1880, the society elected Kemp Battle as its president, an action warmly applauded by the indomitable Mrs. Spencer, who wrote that it had been a mistake in the first place to elect Judge Kerr, who did not live in Chapel Hill, "for the State University is the only proper headquarters for all associations literary and historical. . . ."[46] The following week the

41. Kemp P. Battle to Mrs. Spencer, June 9, 1876, in Spencer Papers, State Archives.

42. "The Historical Society," *University Magazine*, II (October, 1878), 86. Kemp Battle, who soon became president of the university, wrote years later that Mrs. Swain found a paper stating that the bound books in the collection were the property of the Historical Society and that she promptly surrendered them. This may have been the "paper" referred to by Battle above. He also said that Mrs. Swain herself sold "many valuable autographs" to Thomas Addis Emmet of New York for $400. Battle, *History of the University*, I, 487; II, 107. I have not been able to prove conclusively whether the Emmet purchase was made prior to Mrs. Swain's death or afterward by her executor, Walter Clark. See below, p. 263.

43. Battle, *History of the University*, II, 129-30.

44. These were probably the books referred to by Battle. See also Kemp P. Battle to Lyman C. Draper, March 30, 1880, in Draper Manuscripts, Kings Mountain Papers.

45. "The Historical Society," *University Magazine*, II (October, 1878), 85-86.

46. "North Carolina Historical Society," typescript by Mrs. Spencer prepared for the *North Carolina Presbyterian*, 1881, in Spencer Papers, Southern Historical Collection.

executive committee directed its new president to "trace up and obtain the Records and Funds of the Society," and shortly thereafter it adopted a new constitution and bylaws. An annual meeting was to be held at the University of North Carolina in June and a library-museum was authorized in which were to be kept the books, manuscripts, and relics of the society.[47] A printed circular was sent to newspapers appealing for donations of money, documents, and books. Officers, in addition to Battle, were J. F. Heitman of Trinity College, recording secretary, and George T. Winston, treasurer.[48]

Late in 1880, President Battle proposed a meeting of the society in Raleigh during the approaching session of the General Assembly and invited Senator Zebulon B. Vance to be the speaker. Perhaps remembering that Vance had been one of the incorporators of the society five years earlier when it was proposed to be independent of the university, Battle wrote, "The Society is not connected with the University legally, but we give its collections a room & will care for the same."[49] The meeting appears not to have been held, but General Matt W. Ransom delivered the address at its annual meeting at Chapel Hill in June, 1881.[50]

For all intents and purposes, the society, after about 1880, was no longer the one incorporated by the General Assembly in 1875. Its center of activity had been removed from Raleigh to Chapel Hill and it had gradually become, much as the old Swain society had been, an organ of those connected with the university. Even its name had been inverted, though apparently by habit rather than by formal action. It had been unsuccessful in obtaining the Swain collection—except for some printed books —and its own holdings were modest. Meetings were seldom held

47. The constitution was drawn up by a committee in accordance with a resolution passed at the July 3, 1880, meeting. Minutes of the North Carolina Historical Society, 1880-1901, Southern Historical Collection. Interestingly enough, the constitution provided that, should the organization be dissolved, its books and manuscripts were to be transferred to either the State Library or the library of the University of North Carolina.

48. North Carolina Historical Society, *The North Carolina Historical Society. An Appeal to its Friends,* a three-page leaflet dated October 6, 1880, no publisher listed.

49. Battle to Vance, November 16, 1880, in Vance Papers, State Archives.

50. Battle, *History of the University,* II, 234.

and even the traditional addresses during commencement week were not regularly given. Finally, on September 29, 1887, a number of students with several members of the faculty met in President Battle's office "for the purpose of organizing a Historical Society in the University of North Carolina." Battle, who was again elected president, reported that "a charter for a general State Historical Society was obtained in 1875, but that this Society soon came to nought. The present one is to be on a different basis."[51] At the October meeting, however, Professor Winston suggested "that the present organization become a part of the now existing State Historical Society of N.C.," and because a majority of the executive committee of the previous society was then present, "there can be no difficulty about receiving new members." Thereupon, "Dr. Battle, President of the N. C. State Historical Society, after remarking that this Society, the work of which for a number of years has been done by a few individuals, would begin a more vigorous existence, declared the Society ready to receive new members."[52] The new membership consisted almost solely of faculty members and students in advanced classes. The main purpose was to encourage research, and the society proudly announced that "original investigations are carried on at the Hill." Officers in addition to Battle were A. M. Mangum, vice-president; J. F. Heitman, secretary and treasurer; and Stephen B. Weeks, assistant secretary. The executive committee was composed of Battle, Mangum, Weeks, George T. Winston, and Claudius Dockery. All but Heitman—a Trinity College professor —lived in Chapel Hill. Monthly meetings were scheduled with a member, or an invited guest, reading a paper. The new organization claimed direct descent from Swain's 1844 society, but its genealogical sketch was so spurious as to show almost complete lack of familiarity with its predecessors.[53]

The February, 1888, meeting, at which Battle and Dockery

51. Minutes of September 29, 1887, in Minutes of the North Carolina Historical Society, 1880-1901, Southern Historical Collection.

52. Minutes of October 26, 1887, in Minutes of the North Carolina Historical Society, 1880-1901, Southern Historical Collection.

53. "The North Carolina Historical Society," *North Carolina University Magazine,* N.S. VII (December, 1887), 81-83.

read papers,[54] resulted in a new project: the collection of materials—both documents and relics—relating to the Civil War. A circular letter was issued asking for such materials and stating that the university would set apart a "hall for the preservation and display of all relics and documents confided to the care of the Society." Members of the organization would expect to publish articles based on the material collected.[55] The monthly meetings continued during the academic year, and, in 1889, it was reported that "the work of the Society is attracting considerable attention outside of our own State."[56] By 1894, the society claimed a "valuable collection of books, old newspaper files, pamphlets, manuscripts, etc.," many of the books having been loaned to the university library.[57]

But here the tracing of the Historical Society at Chapel Hill can be terminated. Indeed, the only justification for tracing its existence after about 1879 has been to show how a society incorporated by the General Assembly as a state-wide organization with broad purposes was gradually transformed into a club catering almost exclusively to the interests of the university faculty and student body. The act incorporating the Historical Society of North Carolina in 1875 was never repealed or amended. But by changing the name of the organization, by moving its "headquarters" to Chapel Hill, and by changing its nature from that of a corporation to that of a private club, the "North Carolina Historical Society" that emerged with the election of Kemp P. Battle to the presidency in 1880 was, if it could claim descent at all from the 1875 corporation, certainly born out of wedlock. It no longer could be considered a state historical society.[58] Even

54. "North Carolina Historical Society," *North Carolina University Magazine,* N.S. VII (February, 1888), 133-34.

55. "Circular Letter of North Carolina Historical Society, Chapel Hill, Feb. 20, 1888," in Saunders Papers, State Archives.

56. "North Carolina Historical Society," *North Carolina University Magazine,* N.S. VIII (1889), 245.

57. Battle, *History of the University,* II, 510.

58. The Historical Society at the University of North Carolina has remained an active faculty-student organization until the present time. Among its chief contributions to history was its assistance in inaugurating the finest series of historical monographs ever published in North Carolina—*The James Sprunt Historical Monographs.* The first number of the series appeared in 1900 and it

so, it was at the time the only historical society in North Carolina devoted exclusively to the history of the State. In fact, it would not be too much to say that of all the societies established in North Carolina during the nineteenth century, those which were active at Chapel Hill contributed most to the preservation and dissemination of North Carolina history.[59]

THE DISPERSAL OF THE SWAIN COLLECTION, 1880-1930

With the exception of the publication of the colonial and state records, the manuscript collection of David L. Swain[60] constituted the most important single nineteenth-century accomplishment in the preservation of North Carolina history. It was the product of the Historical Society founded in 1844 and

is still being published under the title *The James Sprunt Studies in History and Political Science.*

The manuscripts owned by the Historical Society remained in the custody of President Battle until 1907 when Louis Round Wilson, librarian, and Joseph G. de Roulhac Hamilton, professor of history, transferred them into the new library vault. Some of the papers were exhibited at the state fair in Raleigh in 1901. Louis Round Wilson, "The Acquisition of the Stephen B. Weeks Collection of Caroliniana," *North Carolina Historical Review,* XLII (October, 1965), 425-26. The society's collection became the nucleus around which the Southern Historical Collection has been built. Carolyn Andrews Wallace, "The Southern Historical Collection," *North Carolina Libraries,* XIX (Winter, 1961), 16-21.

59. This study has deliberately excluded private historical societies established during the nineteenth century because it has been primarily concerned with the State and its institutions. Among the private societies, the Trinity College Historical Society, founded in 1892 by Stephen Beauregard Weeks, was and still is the most active. Under the leadership of John Spencer Bassett, that society began in 1894 a collection of manuscripts which formed the nucleus for the Manuscript Department of the Duke University Library. Bassett's successor, William K. Boyd, devoted several decades to building up this collection which, though rich in North Caroliniana, is international in character. For a history of the society, see Nannie M. Tilley, *The Trinity College Historical Society, 1892-1941* (Durham: Duke University Press, 1941). Less pretentious historical societies were formed at other colleges and by special-interest groups. An example of the latter is the Wachovia Historical Society, founded in 1895 for the preservation and study of Moravian history at Salem. See Adelaide L. Fries, "The Wachovia Historical society," North Carolina Historical Commission, *Literary and Historical Activities in North Carolina 1900-1905* (Raleigh: North Carolina Historical Commission, 1907), pp. 169-73. This volume is cited hereafter as *Literary and Historical Activities.*

60. Although in this chapter the manuscripts acquired by Swain will be referred to as the "Swain collection," a good case could be made for referring to them as the "Historical Society collection."

the key factor in the founding of at least three subsequent associations. Following Swain's death it became an important historical prize, and, until it was finally disposed of, it excited historians, inflamed passions, and colored every historical movement.

The pleadings of William A. Graham, William H. Battle, and Cornelia Phillips Spencer in the 1870's were to no avail. Mrs. Swain adamantly refused to give up the manuscripts. She appears, however, to have moved them from the bank to her Raleigh residence around 1880,[61] and the following year Swain's old friend, Charles Phillips, wrote that the papers were "still in the boxes that received them just after his death—i.e., the largest & the more valuable part."[62]

In 1881, Secretary of State William L. Saunders began the collection, copying, and publication of the colonial records, a project so long advocated by David Swain. Mrs. Swain was delighted: Her husband's dream was coming true. But she was old and weary. Her son had been killed in a railroad accident; her daughter, to whom she had planned to leave the collection, was dead; two of her sisters died within a year. Only an older sister and Mrs. Swain's young grandchildren were left. On January 8, 1883, she directed the writing of a new will by Walter Clark and Richard H. Battle whom she appointed her executors. The fourth item read, "The historical collection made by my husband, D. L. Swain, in consideration of his great zeal in providing a good and reliable history of his native State, though unfinished, I leave with the executors of this will to dispose of by a sale, or a gift, as they believe best to ensure a fulfillment of the work to the State of North Carolina."[63]

Almost before the ink of her signature was dry, she decided not to make the State wait until her death to benefit from the papers. In the words of Saunders, writing on February 3, 1883,

61. Kemp Battle wrote that the papers were "probably boxed up in Raleigh at the residence of Mrs. Swain." Battle to Lyman C. Draper, March 30, 1880, in Draper Manuscripts, Kings Mountain Papers.

62. Phillips to Draper, October 18, 1881, in Draper Manuscripts, Kings Mountain Papers.

63. "Last Will and Testament of Eleanor H. Swain," January 8, 1883, printed copy in North Carolina Collection.

". . . a few days past Mrs. Swain . . . has generously made a donation for the public benefit of all the papers it [the Swain
collection] contains of historical value. . . . The Trustees [of the
State Library] cannot refrain from expressing their sense of
the obligation of the people of North Carolina to Mrs. Swain
for her generous and timely donation. . . ."[64] Within a month,
she was dead. Her executors, Clark and Battle, noted as an after-
thought on the inventory of her estate, "also lot of Autographs
and historical papers."[65]

No catalogue was made of the Swain collection in 1868 or
1883. The omission of this detail has plagued historians ever
since. More questions than answers have resulted from it.

The first question that arises is whether the papers turned
over to Saunders by Mrs. Swain were in reality a gift to the State.
The answer appears to be no. Although her will stipulated that
they should be given or sold to the State, Mrs. Swain personally
authorized their delivery to Saunders before her death for his
"examination and classification." Upon hearing of her death,
Saunders wrote her executors, "I will be obliged to you to inform
me where to deliver the MSS papers &c recently entrusted to me
by the late Mrs. D. L. Swain for examination and classification.
The work she was kind enough to suggest that I should undertake has not been completed but under the circumstances I deem
it proper to turn everything over to you as her Executors."[66] The
executors apparently requested that Saunders retain the papers for
the time being and they probably remained in his hands until
1886.

The news of Mrs. Swain's death and of Saunders' custody of
the papers spread rapidly. Charles De F. Burns, a New York
book and manuscript dealer, assuming that the collection would
be for sale, asked for "some general idea of what it consists of
and the price; also, whether, in case it is not intended to dispose

64. "Report of the Trustees of the Library," printed as Document No. 21,
Public Documents, 1883.
65. The inventory is in Eleanor H. Swain Estate Papers, Wake County Records,
Estates, State Archives.
66. Saunders to Battle and Clark, February 27, 1883, in Saunders Papers,
Southern Historical Collection.

of the collection, it would be practicable to obtain any duplicates of Colonial or Revolutionary names that it might contain." Saunders appears to have told him that the bulk of the collection would be retained by the State, for Burns wrote again, "when the selection is made for your State Library I shall be glad to be advised of what there is remaining and the valuation placed on it —if not unreasonable I could probably find a purchaser for it. . . ." He also offered to handle the auction if that method of disposition were decided upon.[67] Charles C. Jones, Jr., a Georgia historian and collector, also inquired about the papers.[68]

Burns continued his periodic inquiries through the next two years[69] and his persistence may have been responsible for the preparation, in 1885, of a catalogue of approximately 325 items in the collection. The catalogue—which excluded practically all materials without autographs and many with them—revealed publicly for the first time the extent of Swain's success in collecting historical materials. Its eight pages listed letters written by scores of men from early colonial times to the mid-nineteenth century, ranging from one to thirty-eight letters each. There were seven from George Washington, four from John Adams (including his "Thoughts on Government"), eleven from Thomas Jefferson, twenty-five from Nathanael Greene, and thirty-eight from Cornelius Harnett. Among the others were letters of Baron de Kalb, Marquis de Lafayette, Baron von Steuben, Talleyrand, and Joseph Bonaparte.[70] It is little wonder that the collection had aroused so much interest.

Saunders wrote Burns late in 1885 that the collection would be sent to "Messrs. Hale & Co." of New York "to enable an examination."[71] Burns, having seen a copy of the catalogue, wrote

67. Burns to Saunders, February 24, March 6, 1883, in Saunders Papers, State Archives.

68. Jones to Saunders, March 16, 1883, in Saunders Papers, State Archives.

69. See, for example, Burns to Saunders, February 2, March 10, May 21, 1884, in Saunders Papers, State Archives.

70. *Catalogue of the Swain Collection of Autograph Letters* (Raleigh: E. M. Uzzell, 1885), pp. 1-8. The catalogue was prepared by K. B. Batchelor for $10.00. Receipt of K. B. Batchelor, September 23, 1885, in Eleanor H. Swain Estate Papers, Wake County Records, Estates, State Archives.

71. Saunders' letter has not been found, but Burns repeated the statement in his letter to Saunders of December 7, 1885, in Secretary of State's Papers, Cor-

that he supposed "the necessary arrangements for the sale have been made, and therefore [I] write you with a request for information as to the price asked and also whether opportunity will be afforded for examination." A few days later he requested several copies of the catalogue and asked, "am I to infer that the catalogue represents the entire collection or only that portion of it which is for sale—if the former is the case can you not designate on one copy which names, & the number of specimens of each, that are for sale."[72]

The private papers of Saunders and Clark are silent on the details of the sale that followed early in 1886 under authority of the executors. But in Clark's account of the estate submitted to the clerk of the Superior Court in Wake County, he recorded the sale of six separate lots of "letters & autographs" between January 20 and March 27. The price ranged from $4.86 to $151.00 per lot, and the total income from the sales was $370.36. The usually meticulous Clark failed to list the names of the purchasers, thus providing for more uncertainty in the effort to trace the Swain collection.[73]

At this point a series of questions arise, the answers to some of which must be based on circumstantial evidence and subject to revisions should additional documentary evidence be found.

1. What portion of the materials originally collected by Swain was not catalogued in 1885? Only about 325 manuscripts, most of which contained autographs of interest to collectors, were included in the catalogue. Not listed were several thousand manuscripts comprising the bulk of the papers acquired by Swain; and, with a few exceptions, Swain's private papers were omitted.[74] The catalogue, therefore, listed only those autographs that com-

respondence, State Archives. Although the word "collection" might have referred to the entire group of papers collected by Swain, I am of the opinion that Saunders intended to send to New York only those items listed in the catalogue. "Messrs. Hale & Co." was E. J. Hale and Sons, 66-68 Reade Street, New York, founded by the North Carolina editor who died in 1883.

72. Burns to Saunders, December 7, 19, 1885, in Secretary of State's Papers, Correspondence, State Archives. Again, Saunders' reply has not been found. The catalogue, of course, listed only a fraction of the entire collection.

73. The account, dated April 23, 1886, is in Eleanor H. Swain Estate Papers, Wake County Records, Estates, State Archives.

74. For an account of the papers not sold in 1886, see below, pp. 267 ff.

manded a market whereas the bulk of the collection—the papers of purely historical as contrasted with autograph value—was retained.

2. Were all of the manuscripts listed in the catalogue sold? The answer is definitely no. John Adams' "Thoughts on Government," the most valuable of all items listed, was retained by Clark and later given to the North Carolina Historical Commission. Other items, including Swain's letters to Howell Cobb and L. O'B. Branch, dated January 31, 1859, were retained by Clark and are now in possession of the State.

3. To whom were the manuscripts sold during the period of January-March, 1886? Until a more complete comparison can be made between the 1885 catalogue and the holdings of other manuscript repositories in the United States, no definite answer can be given.[75] Lacking evidence to the contrary, it is perhaps reasonable to assume that most of the papers listed in the catalogue were sent to Hale and Sons in New York where they were disposed of, just as Saunders indicated they would be. Obviously they were sold at intervals rather than all at once. This fact suggests the possibility that more than one purchaser was involved, but his—or their—identity remains a mystery.

4. The next question is one of the most perplexing of all: Did Mrs. Swain, before her death, or Judge Clark, afterward, sell or give away some of the uncatalogued papers? Evidence suggests that the answer is yes. In 1845, Swain assisted Governor William A. Graham in supervising the copying of the papers of Richard Caswell and Thomas Burke into letter books.[76] The letters copied included those found in the office of secretary of state in Raleigh as well as those in possession of Swain, whose wife was a granddaughter of Caswell. Of the letters to Caswell entered into the letter book, a spot-check shows that at least seven went into private hands. Two originals and two facsimiles were acquired by Thomas Addis Emmet and in 1896 were given to the

75. The catalogue listed the writer, addressee, and year in which each letter was written. It did not, however, give the month and day. Thus positive identification of specific items will be a difficult task.

76. See above, p. 186.

New York Public Library.[77] Three more letters to Caswell that
were copied into the letter books in 1845 have in recent years
been given to the Southern Historical Collection.[78] While the
fact has not been established that these seven letters were in the
Swain collection, it is known that they were available to Swain
at mid-century and consequently they could have been obtained
only from that collection, from the secretary of state's office, or
from someone who may have temporarily loaned them to Swain.
The suspicion that they were actually a part of the Swain collection is given strong support, however, by another singular fact:
Two letters from Cornelius Harnett to William Wilkinson that
were definitely in Swain's possession in 1860 were acquired by
Emmet prior to 1896.[79]

Of particular significance in this connection is the fact that
of all nine letters only three (the Harnett-Wilkinson and the
Rutledge-Caswell letters) could possibly have been listed in the
1885 catalogue, and even these three cannot be positively identified in it. All of this means, of course, that at least two, probably
six, and possibly all nine letters went into private hands from the
Swain collection in some manner other than through the 1886
sales. Kemp P. Battle wrote years later that he had been told that
Mrs. Swain sold many autograph letters to Emmet for $400.[80]
Circumstantial evidence supports Battle's recollection, and based
upon present information it must be concluded that a portion
of the Swain collection was sold, prior to Mrs. Swain's death, to

77. New York Public Library, *Calendar of the Emmet Collection of Manuscripts
Etc. Relating to American History* (New York: New York Public Library, 1900),
passim. The two originals are John Rutledge to Caswell, March 17, 1779, and
John Penn and others to Caswell, October 20, 1777. The two facsimiles, made
from originals in the possession of F. J. Freer of Philadelphia, are John Penn to
Caswell, June 25, 1777, and Joseph Hewes to Caswell, May 12, 1779.

78. These are Penn to Caswell, July 15, 1778; James Iredell to Caswell, December 31, 1778; and Penn, Burke, and William Sharpe to Caswell, July 15, 1779.
Carolyn A. Wallace to H. G. Jones, July 21, 1964, in author's possession. I am
obligated to Mrs. Wallace, Swain's biographer, for giving me aid and comfort in
what to both of us is the intriguing odyssey of the Swain collection.

79. The letters are dated October 20 and November 2, 1777. *North Carolina
University Magazine*, X (1861), 337.

80. Battle, *History of the University*, II, 107. Charles Phillips wrote on October 18, 1881, that "the largest & most valuable part" of the collection was still
boxed up, thus implying that some of the papers were not so preserved. Phillips
to Lyman C. Draper, Draper Manuscripts, Kings Mountain Papers.

Emmet and possibly to others.[81] The only other reasonable answer as to how these letters went into private hands is for Clark to have sold papers that were not included in the 1885 catalogue. No evidence has been found to support this possibility.

5. Another question remains unanswered: Why did Attorneys Clark and Battle sell any of the manuscripts? By her will Mrs. Swain had provided that the papers be disposed of "by a sale, or a gift . . . best to ensure a fulfillment of the work to the State of North Carolina." How could the sale of valuable documents to out-of-state collectors best benefit the State? Particularly in-explicable is Richard H. Battle's role as an executor, for it had been his father and brother who had worked so hard to recover the collection for the State. There appears to be one possible answer: Perhaps Clark and Battle, thinking that the excitement over the Swain collection might be quelled by the sale of a few items, decided that this was the best way of assuring the preservation of the bulk of the papers in North Carolina. There may also have been pressure for some remuneration on behalf of Mrs. Swain's grandchildren, though her estate was estimated to be worth $40,000, not including the manuscripts.[82]

Having considered questions concerning the sale of a portion of the Swain papers, attention may now be turned to the disposition of the remainder of the collection and of Swain's private papers. Even this trail is elusive.

William L. Saunders had been privileged to make copies of any of the materials he desired for the *Colonial Records,* and, in 1886, one of his helpers wrote that the Swain collection would be "committed for preservation to the Historical Society of North Carolina, at Chapel Hill."[83] Not until 1892, however, did the papers come into public view again. In that year the Historical Society examined "a number of the MS. being a portion of those collected by the late David L. Swain, which had been recently

81. I am of the opinion that Emmet did not purchase any of the letters sold by Clark in 1886. A collector of his stature almost certainly would have purchased the John Adams document and the letters of Washington, Adams, and Jefferson.

82. Eleanor H. Swain Estate Papers, Wake County Records, Estates, State Archives.

83. L. C. Vass, "North Carolina Colonial History," *Daily Journal* (New Bern), June 19, 1886.

turned over to the University according to the will of Mrs. Eleanor Swain, the widow of the deceased, David L. Swain, by her executors."[84] About the same time David Schenck of Greensboro intimated that he had a portion of the Burke, Nash, and Sumner papers originally in the collection. He wrote, "I am in receipt of your letter of October 29th, and hope you did not understand my letter as disputing the title of the University of North Carolina to these papers. My recollection is that the title was somewhat mixed, but your letter makes it clear to me that they are the property of the University or of the Historical Society already organized, and I am willing at any time you demand it to send you these papers as your [i.e., the Historical Society's] property."[85]

In 1893, when he took over the task of publishing the state records to 1790, Walter Clark asked for permission to bring back to Raleigh certain of the manuscripts then in Chapel Hill. Replied George T. Winston, the president of the university, "You will protect it, I am sure, you will use it for the State, And you, in fact; secured much of it for us."[86] Three years later Clark asked for additional materials and noted, "The box of papers kindly loaned me (for the State) I have not yet had copied, but they are safely kept & will be copied & returned [to] you this spring."[87] But the following year Clark requested permission to retain the manuscripts. Replied Edwin A. Alderman, the new president of the university, "As I understand it the papers referred to in your letter to Dr. Battle were given to the University and I could not consent to part with them without minute inquiry into the circumstances of their coming into our custody. If you will kindly send them I will make this inquiry and let you know."[88]

Whether Clark returned the papers is not known. The next

84. Minutes of April, 1892, in Minutes of the North Carolina Historical Society, 1880-1901, Southern Historical Collection.
85. D[avid] Schenck to Kemp P. Battle, October 31, 1892, in Battle Family Papers, Southern Historical Collection.
86. Winston to Clark, June 15, 1893, in Brooks and Lefler, *Clark Papers,* I, 265.
87. Clark to Kemp P. Battle, March 23, 1896, in Battle Family Papers.
88. Alderman to Clark, September 1, 1897, in Brooks and Lefler, *Clark Papers,* I, 322.

record of them appears about 1905 when Fred A. Olds, head of the Hall of History,[89] reported that "there has been secured the loan of the Swain collection of autograph letters of noted Colonial and Revolutionary men. . . . Some of the most valuable historical documents of the State are on view. . . ."[90] A year or so later "the large and valuable collection made by Governor David L. Swain and preserved in the archives of the society [North Carolina Historical Society]" was placed in the hands of the newly-created North Carolina Historical Commission for copying.[91] Two years later it was reported that this collection consisting of 1,065 items had been classified and copied.[92] Then, during the next biennium, the commission reported, "To this [the Swain] collection has been added 1,064 exceedingly interesting documents, sent to the Historical Commission by the Hon. Walter Clark, who was the Executor of Governor Swain's estate; and 76 letters and other documents loaned by the North Carolina Historical Society. These, added to the manuscripts previously received for this collection, bring the number of documents comprising it up to 2,205."[93]

Thus it appears that between 1886 and 1892 Clark returned a portion of the Swain collection to the university, while allowing Schenck and perhaps others to take what interested them. Clark himself probably retained a goodly number of documents, and in 1893, when he was appointed to edit and publish the state records through 1790, he borrowed back all or a portion of those papers which he had sent to Chapel Hill only a few years earlier.

89. Then a branch of the State Museum located in the Agricultural Building.

90. F. A. Olds, "The Historical Museum," *Literary and Historical Activities,* p. 29.

91. North Carolina Historical Commission, *The Second Biennial Report [1906-8] of the North Carolina Historical Commission* (Raleigh: North Carolina Historical Commission, 1916), p. 6. These reports, issued biennially, will be cited hereafter as *Biennial Report,* [dates].

92. *Biennial Report, 1908-1910,* p. 7. During the same biennium the Historical Commission acquired from her daughter the papers of Mrs. Cornelia Phillips Spencer. Among these papers were letters that passed between Mrs. Spencer and Mrs. Swain. It is evident that Mrs. Swain, before her death, or Clark after her death, acceded to Mrs. Phillips' request for a return of their personal correspondence. Many of Swain's private papers were later deposited by his descendants in the North Carolina Collection at Chapel Hill.

93. *Biennial Report, 1910-1912,* p. 7.

It is not clear whether he returned any of these papers in 1897, but, if so, he obviously retained many of them. At Olds's request and with the help of Secretary of State J. Bryan Grimes, that portion of the collection still at the university in 1905 was sent to Raleigh and placed on loan in the Hall of History of the State Museum. Between 1906 and 1908 university officials authorized Olds to turn this group of papers over to the North Carolina Historical Commission for classification and copying.[94] Then, in 1911, Judge Clark gave to the Historical Commission in Raleigh another portion of the collection which he had retained in his custody. He also gave to the Historical Commission his own "private" collection which contained some of the manuscripts originally in Swain's possession.

But the story does not end here. Clark did not immediately turn over to the Historical Commission all of the Swain collection still in his custody. Thus the total of 2,205 items in the Historical Commission mentioned above (including the 1,140 documents belonging to the University of North Carolina) was yet only a part of the papers left over after the 1886 sale. In 1913, Clark added 55 items from the collection,[95] and in the next three years he presented to the commission the Cornwallis Order Book acquired by Swain in 1845[96] and papers of William R. Davie, which undoubtedly had been among Swain's collection.[97] Shortly thereafter Clark gave the same repository the letter books of Thomas Burke and Thomas Henderson,[98] and, by 1920, he had added hundreds of "valuable historical manuscripts."[99] By the latter date, a special collection of nearly 2,000 "Walter Clark Manuscripts," not including more than 5,000 of his personal papers, had been accumulated in the Historical Commission. Many of these "Clark Manuscripts" had once been in the Swain collection. Further complicating the tracing of the collection is the fact that

94. These 1,064 manuscripts and the 76 subsequently loaned were returned to the university upon the establishment of the Southern Historical Collection.

95. North Carolina Historical Commission Daily Record, 1910-19, State Archives.

96. See above, p. 189.

97. *Biennial Report, 1914-1916*, pp. 10, 12-13.

98. *Biennial Report, 1916-1918*, pp. 9-10.

99. *Biennial Report, 1920-1922*, p. 15; North Carolina Historical Commission Records of Events, 1918-27, *passim.*

other papers, once having belonged to Swain and the Historical Society, found their way in recent decades to the Southern Historical Collection in Chapel Hill. Such items are found among the papers of John Steele, Thomas Burke, Jethro Sumner, Cornelius Harnett, and Joseph Graham.[100]

It is not possible, therefore, to ascertain the eventual disposition of all of the papers collected by Swain for the Historical Society of the University of North Carolina in the mid-nineteenth century, nor is it possible to determine just where all of his private papers are today. In fact, his collection became so mixed with his private papers that only an item-by-item study of the thousands of scattered papers will reveal which of the manuscripts were legitimately the concern of the Historical Society and which were in fact the private possession of Mrs. Swain and subsequently her heirs. Nevertheless, portions of the combined Swain collection and private papers are in the following collections: (1) the Swain Papers in the Southern Historical Collection; (2) the Swain "Epistolary Correspondence" in the North Carolina Collection; (3) the Swain Papers in the State Archives; (4) the Walter Clark Manuscripts in the State Archives; (5) various individual collections, such as the Thomas Henderson Letter Book and the John Steele Papers in the State Archives, and the Thomas Burke, Jethro Sumner, Cornelius Harnett, and Joseph Graham Papers in the Southern Historical Collection; and (6) the items sold by Mrs. Swain and her executors which are scattered in various collections throughout the country. Finally, some of the manuscripts undoubtedly are still in private hands. Thus even after 98 years the odyssey has not yet ended.

THE ESTABLISHMENT OF A STATE ARCHIVAL-HISTORICAL AGENCY, 1893-1907

It has been pointed out that the Historical Society of North Carolina, incorporated by the General Assembly in 1875 with authority to establish headquarters in the State Capitol, ceased to be a state-wide organization and, instead, eventually took on

100. Carolyn A. Wallace to H. G. Jones, November 19, 1964, in author's possession.

the cloak of a club at the University of North Carolina. Its charter was never changed, but by its own assertion, the group was reorganized in 1887 under a "new regime" made up almost exclusively of faculty members and students at the university. This action marked the end of the incorporated Historical Society of North Carolina. Thus, by 1888, no state historical society existed. This fact appears ironic when it is remembered that the greatest of all the State's historical enterprises—the publication of the colonial records—was then in progress. This publication project was the accomplishment of one of the chief aims of the previous societies and perhaps such an organization was no longer considered to be necessary.

Upon the death of Saunders, apprehension arose as to whether the project would continue when the trustees of the State Library failed to take the action for which they had authority. One person particularly concerned over the question was Edwin A. Alderman, then a professor of history at the State Normal School in Greensboro. Early in 1892, he suggested the indexing of the Saunders volumes and the separate publication of the editor's prefatory notes which he thought were "needed in order to fit that great collection for the student's use."[101]

In June of the same year, the North Carolina Teachers' Assembly met in Morehead City. Two weeks before the meeting, Alderman sent out a circular letter noting that North Carolina did not have an active historical society whereas most states had such organizations "which have been potent influences in stimulating historical investigation and in gathering historical materials." He proposed that "all those interested in historical study" meet during the convention on June 27 "to establish a historical society in North Carolina inter-collegiate in character and seeking to embrace in its membership all earnest historical workers—in or out of school—young or old." The purpose of the society would be to "collect, embody, arrange and preserve" a library of books, pamphlets, manuscripts, and other historical materials and "to take proper steps to promote the study of his-

101. Quoted in *Daily State Chronicle* (Raleigh), March 10, 1892.

tory by lectures and with legislative assistance, to publish and diffuse information relative to the history of the state."[102]

An interested group met with Alderman on the appointed date and proposed the establishment of "The William L. Saunders Historical Society of North Carolina." Editorialized the *News and Observer,*

We are glad to see the successful inauguration of Prof. Alderman's plan to start an Historical Society in North Carolina. The plan has been well matured, and we trust that it will be carried out in the proposed details to a successful conclusion. Historical societies do not achieve great results suddenly. It requires years for them to do their work, collect data and throw light on obscure subjects.

One of the benefits of a Society is that whatever of historical interest is recovered from the ravages of time, is securely preserved, while, on the contrary, the results of the most laborious investigators, working alone, often die with them.[103]

Alderman proposed that his society be incorporated by the General Assembly with an appropriation and authority to continue the publication of the records. Upon learning of a plan for another bill to enable Walter Clark to carry on the project, however, Alderman agreed to support Clark as editor provided the publication be made "a part of the documents of the Historical Society of North Carolina and deposit[ed] . . . with that Society. . . ."[104] His plan was to ask for an annual appropriation of $1,000 and for the use of the old State Library Room in the Capitol as a repository for historical materials. He allowed David Schenck to draw up the bill for him and agreed that the society would publish only those materials selected by the trustees of the State Library.[105]

The Alderman-Schenck bill was introduced "by request" on January 20 by Senator J. L. King of Guilford County. The education committee to which it was referred removed the appro-

102. Circular letter from Edwin A. Alderman, June 14, 1892, in Superintendent of Public Instruction's Papers, 1892, State Archives.

103. *News and Observer* (daily edition, Raleigh), June 30, 1892.

104. David Schenck to Walter Clark, December 14, 1892, in Brooks and Lefler, *Clark Papers,* I, 257.

105. Schenck to Clark, January 17, 1893, in Brooks and Lefler, *Clark Papers,* I, 259.

priation and on the floor the bill was further amended to eliminate the provision for an office in the Capitol. As finally passed
on February 28 the act created a corporation by the name of the
"William L. Saunders Historical Society of North Carolina" with
authority to hold property not exceeding $20,000 in value. It
was to report annually to the trustees of the State Library. The
incorporators were Alderman, Schenck, Kemp P. Battle, Graham
Daves, Richard H. Dillard, Alexander Graham, George W. Graham, Alfred M. Waddell, and Stephen B. Weeks. It is significant
that Walter Clark's name was not among them. The objects of
the society were ". . . to collect, embody, arrange, and preserve
any books, pamphlets, papers and other library material illustrative of the history of North Carolina, and to take proper steps
to diffuse and publish such records as they may be directed to do
by the Trustees of the Public Library of North Carolina. . . ."[106]

Without funds, the society perished before it was ever formally
organized. But the original purpose of the Alderman group was
nevertheless attained when the library trustees appointed Clark
to edit the state records under provisions of the 1881 act. The
efforts, therefore, were not in vain.

During the remaining years of the century, with Clark's
volumes of the state records flowing from the press, perhaps little
thought was given to the need for a state historical agency.[107]
By 1900, however, Clark had virtually completed the copying and
arranging of the materials for his series and, in fact, his eighth
volume was published that year. The basic source materials for
the State's history to 1790 were either in print or soon to be. Led
by the judge himself, a small group of history-minded persons
discussed ways of encouraging the use of the sources because they

106. *Private Laws of 1893*, c. 131.

107. In 1899, Professor John Spencer Bassett of Trinity College lamented that
North Carolina "has had so little real historical interest in it that it cannot support
an historical society outright." He suggested that the "real students of history
in N.C." be organized into a chapter of the American Historical Association.
He thought he might be able to enlist twenty members "who would be really
interested in the matter and who would form the nucleus of a movement which
would eventually build up considerable interest in history." Bassett to Herbert
B. Adams, April 3, 1899, in W. Stull Holt (ed.), *Historical Scholarship in the
United States, 1876-1901: As Revealed in the Correspondence of Herbert B. Adams*
("The Johns Hopkins University Studies in Historical and Political Science," ser.
LVI, no. 4 [Baltimore: The Johns Hopkins Press, 1938]), p. 270.

knew that few individuals would purchase the many volumes of the records and perhaps even fewer would read them. Furthermore, a new spirit was abroad in North Carolina in 1900. Charles B. Aycock was elected governor on a spirited platform of improved education. Torn by the interparty political activities of the 1890's, the people at the turn of the century demonstrated renewed determination to lift the State out of the turmoil and illiteracy that had plagued it following the Civil War. Clark, a radical Democrat with Populist proclivities, was more than a visionary, and his role as a promoter of better education was enhanced by his interest in history. As a descendant of generations of leaders, he sought to revive a sense of pride in the people, and he recognized that pride could best be inculcated through a dissemination of the history of the State.

On September 18, 1900, Clark met in the State Agricultural Building with a small number of like-minded persons and discussed the idea of organizing a society "to stimulate literary and historical activity." They formed a committee to issue a call for a general meeting of interested persons to organize formally a "State Literary and Historical Association." On the committee in addition to Clark were George T. Winston, a former president of the University of North Carolina; William J. Peele, prominent Raleigh attorney; Henry Jerome Stockard, president of Peace Institute; Daniel Harvey Hill, a professor at North Carolina Agricultural and Mechanical College; and Miss Rebecca Cameron and Mrs. John Van Landingham, prominent women leaders of the State. In an address to the public which was carried in most of the major newspapers, the committee proposed that the new organization have as its purposes the promotion of the reading habit among the people, the stimulation of the writing of history and literature, and the collection and preservation of historical material. To carry out these purposes, it was suggested that the society aid in the establishment of public schools, libraries, and literary clubs and that it collect and publish North Carolina literature and history and establish a historical museum.[108]

108. Edward P. Moses, "The State Literary and Historical Association," *Literary and Historical Activities*, pp. 1-3.

To further stimulate interest in the proposed organization, Peele wrote for the newspapers a "card" in which he recognized the existence of a few local societies but he pointed out that none of them could "ever hope to organize the literary talent of the State." He lamented the paucity of good writing, both past and present, and asked, "Is there real literary vitality in North Carolina, or the seeds of it? . . . How far is our character as a people affected by absorbing so much from abroad and producing so little at home?" A state literary and historical association, he predicted, could do much to remedy the State's backwardness.

A "large and representative gathering of gentlemen and ladies from the various sections of the State" met in the Music Hall of the Olivia Raney Library in Raleigh on the evening of October 23 and adopted an elaborate constitution and formally organized "The State Literary and Historical Association." Its purposes, as stated in the constitution, were ". . . the collection, preservation, production and dissemination of our State literature and history; the encouragement of public and school libraries; the establishment of an historical museum; the inculcation of a literary spirit among our people; the correction of printed misrepresentations concerning North Carolina, and the engendering of an intelligent, healthy State pride in the rising generation." Clark was elected president. Other officers chosen were: vicepresidents, Miss Adelaide L. Fries, a Moravian historian of Salem, Edward J. Hale, a Fayetteville businessman and diplomat, and Charles F. Warren, a leading citizen of Washington, North Carolina; secretary and treasurer, Hill; and corresponding secretary, Alex J. Feild, a lawyer of Raleigh.[109] Shortly thereafter, the positions of secretary, treasurer, and corresponding secretary were combined with Feild holding all three jobs. Three resolutions were adopted: to petition the General Assembly to set aside one day each year for the observance of "North Carolina Day" in the public schools; to give a $100 prize for the best biography of Zebulon B. Vance for children; and to publish annually or bien-

109. Minutes of The State Literary and Historical Association, October 23, 1900, in State Literary and Historical Association Records, State Archives. Cited hereafter as Literary and Historical Association Minutes.

nially a "year book containing the best things in our history and literature that have been or shall have been produced." The minute book was opened for autographs of charter members; more than 75 persons signed, including college presidents, professors, ministers, editors, and attorneys.

The program included papers on the stimulation of literature, by Professor B. F. Sledd of Wake Forest College; the publication of what was to be produced, by Editor Hale; and the collection and preservation of material for state and local history, by Professor John Spencer Bassett of Trinity College. Bassett's paper strongly advocated a hall of records to be put in charge of a professionally trained archivist. He said, "As long as history is the production of some man's preconceived notions, there will be no need of keeping records. When history becomes the recording of facts and date[s], then will be felt the absolute necessity of storing and keeping those records. We must have a State archivist and a fire-proof building for the storing of the archives, as well as a law to compel officials to store their records."[110] It is perhaps worthy of note that this was probably the first time the title "state archivist" was used publicly in North Carolina.

Clark entered into his new duties with his usual exuberance and determination. He selected an able executive committee— Peele, Winston, Bassett, Miss Eliza A. Poole of Raleigh, and Professor William Louis Poteat of Wake Forest College, plus the officers. Hill was appointed chairman of the committee on literature and history whose duties were to collect material relating to the history of the State and to promote the production of literature among the people. The committee on libraries, with responsibility to foster the establishment of free libraries, was headed by G. A. Grimsley, superintendent of schools in Greensboro. Fred A. Olds, collector for the Hall of History and formerly quartermaster general of the State Guard, was chosen chairman of the committee on historical museums whose duty was to collect for the association and place in the State Museum "valuable relics and original documents."[111]

110. *News and Observer* (Raleigh), October 24, 1900.
111. The summary of the activities of the association during its first three

Activities were begun almost immediately after the organizational meeting. Within three months all committees were at work and the association had two hundred members. Three bills were drawn up for presentation to the General Assembly. Those to designate October 12 each year as "North Carolina Day"[112] and to appropriate $200 for the purchase of copies of Editor Richard B. Creecy's *Grandfather's Tales of North Carolina*[113] passed without recorded opposition. A more ambitious bill for the establishment of free libraries ran into some difficulty, but with the aid of Editor Josephus Daniels it too was passed in a different form. It amended the Scales Library Act of 1897 by appropriating $5,000 per year to match private and county funds for the purpose of providing a free library in each school district of the State.[114] Within the first year two hundred such libraries had been established or were in the process of being set up.

A missionary zeal permeated the total of five hundred persons who crowded into the Music Hall of the Olivia Raney Library in Raleigh for the second annual meeting of the association on the evening of October 22, 1901. "The Hall was filled with talented and distinguished ladies and gentlemen from all parts of the State, who seemed in thorough sympathy with the spirit of the occasion," Secretary Feild entered into his minutes. Within the previous twelve months the association had accomplished practically all of its objectives. Its bills had been passed, many new libraries had been established, the first North Carolina Day had been held on the theme of the first English settlement in the New World, additional space in the Agricultural Building had been set aside for the State Museum, and editors throughout the State had given warm endorsement to the aims of the organization.[115]

years is taken from Literary and Historical Association Minutes, *passim;* Moses, "Literary and Historical Association," *passim;* and William Burlie Brown, "The State Literary and Historical Association, 1900-1950," *North Carolina Historical Review,* XXVIII (April, 1951), 156-97.

112. *Public Laws of 1901,* c. 164.

113. This resolution is found in *Private Laws of 1901,* p. 1041.

114. *Public Laws of 1901,* c. 662.

115. The Raleigh papers, in particular, carried lengthy articles on the association's activities and frequently printed the addresses delivered at its meetings.

Encouraged by its immediate success, the members turned to new, ambitious projects. Stirred by addresses by Graham Daves, Julian S. Carr, and Governor Charles B. Aycock, the association voted to hold a celebration to commemorate the landings on Roanoke Island and to construct in Nash Square in Raleigh a monument in memory of Sir Walter Raleigh. So moving was Carr's speech on the latter subject that representatives from various areas arose to pledge a penny apiece for all school children in their counties. Not to be outdone, Professor Poteat pledged ten pennies for each student at Wake Forest College, and before the burst of patriotism had subsided pledges had been made on behalf of nearly every college and school system in the State. Governor Aycock, who as chairman of the trustees of the State Library had been unable to find in that library a single book on Sir Walter Raleigh, promised pointedly that readers would soon find available to them not one but many books on the explorer.[116] Other speakers exhorted the people to greater efforts toward education and literary attainments. Judge Henry Groves Connor of Wilson was elected president to succeed Clark. Secretary Feild closed his minutes of the session with the note, "The meeting was thoroughly enjoyable and highly successful, was charged with enthusiasm and the spirit of progress, and showed the association to be in a vigorous, healthy condition."[117]

The third annual meeting was delayed until January 23, 1903.[118] The program included Judge Connor's presidential address, reports on the library movement and the Hall of History,[119] and a review of history and poetry written by North Carolinians during the preceding year. The fact that literary production of the State had been sufficient to warrant a review indicated con-

116. *Morning Post* (Raleigh), October 23, 1901. The monument to Sir Walter Raleigh has not been erected, but the funds raised in 1901 and subsequently (minus the portion lost during bank failures in the 1930's) are still available for the purpose and the movement has been revived in recent years.

117. Literary and Historical Association Minutes, October 22, 1901, State Archives.

118. Thus no session was held in 1902 but two—January 23 and November 12— were held in 1903.

119. The title Hall of History was given to that portion of the State Museum devoted to documents and artifacts when the museum was assigned additional space in the Agricultural Building about 1902.

siderable progress. Professor William Louis Poteat of Wake Forest College was elected president.

The most significant action of the third annual session was the adoption of a resolution to draft a bill for the establishment of a "State Historical Commission."[120] Such a bill was drawn and introduced by Senator R. F. Beasley of Union County exactly a week after the resolution was adopted. Beasley had been a member of the association from its beginning and had served on the publicity committee. The act provided for "an Historical Commission" of not more than five persons, to be selected by the governor for two-year terms and to serve without pay, mileage, or per diem, whose duty it would be "to have collected from the files of old newspapers, from court records, church records and elsewhere valuable documents pertaining to the history of the State." It further provided for the publication of such collected materials, the distribution of which was made the duty of the state librarian under direction of the Historical Commission. Five hundred dollars per year was appropriated for "the collection and transcription of documents."[121] The bill was referred to the committee on education which reported it favorably and it passed into law on March 9, 1903.[122]

Passage of the bill establishing the Historical Commission appears to have encountered no opposition. Undoubtedly the influence of such men as Attorney Peele, Judges Connor and Clark, and Professor Poteat was decisive. Some of the prominent members of the association, however, were not partners to the efforts. John Spencer Bassett wrote his friend William E. Dodd, who had pleaded for the establishment of the commission,[123] "I don't know

120. Interestingly enough, the minutes of the association do not contain a copy of the resolution. The *News and Observer* (January 24, 1903) carried the following: "A resolution passed asking the legislature to secure certain publications and records and a committee was appointed to draft a bill for this purpose. The committee was authorized to request an appropriation of $500."

121. *Public Laws of 1903*, c. 767.

122. The original bill is in the Legislative Papers, 1903, State Archives.

123. Dodd, then teaching at Randolph-Macon College in Virginia, strongly endorsed the bill to create the Historical Commission. In a letter to the *News and Observer,* he pointed out the urgent need for an agency to protect the historical records and source materials. The State Library should have spent less on purchasing books on Europe and more on acquiring manuscript collections

anything about the Hist. Commission in N.C., except that it is got up by some Raleigh fellows for their own advantage. Peele etc. are in it. I have nothing to do with it and I have no idea that I shall have. But if I can do anything to get it in shape I shall gladly do it."[124] Bassett, it will be recalled, had been the most vocal promotor of the idea of the construction of a hall of records and the appointment of a state archivist as early as 1900.[125]

Governor Charles B. Aycock appointed to the commission Peele, James Dunn Hufham of Henderson, Forster Alexander Sondley of Asheville, Richard Dillard of Edenton, and Robert Digges Wimberly Connor of Wilmington. Peele had been a prime mover of the Literary and Historical Association from its beginning and Connor, a young school teacher, was the son of Judge Henry G. Connor, the association's second president. Because of the scattered locations of the members, efforts toward an early meeting were unsuccessful. In the fall of 1903, discouraged by the failure of the group to get together, Peele threatened to "get the Governor to supplement my endeavors with a personal letter."[126] Finally, on November 20, Peele, Connor, and Hufham met in the hotel at Warsaw and officially organized the commission by electing Peele chairman and Connor secretary. After discussing the functions of the agency, they agreed to offer prizes of $100 each for the best biographical sketch of a North Carolinian, the best history of one particular decade in North Carolina during the period 1781-1861, and the best history

---

such as that of the late John H. Wheeler, he wrote. Of particular concern to him was the neglect of county records. In one county seat he "found five or six large boxes of records stored away in the attic of the courthouse. No one knew anything of their contents; no one was charged with their preservation. I pried into one of the boxes and found an old marriage bond dating back to 1686!" He surmised that the records had been hurriedly packed up in a "panic" during the Civil War. Valuable private papers, too, were being lost each year, he said; one example was a "meat box" full of the correspondence of Nathaniel Macon which had been destroyed at Warrenton ten years before. "Few more significant moves have been made in North Carolina" than the effort to establish a Historical Commission, he wrote. Dodd to the Editor, *News and Observer*, February 8, 1903.

124. Bassett to Dodd, March 25, 1903, in William E. Dodd Papers, Library of Congress (photocopy in Duke University Library).

125. See above, p. 275.

126. Peele to Connor, October 29, 1903, in North Carolina Historical Commission Records, Correspondence of the Secretary, 1903, State Archives.

of a county. Fifty dollars was authorized to be expended for photographing the DeBry engravings of Indian life for exhibition in the Hall of History. The remaining $150 was to be devoted to collecting and transcribing "old files of newspapers, records, and documents," and to placing an advertisement on the competition in the *North Carolina Booklet*.[127]

During the second year of its existence, the commission held not a single formal meeting. Through correspondence, however, it was decided to issue the first of a proposed series of volumes in which would be published the main addresses and a review of historical activities. Clarence H. Poe, secretary of the Literary and Historical Association, and Peele, assisted by Edward P. Moses, a founder of the organization, compiled and edited the material, which went to the press in 1904 but was not finally issued in bound form until 1907. The volume, *Literary and Historical Activities in North Carolina, 1900-1905*, was a remarkable potpourri of historical articles, reports, and exhortations. Its contents ranged from a series of articles supporting North Carolina's claims to distinction in the Civil War to selections of John Henry Boner's poetry, and from bibliographies of North Carolina history and literature for 1902-5 to a listing of books on the State's history in the State Library. It stands today as a major contribution of the early years of the Historical Commission.[128]

Other accomplishments of the first two years included the copying of the parish records of St. Paul's Church of Edenton, the editing by Moses of the debates of the constitutional conventions of 1788 and 1789, and the reproduction of the DeBry engravings.

On December 1, 1904, Connor, for the commission, prepared its first biennial report.[129] After outlining the commission's work, he exhibited flashes of the wisdom that would, in fifteen years,

127. Commission Minutes, November 20, 1903, in North Carolina Historical Commission Records, State Archives.
128. The volume was numbered one, but no subsequent volumes of the series were issued.
129. North Carolina Historical Commission, *Report of the Historical Commission to Governor Charles B. Aycock, 1903-1905* (Raleigh: North Carolina Historical Commission, 1904).

bring to fruition many of the accomplishments which, at the age of twenty-six, he envisaged. He wrote, "The people of North Carolina are realizing more and more every day that it is not safe to trust the future to the control of a people who are ignorant of their past; and that no people who are indifferent to their past need hope to make their future great." He continued,

The real work [of the commission] lies in collecting, transcribing and editing original sources. The importance of this work is equalled only by the almost insuperable difficulties in the way. Many hundreds of invaluable historical documents and records have been lost or destroyed through the indifference of the State and the ignorance and carelessness of their possessors. These are hopelessly gone, but many others remain which should be preserved. Stuffed away in dark corners and dusty archives, in pigeon-holes, vaults, desks and cellars, all over North Carolina, are many documents, records, private and public letters, and other manuscripts, which as matters now stand are of absolutely no value to their possessors or to the public; but if properly collected, edited and published they will be of incalculable value in throwing light on our history.

It is the duty of the Historical Commission to do this work. All patriotic citizens should aid in it. Those who possess such documents, or know of their whereabouts, will render a service to the State by placing them, or copies of them, in possession of the commission.

The work, he said, would not be accomplished within a year, "nor within two years, but is rather the work of a generation. . . ."

In October, 1904, Connor resigned his principalship at Wilmington High School and joined the staff of the State Department of Public Instruction in Raleigh. Thereafter, though he received no salary for his work with the commission for the next three years, he was in a position to work with Peele and others vitally interested in historical activities. From the beginning, Connor and Peele had been the moving forces of the commission, and their leadership continued after 1905 when Governor Robert B. Glenn reappointed them. The other three initial members—Hufham, Sondley, and Dillard—were replaced by Thomas W. Blount, Charles Lee Raper, and Secretary of State J. Bryan Grimes. The annual appropriation to the commission continued at only $500 per year, however, and its activities were limited thereby. But the lack of funds did not deter Connor from carrying on a busy correspondence with other historians throughout the nation, seeking advice on the direction that the commission should take. All proposals had the same prerequisite: more funds and additional legislation.

The prestige of the members made it relatively easy to persuade the 1907 General Assembly to amend the original act. Legislation that year provided: (1) staggered terms for members of the commission and payment for their travel expenses; (2) an annual appropriation of $5,000 for the employment of a full-time secretary, outfitting of an office for the secretary, and copying historical materials; (3) broadened authority to collect and publish historical materials and to mark and preserve historic sites; and (4) authority for public officials to turn over to the commission for preservation "any official books, records, documents, original papers, newspaper files, printed books or portraits, not in current use. . . ."[130] To carry out its broadened responsibilities, the commission elected Connor[131] as its full-time secretary.

Thus, within seven years after Walter Clark and a small group of interested persons met to organize a state literary and historical society, the State had, for the first time, a true archival-historical agency.

130. *Public Laws of 1907,* c. 714.
131. For a biographical sketch of Connor, see Hugh T. Lefler, "Robert Digges Wimberly Connor," in Clifford L. Lord (ed.), *Keepers of the Past* (Chapel Hill: The University of North Carolina Press, 1965), pp. 109-23.

Postscript

1966

The story of twentieth-century historical activities is yet to be written. It is perhaps proper, however, that a brief note be added concerning the status of historical preservation as North Carolina enters its fourth century.

In 1963, during the three-hundredth anniversary of the granting of the Carolina Charter, the Society of American Archivists and the American Association for State and Local History held concurrent meetings in Raleigh. Governor Terry Sanford told the delegates, ". . . you are meeting today in a historically-minded State. You are among a people who love to study their past and to preserve the best of it. But, perhaps most important of all, you are among a people who know the difference between studying the past and living in it. We learn from the past in this State, but we do not worship it. Our adversities and mistakes of bygone days help us chart our course for the future." He then summarized the current state of history in North Carolina:

. . . within the past few years there has occurred in our State a veritable historical renaissance. The number of local historical organizations has shown a phenomenal increase, from one or two at the turn of the century to a total of approximately fifty today. We are preserving our historic sites as never before. Our State historical museum has become one of the best of such institutions in the entire South, and creditable historical museums are springing up in all parts of the State. Both at Chapel Hill and at Duke are two large collections of private and unofficial historical manuscripts which draw scholars from many parts of the free world. Our two university presses and our commercial presses are turning out a steady stream of works relating to our history. Our graduate schools draw students from all over the Nation and through research and writing contribute much to the knowledge of our State history. There is a powerful movement to secure the more adequate coverage of our State and local history in our public schools. There can be no doubt that, more than ever before, our people are conscious of and interested in their history.[1]

This speech by the governor is revealing on two counts: It calls attention to the historical renaissance that has occurred in North Carolina since 1900, and it points to new dimensions in the study of history. No longer is history the monopoly of the professional. Instead, it is common property and is taught not merely by manuscripts and books but also by visual displays in museums, by preservation and restoration of historic sites, by outdoor as well as indoor dramas, by programs of historical groups, and by radio, television, and motion pictures.

These new techniques, as effective and as important as they are, have not denigrated the traditional study of history through the written record, and the twentieth-century developments in the preservation and use of the written and printed word have been no less striking. Indeed, the story of these changes, when it is written, will be far more dramatic than that of the first two and a half centuries of North Carolina historical activity.[2]

Not even the visionary Archibald D. Murphey could have foreseen the flow of scholarly monographs that followed the publication of the colonial and state records; the dozens of volumes of documentaries; the historical quarterly; the ever-increasing number of grade-school-level booklets; the meticulously-researched general histories of Ashe, Boyd, Connor, Hamilton, Henderson, Newsome, and Lefler; the scores of doctoral dissertations and masters' theses on North Carolina subjects. Nor could he have foreseen the establishment of the nation's largest and most comprehensive state archival-records management program, two of the finest private manuscript repositories and more than two dozen other institutions preserving unpublished materials,

1. Terry Sanford, "North Carolina—Three Hundredth Birthday," *American Archivist*, XXVII (January, 1964), 15-19.

2. Although no comprehensive survey of historical activities in the twentieth century has been written, two articles summarize them: J. G. de Roulhac Hamilton, "The Preservation of North Carolina History," *North Carolina Historical Review*, IV (January, 1927), 3-21; and Christopher Crittenden, "We've Come a Long Way: History and Historical Activities in North Carolina," *North Carolina Historical Review*, XXXVI (April, 1959), 153-61.

and the great research libraries housing millions of books. It is perhaps coincidental but nevertheless fitting that two of the outstanding graduate schools of history now train scholars within fifteen miles of Murphey's grave.

The North Carolina Historical Commission became, in time, one of the most respected state archival-historical agencies in the nation. To its original emphases upon documentary preservation and publication were added new functions: records management, newspaper microfilming, museums, historic sites, and other specialized areas of activity. To reflect these broadened interests, the name of the commission was changed in 1943 to the State Department of Archives and History.[3] Its record of preservation of the public records won in 1964 the Society of American Archivists' first Distinguished Service Award for "outstanding service to the American people and exemplary contributions to the archival profession."

At the University of North Carolina two outstanding research collections have been built upon the foundations laid by David L. Swain and Kemp P. Battle—the Southern Historical Collection[4] of manuscripts and the North Carolina Collection of printed materials. Only a few miles away, the younger Duke University Library has established its own extensive manuscript department[5]

3. The most complete story of the programs of the State Department of Archives and History is found in its *Biennial Reports*. For secondary accounts, see the following: Henry S. Stroupe, "The North Carolina Department of Archives and History—The First Half Century," *North Carolina Historical Review*, XXXI (April, 1954), 184-200; *The North Carolina Historical Commission: Forty Years of Public Service, 1903-1943* (Raleigh: North Carolina Historical Commission, 1942); *The First Half Century: The North Carolina Department of Archives and History, A Record of Achievement 1903-1953* (Raleigh: State Department of Archives and History, 1953); H. G. Jones, "The Archival-Records Management Program of an American State: North Carolina," *Indian Archives*, XVI (1965) [in preparation]; H. G. Jones, "State Department of Archives and History," *North Carolina Libraries*, XIX (Winter, 1961), 5-15; Ernst Posner, *American State Archives* (Chicago: University of Chicago Press, 1964), pp. 202-11; and H. G. Jones, A. M. Patterson, and T. W. Mitchell, "Records Management in North Carolina," *Records Management Journal*, IV (Autumn, 1966) [in preparation].

4. For a brief history and description of the collection, see Carolyn Andrews Wallace, "The Southern Historical Collection," *American Archivist*, XXVIII (July, 1965), 427-36.

5. Mattie Russell, "The Manuscript Department in the Duke University Library," *American Archivist*, XXVIII (July, 1965), 437-44, reviews the growth of this department.

upon the beginnings made by Stephen B. Weeks, John Spencer Bassett, and William K. Boyd. At least twenty-six other institutions throughout the State now preserve some manuscript materials, many of them concerned primarily with sources relating to special-interest groups.[6] The State Library in Raleigh has acquired an enviable number of volumes of printed North Caroliniana.

Annual reviews of books by North Carolinians and about North Carolina become lengthier, and the Mayflower Cup for non-fiction has come to be the most prestigious award for a North Carolina literary work. The *North Carolina Historical Review* has carried an impressive number of scholarly articles. North Carolina books by the scores have been published by the two university presses and the various commercial printeries, and the State Department of Archives and History has produced hundreds of documentary volumes, booklets, and leaflets for both scholar and layman.[7] The observance of the tercentenary of the granting of the Carolina Charter and the centennial of the Civil War led to the beginning, respectively, of a new series of the colonial records and a new roster of North Carolina troops. Newspapers and special-interest magazines have found history a profitable feature. Microfilm and copying devices have brought printed and manuscript sources within reach of more and more researchers.[8] North Carolina history is taught in all public elementary schools, and advanced courses are given in many of the colleges and universities. District and local historical societies have be-

6. H. G. Jones, "Archives and Manuscript Collections in North Carolina," in Robert B. Downs (ed.), *Resources of North Carolina Libraries* (Raleigh: Governor's Commission on Library Resources, 1965), 197-212.

7. It is revealing to note that when Weeks published his bibliography in 1895 he knew of only 1,491 items of printed North Caroliniana. Six decades later Thornton was able to list 15,519 unofficial and 4,143 state publications. Stephen B. Weeks, *A Bibliography of the Historical Literature of North Carolina* (Cambridge: Library of Harvard University, 1895); Mary L. Thornton (comp.), *Official Publications of the Colony and State of North Carolina, 1749-1939: A Bibliography* (Chapel Hill: The University of North Carolina Press, 1954); and Mary L. Thornton (comp.), *A Bibliography of North Carolina, 1589-1956* (Chapel Hill: The University of North Carolina Press, 1958). A serial publication, of course, is listed as only one item in the Thornton bibliographies.

8. For the availability of newspapers on microfilm, see H. G. Jones and Julius H. Avant (eds.), *North Carolina Newspapers on Microfilm* (3rd ed.; Raleigh: State Department of Archives and History, 1965).

come more numerous and active, and various state-wide historical groups hold annual joint meetings in Raleigh during "Culture Week," a term used at first derisively, now respectfully.

In 1899, John Spencer Bassett expressed the opinion that there were no more than twenty persons in the State "really interested" in their history.[9] A year later, the State Literary and Historical Association was formed to stimulate the study and writing of history, and within three more years an official state archival-historical agency was established. What has transpired in the intervening six decades has indeed been nothing less than a historical renaissance.

9. See above, p. 272, n. 107.

Selected Bibliography

I. PRIMARY SOURCES

A. Manuscripts

Unless otherwise indicated, all manuscripts listed below are in the North Carolina State Department of Archives and History, Raleigh, North Carolina.

Adjutant General's Department. Records, 1862-1865.

Barringer, Daniel Moreau. Papers, 1832. Southern Historical Collection, The University of North Carolina Library, Chapel Hill, N.C.

Battle Family. Papers, 1865-1900. Southern Historical Collection.

Beauregard, P. G. T. Papers, 1865. Manuscript Department, Duke University Library, Durham, N.C.

Carter, David Miller. Papers, 1866-67. Southern Historical Collection.

Chatham, Thurmond. Collection, 1664-75.

Chowan County, North Carolina. Records, 1795-1800. [Subgroup: Miscellaneous.]

Clark, Walter. Collection, 1783-1920.

Dodd, William E. Papers, 1903. Library of Congress, Washington, D.C. (Photocopy in Duke University Library.)

Draper, Lyman C. Collection, 1840-90. State Historical Society of Wisconsin, Madison, Wisconsin. (Microfilm copy in North Carolina State Department of Archives and History.)

Emmet, Thomas Addis. Collection, 1757-1847. New York Public Library, New York, N.Y. (Typewritten copies of items relating to North Carolina in North Carolina State Department of Archives and History.)

General Assembly. Legislative Records, 1689-1903.

General Court, Province of Carolina. Minutes, 1690-1767.

Governor's Office. Papers and Letter Books, 1694-1903.

Graham, William A. Papers, 1779-1918.

Hawks, Francis Lister. Papers, 1850.

Hawks, Francis Lister. Collection, c.1836-c.1866. Church Historical Society, Austin, Texas. (Microfilm copies in North Carolina State Department of Archives and History.)

Miscellaneous Papers [an artificial collection of private papers]. Papers, 1697-1912.

Murphey, Archibald Debow. Papers, 1797-1852.

Murphey, Archibald Debow. Papers, 1793-1826. Southern Historical Collection.

North Carolina Historical Commission. Records, 1903-10. [Sub-groups: Correspondence, Minutes.]

North Carolina Historical Society. Minutes, 1880-1901. Southern Historical Collection.

North Carolina State Library. Records, 1877-1914.

Orange County, North Carolina. Records, 1868. [Subgroup: Wills (David L. Swain).] Orange County Courthouse, Hillsborough, N.C. (Microfilm copy in North Carolina State Department of Archives and History.)

Perquimans Precinct (County), North Carolina. Records, 1659-1820. [Sub-groups: Court Minutes, "Births, Marriages, Deaths, and Flesh Marks."]

Perquimans Precinct (County), North Carolina. Records, 1681. [Sub-group: Deeds.] Perquimans County Courthouse, Hertford, N.C. (Microfilm copies in North Carolina State Department of Archives and History.)

Saunders, William Laurence. Collection, 1775-1891.

Saunders, William Laurence. Papers, 1776-1869. Duke University Library.

Saunders, William Laurence. Papers, c. 1775-1891. Southern Historical Collection.

Secretary of State's Office. Records, 1663-1891. [Sub-groups: Boundary Commissioners, Correspondence, Miscellaneous, Receipts, Wills.]

Smith, L. W. Collection, 1792. Morristown National Historical Park, Morristown, New Jersey. (Photocopy in North Carolina State Department of Archives and History.)

Spencer, Cornelia Phillips. Papers, 1859-1905.

Spencer, Cornelia Phillips. Papers, 1833-1924. Southern Historical Collection.

State Archivist. Files, 1961-1965.

State Literary and Historical Association. Records, 1900-5.

Superintendent of Public Instruction's Office. Records, 1892-95.

Swain, David Lowry. Collection and Diary, 1763-1895.

Swain, David Lowry. Papers, 1854-60. Duke University Library.

Swain, David Lowry. Papers, 1740-1896. Southern Historical Collection.

Swain, David Lowry. Epistolary Correspondence, c. 1801-68. North Carolina Collection, The University of North Carolina Library.

Treasurer's and Comptroller's Departments. Records, 1731-1900.

[Sub-groups: Accounts, Capital Buildings, Executive Offices, Journals and Ledgers.]

United States Adjutant General's Office. Record Group 94, 1865. [Sub-groups: Copybook of Letters Sent, Document File.] National Archives, Washington, D.C. (Microfilm copies in North Carolina State Department of Archives and History.)

United States Army Commands. Record Group 98, 1865. [Sub-groups: Headquarters, Department of North Carolina—Copybook of Letters Sent, Copybook of Telegrams Sent, Document File; Headquarters, 3rd Division, 23rd Army Corps—Copybook of Letters Sent.] National Archives. (Microfilm copies in North Carolina State Department of Archives and History.)

United States Department of State. Record Group 59, 1806. [Sub-group: Diplomatic Despatches, Great Britain.] National Archives. (Photocopy in North Carolina State Department of Archives and History.)

United States Secretary of War. Record Group 107, 1865-88. [Sub-group: Document File.] National Archives. (Microfilm copies in North Carolina State Department of Archives and History.)

Vance, Zebulon B. Papers, 1827-1903.

Wake County, North Carolina. Records, 1883-90. [Sub-groups: Estates Papers, Inventories (Eleanor H. Swain).]

War of the Regulation. Collection, c. 1768-71.

Wheeler, John Hill. Papers and Diary, c. 1800-81. Library of Congress, Washington, D.C. (Microfilm copies in North Carolina State Department of Archives and History.)

Wheeler, John Hill. Papers, 1837-64. Southern Historical Collection.

Williamson, Hugh. Papers, 1780-90.

B. Collected Documents and Papers and Finding Aids

Adams, Henry Baxter. *The Life and Writings of Jared Sparks Comprising Selections from His Journals and Correspondence.* 2 vols. Boston and New York: Houghton, Mifflin and Co., 1893.

[Batchelor, K. B. (comp.).] *Catalogue of the Swain Collection of Autograph Letters.* Raleigh: E. M. Uzzell, 1885.

Brooks, Aubrey Lee, and Hugh Talmage Lefler (eds.). *The Papers of Walter Clark.* 2 vols. Chapel Hill: The University of North Carolina Press, 1948.

Butterfield, Lyman H. (ed.). *The Adams Papers: Series I, Diary and Autobiography of John Adams.* 4 vols. Cambridge: Belknap Press of Harvard University Press, 1961.

Clark, Walter (ed.). *Histories of the Several Regiments and Battalions from North Carolina in the Great War 1861-'65.* 5 vols.

Raleigh: State of North Carolina [E. M. Uzzell, printer], 1901, and Goldsboro: Nash Brothers, 1901.

Clark, Walter (ed.). *The State Records of North Carolina.* 16 vols. Winston, Goldsboro, and Charlotte: State of North Carolina, 1895-1907.

Coon, Charles L. (ed.). *The Beginnings of Public Education in North Carolina: A Documentary History 1790-1840.* 2 vols. Raleigh: North Carolina Historical Commission, 1908.

Crittenden, Charles C., and Dan Lacy (eds.). *The Historical Records of North Carolina: The County Records.* 3 vols. Raleigh: North Carolina Historical Commission, 1938-39.

Graham, William A. *General Joseph Graham and His Papers on North Carolina Revolutionary History.* Raleigh: Edwards and Broughton, 1904.

Hamer, Philip M. (ed.). *A Guide to Archives and Manuscripts in the United States.* Compiled for the National Historical Publications Commission. New Haven: Yale University Press, 1961.

Hamilton, J. G. de Roulhac (ed.). *The Correspondence of Jonathan Worth.* 2 vols. Raleigh: North Carolina Historical Commission, 1909.

Hamilton, J. G. de Roulhac (ed.). *The Papers of Thomas Ruffin.* 4 vols. Raleigh: North Carolina Historical Commission, 1918-20.

Hamilton, J. G. de Roulhac (ed.). *The Papers of William Alexander Graham.* 4 vols. Raleigh: State Department of Archives and History, 1957-61.

Hathaway, J. R. B. (ed.). "Births, Deaths and Marriages in Berkeley, Later Perquimans Precinct, N. C.," *North Carolina Historical and Genealogical Register,* III (1903), 199-220, 363-410.

Holt, W. Stull (ed.). *Historical Scholarship in the United States, 1876-1901: As Revealed in the Correspondence of Herbert B. Adams.* ("The Johns Hopkins University Studies in Historical and Political Science," ser. LVI, no. 4.) Baltimore: The Johns Hopkins Press, 1938.

Hoyt, William H. (ed.) *The Papers of Archibald D. Murphey.* 2 vols. Raleigh: North Carolina Historical Commission, 1914.

Jones, H. G., and Julius H. Avant (eds.). *North Carolina Newspapers on Microfilm.* Raleigh: State Department of Archives and History, 1965.

Jones, H. G., and Julius H. Avant (eds.). *Union List of North Carolina Newspapers 1751-1900.* Raleigh: State Department of Archives and History, 1963.

Jones, Johnstone (comp.). *Roster of North Carolina Troops, in the War with Mexico. Being the Muster-out Rolls of the First Regiment of North Carolina Foot Volunteers: and Companies "G" and "I" of the Twelfth United States Infantry, Prepared, by Authority of the Legislature of 1887, by Brigadier General Johnstone Jones, Adjutant General of the State of North Carolina.* Raleigh: State of North Carolina [Josephus Daniels, printer], 1887.

Library of Congress (comp.). *The National Union Catalog of Manuscript Collections 1959-1961.* Ann Arbor: J. W. Edwards, 1962.

McRee, Griffith J. *Life and Correspondence of James Iredell, One of the Associate Justices of the Supreme Court of the United States.* 2 vols. New York: Appleton and Co., 1857, 1858.

Moore, John H. "Jared Sparks in North Carolina," *North Carolina Historical Review,* XL (July, 1963), 285-94.

Moore, John Wheeler (comp.). *Roster of North Carolina Troops in the War Between the States, Prepared by Order of Legislature of 1881.* 4 vols. Raleigh: State of North Carolina [Ashe and Gatling, printer], 1882.

Newsome, A. R. (ed.). "A British Orderly Book, 1780-1781," *North Carolina Historical Review,* IX (January, 1932), 57-78; IX (April, 1932), 163-86; IX (July, 1932), 273-98; and IX (October, 1932), 366-92.

New York Public Library (comp.). *Calendar of the Emmet Collection of Manuscripts Etc. Relating to American History.* New York: New York Public Library, 1900.

North Carolina, Adjutant General's Department. *Muster Rolls of the Soldiers of the War of 1812: Detached from the Militia of North Carolina, in 1812 and 1814.* Raleigh: State of North Carolina [Ch. C. Raboteau, printer], 1851. [A second edition was published in 1873.]

North Carolina, Adjutant General's Office. *Roster of the North Carolina Volunteers in the Spanish-American War, 1898-1899.* Raleigh: State of North Carolina [Edwards and Broughton, E. M. Uzzell, printers], 1800.

Parker, Mattie Erma Edwards (ed.). *The Colonial Records of North Carolina: North Carolina Charters and Constitutions, 1578-1698.* Raleigh: Carolina Charter Tercentenary Commission, 1963.

Powell, William S. (ed.). *Y^e Countie of Albemarle in Carolina: A Collection of Documents 1664-1675.* Raleigh: State Department of Archives and History, 1958.

Saunders, William L. (ed.). *The Colonial Records of North Carolina.* 10 vols. Raleigh: State of North Carolina, 1886-90.

Scott, R. N., *et al.* (eds.). *The War of the Rebellion: A Compilation of the Official Records of the Union and Confederate Armies.* 70 vols. [127 books, atlases, and index]. Washington, D.C.: Government Printing Office, 1880-1901.

Shanks, Henry T. (ed.). *The Papers of Willie Person Mangum.* 5 vols. Raleigh: State Department of Archives and History, 1950-56.

[Stokes, Montford (ed.).] *The Declaration of Independence by the Citizens of Mecklenburg County, on the Twentieth Day of May, 1775, with Accompanying Documents, and the Proceedings of the Cumberland Association. Published by the governor, Under the authority and direction of the General Assembly of the State of North Carolina.* Raleigh: State of North Carolina [Lawrence & Lemay, printer], 1831.

Thornton, Mary Lindsay (comp.). *A Bibliography of North Carolina 1589-1956.* Chapel Hill: The University of North Carolina Press, 1958.

Thornton, Mary Lindsay (comp.). *Official Publications of the Colony and State of North Carolina 1749-1939: A Bibliography.* Chapel Hill: The University of North Carolina Press, 1954.

Wagstaff, H. M. (ed.). *The Papers of John Steele.* 2 vols. Raleigh: North Carolina Historical Commission, 1924.

Weeks, Stephen B. *A Bibliography of the Historical Literature of North Carolina.* ("Library of Harvard University. Bibliographical Contributions," edited by Justin Winsor, no. 48.) Cambridge: Library of Harvard University, 1895.

Weeks, Stephen B. (comp.). *Index to the Colonial and State Records of North Carolina, Covering Volumes I-XXV.* 4 vols. Goldsboro, Charlotte, and Raleigh: State of North Carolina, 1909-14. [These four volumes comprise vols. XXVII-XXX of the combined series. Weeks's "Historical Review" appears in Vol. IV (XXX of the combined series).]

Wheeler, John Hill (comp.). *Catalogue of the Library of John H. Wheeler, the Historian of North Carolina . . . to be Sold at Auction, Monday Afternoon, April 24, 1882, by Bangs and Co.* N.p.: n. pub., n.d.

[Wheeler, John H. (ed.).] *Indexes to Documents Relative to North Carolina During the Colonial Existence of Said State: Now on File in the Offices of the Board of Trade and State Paper Offices in London: Transmitted in 1827: By Mr. Gallatin, Then the American Minister in London, and Now Published By Resolution of the Legislature of 1842-43: Under the Direction of the Public Treasurer.* Raleigh: State of North Carolina [T. Loring, printer], 1843.

Wheeler, John H. (ed.). *The Narrative of Colonel David Fanning.* Richmond: Privately printed, 1861.

C. *Printed Laws, Journals, and Reports*

Historical Society of the University of North Carolina. *First Report of the Historical Society of the University of North Carolina, June 4, 1845.* Hillsborough: Dennis Heartt, 1845.

Iredell, James (comp.). *Laws of the State of North-Carolina.* Edenton: State of North Carolina [Hodge and Wills, printer], 1791.

Martin, Francois-Xavier (reviser). *The Public Acts of the General Assembly of North-Carolina.* 2 vols. in 1. Newbern: State of North Carolina [Martin and Ogden, printer], 1804.

North Carolina, General Assembly. *Acts Passed by the General Assembly of the State of North Carolina, at its Session Commencing on the 25th of December, 1826.* Raleigh: State of North Carolina [Lawrence and Lemay, printer], 1827. [The title of the printed laws changed from session to session. All volumes for the period 1791-1903 were examined and citations in the text, after the initial reference, are to the short title, *Laws of (appropriate session).* The words *Public* or *Private* have been added whenever necessary. Laws prior to 1791 are printed in compilations by Clark, Iredell, Martin, and Saunders, listed separately herein.]

North Carolina, General Assembly. *Collection of All the Public Acts of Assembly in the Province of North Carolina Now in Force and Use, Together with the Titles of all Such Laws As Are Obsolete, Expir'd or Repeal'd and Also an Exact Table of the Titles of the Acts in Force; Revised by Commissioners Appointed by an Act of the General Assembly of the Said Province for that Purpose, and Examined with the Records and Confirmed in Full Assembly.* Newbern: Province of North Carolina [James Davis, printer], 1751.

North Carolina, General Assembly. *Documents Printed By Order of the General Assembly . . . 1842-43.* Raleigh: State of North Carolina [Weston R. Gales, printer] 1843. [The title and printer of this series of documents varied from session to session. All issues through the year 1900 were examined and citations within the text, after the initial reference, are to the short title, *Public Documents,* with the appropriate dates.]

North Carolina, General Assembly. *The Journal of the House of Burgesses of the Province of North-Carolina.* Newbern: Province of North Carolina [James Davis, printer], 1749. [The journals of most sessions prior to 1791 are printed in Saunders, *Colonial Records,* and Clark, *State Records,* listed separately herein. Journals subsequent to that date are available, under varying titles, for each session.]

North Carolina, General Assembly. *Report of the Comptroller's Department . . . for the Fiscal Year, Ending November 1st, 1845.*

Raleigh: State of North Carolina [W. R. Gales, printer], 1845. [Reports of the comptroller and other state officers were customarily printed in *Public Documents,* listed separately herein. However, upon occasion reports were printed as separate pamphlets, many of which are found in the Treasurer's and Comptroller's Papers, State Archives.]

North Carolina, General Assembly. *Revisal of 1905 of North Carolina.* 2 vols. Raleigh: State of North Carolina [E. M. Uzzell, printer], 1905.

North Carolina, General Assembly. *True and Faithful Narrative of the Proceedings of the House of Burgesses of North-Carolina, Met in Assembly for the Said Province at New-Bern, February 5th, 1739, on the Articles of Complaint Exhibited Before Them Against the Honourable William Smith, Esq., Chief Justice of the Said Province.* Williamsburg, Virginia: William Parks, 1740.

North Carolina Historical Commission. *Literary and Historical Activities in North Carolina 1900-1905.* Raleigh: North Carolina Historical Commission, 1907.

North Carolina Historical Commission. *The North Carolina Historical Commission: Forty Years of Public Service 1903-1943.* Raleigh: North Carolina Historical Commission, 1942.

North Carolina Historical Commission. *The North Carolina Historical Commission. General Information. 1911.* Raleigh: North Carolina Historical Commission [E. M. Uzzell, printer], [1911].

North Carolina Historical Commission. *Proceedings and Addresses of the Fifteenth Annual Session of the State Literary and Historical Association.* Raleigh: North Carolina Historical Commission [Edwards and Broughton, printer], 1915.

North Carolina Historical Commission. *Proceedings of the Eleventh and Twelfth Annual Meetings of the State Literary and Historical Association.* Raleigh: North Carolina Historical Commission [Edwards and Broughton, printer], 1912.

North Carolina Historical Commission. *Report of the Historical Commission to Governor Charles B. Aycock, 1903-1905.* Raleigh: North Carolina Historical Commission, 1904. [Subsequent reports were titled *Biennial Report . . . ,* and were issued in even-numbered years. The reports through 1910 have been cited in this study.]

North Carolina Historical Society. *The North Carolina Historical Society. An Appeal to its Friends.* N.p.: n. pub., 1880.

North Carolina State Convention. *The Journal of the Convention of North-Carolina at a Convention Begun and Held at Hillsborough, on the Twenty-First Day of July, in the Year of Our Lord*

One Thousand Seven Hundred and Eighty-Eight. . . . Hillsborough: State of North Carolina [Robert Ferguson, printer], n.d.

North Carolina, State Convention. *Ordinances and Resolutions Passed by the State Convention of North Carolina. First Session in May and June, 1861.* Raleigh: State of North Carolina [John W. Syme, printer], 1862.

North Carolina State Department of Archives and History. *The First Half Century.* Raleigh: State Department of Archives and History, 1953.

[Patterson, A. M.] *North Carolina's Local Records Program.* Raleigh: State Department of Archives and History, 1964.

[Swain, David L.] *Report of Hon. David L. Swain, LL.D., on the Historical Agency for Procuring Documentary Evidence of the History of North-Carolina.* Raleigh: Holden & Wilson, 1857.

D. Contemporary Newspaper and Periodical Articles

"Bishop Ives' Introductory Address: Delivered before the Historical Society of the University of North Carolina, June 5, 1844," *North Carolina University Magazine,* I (July, 1844), 201-16.

Daily State Chronicle (Raleigh), March 10, 1892.

[Davis, James.] "Newbern's Remembrancer: Or, An Essay on the Seat of Government," *The North-Carolina Magazine* (New Bern), I (August 17-24, 1764), 94-95.

Fayetteville Observer, February 4, 1832.

"The Historical Society," *University Magazine,* N.S. II (October, 1878), 85-86.

Martin's North-Carolina Gazette (New Bern), July 11, 1787.

Morning Post (Raleigh), October 23, 1901.

News and Observer (daily edition, Raleigh), October 24, 1900; June 30, 1892; January 24, 1903; February 8, 1903.

North-Carolina Gazette (New Bern), February 24, 1798.

The No^th. Carolina Gazette, Or New-Bern Advertiser, November 3, 1785.

"The North Carolina Historical Society," *North Carolina University Magazine,* N.S. VII (December, 1887), 81-83.

"North Carolina Historical Society," *North Carolina University Magazine,* N.S. VII (February, 1888), 133-34.

"North Carolina Historical Society," *North Carolina University Magazine,* N.S. VIII (1889), 245.

North Carolina Standard (Raleigh, weekly edition), June 22, 1870.

North Carolina University Magazine [title varies], 1844; 1852-61; 1878; 1882-90.

"Official Proceedings of the First Meeting of the North Carolina

Historical Society," *Our Living and Our Dead,* III (July, 1875),
62-64.

Raleigh Register (weekly edition), December 23, 1814; June 23, 1815;
June 14, 1816.

Raleigh Register, and North-Carolina Gazette (semi-weekly edition),
September 3, 1841; January 26, 1844.

Raleigh Register, and North-Carolina Gazette (weekly edition),
January 13, June 23, 30, 1831; November 18, 1834; February 12,
November 5, 1838.

The Sentinel (daily edition, Raleigh), October 30, 1865; April 16,
1866.

Star, and North Carolina State Gazette (Raleigh), June 23, 30, 1831.

[Swain, David L.] "The Historical Society of the University of North
Carolina," *North Carolina University Magazine,* I (April, 1844),
82-84.

Vass, L. C. "North Carolina Colonial History," *Daily Journal* (New
Bern), June 19, 1866, p. 1.

Virginia Gazette (Williamsburg, Virginia), April 28, 1738; May 25,
June 22, 1739.

II. SECONDARY SOURCES

A. Published Works

Ashe, Samuel A. *History of North Carolina.* 2 vols. Greensboro:
C. L. Van Noppen, 1905, 1925.

Ashe, Samuel A., *et al.* (eds.). *Biographical History of North Carolina
from Colonial Times to the Present.* 8 vols. Greensboro: C. L.
Van Noppen, 1905-17.

Atkinson, Thomas. *Address Delivered Before the Historical Society
of the University of North-Carolina, June 6, 1855, By Rt. Rev.
Bishop Atkinson.* Raleigh: Holden & Wilson, 1855.

Bassett, John Spencer. *The Middle Group of American Historians.*
New York: The Macmillan Co., 1917.

Battle, Kemp P. *History of the University of North Carolina. . . .*
2 vols. Raleigh: Edwards & Broughton, 1907, 1912.

Battle, Kemp P. "Raleigh and the Old Town of Bloomsbury," *North
Carolina Booklet,* II (November, 1902), 1-20.

Brewer, Fisk P. *Library Circular.* Chapel Hill: The University of
North Carolina, 1870.

Brooks, Aubrey Lee. *Walter Clark[,] Fighting Judge.* Chapel Hill:
The University of North Carolina Press, 1944.

Brown, William Burlie. "The State Literary and Historical Association 1900-1950," *North Carolina Historical Review,* XXVIII
(April, 1951), 156-97.

Butterfield, Lyman H. "Documentary Enterprises: Guidance by Remote Control," *American Archivist*, XXV (July, 1962), 393-94.

Chalmers, George. *Political Annals of the Present United Colonies From Their Settlement to the Peace of 1763: Compiled Chiefly from Records, and authorised often by the Insertion of State-Papers.* London: The Author, 1780.

Clarke, Desmond. *Arthur Dobbs Esquire 1689-1765.* Chapel Hill: The University of North Carolina Press, 1957.

Connor, R. D. W. *The Colonial and Revolutionary Periods, 1584-1783.* ("History of North Carolina," edited by R. D. W. Connor, William K. Boyd, J. G. de Roulhac Hamilton, Vol. I.) Chicago and New York: Lewis Publishing Co., 1919.

Connor, R. D. W. *North Carolina: Rebuilding an Ancient Commonwealth, 1584-1925.* 4 vols. Chicago: American Historical Society, 1929.

Corbitt, David Leroy. *The Formation of North Carolina Counties 1663-1943.* Raleigh: State Department of Archives and History, 1950.

Craven, Wesley Frank. *The Southern Colonies in the Seventeenth Century 1607-1689.* ("A History of the South," edited by Wendell H. Stephenson and E. Merton Coulter, Vol. I.) Baton Rouge: Louisiana State University Press, 1949.

Crittenden, Christopher. "We've Come a Long Way: History and Historical Activities in North Carolina," *North Carolina Historical Review*, XXXVI (April, 1959), 153-61.

Dill, Alonzo T. *Governor Tryon and His Palace.* Chapel Hill: The University of North Carolina Press, 1955.

Dowd, Clement. *Life of Zebulon B. Vance.* Charlotte: Observer Printing and Publishing House, 1897.

Duyckinck, Evert A. *A Memorial of Francis L. Hawks, D.D., LL.D.* New York: Privately printed, 1871.

Foote, William H. *Sketches of North Carolina, Historical and Biographical.* New York: Robert Carter, 1846.

Gilpatrick, Delbert Harold. "Contemporary Opinion of Hugh Williamson," *North Carolina Historical Review*, XVII (January, 1940), 26-36.

Grant, Daniel Lindsey (ed.). *Alumni History of the University of North Carolina.* 2nd ed. Chapel Hill: General Alumni Association, 1924.

Guess, William Conrad. *County Government in North Carolina.* ("The James Sprunt Historical Publications," Vol. XI.) Chapel Hill: The University of North Carolina Press, 1911.

Hamilton, J. G. de Roulhac. "The Preservation of North Carolina

History," *North Carolina Historical Review,* IV (January, 1927), 3-21.

Hamilton, J. G. de Roulhac. "Three Centuries of Southern Records, 1607-1907," *Journal of Southern History,* X (February, 1944), 1-36.

Harrison, Fairfax. "The Colonial Post Office in Virginia," *William and Mary Quarterly,* IV (April, 1924), 73-92.

Hawks, Francis L. *History of North Carolina: With Maps and Illustrations.* 2 vols. Fayetteville: E. J. Hale & Son, 1857, 1858.

Henderson, Archibald. "Buncombe's D. L. Swain, Founder of Historical Society of North Carolina," *Durham Morning Herald,* April 13, 1956.

Henderson, Archibald. *The Campus of the First State University.* Chapel Hill: The University of North Carolina Press, 1949.

Henderson, Archibald. "Historical Society of North Carolina," *Asheville Citizen,* August 10, 1956.

Henderson, Archibald. *North Carolina, the Old North State and the New.* 2 vols. Chicago: Lewis Publishing Co., 1941.

Hosack, David. *A Biographical Memoir of Hugh Williamson . . . Delivered on the First of November, 1819, at the Request of the New-York Historical Society.* New York: C. S. Van Winkle, 1820.

Hoyt, William H. "Reminiscences of a Collector of Books and Manuscripts," *The Bookmark* [a publication of the University of North Carolina Library], No. 23 (June, 1955).

Jarvis, Thomas J. "North Carolina Must Preserve Its Historical Records," *Proceedings of the Eleventh and Twelfth Annual Meetings of the State Literary and Historical Association.* Raleigh: Edwards & Broughton, 1912.

Johnson, Allen, and Dumas Malone (eds.). *Dictionary of American Biography.* 20 vols. New York: Charles Scribner's Sons, 1943.

Johnson, Charles Earl. "History of the Capitol," *North Carolina Booklet,* V (October, 1905), 73-89.

Johnson, William Perry. "Wake County Deeds, 1771-1832," *The North Carolinian,* IV (September, 1958), 455-58.

Jones, H. G. "The Archival-Records Management Program of an American State: North Carolina," *Indian Archives,* XVI (1965).

Jones, H. G. "Archives and Manuscript Collections in North Carolina," in Robert B. Downs (ed.), *Resources of North Carolina Libraries.* Raleigh: Governor's Commission on Library Resources, 1965.

Jones, H. G. (ed.). *Guide to State and Provincial Archival Agencies.* Raleigh: Society of American Archivists, 1961.

Jones, H. G. "North Carolina's Local Records Program," *American Archivist,* XXIV (January, 1961), 25-41.

Jones, H. G. "State Archival-Records Management Programs in the United States," *Archivum,* XI (1961), 135-42.

Jones, H. G. "The State Department of Archives and History," *North Carolina Libraries,* XIX (Winter, 1961), 5-15.

Jones, H. G. "Stephen Beauregard Weeks: North Carolina's First 'Professional' Historian," *North Carolina Historical Review,* XLII (Autumn, 1965), 410-23.

Jones, H. G., A. M. Patterson, and T. W. Mitchell, "Records Management in North Carolina," *Records Management Journal,* IV (Autumn, 1966).

Jones, Jo[seph] Seawell. *A Defence of the Revolutionary History of North Carolina From the Aspersions of Mr. Jefferson.* Boston: Charles Bowen, and Raleigh: Turner and Hughes, 1834.

Jones, Jo[seph] Seawell. *The Mammoth Humbug, or, The Adventures of Shocco Jones, in Mississippi, in the Summer of 1839, including the History of His Visit to Alabama and "The way he come it over" Certain Members of its Legislature, &c., &c.* Memphis: Privately printed, 1842. *N.V.*

Jones, Jo[seph] Seawell. *Memorials of North Carolina.* New York: Scatcherd and Adams, 1838.

Lee, Lawrence. *The Lower Cape Fear in Colonial Days.* Chapel Hill: The University of North Carolina Press, 1965.

Lee, Sidney (ed.). *Dictionary of National Biography.* 63 vols. New York: The Macmillan Co., 1897.

Lefler, Hugh T. "Robert Digges Wimberly Connor," in Clifford L. Lord (ed.). *Keepers of the Past.* Chapel Hill: The University of North Carolina Press, 1965.

Lefler, Hugh Talmage, and Albert Ray Newsome. *North Carolina: The History of a Southern State.* Chapel Hill: The University of North Carolina Press, 1954.

London, Lawrence F. *Bishop Joseph Blount Cheshire.* Chapel Hill: The University of North Carolina Press, 1941.

McGehee, Montford. *Life and Character of the Hon. William A. Graham. A Memorial Oration.* Raleigh: News Job Office and Book Bindery, 1877.

McMahon, John Alexander. "A County Official Looks at a State-Supervised County Records Program," *American Archivist,* XXV (April, 1962), 211-18.

McMahon, John Alexander. "The Local Records Program in North Carolina," *North Carolina Historical Review,* XXXIX (Spring, 1962), 165-74.

McPherson, Elizabeth Gregory. "Nathaniell Batts, Landholder on Pasquotank River, 1660," *North Carolina Historical Review,* XLIII (Winter, 1966), 66-81.

Martin, Francois-Xavier. *The History of North Carolina, from the Earliest Period.* 2 vols. New-Orleans: A. T. Penniman & Co., 1829.

Miles, Edwin A. "Joseph Seawell Jones of Shocco—Historian and Humbug," *North Carolina Historical Review,* XXXIV (October, 1957), 483-506.

Moore, John Wheeler. *History of North Carolina From the Earliest Discoveries to the Present Time.* 2 vols. Raleigh: Alfred Williams & Co., 1880.

Moore, John Wheeler. *School History of North Carolina.* Raleigh: Alfred Williams & Co., 1879.

Morgan, Lawrence N. *Land Tenure in Proprietary North Carolina.* ("The James Sprunt Historical Publications," Vol. XII.) Chapel Hill: The University of North Carolina Press, 1912.

Olds, Fred A. *Story of the Counties of North Carolina With Other Data.* Oxford, N.C.: Oxford Orphanage Press, 1921.

Posner, Ernst. *American State Archives.* Chicago: University of Chicago Press, 1964.

Powell, William S. *The Proprietors of Carolina.* Raleigh: Carolina Charter Tercentenary Commission, 1963.

Rankin, Hugh F. *North Carolina in the American Revolution.* Raleigh: State Department of Archives and History, 1959.

Rowland, Dunbar. *History of Mississippi, The Heart of the South.* 2 vols. Chicago-Jackson: S. J. Clarke Publishing Co., 1925.

Russell, Mattie. "The Manuscript Department in the Duke University Library," *American Archivist,* XXVIII (July, 1965), 437-44.

Sanders, John L. *Housing State Government: A Review 1792-1957.* Chapel Hill: Institute of Government, 1958.

Sanford, Terry. "North Carolina—Three Hundredth Birthday," *American Archivist,* XXVII (January, 1964), 15-19.

Saunders, William L. *Lessons from Our North Carolina Records: An Address Read Before the Faculty and Students of Trinity College, November 27, 1888.* ("Trinity College Publications," No. 1.) Trinity College, N.C.: Trinity College, 1889.

Schellenberg, Theodore R. *Modern Archives: Principles and Techniques.* Chicago: University of Chicago Press, 1956.

Smith, William. "The Colonial Post-Office," *American Historical Review,* XXI (January, 1916), 258-75.

Stroupe, Henry S. "The North Carolina Department of Archives and History—The First Half Century," *North Carolina Historical Review,* XXXI (April, 1954), 184-200.

Tilley, Nannie M. *The Trinity College Historical Society, 1892-1941.* Durham: Duke University Press, 1941.

United States, Congress. *Biographical Directory of the American*

Congress 1774-1927. House Document No. 783. 69th Cong., 2nd Sess., 1927.

Vance, Zebulon B. "The Life and Character of Hon. David L. Swain," *North Carolina University Magazine,* 2nd ser. I (May, 1878) , 73-93.

Waddell, Alfred Moore. *The Life and Character of William L. Saunders, LL.D., An Oration Delivered before the Alumni Association of the University of North Carolina, Tuesday, May 31st, 1892.* Wilmington: Jackson and Bell, Steam Power Presses, 1892.

Wallace, Carolyn Andrews. "The Southern Historical Collection," *American Archivist,* XXVIII (July, 1965) , 427-36.

Wallace, Carolyn Andrews. "The Southern Historical Collection," *North Carolina Libraries,* XIX (Winter, 1961) , 16-21.

Weeks, Stephen B. "The North Carolina Historians," *Proceedings and Addresses of the Fifteenth Annual Session of the State Literary and Historical Association.* Raleigh: North Carolina Historical Commission, 1915.

Wheeler, John H. *The Early Times and Men of Albemarle; An Oration Delivered at Elizabeth City, N.C., on 7th of August, 1877, at request of the Albemarle Historical Society.* [Elizabeth City?]: Albemarle Historical Society, 1877.

Wheeler, John H. *Historical Sketches of North Carolina, From 1584 to 1851. Compiled from Original Records, Official Documents, and Traditional Statements. With Biographical Sketches of Her Distinguished Statesmen, Jurists, Lawyers, Soldiers, Divines, Etc.* 2 vols. bound as 1. Philadelphia: Lippincott, Grambo and Co., 1851.

Wheeler, John H. *The Lives and Characters of the Signers of the Mecklenburg Declaration of Independence, on the 20th of May, 1775; delivered at Charlotte, N.C., on the 24th day of May, 1875, at the request of the Mecklenburg Historical Society.* Charlotte: Observer Book and Job Power Press Print, 1875.

Wheeler, John H. *Reminiscences and Memoirs of North Carolina and Eminent North Carolinians.* Columbus, Ohio: Columbus Printing Works, 1884.

Wheeler, John H. *Sketch of the Life of Richard Dobbs Spaight of North Carolina.* Baltimore: W. K. Boyle, printer, 1880.

Williamson, Hugh. *The History of North Carolina.* 2 vols. Philadelphia: Thomas Dobson, 1812.

Wilson, Peter Michel. *Southern Exposure.* Chapel Hill: The University of North Carolina Press, 1927.

Winborne, Benjamin B. *The Colonial and State Political History of Hertford County, N.C.* Raleigh: Edwards & Broughton for the Author, 1906.

Wood, Richard G. "Richard Bartlett, Minor Archival Prophet," *American Archivist,* XVII (January, 1954), 13-18.

Yearns, W. B. "Francois X. Martin and His History of North Carolina," *North Carolina Historical Review,* XXXVI (January, 1959), 17-27.

Zuber, Richard L. *Jonathan Worth: A Biography of a Southern Unionist.* Chapel Hill: The University of North Carolina Press, 1965.

B. *Unpublished Works*

Irvine, Dallas. "The Story of Governor Vance's Confederate Letter Books." Unpublished manuscript. (Photocopy in North Carolina State Department of Archives and History.)

Irvine, Dallas. "What Happened to the Archives of North Carolina in 1865?" Unpublished manuscript. (Photocopy in North Carolina Department of Archives and History.)

Johnson, Elmer D. "The War of the Regulation: Its Place in History." Unpublished M.A. thesis, The University of North Carolina, 1942.

Jones, H. G. "William Laurence Saunders and the Publication of *The Colonial Records of North Carolina.*" Unpublished manuscript, 1965, in files of the Historical Society of North Carolina.

McCain, Paul M. "The County Court in North Carolina Before 1750." Unpublished Ph.D. dissertation, Duke University, 1950.

Riggs, John Beverley. "The Acquisition of Foreign Archival Sources for American History to the Year 1940." Unpublished Ph.D. dissertation, Yale University, 1955.

Wallace, Carolyn Andrews. "David Lowry Swain 1801-1835." Unpublished Ph.D. dissertation, The University of North Carolina, 1954.

INDEX

Index

PEACE

PERSON

HALIFAX

SALISBURY

JONES

JOHNSON

ELM

LANE

SAUNDERS

HARRINGTON

HILLSBORO

BOYLAN AV.

PENITENTIARY (In Construction)

BIRD'S EYE

NOR